THE SEXUAL ABUSE
OF CHILDREN

Jeffrey J. Haugaard
N. Dickon Reppucci

THE SEXUAL ABUSE
OF CHILDREN

*A Comprehensive Guide
to Current Knowledge
and Intervention Strategies*

 Jossey-Bass Publishers

San Francisco • London • 1988

THE SEXUAL ABUSE OF CHILDREN
A Comprehensive Guide to Current Knowledge and Intervention Strategies
by Jeffrey J. Haugaard and N. Dickon Reppucci

Copyright © 1988 by: Jossey-Bass Inc., Publishers
350 Sansome Street
San Francisco, California 94104
&
Jossey-Bass Limited
28 Banner Street
London EC1Y 8QE

Library of Congress Cataloging-in-Publication Data

Haugaard, Jeffrey J., date.
  The sexual abuse of children.

  (The Jossey-Bass social and behavioral science series)
  Bibliography: p.
  Includes index.
  1. Child molesting—United States. 2. Sexually abused children—Services for—United States. 3. Child abuse—Law and legislation—United States. I. Reppucci, N. Dickon. II. Title. III. Series.
  HQ72.U53H36   1988   362.7′044   87-46345
  ISBN 1-55542-077-X (alk. paper)

Manufactured in the United States of America

The paper in this book meets the guidelines for permanence and durability of the Committee on Production Guidelines for Book Longevity of the Council on Library Resources.

JACKET DESIGN BY WILLI BAUM

FIRST EDITION

Code 8807

The Jossey-Bass
Social and Behavioral Science Series

CONTENTS

PREFACE

*T*he past few decades have seen a dramatic increase in the attention paid to all forms of child abuse. Much of this attention is now being focused on the sexual abuse of children by adults. This topic, once the concern of only a few, now receives considerable attention from professionals in the academic, medical, mental health, social work, and legal fields. Since the 1970s, the mass media have helped to focus the attention of the general public, which has become increasingly aware of the victims of child sexual abuse. The research, treatment, and legal literature regarding child sexual abuse has burgeoned. Many investigations of the prevalence, etiology, and consequences of child sexual abuse have been reported. Writers in social work, psychology, and medicine have described a multitude of interventions for victims of child sexual abuse and their families and for perpetrators. Numerous articles on the involvement of victims in the legal system have been published in legal journals, as well as debates about the constitutionality of reforms designed to reduce what some have described as the further abuse of victims during the prosecution of alleged perpetrators.

Few attempts have been made to integrate the accumulated knowledge from the research, treatment, and legal literature. Our goal is to accomplish this task. An integration is important at this point if our knowledge about child sexual abuse is to expand and if the ways in which we intervene with victims and their families are to improve. Professionals from many fields now have increased interactions with child sexual abuse victims and their families, and, as a result, the interactions among these professionals have also increased. The knowledge gained by each type of professional within this diverse group can be of value to the others. Each type of professional may have a slightly different perspective on victims, families, and perpetrators, and a sharing of these perspectives should promote increased understanding of the phenomenon of child sexual abuse for all. Moreover, such understanding may help to bridge the gaps between the often different goals and concerns of each group, resulting in an increased likelihood that the most effective services for child victims and families will be provided.

We believe that the integration of the literature presented in this book will be of value to anyone concerned with the topic of child sexual abuse. Service providers to victims and their families may be able to improve the effectiveness of their interventions as they learn about the successes and failures of others. They can also gain by understanding the various theoretical perspectives and empirical findings about the causes and consequences of child sexual abuse. Researchers will be better able to develop meaningful research projects by having both a thorough knowledge of previous research and an understanding of the problems and concerns faced by those providing services. Furthermore, the material presented in this book should be of value to all who are, or who plan to be, regularly involved in any capacity with children and their families. Child sexual abuse occurs throughout our society, and its effects may be felt by many children who have never been identified as victims. Knowing about the prevalence, consequences, treatment, and prevention of child sexual abuse will be valuable to teachers, counselors, members of the clergy, and others who have regular contact with children, as well as to parents and other concerned citizens.

Throughout this book we not only report the information available in the literature but also try to provide the reader with a framework within which to analyze it. Most of the literature in this area is relatively new, with many discrepancies and areas in which information is scarce. In addition, there are important limitations to much that has been written. Understanding the literature and using it properly require an appreciation of both its assets and its limitations. As will be seen, able researchers and clinicians often disagree about the meaning of a particular finding or about the most effective way of handling a particular situation. Other authors have dealt with these disagreements by expounding the process or method that they have found to be the best. We take a different approach. We discuss the various positions that have been taken on an issue and then describe the aspects of the situation that we believe should be considered as a decision is reached about it. We believe that this approach is most beneficial in helping each individual come to conclusions about how to consider or resolve one or more of the many thorny issues in this field.

We outline both what is known about child sexual abuse and what is unknown. We argue throughout the book that too little is known for anyone to make firm statements about nearly any topic in the field. Although our knowledge is steadily increasing, it must expand much further before "the truth" begins to emerge. Although some may suggest that more should be known before a book such as this is undertaken, we disagree. Distinguishing between what is known, what is hypothesized, and what is unknown is an important step in the further development of this field. We hope that this book will be a stepping stone in the development of a comprehensive body of knowledge about child sexual abuse.

We begin the book with a general introductory chapter that describes how society has dealt with the sexual abuse of children in the past and the problems we encounter in dealing with it today. The chapters in Part One present basic information about child sexual abuse. In Chapter Two, we address the issue of defining child sexual abuse. The development of legal, research, and clinical definitions is discussed, and implications of the use of differing definitions by those in these fields are explored. In Chapter Three, we review research on the prevalence of child sexual abuse in our society and the form that it takes with boys and girls of various ages and backgrounds. An examination of the consequences experienced by victims of child sexual abuse, as well as of the factors that appear to increase or decrease those consequences, is the focus of Chapter Four. In the last chapter of Part One, theories concerning incest and the families in which it occurs are reviewed.

This basic information is integral to an understanding of child sexual abuse and thus is an important foundation for the following chapters. How one defines child sexual abuse determines which children and families will be intervened with by legal and clinical agencies. Information about prevalence influences the extent of the effort that must be made to counteract any negative effects and suggests which children face the greatest risk of being abused. Methods for assessing whether a child has been sexually abused or for providing therapeutic interventions to victims and families should be based on findings about the specific consequences of child sexual abuse and theories about the causes of these consequences. Methods for dealing with incestuous families differ depending on conceptualizations about the ways that a family becomes incestuous.

Part Two discusses the identification of child sexual abuse victims. Chapter Six focuses on the various signs that suggest that a child or adult who is in therapy for some other reason is a victim of child sexual abuse. Many authors are beginning to comment on the importance of recognizing victims so that the consequences of their abuse can be directly addressed in therapy. Chapter Seven outlines procedures that have been used to assess whether a child who claims to be a victim is telling the truth. An increasing number of clinicians are being asked to assess children who claim to have been abused, and knowledge of the procedures used in this assessment is important for anyone who has contact with these apparent victims. We have kept these chapters apart from those dealing exclusively with therapeutic interventions in order to emphasize the difference between these two processes and the importance of keeping them separate.

The six chapters in Part Three focus on clinical interventions used with child sexual abuse victims and their families. Chapter Eight provides a discussion of several issues of general concern to those intervening in these cases. These issues include countertransference while working with victims and perpetrators, the benefits and limitations of legal coercion for treatment, and the need for interagency cooperation. Chapters Nine through Twelve outline the procedures generally used during the treatment of children and families and with adult victims of child sexual abuse—crisis intervention, individual treatment, group treatment, and family therapy. Chapter Thirteen concerns the development, implementation, and evaluation of prevention programs for children, parents, and professionals.

The goal of Part Three is to present a compilation of the treatment styles used by many clinicians. As a result, it is quite different from most writings on the treatment of child sexual abuse, which usually focus on the treatment program developed and used by the author. We do not present the reader with a blueprint for treating victims and families; rather, we describe many treatment issues and the ways they have been handled by various clinicians. Our aim is to provide information about the variety of therapeutic styles and programs that have been established in order to assist those interested in developing or improving a treatment program or evaluating the programs of others. By discussing several unresolved therapeutic issues, we hope also to provide researchers with directions for meaningful future investigations.

Part Four is on relevant legal issues. Chapter Fourteen deals with the child and clinician as witnesses in child sexual abuse trials. The questions addressed are whether young children are competent to testify about an abuse experience and when it is appropriate for a clinician to provide expert testimony in child sexual abuse trials. Many in the legal, mental health, and social science fields are debating the effects on victims' and defendants' rights of innovations such as the increased use of hearsay testimony, videotaped testimony of the victim, and shielding the defendant from the victim during the trial. The legal and clinical arguments for and against these innovations are presented in Chapter Fifteen. With the increased involvement of victims and clinicians in the legal system, an understanding of these proposed changes will help clinicians think about them clearly.

Chapter Sixteen, a concluding summary, highlights the major themes found throughout the book. It also suggests some directions for future research and action.

Because the overall focus of this book is on the victims of child sexual abuse and their families, we do not provide a review of the literature concerning the etiology of pedophilia or child molesting in general. We do discuss perpetrators if they are family members, because we believe that in many cases the treatment of the incest perpetrator has a major impact on the well-being of the victim and family. Consequently, there is some information on the etiology of sexually abusive behavior in adults in Chapter Five and some material on the treatment of the incest perpetrator in Chapters Ten, Eleven, and Twelve. For a thorough review of theory and research concerning the perpetrator, the reader is referred to Cook and Howells (1981), Finkelhor and Associates (1986), Langevin (1983), and Lanyon (1986).

An initial short review of research literature (Haugaard and Reppucci, 1986) led to the writing of this book and was funded by the Virginia Treatment Center for Children. We gratefully acknowledge this support and the continued encouragement of the center's director, Robert Cohen. Richard Bonnie, director of the University of Virginia's Institute for Law, Psychiatry, and Public Policy, provided financial resources near the end of this project. The thoughtful comments of Richard Barth, Lucille Berliner, William Henry, and an anonymous reviewer on drafts of this book contributed much to its final form. Carolyn Williams provided insightful comments about the differences between victims' psychological and legal guilt, and her encouragement was valuable throughout this project. Mary Alice Fisher provided guidance on ways for clinicians to understand their roles in sexual abuse cases. Elizabeth Scott's mentorship regarding legal issues was also valuable, as were her clarifying comments on the two legal chapters. Moreover, the Center for the Study of Law and Children, which she directs, has contributed greatly to the intellectually stimulating environment at

the University of Virginia. Our colleagues Mark Aber, Jinger
Atteberry-Bennett, Robert Emery, Edward Mulvey, John Monahan, Christine Reppucci, Mindy Rosenberg, Jeanne Smith, and
Janet Warren helped over the years to clarify our thinking on
several important issues discussed in this book. We owe much
gratitude to each of these individuals. Our thanks go also to
Deborah Mundie, who typed the initial draft of the bibliography, and Anna Reppucci, who spent many hours cross-check-
ing the references, both singularly unrewarding tasks. Lastly, we
would like to acknowledge those who pioneered the recognition
of child sexual abuse as an important national problem. These
researchers and clinicians provided the foundation for today's
research by their early efforts and guided the development of
treatment programs by their innovative approaches to the children and their families. The reader will find their names throughout this book.

Charlottesville, Virginia   Jeffrey J. Haugaard
February 1988   N. Dickon Reppucci

For
Mary-Lois and Viggo Haugaard,
Theresa and Patrick Walsh
J.J.H.

For my mother, Bertha E. Reppucci,
and my family, Christine, Nicholas, Jonathan, and Anna Reppucci
N.D.R.

THE AUTHORS

*J*effrey *J. Haugaard* is a doctoral candidate in child clinical psychology in the Department of Psychology at the
University of Virginia. He received a B.A. from the University
of California, Santa Cruz (1973), with majors in psychology and
politics; an M.A. in marriage, family, and child counseling from
Santa Clara University (1984); and an M.A. in psychology from
the University of Virginia (1987).

After receiving his bachelor's degree, he worked for ten
years at a private elementary and junior high school as boarding
program director and school counselor. His current research and
clinical interests include child sexual abuse, divorce mediation,
and the interface of psychology and the law. He has written
articles on the competence of child witnesses, methodological
issues in child sexual abuse, and coercive sexual experiences between children. In 1986 he coauthored with Edward Mulvey the
report of the Surgeon General's Workshop on Pornography and
Public Health.

N. *Dickon Reppucci* is professor of psychology and director
of graduate studies in the Department of Psychology at
the University of Virginia. He received his B.A. in psychology
from the University of North Carolina at Chapel Hill (1962), his

M.A. in social relations from Harvard University (1964), and his Ph.D. in clinical psychology from Harvard University (1968).

Reppucci's main research activities have been in the areas of community and preventive psychology; juvenile correctional institutions; child abuse; and children, mental health, and the law. His experience includes being an assistant and associate professor at Yale University (1968-1976). He has served on the editorial boards of the *American Journal of Community Psychology* (1974-1983; 1988-1991), *Journal of Consulting and Clinical Psychology* (1973-1979; 1986-1987), *Professional Psychology* (1987-present), and *Law and Human Behavior* (1985-1987; associate editor, 1988-1990), and on the National Institute of Mental Health internal review committees on criminal and violent behavior (1980-1983) and on child and family and prevention (1987-1989). He served as chair of the American Psychological Association Task Force on Psychology and Public Policy (1980-1984), as a member of the American Psychological Association Task Force on Psychology and the Criminal Justice System, and was chosen as a G. Stanley Hall Lecturer (1985). He served as president of the American Psychological Association's division of community psychology (1986) and is a fellow of that division and those of clinical psychology, law and psychology, and children, youth, and families. He was organizer of the first Biennial Conference on Community Research and Action (1987). He is the author or coauthor of more than sixty professional articles and book chapters, and with Lois Weithorn, Edward Mulvey, and John Monahan is editor of *Children, Mental Health, and the Law.*

Reppucci is an associate of the University of Virginia's Institute of Law, Psychiatry and Public Policy, and cofounder of its Center for the Study of Law and Children. He is also a member of the Virginia Department of Mental Health and Mental Retardation's Advisory Council on Prevention and Promotion (1987-1989).

THE SEXUAL ABUSE
OF CHILDREN

Child Sexual Abuse: A Critical Social Problem

P rohibitions have existed against the sexual abuse of children in the form of incest since ancient times (Wulkan and Bulkley, 1985). Both primitive and modern cultures have provided strong penalties for breaking these prohibitions, including death, which perhaps indicates the intense emotional reactions provoked in many people by such acts (Meiselman, 1978). Considering the universality of this negative reaction to incest, it is surprising that only in the last few decades has the sexual abuse of children been acknowledged as an important social problem by both professionals and the general public (Sgroi, 1982b).

Inattention to child sexual abuse may have its roots in the historic view of children as miniature adults, owned by their parents (Aries, 1962; Greenleaf, 1978). Ancient Roman law used the concept of *patria potestas* to give the father complete power, including the right to commit infanticide and to sell his children into slavery (Avery and Sand, 1975). Moreover, deMause (1974) documents that in ancient Greece and Rome sexual use of children in some form was prevalent; for example, boy brothels flourished in many cities. The first glimmerings of the concept of children as distinctive individuals did not occur until the Renaissance, and not until the present century did children gain a new status as individuals with independent rights.

Despite these views, children have had some protections since the early 1700s. In 1722 the English monarch was given the *parens patriae* power: the obligation to defend the rights of "children, idiots, and lunatics" who were incapable of protecting themselves (Avery and Sand, 1975). Current laws in the United States that grant the state the power to protect children and to intervene in the family are based on this *parens patriae* concept. However, the right and obligation of the state to intervene on the behalf of children have had to be balanced against the legal tradition that the right to family privacy is inviolate except in exceptional circumstances. Giovannoni, Conklin, and Iiyama (1978) suggest that the traditional imbalance in favor of the sanctity of the family is one of the major reasons why child abuse of any sort has been acknowledged as a problem of significant proportions only since the 1960s.

Although professional interest in child sexual abuse probably began with the publication of several incest histories in Krafft-Ebing's *Psychopathia Sexualis* in 1886, Freud's ([1933], 1965) discussion of incest fantasies by females ensured that most reports were considered as just that—fantasy. The professional interest that did exist remained focused either on incest cases, as illustrated by the increasing number of case histories that began appearing in the professional literature in the 1950s (Meiselman, 1978), or on the perpetrator of the abuse. Psychiatrists labeled the problem *sexual psychopathy,* a term that first appeared in legal nomenclature in statutes enacted during the late 1930s (Weisberg, 1984). Public attention became focused on extrafamilial sexual abuse and the sexual psychopath following sensational publicity surrounding the 1949 sex murder of a child in California and the passage of sexual psychopath laws (Sutherland, 1950). In the 1950s, increased attention was paid to the criminal aspects of child sexual abuse, although psychiatrists encouraged relabeling sexual psychopaths to emphasize the idea of perpetrators as patients; in California, they were termed *mentally disordered sex offenders* (Weisberg, 1984).

Calls from the public sector for help in stopping child sexual abuse tended to be ignored by professionals, probably because they believed that child sexual abuse of any variety was a relatively rare phenomenon. Moreover, Finkelhor (1979) suggests that many professionals in the 1950s and 1960s were interested in liberalizing sexual mores, and this agenda may have influenced them to cite research and theory that downplayed the importance of sexual abuse. However, beginning with the vast increase in attention to the problem of physical child abuse as a result of Kempe and others' (1962) landmark article on the "battered child syndrome" and the subsequent institution of child abuse reporting laws in the late 1960s, the incidence of child sexual abuse, either internal or external to the family, could no longer be denied (Rosenfeld, 1977).

In the 1970s, advocates for children and feminist groups helped make the public and professionals aware of child sexual abuse (Finkelhor, 1986). The label *child sexual abuse* first appeared in the federal Child Abuse Prevention and Treatment Act of 1974. Weisberg (1984) claims that psychologists and social workers replaced psychiatrists as the new experts during this period. The focus shifted from the extrafamilial offender to the familial offender, usually the father or stepfather, and interventions often included some form of family counseling rather than hospitalization or civil commitment of the perpetrator. For the first time, experts viewed the entire family, rather than the perpetrator alone, as the source of the problem. In addition, and most significantly, attention focused on the child victim, for whom treatment was also recommended. Weisberg (1984) credits a California psychologist, Henry Giarretto, with playing a prominent role in this development (see Chapter Twelve for details), and a social worker and lawyer, Vincent DeFrancis, with being especially influential in broadening the federal definition of child abuse to include sexual abuse. The federal government required states to accept this broadened definition in order to qualify for federal funds for the treatment and prevention of abuse.

Since 1974, there has been an explosion of interest in and concern about child sexual abuse of all types. A study by Kinsey, Pomeroy, Martin, and Gebhard (1953), indicating that many children had sexual experiences with adults, was revived. Large-scale surveys using relatively broad definitions of child sexual abuse, such as Finkelhor's 1979 study of college students and Russell's 1983 study of urban women, indicated that such abuse was much more widespread than previously believed and that it cut across all social and economic boundaries. These surveys added impetus to the development of treatment and prevention programs. Between 1976 and 1981, the number of treatment programs for offenders and their families in the United States grew from 20 to 300 (Bulkley, 1985b). Many schools now offer sexual abuse prevention programs; such a curriculum was for the most part unheard of even in the early 1980s.

In 1984, the issue of child sexual abuse was dramatically brought to the public's attention with the arrest in Manhattan Beach, California, of Virginia McMartin and six of her employees for allegedly sexually abusing 125 children over a ten-year period at a daycare center. These arrests were followed by another highly publicized case in which indictments were brought against twenty-four parents and other adults for allegedly sexually abusing over fifty children in Jordan, Minnesota. *Newsweek* ran a cover story on child sexual abuse in May 1984, and *Life* ran a similar story in November of that year. "Sixty Minutes," "20-20," and "Nightline" featured reports on child sexual abuse, and the Public Broadcasting System televised a four-part series on its prevention. Public attention had become riveted on the problem. In addition, the pictures of missing children that appeared on milk cartons, billboards, and telephone books were constant reminders that untold numbers of children were disappearing, possibly to become victims of sexual abuse and perhaps murder.

Professionals in several fields reacted to this previously underrecognized but now significant and politicized problem. Lawyers and legislators responded by developing new legal procedures to reduce the apparent trauma suffered by many victims as they became involved in the prosecution of alleged perpetrators. In addition, in the late 1970s several states changed their sexual abuse laws to increase punishment for perpetrators from outside the family, while at the same time providing "humanistic" treatment for incest perpetrators, many of whom could receive reduced sentences in exchange for participation in therapeutic programs (Weisberg, 1984). Those in the academic, medical, and mental health fields developed numerous research projects, therapeutic interventions, and prevention programs. They made a concerted effort to learn about the causes, effects, treatment, and prevention of child sexual abuse. The need for this knowledge was immediate—more and more victims of sexual abuse were being discovered, and many of the victims had been adversely affected by their experiences.

Although this effort to learn about child sexual abuse continues, its urgency seems to have abated somewhat in the public mind, perhaps because the impression exists that we are now taking meaningful action. We believe, however, that the problem of child sexual abuse has not diminished and that our knowledge about child sexual abuse is still at a rudimentary level. The development of this knowledge is at an important turning point. Either we can continue to provide legal and therapeutic services to victims, families, and perpetrators based on what we think we know—which is sufficient to have gotten us started—or we can review what we actually know about child sexual abuse, look for the gaps in our knowledge or the places where our assumptions and prejudices have been inserted to fill these gaps, and then begin a new effort to learn more. We clearly believe that the second alternative is preferable, even though it is more difficult to pursue. Discovering what one does not know is immeasurably harder than espousing what one does know. Recognizing and dealing with the nuances of a problem are more difficult than the initial plunge into its solution.

In order to highlight some of the subtle difficulties that now face those working with victims of child sexual abuse and their families, we present three short vignettes from our own experience. We offer other vignettes throughout the book to illustrate the complexity of the issues being discussed.

> A mother brings her two young children to a child guidance clinic. Both children are exhibiting signs of emotional stress and are having behavior problems at home and school. She explains that both children had been sexually abused by their father,

often brutally, during monthly visits to him after the mother and father were divorced. Once the abuse was discovered, the father was jailed, and the mother moved to a new town and put the children in a daycare center. While there, they and other children were sexually abused by several employees. She has now moved to a new state out of fear of the father, who is due to be released from prison in a few months. The mother is very upset.

A sixth-grade girl who has just seen a sexual abuse prevention program at school reports to her teacher that about six years earlier her father had fondled her genitals on two occasions. The girl reports that after the second incident she told her father that she did not like what he was doing and he stopped. The father has made no other advances to her, and she generally has a nice relationship with him. She has never told anyone of the incidents and is reporting them now because the sexual abuse prevention program indicated that she should do so. The teacher reports the abuse to the principal, who calls protective services. Soon thereafter the father is arrested. He, the child, and the child's mother go through a series of interviews with police and psychologists. No evidence indicates that family pathology occurred before the child revealed the sexual activity, and the girl shows no indications of individual pathology. Eventually the charges against the father are dismissed. The family, which before the revelation of the abuse appeared to be functioning well, is distraught and fragmented but vows to stay together.

A seventh-grade boy reveals that a school employee has fondled his genitals and has had oral sex with him over a period of two years. The perpetrator is arrested, pleads guilty, and is jailed. The boy continues to perform well at school and at home. Although upset about the incident, he is able to talk about it and does not show any signs of an unhealthy emotional or social response.

What should be done with each of these children or families? Are any or all of them in need of therapeutic intervention? Is there any information from empirical research or clinical reports that indicates which of these children might be in the most or the least need of therapy, or which type of therapy would be the most effective? In what types of legal proceedings might these children and their families become involved, and with what effect?

Books and articles have often provided answers to these and other questions about child sexual abuse, partially because of the authors' need to take strong stands in order to bring child sexual abuse to the attention of policy makers, mental health and medical professionals, and the public. Now that child sexual abuse has been acknowledged as a meaningful problem and many clinical and experimental reports on victims and their families have been published, it is possible, and important, to stand back and take a critical and objective view of the field. When we do, we often find ourselves unable to provide unequivocal answers to such questions. We believe that this book, however, will make readers aware of the answers currently available, of the questions that still remain, and of the directions in which we might search for their solutions.

Part 1

UNDERSTANDING CHILD SEXUAL ABUSE

*T*he first part of this book is devoted to the theories, hypotheses, clinical observations, and empirical research concerning the basic issues of child sexual abuse: What is child sexual abuse? To whom does it happen? What are the consequences when it occurs? This material is presented first because we believe that (a) it is integral to understanding the phenomenon of child sexual abuse and (b) anyone doing research in the area or providing services to victims and their families needs to have as complete an understanding of the phenomenon as possible. Much as medical researchers and practitioners must understand both the mechanisms of the normal and cancerous cell and the theories concerning the process by which a normal cell becomes cancerous in order to provide the best services to cancer patients, those dealing with sexual abuse victims and their families must understand the theories and facts that pertain to a certain child or family.

In Chapter Two we discuss a subject often assumed to need no discussion: What is child sexual abuse? When individuals in the same or different professions discuss such abuse, they generally assume that they are talking about the same phenomenon. However, this assumption may not always be accurate. We outline the definitions of child sexual abuse that have been employed by researchers and practitioners in various fields, and we discuss the implications and possible problems that can occur if those in the agencies that deal with child sexual abuse define it differently.

In Chapter Three, we review clinical and empirical research about the prevalence of child sexual abuse. Knowing how many children experience sex with an adult and what form these experiences take should provide valuable information for those concerned with treating and preventing the sexual abuse of children. We attempt to reconcile the diverse estimates of the prevalence of child sexual abuse in our society and to help the reader understand why these estimates have ranged from 10 to 60 percent.

Chapter Four focuses on the consequences of child sexual abuse. The goal is to provide information to those interacting with victims about the consequences that their clients might be experiencing. We also review the theories used to explain the processes by which having sexual relations with an adult becomes a negative experience for so many children.

Chapter Five presents theories about the incest taboo and why it is broken in some families. The literature suggests that although most child sexual abuse is perpetrated by persons not in the child's nuclear family, most children referred to therapy have experienced incest. Consequently, an understanding of the theories explaining how a family becomes incestuous should be important to anyone dealing with identified victims of child sexual abuse.

As will be seen throughout these four chapters, competing theories and hypotheses are prevalent in most areas of child sexual abuse. Although each theory has its advocates, none of them has been shown to be clearly superior in explaining or understanding this phenomenon. Most of them are valuable in some instances and relatively valueless in others. Some empirical research and clinical observations support one theory, while other research and observations contradict that theory and support another. We do not believe that this state of affairs indicates that the theories are all fatally flawed; rather, we believe that it reflects the complex interaction between the many forms of child sexual abuse and the idiosyncratic nature of each abuse victim. We doubt that any overarching theory will adequately explain this extraordinarily complex area, and we are concerned that efforts to formulate such a theory may constrict rather than enhance our ability to conceptualize and successfully handle as many child sexual abuse cases as possible.

When appropriate, we present these competing theories and discuss their apparent strengths and weaknesses. We refrain from endorsing one or another because we believe that any such endorsement is premature at this stage. By presenting a variety of theories, we hope to expand the ability of the reader to conceptualize the process of child sexual abuse and to understand how that process interacts with the individuals involved to produce certain consequences. Readers should then be able to gain an understanding of specific cases of child sexual abuse that may not have been understandable before.

Throughout this book, we use the title *clinician* to refer to the person who works directly with the victim or family in a therapeutic fashion. Terms such as *mental health professional* might be more generic but are more bulky. The use of *therapist* on some pages, *counselor* on others, and *social worker* on still others would indicate the types of professionals who intervene with victims and their families, but the use of different terms might be confusing and might suggest incorrectly that only certain types of professionals work with certain types of situations. The term *clinician* may not be directly applicable to individuals from social work or legal agencies who manage a case without providing direct clinical services, but we assume that much of the information of concern to clinicians will also be of concern to case managers.

CHAPTER TWO

Definitions of Abuse

*T*he term *child sexual abuse* is used widely by both professionals and laypeople with the implicit, if not explicit, understanding that the term has the same meaning for all. As a result of this myth of shared meaning, almost any statistic or comment about child sexual abuse is accepted as if the phenomenon being described is uniquely defined. However, close examination reveals that nothing could be further from the truth. As Atteberry-Bennett and Reppucci (1986) note, "A review of the literature suggests that total agreement, even in cases where sexual intercourse has taken place between an adult and child, does not exist" (p. 1). Not only do public and professional groups have differing definitions but mental health, legal, and social service professionals frequently differ among themselves; and differences exist within professional groups—for instance, mental health researchers commonly use different definitions when investigating the phenomenon. This lack of a shared definition has profound implications for our knowledge and understanding of the entire field of child sexual abuse. In this chapter, we discuss the importance of definition, review research and legal definitions, and discuss contrasting definitions used by professional groups and laypersons.

Importance of Definition

As with other social concerns, definition can be of critical importance in the area of child sexual abuse because problem solutions are frequently determined on the basis of problem definition (Caplan and Nelson, 1973). For example, if child sexual abuse is defined as an individual problem, the solution will involve individual interventions, whereas if it is defined as an environmental or situational problem, solutions or interventions will focus on the environment. Definition also determines which acts are dealt with in which ways. For instance, if exhibitionism and engaging in intercourse with children are both included in the same definition, the perpetrators of these acts may be dealt with similarly. The extent to which the acts are defined differently may determine differential treatment of the perpetrators.

Definitional issues are critical in all areas of child maltreatment because operational definitions are used to determine when intervention into the privacy of the family is permissible. At the core of this ethical and legal dilemma are the competing interests of protecting the constitutionally guaranteed right of family privacy while at the same time using the *parens patriae* power of the state to protect children. Throughout the area of child maltreatment remarkably little consensus exists as to when a court should find a child abused (Bourne and Newberger, 1977; Gelles, 1980; Wald, 1975) or as to what is in the child's best interests. Rosenberg and Hunt (1984) point out that mental health and legal professionals disagree about the evidence necessary to prove abuse in general and consequently disagree about the point at which it is justifiable to intervene in a family. On one end of the continuum, those favoring protection of family privacy argue for limiting state intervention to only the most extreme cases (see Goldstein, Freud, and Solnit, 1979). They recommend definitions of abuse that are purposefully specific and narrow. Critics who agree with this position contend that current definitions of abuse are unconstitutionally vague, thereby permitting interventions based on subjective opinion (Day, 1977–1978). On the other end of the continuum are those favoring protection of the child at all costs. These individuals recommend interventions based on suspicions of abuse, defined quite broadly, in order to prevent an escalation of the abuse to extreme forms (Bourne and Newberger, 1977; Feshbach and Feshbach, 1978).

Definitional Standards

Garbarino and Gilliam (1980) describe the difficulty in defining all forms of child abuse by emphasizing that the definition depends on the circumstances in which the behavior occurred. They suggested that abusiveness should be determined by using such factors as "(1) the intention of the actor, (2) the act's effects upon the recipient, (3) an observer's value judgments about the act, and (4) the source of the standard for that judgment" (p. 5). They propose, for example, that intention be used to discriminate between acts performed for the sexual stimulation of the offender and acts performed simply to convey feelings of affection.

All these factors have clear relevance for a definition of child sexual abuse but may be difficult to apply to actual cases. Consider, for example, the following:

> A family living in a commune consists of a father, mother, five-year-old boy, and seven-year-old girl. The children and parents participate in mutual massage while naked as part of their normal family routine. They do not directly manipulate genitalia, but as a result of the massage both the parents and the children occasionally become sexually stimulated; such stimulation does not appear to be viewed as a problem by either the parents or the children.

In what ways are we to judge the intentions of the parents and distinguish them from those of a father who fondles his daughter when the mother is not at home? How are we to judge the effects on the children, especially if, as authors such as Gelinas (1983) hypothesize, the effects of child sexual abuse may not become apparent for years? What community standards should be brought to bear—those of the commune in which these parents live or those of the county in which the commune is located? As this example demonstrates, arriving at a definition can be quite difficult, and if this definition determines whether this family will be intervened with, the definition is of great importance to each member of the family.

Value judgments based on prevailing community standards, normative family behavior, and our scientific understanding of parent/child relations are commonly used to define sexually abusive acts. However, these criteria are clearly imprecise and subject to interpretation that will vary as a result of professional beliefs and biases, cultural and community standards, and personal values.

Garbarino, Guttman, and Seeley (1986) suggest that the definitions of psychological maltreatment of children be developmentally based because acts that may be maltreatment at one point in the child's development may not be so earlier or later. Such a perspective might be valuable in the area of child sexual abuse also, but the specific ages at which some acts, such as bathing a child, are appropriate are difficult to determine.

Acknowledging the difficulties in defining child sexual abuse, Finkelhor (1979) describes three standards that influenced the development of his research definition: the consent standard, the report of the victim, and the community standard. The consent standard maintains that an act is abusive if a child does not consent to it. Children, however, may report later that they felt victimized by the act but did not openly object because they did not think they could say no to an adult. In addition, there is the question of whether it is possible for children to give informed consent to a sexual act because of their lessened awareness of its meaning and possible consequences. Finkelhor resolves this issue by asserting that children cannot give informed consent to participate in a sexual act with an adult. The specific age at which childhood ends, however, may be open to debate. For instance, the American Psychological Association has argued that a fourteen-year-old is competent to consent to an abortion (Bales, 1987), and one wonders whether it should be assumed that the fourteen-year-old was unable to consent to the sex that caused her pregnancy. In a similar fashion, Finkelhor rejects the standard of feeling victimized; he asserts that victimization can occur even if the victim does not feel victimized. Thus, he includes in his data some respondents who describe their experiences as positive.

Finally, Finkelhor considers the community standard as the most critical because it is based on the age of both victim and perpetrator as well as on the relationship between the two and because legal definitions are often based on these criteria. As just noted, however, which community should supply the standard is often open to question. Although some acts of physical contact between children and adults may generally be seen as sexual abuse, for many other acts general agreement may not be possible. Many definitions (such as "acts designed to stimulate the adult") have been kept vague because of the impossibility of listing every conceivable act as either abusive or not. The vaguenesᵣ of these definitions may cause differences in the treatment of adults, children, and families in different locales.

A final difficulty in the definition of abusive acts is the use of varying terminology to convey a certain attitude about them. Adams and Fay (1981) prefer the term *sexual assault* because it suggests the seriousness and harmfulness of the act. Constantine (1981) recommends using *sexual misuse* or *sexual exploitation* to separate abusive from nonabusive sexual encounters between children and adults. The National Legal Resource Center for Child Advocacy and Protection (1984) suggests using the term *sexual abuse* to refer to an act "generally perpetrated by an adult the child knows, most often a parent, guardian, or a person with authority over the child, and [that] generally has no commercial element" (p. 1) and the term *sexual exploitation* for an act that "usually involves a commercial element: children selling themselves or being sold as prostitutes or models" (p. 1).

Research Definitions

In general the term *sexual abuse* is used by researchers to cover a multitude of vaguely defined acts. Peters, Wyatt, and Finkelhor (1986) report that the definition of child sexual abuse used in many studies combines contact abuse, such as all behaviors that involve intercourse, oral and anal sex, and fondling of breasts and genitals, with noncontact abuse, which usually refers to encounters with exhibitionists and solicitation to engage in sexual activity. In response to the belief that noncontact abuse may not be of the same seriousness as contact abuse, a few researchers, such as Russell (1983) and Wyatt (1985), have reported their results separating noncontact and contact abuse. Prevalence rates, as we will see in Chapter Three, were clearly increased by using noncontact abuse as part of the definition. Another definitional criterion is the inclusion or exclusion of peers as perpetrators. Some investigators include only incidents with adult perpetrators (Fritz, Stoll, and Wagner, 1981), while others include some peer experiences if they were reported as unwanted (Russell, 1983) or coercive (Wyatt, 1985).

Wyatt and Peters (1986) use four of the most cited large-scale survey studies (Finkelhor, 1979, 1984; Russell, 1983; Wyatt, 1985) to describe differences in the definitions used and their impact on the reported prevalence of child sexual abuse. Finkelhor's 1979 study used male and female college students, and his 1984 investigation used male and female parents of children six to fourteen years of age. In both studies, all types of contact and noncontact acts were included, from intercourse and genital fondling to exhibition of genitals to hugging, kissing, or fondling in a sexual way to sexual overtures. In the 1979 study, Finkelhor included three age ranges: experiences between a child twelve and under with an adult eighteen or over, experiences between a child twelve and under and a person under eighteen but at least five years older than the child, and experiences between adolescents aged thirteen to sixteen with adults at least ten years older. The same criteria were used in Finkelhor's 1984 study except that the subject had to consider the experience to have been sexual abuse.

In contrast to Finkelhor, Russell (1983) and Wyatt (1985) both used urban community samples composed entirely of women, the upper age limit was seventeen, and contact and noncontact abuse were separated for analyses. Russell included intrafamilial contact abuse at all ages, but for adolescents aged fourteen to seventeen extrafamilial contact was included only if it was completed or attempted forcible rape. No age discrepancy between victim and perpetrator was required, meaning that peer abuse was included. Wyatt's definition of abuse used the consent standard: For incidents that took place when the victim was twelve or younger and that involved an older partner, experiences were considered abusive regardless of consent. For youth from thirteen to seventeen years old, voluntary experiences with older partners were not defined as sexual abuse.

The result of varying the factors of age of victim, age of perpetrator, and type of act is that prevalence-rate differences occur that appear to be the result of definition alone (Wyatt and Peters, 1986). For example, Finkelhor (1979) and Russell (1983) used somewhat more restrictive definitions than did Wyatt (1985). Imposition of these more restrictive criteria on Wyatt's sample resulted in a 14 percent decrease in the number of women identified as abused.

Legal Definitions

According to Bulkley (1985a), definitions of child sexual abuse are found in child sex offense, incest, and child protection statutes. A fourth type of statute, regarding domestic violence and sexual psychopaths, may be invoked to protect children from intrafamilial sexual abuse. In this section, we briefly examine the three types of statutes that provide legal definitions. The information is drawn almost exclusively from Bulkley's 1985 edition of *Child Sexual Abuse and the Law*, which provides state-by-state information on all laws in existence. This volume is an essential reference for anyone concerned about these issues. Because laws are frequently changed or modified, however, specific references to states may become inaccurate.

Child Sex Offense Statutes. Sexual activity with children by adults is a crime in every state of the Union. Sex offense statutes were developed with the goal of protecting young children (Kocen and Bulkley, 1985). Until the late 1800s, most states used the terms *carnal knowledge, carnal abuse,* or *sexual intercourse* to refer to the prohibition of sex with females under the age of ten. By the 1950s and 1960s, the age of prohibition had been raised to as high as seventeen in several states, necessitating the development of statutory rape laws. The goals of these laws were the prevention of sexual exploitation and the promotion of certain moral attitudes regarding sexuality.

Reforms in these laws have led to more specific definitions of prohibited acts. For example, forty-two states and two territories explicitly define *deviate sexual intercourse* as anal or oral intercourse or as fellatio, cunnilingus, and analingus, instead of leaving it to the judge or jury to interpret its meaning. A tiered structure of offenses with penalties based on the age of the victim or the perpetrator or both is now used in many states. For example, in the state of Washington, intercourse with a child under eleven is criminal only if the perpetrator is over thirteen; with a child eleven, twelve, or thirteen, it is criminal when the perpetrator is over sixteen; and with a child fourteen or fifteen, when the perpetrator is over eighteen. (Note that the age differences in legal definitions are considerably smaller than those in the research definitions just reviewed.) When the child is older, the penalties are lower. Relationships between child and perpetrator are also taken into account in that special protections from abuse by family members or other caretakers are often included in these laws. Thus, consenting intercourse may be specifically prohibited if the adult is a parent or legal guardian; someone acting *in loco parentis;* a custodian, in charge of care or supervision of the child; a foster parent; a blood or affinity (by marriage) relative; a household member; or a person in a position of authority over the child, such as a teacher.

Despite these reforms, there are numerous inconsistencies in the laws across states. The lower age at which children can consent to sexual activity ranges from eleven to seventeen years. Although some states do not penalize voluntary intercourse between adolescents close in age, others supply minimum penalties. Penalties for perpetrators range from one year in prison to life imprisonment or death. Finally, the definitions of prohibited acts vary widely: Some state statutes still use terms such as *carnal knowledge* without defining them; other statutes specifically state the organs considered intimate and prohibit touching them or the clothing covering them directly.

Incest Statutes. All states except New Jersey have incest laws; however, every state with incest laws limits the criminal act of incest to sexual intercourse. Prosecutions involving other sexual contact, even anal and oral sodomy, must be brought under other laws, as is the case for incestuous acts in New Jersey. Wulkan and Bulkley (1985) state that incest laws in the United States were originally passed "primarily to protect against biological risk of dysgenic effect on the offspring of consanguineal relations" (p. 53) and thus prohibited only sexual intercourse between blood relatives. More recently, many states have revised their laws to protect family solidarity and thus forbid nonconsanguineous sexual relationships between adoptive parents or stepparents and children. These reforms appear to reflect a desire to protect children from sexual abuse by guardians and others who act *in loco parentis,* and indicate movement away from viewing incest as posing primarily a biological threat. However, four states—Michigan, New Hampshire, Ohio, and Vermont—have repealed their criminal incestuous provisions and therefore do not have incest laws that specifically cover the sexual abuse of children. These states do prohibit sexual intercourse between adult relatives and children in their general criminal statutes regarding sexual offenses. Moreover, in fifteen states incest is still a crime only between blood relatives. Penalties vary widely from imprisonment of less than one year to ten years or more, and fines range from $500 to $150,000.

Atteberry-Bennett (1987, pp. 15–16) uses the state of Virginia as an example of the impact of the definition of incest:

> In Virginia, incest that occurs as intercourse between sibling, half sibling, adoptive sibling, uncle/ aunt, and uncle/aunt of half blood is considered a misdemeanor (punishable by one to ten years in prison, and less than or equal to a $1,000 fine). Incest with a daughter or granddaughter, a son or grandson, or a father or mother is considered a class 5 felony (punishable by not less than one year and not more than ten years in prison or one year

in prison and/or a $1,000 fine). However, the age of the child involved is taken into consideration in defining the seriousness of the crime. If a parent has intercourse with a child at least thirteen years old but less than fifteen years of age, the parent is guilty of a class 3 felony (punishable by not less than five years nor more than twenty years in prison). Notice that in the case of incest, intercourse with an older child is considered a more serious crime, whereas in the case of an extrafamilial sexual contact (as written in the child sex-offense statutes) intercourse with an older child is considered a less serious crime.

Child Protection Statutes. Two types of civil statutes, reporting laws and juvenile or family court jurisdiction acts, have as their primary purpose the protection of abused and neglected children. Statutory definitions in every state can be interpreted to include sexual abuse even if it is not explicitly mentioned. More than twenty states now specifically include sexual abuse, but only one state, Kansas, defines which acts constitute sexual abuse (Bulkley, 1985a). A child protection proceeding can be brought against the passive parent as well as the abusive parent if the passive parent fails to prevent the abuse from occurring. Because the father is usually the abusive parent, the culpability of the mother becomes important in determining whether a child-neglect or criminal proceeding against her is appropriate. For instance, in *Sutton* v. *Commonwealth of Virginia* (1985) the conviction of a woman as a principal in the second degree in the rape of her niece (who was living with her) by her husband was upheld because the woman had encouraged the niece to have sex with her husband and later had threatened her if she did not do it. Although the woman was not present physically during the sexual intercourse, her "constructive presence" had been established to the court's satisfaction.

Although reporting laws in all fifty states require certain persons who work with or care for children, such as physicians and teachers, to report suspected abuse or neglect to public child protective agencies, data from the 1979–1980 National Incidence Study (NIS) suggest that professionals report only about 33 percent of suspected cases (Burgdorf, 1981). However, sexual abuse was more likely (56 percent) to be reported than other forms of abuse and maltreatment. In a separate investigation of physician reporting practices in Virginia, Saulsbury and Campbell (1985) found that 38 percent of the 307 physicians sampled justified nonreporting on the grounds of not being certain of the diagnosis. Kalichman, Craig, and Follingstad (1987) found that 19 percent of 144 mental health professionals would not report a presented case of child abuse and that the factor most influential in this decision was their lack of confidence that abuse had occurred. Diagnosis, as will be seen in Chapters Six and Seven, may be based on many sources of data, but the definition of sexual abuse is not the least of these. It may be that failure to clearly define which acts constitute child sexual abuse has a meaningful impact on reporting rates. Few states define child sexual abuse, and ten states use their criminal statutes regarding sexual offenses to define it. Even in the few states with specific definitions, the definitions for purposes of criminal prosecution may be different from those for a child protection proceeding. Bulkley (1985a) strongly suggests that legislatures provide specific definitions of sexual abuse within the civil statutes themselves as a way of encouraging reporting.

Summary. Finkelhor's (1979) notion that laws concerning sexual abuse can be considered reflections of community standards and therefore can provide some useful guidelines for definitions of child sexual abuse appears to have some validity. The criteria that most legal definitions depend on tend to be the ages of the child and the perpetrator and the type of act. However, wide variations exist from state to state, especially in regard to the specific acts that are defined as constituting sexual abuse. In general, children under the age of eighteen are protected from sexual activity with a parent or anyone who is in a parental or custodial position. Children who are thirteen or fourteen tend to be protected from sexual activity with anyone three or more years older than they are. Children under the age of thirteen are protected from all sexual activity. Children over the age of fourteen tend to be protected from sexual activity with someone other than a custodial figure only if they do not consent to the sexual activity.

Empirical Investigations of Definitions
Used by Professionals and Laypeople

Various professional groups are involved in each individual case of child sexual abuse (Atteberry-Bennett, 1987), and these groups tend to use definitional criteria that are most in line with the goals of their own profession (Caplan and Nelson, 1973). Protective service social workers are mandated by law to investigate suspected cases of child sexual abuse in order to protect the interests of children. Legal professionals are involved in the prosecution and defense of the offenders. Mental health professionals are involved in providing assessment and treatment to victims, offenders, and their families. Numerous other professionals who work with children, such as teachers, physicians, and police officers, can also be involved in these cases. Each of these groups, as well as the general public, may have quite different definitions of child sexual abuse, and this can lead to confusion in selecting treatment and making legal decisions about a particular case.

Since the 1970s, a few researchers (Giovannoni and Becerra, 1979; Christopherson, 1983) have taken this issue seriously and have systematically studied definitions of child abuse in general among various professional groups and the public. Finkelhor and Redfield (1984), Atteberry-Bennett (1987), and Atteberry-Bennett and Reppucci (1986) have examined these matters specifically with regard to child sexual abuse.

Finkelhor and Redfield (1984) used a series of vignettes to study laypersons' definitions of sexual abuse. Across vignettes, the investigators varied nine factors selected as sources of controversy in definitions: the age and sex of the victim, the age and sex of the perpetrator, the relationship between the victim and the perpetrator, the sexual act, consent, the consequence of the abuse, and the sex of the respondent. Using multiple regression analysis, they analyzed 9,839 vignettes from 521 adult respondents living in the Boston area and found that the age of the perpetrator, if under twenty, and the type of act committed were the most significant components of the definitions. If the perpetrator was over twenty, there was virtually no distinction by age, but teen perpetrators were viewed as less abusive than adults and more abusive than younger children. In terms of acts committed, intercourse, attempted intercourse, and genital fondling were all rated as highly abusive. Verbal abuse with a sexual theme was rated as the least abusive act. Other findings included less abusive ratings when the perpetrators were women, with male respondents rating situations with women perpetrators less serious than did the women respondents. The age of the victim had some influence, with less abusive ratings when the victims were either younger or older than pre- or early adolescence. The consequence of the abuse was the least important variable.

Atteberry-Bennett (1987) and Atteberry-Bennett and Reppucci (1986) have completed preliminary analysis of definitional data obtained from four groups of professionals most likely to be involved in cases of child sexual abuse—legal professionals, protective service workers, probation and parole workers, and mental health professionals—and a group of parents not in these professions. Using a five-point rating scale that ranged from definitely sexual abuse to definitely not sexual abuse, a total of 255 participants responded to a series of forty-eight vignettes that varied according to the age of the child (five, ten, and fifteen), the sex of the parent/child combination (mother/son or father/daughter), and the act involved (the parent hugs the child, kisses the child on the lips as the parent goes to work in the morning, sleeps in the same bed with the child, enters the bathroom without knocking while the child is bathing, is nude in front of the child, photographs the child in the nude, touches the child's genitals, and has sexual intercourse with the child). The term *often* was used in each vignette; thus, all acts were stated as occurring with the same frequency. As an example: "A mother often sleeps in the same bed with her ten-year-old son." Because this is the only study that has investigated professionals' responses to possible instances of child sexual abuse, we summarize its findings in some detail.

Across all groups, the acts involving fathers and daughters were rated as more abusive than the same acts involving mothers and sons. For instance, a mother touching a five- or ten-year-old son's genitals was rated as less abusive than the same act involving a father and daughter. Such results suggest that mothers may be allowed more leeway in what is recognized as acceptable behavior than fathers, possibly because of mothers' caretaker role. All acts increased in ratings of abusiveness with an increase in age of the child, with the exception of sexual intercourse, which was perceived as equally abusive at all ages. This result differs from Finkelhor and Redfield's (1984) finding that acts involving preadolescents were viewed as more abusive than those involving older children. Note, however, that in both studies, acts with young children (except for intercourse) were viewed as less abusive than similar acts with children in puberty, reflecting, perhaps, a view that sexual behavior of any type has less impact on supposedly asexual young children. Sexual intercourse was clearly seen as the most abusive act and hugging as the least abusive act, but there was a mixture of ratings on all other acts.

When the five respondent groups were compared, the mental health and the legal professionals were consistently significantly different from one another in their definitions of abuse. Mental health professionals rated almost all vignettes involving parents being nude in front of five- and ten-year-olds as significantly more abusive than did the legal professionals. In addition, mental health professionals rated the vignettes involving parents and children sleeping in the same bed as significantly more abusive than did any other group. Legal professionals rated the act of a parent touching a child's genitals as significantly less abusive than did any other group.

In order to assess the seriousness of any given act, respondents were asked to rate several possible intervention strategies that they might recommend in regard to the various vignettes. They were asked first to choose whether they felt any intervention was necessary. There was complete agreement that some intervention was necessary when the act involved sexual intercourse, regardless of the age of the child or parent/child relationship. A high level of agreement also occurred when the act involved touching genitals or photographing a child in the nude, regardless of age or parent/child dyad. For the other acts, the results were diverse. The age of the child was a major factor with some acts. For example, often hugging a five-year-old child yielded a 90 percent agreement that no intervention was required. However, often hugging a ten- or fifteen-year-old child resulted in 20 percent of the respondents suggesting some sort of intervention. The act of often kissing a child on the lips resulted in even more disagreement. Although most of the respondents felt that no intervention was necessary when a parent often kissed a five-year-old child on the lips, a range of 44 percent to 67 percent of the respondents felt that some intervention should be undertaken when parents often kissed ten- and fifteen-year-old children on the lips. Similarly, 90 percent of the respondents felt that some type of intervention was called for when a parent often appeared nude in front of a ten- or fifteen-year-old child, but only 75 percent thought it was appropriate when the child was five years old.

For other acts, respondents appeared to consider the parent/child dyad as opposed to age when determining whether intervention was indicated. Although 90 percent of the respondents agreed that some sort of intervention was necessary when either parent often enters a bathroom while a fifteen-year-old of the opposite sex is bathing, intervention was dependent on the parent/child combination for younger children. Although only 25 percent of the respondents suggested intervention when a mother often enters the bathroom on a five-year-old son, 52 percent considered this a situation for intervention when the actors were father and daughter. Likewise, although 79 percent felt intervention was needed when a mother often enters a bathroom while her ten-year-old son is bathing, an even larger 90 percent viewed intervention as called for when the father/daughter dyad was involved. When the act was a parent often sleeping with or being nude in front of a five-year-old child, the need for intervention was lessened but still greater for a father/daughter combination than for a mother/son dyad.

If the respondents recommended intervention, they were asked to rate eight possible interventions on a five-point scale from "definitely would not recommend" to "definitely would recommend." The eight interventions were educational counseling, family therapy, therapy for the child, therapy for the adult, investigation by a child protective service agency, removal of the child from the home, removal of the adult from the home, and prosecution of the adult in court. Mental health professionals recommended family, child, and adult therapy significantly more often than did legal professionals. Protective service workers were most in favor of referrals to child protective service agencies for investigation, while parents and legal professionals were least in favor of this intervention. Agreeing with professionals in the Finkelhor, Gomes-Schwartz, and Horowitz (1984) investigation of proposed interventions in a hypothetical case of child sexual abuse, no group was highly in favor of removal of the child from the home. Surprisingly, parents were less opposed to this intervention than were the professional groups. Mental health professionals were significantly more willing to remove the adult from the home than were either legal professionals or probation and parole workers, and even though this intervention was not highly favored, it was preferred to removal of the child. Although prosecution of the perpetrator was not highly endorsed by any group, legal professionals, parents, and probation and parole workers were significantly less in favor of this intervention than were mental health professionals.

The relatively small samples of approximately fifty persons in each group, consisting entirely of Virginians, and the use of a restricted number of one-line vignettes limits the definitiveness of these findings. In addition, the fact that all vignettes were part of a questionnaire asking specifically about child sexual abuse may have skewed the respondents' ratings of abuse and recommendations for intervention. However, because professionals usually get involved only when there is a suspicion of child sexual abuse, the characteristics of that situation may be more similar to, than different from, those of the questionnaire situation. Regardless of these possible methodological limitations, the results suggest that definitions of child sexual abuse vary between parents and professionals and between professional groups, and that these definitions influence the interventions that may be recommended in various situations.

The greater discrepancies in response between the legal

and mental health professionals than between the other groups may be a function of their respective professional roles. To define a behavior as abusive for a mental health professional may simply mean that a child or family should be given help in the form of a therapeutic intervention. Given that these interventions are believed to be beneficial for the family and child, a broader definition of abuse would allow for more families to be helped. For legal professionals, however, a finding of abuse may require legal action, and because such action increases the chance of subsequent disruption in the life of an individual or a family, legal definitions of child sexual abuse are limited to only the most clear-cut cases.

Conclusions

As we stated in the beginning of this chapter, a myth of shared meaning surrounds the general area of child maltreatment and the specific area of child sexual abuse. By examining the various definitions that have been used by researchers to determine estimates of prevalence, by the legal system to determine when to intervene either to protect the child or to prosecute the perpetrator, and by professional helpers and the general public to decide whether and what kind of intervention is necessary, we have tried to demonstrate just how important shared definitions are. The task of communicating about an issue is infinitely more difficult when the same term does not convey identical meaning because the implications can be so different. Child sexual abuse is just such a term. If different professional groups do not have consensual definitions, they should become aware of their differences in order to coordinate their efforts and increase the probability of outcomes that are in the public interest. Because there is every reason to believe that mental health professionals will be called on increasingly to provide expert opinion to clarify legal definitions of child sexual abuse, it is vitally important that legal and mental health professionals be able to communicate and to work cooperatively with each other. Their differences should not be allowed to exacerbate the trauma to the child victims and their families.

The use of a broad and encompassing definition of child

sexual abuse dramatically increases the number of children who can be categorized as having been abused. Thus, a broad definition has been valuable in alerting professionals and the public to the widespread nature of these abusive experiences. However, now that we have been alerted and want to study the phenomenon closely, too broad a definition may be an impediment. The broad definition yields such a heterogeneous group that an investigation of it is often meaningless, just as studying the effects of television on children might be meaningless if researchers looked at a group of fifty three- to seventeen-year-old boys and girls from a variety of cultural backgrounds. Any effect of a specific type of abuse or of abuse on a specific type of child might become lost in the varying effects of other types of abuse on other children. For example, the effects on a diverse group of sexually abused children might appear to be minimal because the meaningful negative effects on a small group of children who experienced intercourse were masked by the minimal effect on a larger group who only saw an exhibitionist. In this situation, misleading information might be given about the effects of abuse on children experiencing intercourse.

For this reason, we do not believe it appropriate to develop a specific definition of child sexual abuse for use throughout the field (even if this were possible, which is doubtful). We do, however, need careful descriptions of specifically which types of child sexual abuse are being studied or which types of victims are being intervened with. Terms like *child sexual abuse* should be used sparingly and only in the most general sense, with detailed descriptions used whenever possible. For instance, phrases that are relatively specific, such as *children molested by their parents,* or even more specific, such as *adolescents who have had intercourse with their fathers,* provide much more meaningful information than does *child sexual abuse victims.* Keeping in mind how both our cultural values and our mores affect our definitions of child sexual abuse, we can understand why clear definitions are critical to developing a reasonable research, clinical, legal, and social agenda for the future.

CHAPTER THREE

Extent of the Problem

*T*he incidence of child sexual abuse received scant attention in the first half of this century. The first well-known report came from Kinsey and others' 1953 study of female sexual behavior. The surge of interest since the 1960s in child sexual abuse has prompted many researchers to examine closely the incidence of the various forms of child sexual abuse. These studies are discussed in this chapter.

Initially, we provide a short summary of the value of this line of research, followed by a discussion of its strengths and limitations. The results of the studies are then presented. Although the data may be a bit dry, they provide the basis for much of what we know about child sexual abuse. We have tried to compare the results of the studies when possible. We have been quite limited in this endeavor because (a) this line of research has just recently emerged, (b) few studies have been done to replicate previous work, and (c) the basic pattern has been for each researcher to investigate a different segment of the population using a different method of investigation. Not only do these limitations make comparison of studies difficult, but the comparisons may be misleading. We are therefore cautious in this area.

Value of the Research

Incidence research provides an understanding of the extent to which the sexual abuse of children occurs, both in general and in various segments of our society. This information alone has made a great difference in the way that child sexual abuse is perceived by professionals and the general public. Despite the study by Kinsey, Pomeroy, Martin, and Gebhard (1953), it had been commonly assumed that child sexual abuse occurred rarely and that when it did occur it usually involved chance encounters with strangers or relationships between mentally disturbed adults and low-functioning children. Most likely, these assumptions were based partially on the widespread belief in Freud's theory of development and his clear rejection of the tenet that fathers could be sexually interested in their daughters. Recent systematic research has shown both these assumptions to be false. Much of today's increased interest in the identification and treatment of sexually abused children, as well as in the prevention of sexual abuse, can be attributed to the research on prevalence, as it has shown that child sexual abuse occurs in all segments of our society and that children in any family can experience sexual abuse.

The results of the research and the subsequent public acceptance of child sexual abuse as a significant problem have made it increasingly easy for sexually abused children, or adults who were sexually abused as children, to reveal their abuse, to be taken seriously, and to seek help if it is needed. Interviews with many sexual abuse victims reveal that they often believe themselves to be the only ones who have suffered abuse. Making the true prevalence known may have helped many victims take steps to ameliorate the effects of their earlier abuse as they came to see their experience and their reaction to it as less unique. These studies have also provided some valuable preliminary information about the children who have the greatest risk of being sexually abused. This knowledge can be used to aim preventive efforts toward these groups of children.

Strengths and Weaknesses of the Research

Three types of subjects have generally been used in this research. The first consists of "normal" individuals who have been recruited from college campuses, metropolitan areas, and national samples. These large-scale studies are done by asking, for instance, all the students in a college class or randomly selected individuals in a city to reveal any previous sexual abuse experiences on a survey form or through individual interviews. The second group includes those who have come to the attention of mental health, social service, or legal agencies for a variety of reasons. Groups of delinquents, prostitutes, and clients in mental health clinics have been studied. As in the large-scale surveys, individuals in these groups are asked to reveal child sexual abuse experiences. The third group comprises children or adults who have previously been identified as victims of child sexual abuse because they either have asked for therapy or have become involved in the legal or child protective systems. Before we review the results of the research, it would be wise to discuss its strengths and weaknesses. An understanding of these strengths and limitations will allow the reader to assess the degree of accuracy with which we can presently judge the incidence of child sexual abuse.

General Limitations

Some factors affect the results of all research. We mention them briefly here and note later the specific ways in which they have an impact on each type of research.

Rate of Participation. One important consideration when viewing the results of any survey is the rate of participation among the group of possible subjects. It is generally believed that a high rate of participation of all those eligible is important if one wants to ensure that the results of a survey are representative of the particular group examined and not just representative of those from that group who are willing to participate. If a factor systematically eliminates or reduces the participation of some segment of the group, then those who do participate are not representative of the entire group. This concern is magnified in child sexual abuse research because of the sensitive nature of the topic. Some individuals may not want to become involved in a survey because they do not want to admit to or discuss their sexual abuse experiences. Victims of certain types of abuse may be less willing than other victims to participate. Nonabused individuals may decline to participate because they may feel that if they do, others will assume that they have been abused.

Honesty. Honesty is closely tied to rate of participation because a researcher wants a high rate not merely of participation but of honest participation. Again, this problem is magnified in research of a sensitive nature. Abused individuals may not be willing to admit abuse, and victims of serious types of abuse may be the least willing to describe it. In such a case, the rates of abuse or of a particular type of abuse may be underreported by surveys.

Large-Scale Surveys

Choice of Sample. Large-scale surveys provide information that is not available from more limited samples because the experiences of a wide range of individuals can be examined. Consequently, a picture of the incidence of sexual abuse across segments of the population can be provided. However, several factors limit the information that can be obtained from these surveys. The most obvious involves the choice of a particular group to be surveyed. Several surveys have been done with college undergraduates; however, the typical college undergraduate is not representative of all of his or her peers. If sexual abuse is debilitating, and if the colleges require a demonstration of above-average academic and social ability in the students who are admitted, one would expect that the college surveys would produce a lower number of abused victims than would be found in the general population and that those who are found might show fewer consequences of the abuse.

Surveys of more varied population samples, such as those in metropolitan areas, provide information about the sexual abuse of a diverse group of individuals. The location of the survey may influence the results, however, because sexual abuse victims may be more numerous in some locales than in others. For instance, surveys of areas with high concentrations of individuals in low and lower-middle socioeconomic groups might indicate high rates of sexual abuse. Children with lower socioeconomic status are at a higher risk for abuse than are children with higher socioeconomic status (Finkelhor, 1980a); and if the effects of child sexual abuse are debilitating, victims may be less able to function well in society and consequently may be overrepresented in the lower economic groups. Consequently, generalizing results from a lower socioeconomic area to the general population might be misleading. (A high rate of child sexual abuse in lower socioeconomic areas is still, however, a meaningful problem.) Also, victims in certain locales might be more willing to reveal sexual abuse experiences than victims in other areas; survey results from a candid, unreserved group would be likely to provide a more accurate estimate of the prevalence rate than results from a survey of a more inhibited sample. Russell (1984), for instance, stated that she interviewed women in San Francisco in part because of her belief that women in that city would be more willing to reveal abuse experiences than would women elsewhere. We have no way of knowing how accurate her belief is, and we have no information in general that clarifies the ways in which the choice of certain samples can influence the prevalence rates estimated by large-scale surveys.

Rate of Participation. Following the common social science belief that high participation rate increases the accuracy of prevalence-rate estimates, researchers have attempted to maximize participation in their studies by various methods. Finkelhor (1979) had college students complete an anonymous questionnaire in class, with a resulting 90 percent participation rate. To ensure that the respondents felt as comfortable as possible while answering questions, Russell (1984) and Wyatt (1985) matched their interviewers by race and gender to those interviewed and provided the interviewers with extensive training. These two surveys had response rates of between 81 percent or 64 percent for Russell and 73 percent or 61 percent for Wyatt, depending on how those who refused to participate are defined.

In any case, one is left with the problem of identifying the characteristics of those who refused to participate.

Haugaard (1987) provides some preliminary information in this area. After completing a survey of college students' sexual abuse experiences, he returned to several of the classes and distributed a second questionnaire, which was completed in class. On this questionnaire the students indicated whether they had returned the original survey, the reason for not returning it if they had not, and whether they had experienced sexual abuse (they were not asked to describe the abuse, merely to indicate whether they had experienced any). Results showed that in classes with a low participation rate (25 percent and 42 percent) the prevalence rate reported by those who completed the original survey was higher than that of the entire class as indicated by the second survey. In a class with a 78 percent participation rate (where the students received credit for returning the original survey), the prevalence rate reported by those who completed the original survey was lower than that of the entire class. The explanation Haugaard puts forward for this phenomenon is that a certain percentage of abused students in each class found their experiences too difficult to recount on the survey. In the classes where no credit was given for returning the original survey, a higher percentage of nonabused subjects failed to return it, overcompensating for the abused students who did not return it. In the class where credit was given, the percentage of nonabused subjects who did not return the survey was low and did not compensate for the number of abused subjects who did not. Apparently, then, the participation rate may have an important influence on the results of large-scale surveys. Unfortunately, we have no information on those individuals who do not participate in large-scale surveys, and so we do not know to what extent the surveys accurately represent sexual abuse experiences.

Honesty. Issues of honesty may have several effects on large-scale surveys. For instance, what effect do personal, face-to-face interviews have on the respondents in surveys such as those by Russell and Wyatt? Each of these investigators found a very high incidence of abuse (especially Wyatt, who reported a 62 percent rate). Does this type of interviewing suggest that sexual abuse is common and thus encourage some of the respondents to exaggerate previous experiences so that they can be included as abuse? Or are many women too embarrassed about a sexual abuse experience to reveal it in a face-to-face interview, regardless of the warmth and understanding of the interviewer? If so, then even these high rates may underestimate the frequency of sexual abuse.

Problems of honesty also exist in written surveys. As just noted, Finkelhor (1979) had his student sample complete the survey forms in class in order to increase the rate of participation. As is often the case in classroom situations, it may have been easy for one student to see what another was writing on the survey form. Consequently, some students may have been inhibited from reporting abuse experiences, especially those experiences that are the least socially acceptable. Some of this problem is eliminated by allowing the students to complete the surveys out of class, but other concerns remain, such as the problem of those who might manufacture an especially horrible experience as a form of amusement.

Surveys of Special Samples

One advantage to studying sexual abuse in special samples is that a large proportion of those surveyed may have been abused and a relatively large sample of abuse victims can be gathered without having to survey many people. Another advantage is that specific effects of sexual abuse, such as sexual promiscuity or clinical depression, may be identified if groups such as prostitutes or depressed patients report a higher rate of child sexual abuse than does the general population. One major drawback to this approach, however, makes it important to interpret research results cautiously. Victims of incest or other forms of sexual abuse often come from disorganized families or have experienced some other sort of trauma. For instance, Herman (1983) found that 50 percent of the fathers in incestuous families were physically abusive toward members of the family. Because the effects of these other possibly debilitating situations are not taken into account, certain outcomes such as depression or prostitution cannot be attributed specifically to the sexual abuse. Although the abuse may have contributed to some of the problems, the unique role that it and the other aspects of a victim's life have played in his or her development cannot be ascertained.

Honesty. The concern over honesty may be relatively more important when interviewing certain groups of individuals. For instance, a number of studies have shown that convicted criminals report a high rate of both physical and sexual abuse. But are the prisoners overreporting abuse because they feel that it gives them an excuse for their criminal behavior or that it might induce sympathy among parole-board members if such information is in their files? Overreporting of sexual abuse may be especially common in sexual offenders because it may give them a ready excuse for their molesting others. Or do they underreport sexual abuse because they are embarrassed to admit that they were once in the position of being helpless victims? Unfortunately, we have no information to judge the honesty with which the surveys were answered.

Studies of Sexual Abuse Victims

It is often possible to collect large groups of identified victims, especially if the source of information is records that extend for several years. With such large groups, it may be possible to explore whether the abuse experience varies across the different subgroups of victims. For instance, it could be determined that young boys are more susceptible to abuse by a certain type of a perpetrator while older girls are more often abused by someone with other characteristics. This information may be important for preventive programs. A meaningful limitation to this line of research is that by including only identified victims, one may form an incorrect impression of the experience of all abuse victims because only a minority of abuse victims reveal their abuse, and those who do may be unrepresentative of all abuse victims. Consequently, although results from research with identified groups of victims may tell us about those individuals who come to the attention of professionals in the legal or mental health fields, generalization of the findings to all abuse victims must be done with caution, if at all.

Conclusion

From this discussion of the limitations of research into the incidence of child sexual abuse, the impression may be conveyed that each type of research is so flawed that there is little reason in doing any of it. This is not the case. Although research with each type of sample has its limitations, research with other types of samples can, in some ways, compensate for these. Consequently, research using a wide range of samples is necessary for a full understanding of the phenomenon of child sexual abuse. Most of the concerns about the validity of sexual abuse surveys have not been addressed. A number of questions, such as the honesty of reports, may be impossible to answer, and others can be only partially answered. We do not mention these concerns as a way of discounting the results of the studies. However, we believe that it is important for the reader to recognize that limitations do exist and consequently that the survey results cannot be taken as an absolutely accurate estimate of the prevalence of child sexual abuse. Having pointed out the strengths and limitations of surveys, we now turn to the prevalence studies and their results.

Large-Scale Surveys

As noted earlier, large-scale surveys have been conducted with college students, women in metropolitan areas, and national samples. As well as using different samples, researchers used different methods to gather the data, and different definitions of child sexual abuse to form the group of victims. The diverse rates of reported abuse may reflect true differences between the samples; however, the use of different methods and definitions may have artificially magnified or diminished these differences. In this section, we summarize the sample, method, and definition of child sexual abuse used in each study, present the overall prevalence rates reported, and compare these prevalence rates when possible. We then provide specific information about the sexual abuse experiences.

Description of the Studies and Their Prevalence Rates

National Samples. One of the earliest estimates of the prevalence of child sexual abuse came from the studies of Kinsey and his associates in the 1940s (Kinsey, Pomeroy, Martin, and Gebhard, 1953). The authors conducted personal interviews with 5,940 white females, and questioned 4,441 of those respondents about childhood sexual experiences with an adult. Although their sample included women from all forty-eight states, it was not random. The authors secured the cooperation of various academic, community, and social groups, and presented their request for subjects to them. As a result, the sample was not representative of all women in the United States. Most of the women were between sixteen and fifty years of age and came from middle to upper socioeconomic backgrounds. Ninety percent of the women were from an urban area. The authors did not state specifically the rate of participation. They noted that 15 percent of the reports came from groups with 100 percent participation of their members, and that the remainder came from groups with participation rates from 50 to 90 percent. Their definition of child sexual experience included sexual activity between a prepubertal female and a postadolescent male at least five years older than the female. Experiences involving either physical contact or nonphysical contact (such as with an exhibitionist) were included (see Table 1 for summary). Twenty-four percent of the women reported an experience with an adult while they were children. When the authors excluded those who had experienced only unsuccessful approaches for sexual activity, the prevalence rate fell to 22 percent. When only sexual activity involving physical contact was considered, the rate fell considerably, to 9.2 percent.

In 1983, the Canadian Government authorized the Na-

Table 1. Definitions of Child Sexual Abuse Used in Prevalence Research.

Study	Size	Sample	Maximum Age of Victim	Minimum Age of Perpetrator	Age Differential	Contact Required	Wanted or Unwanted
Kinsey and others (1953)	4,441	Nonrandom American females	Prepubertal	15	5 years	No	Either
Canadian Population Survey (1984)	2,008	Probability sample of Canadians	15	None	None	No	Unwanted
Russell (1984)	930	Probability sample, women in San Francisco	17	None	None	No	Extrafamilial, unwanted Intrafamilial, either
Wyatt (1985)	248	Probability sample, women in Los Angeles	17	None	Peer abuse, none Other, 5 years	No	If victim ≤ 12, either If victim ≥ 13, unwanted
Finkelhor (1979)	796	Male and female undergraduates	16	None	If victim ≤ 12, 5 years If victim ≥ 13, 10 years	No	Either
Fritz, Stoll, and Wagner (1981)	952	Male and female undergraduates	Prepubertal	Postadolescent	None	Yes	Either
Sedney and Brooks (1984)	310	Female undergraduates	?	?	?	No	?
Fromuth (1986)	383	Female undergraduates	16	None	If victim ≤ 12, 5 years If victim ≥ 13, 10 years	No	Either
Haugaard (1987)	1,089	Male and female undergraduates	16	16	5 years	Yes	Unwanted

tional Population Survey (Committee on Sexual Offenses Against
Children and Youth, 1984; referred to here as the Canadian
Population Survey). This survey examined the prevalence of
sexual assault among Canadian men and women. The Canadian
Gallup Poll formed a sample of 2,135 individuals eighteen years
and older that was statistically representative of the Canadian
population. Each possible subject was visited by a member of
the survey team who explained the project and asked the subject to complete an anonymous questionnaire. While the team
member waited, the respondents completed the questionnaire
privately, sealed and returned it. Thirteen people refused to take
the questionnaire, and 114 returned theirs incomplete, for a completed response rate of 94 percent. Although the survey was concerned with sexual assault against both children and adults, the
results were reported in such a way that the incidence of sexual
assault against children could be isolated. From a definitional
perspective, the survey included only unwanted experiences, and
we will consider the sexual experiences of those fifteen years and
younger. There was no minimum age for the perpetrator nor an
age differential required between the victim and perpetrator.
Twenty-eight percent of the women and 10 percent of the men
surveyed had experienced some sort of contact or noncontact
child sexual abuse. However, unwanted sexual experiences that
involved someone either the same age as or younger than the
victim constituted 40 percent of the total number of reports,
and about 50 percent of the incidents involved physical contact.
From the figures supplied by the Survey, it is impossible to determine the specific number of children who experienced abuse
from a peer or those who experienced contact abuse. Clearly,
though, the percentage of children who were abused by an adult
is lower than 28 percent and 10 percent.

   Samples of Urban Women. Two major surveys have been
taken of women in metropolitan areas (Russell, 1983, 1984;
Wyatt, 1985). In Russell's study, 930 women participated in
personal interviews conducted by an extensively trained staff of
women. The sample consisted of women who were eighteen
years old or older from a probability sample of households in
San Francisco. Each home in the probability sample was visited,

and if a woman meeting the criteria lived there, she was asked to participate. In 17 percent of the homes it was impossible to discover whether a woman meeting the criteria resided there, or the woman refused to cooperate before discovering the nature of the survey. An additional 19 percent who were initially coopera-tive refused to participate once they knew the topic of the inter-view, so the refusal rate was either 19 percent or 36 percent de-pending on the criteria used to determine refusal (Wyatt and Peters, 1986, prefer the lower figure). Russell distinguished be-tween intrafamilial and extrafamilial abuse. Extrafamilial sexual abuse was defined as "one or more unwanted sexual experiences with persons unrelated by blood or marriage, ranging from pet-ing . . . to rape before the victim turned fourteen years, and com-pleted or attempted forcible rape experiences from the ages of fourteen to seventeen years (inclusive)" (Russell, 1983, p. 135). Intrafamilial child sexual abuse was defined as "any kind of ex-ploitive sexual contact that occurred between relatives, no mat-ter how distant the relationship, before the victim turned eigh-teen years old" (p. 136). An experience with a relative less than five years older that was wanted was not regarded as sexual abuse.

Russell reported that 38 percent of the women inter-viewed had experienced some form of sexual abuse involving physical contact before they were eighteen. Twenty-eight per-cent of them had experienced the abuse before their fourteenth birthday. If instances of noncontact abuse, such as with an ex-hibitionist, were also considered as sexual abuse, the number of women reporting an abuse experience before they were eighteen increased to 54 percent.

In a study by Wyatt (1985), personal interviews were completed with 126 black and 122 white women between the ages of eighteen and thirty-six by trained women interviewers matched by race to the subjects. Subjects were selected through randomly generated phone numbers for the metropolitan Los Angeles area. Wyatt states that from the 1,348 households in which a woman resided, 709 women agreed to participate and 266 refused. It was not possible to know whether the women met the demographic requirements in 335 households. (The in-consistency in the figures was not explained.) Consequently, the refusal rate was either 27 percent or 45 percent. From those agreeing to take part, the first 248 were selected. Sexual abuse was defined as both contact and noncontact sexual experiences in which the victim was below eighteen years of age and the perpetrator was at least five years older. If the victim was twelve years or younger, all experiences were considered, whether or not the victim wanted them to occur. For victims who were thirteen to seventeen, only unwanted experiences were considered.

Wyatt found that 59 percent of her sample reported some form of contact or noncontact abuse before their eighteenth birthday. When examined by race, 54 percent of the black women and 65 percent of the white women had had such an experience. When the definition of sexual abuse was expanded to include unwanted experiences with peers less than five years older, the prevalence rate rose to 62 percent, with 57 percent of blacks and 67 percent of whites reporting an incident. Of those falling into this broad definition, 40 percent of the black women and 51 percent of the white women had an experience that involved some sort of physical contact.

College Surveys. Landis (1956) surveyed 1,800 college students over a three-year period, using an anonymous questionnaire. No specific definition of child sexual abuse was stated, although both contact and noncontact experiences were included and any experience prior to the completion of the questionnaire appears to have been considered. Thirty percent of the males and 35 percent of the females reported an abuse experience. Fifty-five percent of the women reporting an abuse incident had only a noncontact experience with an exhibitionist, and 84 percent of the men had experienced a "homosexual approach," the nature of which was not defined in the report.

Finkelhor (1979) surveyed 796 male and female undergraduates from six New England colleges. Anonymous questionnaires were completed in class voluntarily, and 90 percent of the students participated. The victim group included children under twelve who had a wanted or unwanted experience with someone at least five years older, and children thirteen to sixteen years old who had a wanted or unwanted experience with someone at least ten years older. Both contact and noncontact experiences were included. Finkelhor reported that 19 percent of the women and 9 percent of the men in his sample had experienced either contact or noncontact abuse. About 20 percent of all the abuse of girls involved a noncontact experience with an exhibitionist, making those experiencing contact abuse about 15 percent.

Fromuth (1986) used the same definition of sexual abuse as Finkelhor and gave questionnaires to 383 female undergraduates who had previously agreed to participate. Because of the recruiting procedure, the rate of participation of those eligible was not calculable. Fromuth found a 22 percent rate for her sample of women, a rate comparable to that found by Finkelhor.

Haugaard (1987) distributed questionnaires to 1,784 male and female undergraduates at a mid-Atlantic university. The number returned was 1,089, for a return rate of 61 percent. When using a definition similar to that of Finkelhor, Haugaard found a prevalence rate of 11.9 percent for women and 5 percent for men, a lower rate than that found in comparable studies with college students. When only experiences involving unwanted physical contact were considered, the prevalence rate was 10 percent for women and 3.1 percent for men.

Fritz, Stoll, and Wagner (1981) administered a questionnaire to 952 male and female undergraduates. They did not state the response rate to their questionnaire. Sexual abuse was defined as a prepubertal child having a sexual experience involving physical contact with a postadolescent. They found a prevalence rate of 7.7 percent for females and 4.8 percent for males.

Sedney and Brooks (1984) received questionnaires from 301 undergraduate women. The number of questionnaires distributed was not stated. Both contact and noncontact sexual experiences were included. Specific age requirements and whether the experience had to have been unwanted were not stated. The authors reported a 16 percent rate of abuse for women.

Comparing Prevalence Rates

As mentioned, it is difficult to compare the prevalence figures from these studies because of their use of different samples, methods of gathering data, and definitions of child sexual abuse. We will make a few comparisons, but they only suggest possible trends; strict comparisons cannot be made. The principal trend appears to be that the samples of urban women report the highest rates of abuse, followed by the national samples, and then by the samples of college students.

In the samples of urban women, Wyatt reported somewhat higher rates than Russell. Although their definitions were not identical, when the categories that appear to be most similar are compared, Wyatt reported a total rate of 62 percent, and Russell 54 percent for both contact and noncontact abuse involving both peers and older persons. Wyatt (1985) noted that when Russell considered only those subjects in the same age range interviewed by Wyatt (eighteen to thirty-six), the differences between the studies almost disappeared. Also, when Wyatt recalculated the percentage of abused women using a definition more similar to Russell's, the results of the two surveys were close, with both showing about 40 percent of the women experiencing contact abuse before the age of eighteen and 53 percent experiencing either contact or noncontact abuse (Wyatt and Peters, 1986). This finding suggests that the abuse rate among urban women in different areas is comparable, and it highlights the effects that definitional differences can have on prevalence estimates.

It is difficult to compare the results of the two national surveys because they used quite different methodologies and samples. Clearly, though, both of them indicated a much lower prevalence of abuse than did those by Russell or Wyatt. The differences between the urban and national samples may reflect a true difference in prevalence among urban women and that of the national average. A higher incidence of sexual abuse has been linked to lower socioeconomic status (Finkelhor, 1980a) and the overcrowding that often occurs in urban areas (Bagley, 1969). If urban areas include more women with a poorer and more crowded life than the national average, then they may have a higher rate of child sexual abuse.

The rates found in samples of college students fall below the rates in both the national samples and far below the prevalence rates from studies involving urban women. The sexual abuse experience may be debilitating to the point that it disrupts the lives of many who could attend college so that they cannot achieve what is needed for admission. However, the types of environments that place children at risk for sexual abuse may also be those from which children do not generally attend college. The relative influence of these two factors in causing the lower prevalence rates seen in the college samples is not clear. This question will also arise in our discussion of the consequences of child sexual abuse in Chapter Four: Is it the sexual abuse itself that causes the negative consequences, or is the sexual abuse simply part of a family environment that is harmful, with the abuse playing a peripheral role in the observed symptoms of the child?

Other Survey Results

Identity of the Perpetrator. Most of the studies indicate that the perpetrator is known by the victim in most cases, although there are some exceptions. In samples of women, the percentage abused by strangers has varied from 52 percent (Kinsey) to 11 percent (Fromuth, Russell). Wyatt found a relatively high rate of abuse by strangers and found that white women experienced abuse by a stranger more often than black women (51 percent to 37 percent). In studies involving both men and women, Finkelhor found that boys were abused more often by a stranger than were girls (30 percent to 24 percent), while Haugaard found the opposite, that girls experienced abuse by a stranger more often (27 percent to 5 percent). The differences between the studies may be attributed partially to whether noncontact experiences were included as sexual abuse. When both contact and noncontact experiences are considered, Haugaard's rate for girls abused by strangers is close to that of Finkelhor, who also considered both types of experiences. However, if only the experiences involving physical contact from the Haugaard sample are considered, his rate for girls abused by a stranger falls to 12 percent, similar to the rate reported by Russell when she considered only contact experiences. Strangers, therefore, seem to be involved principally in exhibitionism when they are counted in the surveys.

The percentage of abuse attributed to one type of perpetrator affects the percentage that can be attributed to others.
However, all the studies report that members of extended and
nuclear family are the perpetrators in quite a few cases. Finkelhor found the highest percentage of family members as perpetrators (43 percent for females and 17 percent for males). Russell, Haugaard, Kinsey, and the Canadian Population Survey all
found the rate for family members to be between 20 percent
and 30 percent. Instances in which fathers, stepfathers, or other
father figures were implicated are 10 percent for black women
and 6 percent for white women in Wyatt's sample, 8 percent in
the Haugaard sample, 6 percent in the Finkelhor sample, and
8.7 percent in the Russell sample. Overall, then, the stereotype
of children being molested mainly by strangers is not accurate.
And the impression that could be obtained from many current
reviews of clinical cases, that most abuse is perpetrated by a father or father figure, is equally inaccurate.

The perpetrators of sexual abuse against girls are almost
exclusively male. The percentage of girls abused by women was
2 percent (Russell), 1 percent (Wyatt, Canadian Population Survey), or none at all (Haugaard). A higher figure, 10 percent, was
reported by Fritz, Stoll, and Wagner. More variability has been
found in the percentage of boys involved with female perpetrators. The Canadian Population Survey found that 3 percent of
the abusers of boys were women, Finkelhor found 16 percent of
the boys had been molested by females, Haugaard 38 percent,
and Fritz, Stoll, and Wagner 60 percent. One explanation for
these differences may be the definitional issue of whether the
sexual experience was wanted by the child. In Haugaard's sample, seven boys had heterosexual experiences that they rated
as very positive. If these experiences were to be considered
sexual abuse, the percentage of female perpetrators with boys
in his sample rises to 60 percent. A number of males may
not report pleasurable experiences with older women if they
feel that they are to report only abuse experiences. The large
difference between the Finkelhor and Haugaard studies (16 percent to 60 percent) remains unreconcilable because they both
included wanted and unwanted sexual activities. At any rate,

the conclusion of Russell (1984) that women are rarely involved in child sexual abuse may be premature if the Haugaard and Fritz, Stoll, and Wagner findings have any validity.

Child's Age. Most studies indicate that the average age of abuse victims is below puberty. Finkelhor found the mean age of girls to be 10.2 and of boys to be 11.2 years. Haugaard found that the average age of girls was 10 and of boys was 9.8. Sedney and Brooks found the median age of the onset of abuse with their sample of females to be nine years. Wyatt reports that abuse occurred most often for white girls from six to eight, and for black girls from nine to twelve. The exception to this trend comes from the Canadian Population Study. They found that abused females were from twelve to fifteen 59 percent of the time, and males were in that age range 60 percent of the time. Recall, however, that these figures also included a much larger percentage of abuse by peers than that found in other studies, which may be the cause for a higher percentage of victims in the older age range.

Number of Occurrences. Single occurrences constitute most of the sexual abuse cases in every study. The lowest rate of one-time occurrences comes from Sedney and Brooks (58 percent of the occurrences), and the highest rate from the Canadian Population Survey, where 93 percent of the males had a one-time occurrence. A relatively small percentage of cases continue for more than one year: Fromuth showed 13 percent, Sedney and Brooks 14 percent, and Haugaard 15 percent. These cases usually involved family members as abusers.

Types of Sexual Activity. The most common type of sexual activity reported in most surveys is nongenital or genital fondling (Canadian Population Survey, 36 percent; Kinsey, 58 percent; Finkelhor, 40 percent; Haugaard, 52 percent). Cases of intercourse are rare. For instance, Finkelhor reported 4 percent of the cases involved intercourse, and Haugaard found 5 percent. However, in the Haugaard sample, if oral sex is considered intercourse (as it often is legally), then the rate rises to 17 percent because of a rate of oral sex among the boys of 30 percent and among the girls of 5 percent. Wyatt found a higher rate of vaginal intercourse (11 percent) among her sample of urban women than that found among college samples; and the Russell study also showed a higher rate of intercourse than that found in college samples. When noncontact experiences are included as abuse, they usually represent 20 to 30 percent of the cases, with the exception of the Kinsey study, in which they constituted 53 percent.

Russell notes differences in types of sexual activity between cases of extra- and intrafamilial abuse. Extrafamilial cases involved completed or attempted intercourse 53 percent of the time, which was much more than the 23 percent reported for intrafamilial abuse. Twenty-seven percent of the extrafamilial and 41 percent of the intrafamilial cases involved genital fondling or digital penetration, and 20 percent of the extrafamilial and 36 percent of the intrafamilial cases involved nongenital fondling, sexual touching, and forced or unforced kissing. These percentages can be misleading however. Russell's definition of extrafamilial abuse included only girls fourteen to seventeen years old who had experienced attempted or completed intercourse, and she did not have this requirement for intrafamilial abuse. Consequently, one would expect a higher rate of intercourse in the extrafamilial abuse group, and this finding might not indicate that perpetrators outside the family are more likely than those in the family to engage in intercourse.

Telling About the Experience. There is general agreement that only a minority of abused children ever tell anyone of their experience. The cases reported to someone in the legal, medical, or mental health fields are a smaller proportion still. Specific patterns of those who do or do not reveal the abuse are not well defined. Landis (1956) reports that girls were more likely to tell their parents of an abuse experience than boys, and that those who experienced abuse by a stranger were more likely to tell than those who were abused by someone they knew. Gagnon (1965) also found that girls experiencing an accidental encounter with an abuser were more likely to tell their parents (86 percent) than those experiencing ongoing abuse (31 percent). He also found that abuse by a stranger was reported to the police more than was abuse by a perpetrator the child knew. This result is similar to Russell's findings that those experiencing intrafamilial abuse were less likely to report it to the police than were those experiencing extrafamilial abuse.

Summary

Prevalence rates of child sexual abuse have varied considerably in large-scale surveys—from about 10 percent to about 60 percent. The use of different samples, methods for gathering data, and definitions makes the results of the studies difficult to compare. As a whole the large-scale surveys indicate that most victims of child sexual abuse are girls, that the average age of a victim is about ten, and that many victims are abused one time by a male that they know. The form of abuse they experience most often is fondling. As we will see next, the victims surveyed using special samples or samples of abuse victims have often experienced forms of abuse quite different from those experienced by victims responding to large-scale surveys.

Surveys of Special Populations

Two studies have examined the prevalence of child sexual abuse among groups of prostitutes. James and Meyerding (1977) interviewed 136 prostitutes, all of whom agreed to participate. Sixty-seven percent of the prostitutes were contacted on the street, the rest were contacted through jails or treatment programs. Each subject was asked, "Prior to your first intercourse, did any older person (more than ten years older) attempt sexual play or intercourse with you?" (p. 35). Fifty-two percent reported some type of sexual abuse experience.

Silbert and Pines (1981) interviewed 200 prostitutes in the San Francisco Bay area. Sixty percent were sixteen years old or younger, and 78 percent claimed that they had started prostitution as a juvenile. Child sexual abuse was defined as sexual activity forced on a child younger than sixteen. Sixty percent of the prostitutes had experienced sexual abuse before leaving home. The slightly higher percentage than that found in the James and Meyerding sample may reflect the more circumscribed definition of child sexual abuse used by James and

Meyerding. Two-thirds of the victims in the Silbert and Pines sample had been abused by their father or father figure. Although differences in definitions make direct comparisons difficult, overall, the prevalence rates from the two studies of prostitutes are higher, but not much higher, than those found in Russell's and Wyatt's samples of urban women. The percentage of abuse by fathers and other family members is much higher in the prostitute samples however. Silbert and Pines suggest that this result is due to the greater use of running away as a method of escaping incestuous abuse and to the runaway child's need to turn to prostitution as a means of financial support. This explanation implies that the prostitution is not a direct result of the previous sexual activity; in other words, the children are not compulsively repeating sexual activity with an exploitive adult because of some unconscious response to their previous experience. Thus, one of the reasons that abuse by a father or father figure may be especially harmful is that the child may need to go to great lengths to escape it. No available information suggests how many sexually abused children eventually turn to prostitution or which factors lead some incestuously abused children to run away while others do not.

McCormack, Janus, and Burgess (1986) interviewed 149 runaway children in a shelter in Toronto. They defined sexual abuse as "(1) having had sex against his/her will, (2) having been sexually molested, or (3) having been forced to view the sex act as in pornographic films" (p. 389). The results indicated that 73 percent of the female and 38 percent of the male runaways had been sexually abused. Unfortunately, problems with the data reduce the value of this study. The investigators included abuse that happened both prior and subsequent to running away from home, so there is no way to determine whether previous sexual abuse may have been a factor in running away. Also, their definition of sexual abuse included a category that is not included in any other author's definition of sexual abuse (being forced to watch pornographic films), thereby making it difficult to compare this sample to any other.

Jones, Gruber, and Timbers (1981) interviewed forty-two female and twenty-four male adolescents involved in various residential delinquency-treatment programs in the central Appalachian region. Of those contacted, 82 percent of the females and 60 percent of the males agreed to participate. The specific definition of sexual abuse used is not stated. The authors found that 33 percent of the females had been raped and that another 16 percent had experienced some other type of sexual assault. None of the males in their sample reported any type of sexual assault. Nineteen percent of the females had been assaulted by their stepfather or foster father, 71 percent had been assaulted by a friend, and 10 percent were assaulted by a stranger. The surprising lack of abuse in the male sample may support the belief of some researchers that it is more difficult for a male than for a female to admit to being the victim of sexual abuse (Nasjleti, 1980; Rogers and Terry, 1984). The relatively high rate of males who refused to participate in the study (40 percent) may also indicate males' unwillingness to admit to an experience in which they felt helpless.

Bess and Janssen (1982) randomly selected eighteen male and fourteen female patients during their initial visit to a psychiatric walk-in evaluation unit of an urban hospital. All the subjects completed an intake interview that included questions about incestuous experiences involving some sort of physical contact. They found that 31 percent of the patients had an incestuous history. The age at onset of the abuse ranged between five and fourteen years, with the males being abused earlier in life. All of the male and three of the female abuse cases involved a sibling or stepsibling. The sexually abused patients had been physically abused as children more often than the nonsexually abused patients. It is hard to determine the extent to which the sexual abuse contributed to the later hospitalization because it appears that the patients came from quite disorganized families.

Goodwin, McCarthy, and DiVasto (1981) distributed anonymous questionnaires to 500 "normal" women in community groups and 100 mothers receiving counseling after coming to the attention of child protective agencies for physically abusing or neglecting their own children. The questionnaire asked about "upsetting sexual events in childhood" (p. 88). The participation rate was not stated. Thirty-eight percent of the mothers who had abused or neglected their own children had themselves experienced earlier sexual abuse, compared with 24 percent of the control sample. The mothers of abused children were four times as likely as those in the control group to have experienced incestuous abuse. Along with the surveys of prostitutes, this finding implies that incestuous abuse may have more detrimental effects than nonincestuous abuse. As mentioned before, however, one must be cautious in making this interpretation because the general family atmosphere of those who experienced intrafamilial abuse might have been quite different from that of those who experienced extrafamilial abuse. This general atmosphere, along with or rather than the incest, may have been a major influence in the mothers' later behavior.

In summary, the rates of sexual abuse experienced by these special samples are generally higher than those found in college samples and are similar to those found in samples of urban women. The main disparity between the special samples and urban women appears to be the higher rate of incestuous experiences in the special samples. These findings may indicate either that an incestuous experience is generally more devastating to a child than a nonincestuous sexual abuse experience or that the effects of living in the type of family in which incest occurs can be devastating. It is not possible to distinguish clearly the relative impact of these two aspects of an incestuous experience, and they may both play a meaningful role in the negative consequences experienced by victims of incest.

Samples Including Only Sexually Abused Children

Several researchers had examined records of groups of children who have been identified as sexual abuse victims. Most of these records have come from hospitals to which sexually abused children have been referred for medical and psychiatric evaluations; some are from the records of child protective services. Examining this research allows us to understand the children who appear in legal or medical settings and to compare some of the characteristics of these sexually abused children with those of sexually abused children in other types of samples. This comparison may provide us with an understanding of the factors that cause some cases to be reported to the authorities.

Description of the Samples

Numerous studies use medical records. Scherzer and Lala (1980) reviewed the seventy-three cases of sexual abuse of children fourteen years or younger referred to the Baltimore City Hospital in 1978. Tilelli, Turek, and Jaffee (1980) report on all the referrals for sexual abuse of children sixteen years and younger during a period of a year and a half at a medical center in Minneapolis. Rimsza and Niggemann (1982) reviewed the records of all 311 children seventeen years and younger who were referred for sexual abuse evaluations to the Maricopa General Hospital in Phoenix, Arizona. Showers and others (1983) and Farber and others (1984) report on all eighty-one sexually abused boys and on eighty-one sexually abused girls matched by age who were seen over a three-year period at a midwestern hospital. They included children seventeen years old and younger. Spencer and Dunklee (1986) evaluated the records of 1,748 children seen over a five-year period for evaluation of sexual abuse at the Children's Hospital in San Diego, California. Mian and others (1986) examined the records of 125 children under the age of seven who were referred to the Hospital for Sick Children in Toronto for sexual abuse during a two-year period. Reinhart (1987) reports on all 189 sexually abused boys seen at the University of California, Davis, Medical Center from 1983 to 1985 and on a group of 189 sexually abused girls matched to the boys by age and race.

Other studies have used records from police departments or child protective services. Jaffee, Dynnesson, and ten Bensel (1975) reviewed the records of the Minneapolis Police Department from 1970. They found 291 cases of sexual offenses against children fifteen years old or younger. Pierce and Pierce (1984, 1985) report on 205 sexually abused children who were reported over a four-year period through the Illinois Child Abuse Hotline. Jason, Williams, Burton, and Rochat (1982) considered the 735 cases of child sexual abuse and the 3,486 cases of physical abuse that were reported in Georgia over four and a half years. They included victims under the age of eighteen.

Study Results

Specific Findings. As with broad samples, these studies show that girls are sexually abused far more often than boys. Scherzer and Lala (1980) and Reinhart (1987) report one of the lower ratios of girl-to-boy abuse, with about 80 percent of their abused samples overall being girls. Other studies report more than 90 percent of their victims to be girls (Jason, Williams, Burton, and Rochat, 1982; Spencer and Dunklee, 1986). The percentage of girls found in these groups of identified victims is higher than the percentage seen in surveys including both identified and unidentified victims. This finding suggests either that girls are more likely than boys to tell someone about an abuse experience or that parents are more likely to report abuse of a daughter than of a son to a legal or social service agency (or both these possibilities may be occurring).

The average age of the victims in these reports is generally between nine and eleven, although comparing the studies on the age variable can be misleading because they vary in the upper age of the victim. Most researchers report that boy victims are younger than girl victims, although one study reported no significant age differences (Tilelli, Turek, and Jaffee, 1980). For instance, the average age for boys and girls has been reported as 8.6 years and 10.6 years (Pierce and Pierce, 1985) and as 7.8 years and 9.2 years (Rimsza and Niggemann, 1982). The ages of victims in these studies are somewhat lower than those reported in the large-scale samples, suggesting that younger children come to the attention of authorities more often than do older children.

The perpetrator in these studies was almost always male, even more so than in reports from more general samples. Also similar to the large-scale studies is the finding that the perpetrator is known to the child in most cases. There is a higher percentage of fathers as perpetrators in the samples of both boy and girl identified victims. Rimsza and Niggemann (1982) report that 20 percent of the perpetrators were fathers, and Mian and others (1986) report an even higher figure, 37.5 percent. Reinhart (1987) found that 25 percent of the boys and 28 percent of the girls had been abused by their fathers. When these figures are compared with the 6 to 8 percent of cases in which fathers are the perpetrators in the large-scale surveys, it may indicate that more cases of incest than cases involving other perpetrators are reported to authorities. Teenagers were also the perpetrators in a relatively high number of reported cases. Scherzer and Lala (1980) found that one third of the perpetrators were teenagers, and Showers and others (1983) report a 57 percent figure. Reinhart (1987) found that a higher percentage of male victims (19 percent) had been abused by teenagers than female victims (8 percent).

There is also a difference in the types of sexual activity that are reported in victim-only studies and studies of general samples. A higher percentage of the cases in the victim-only studies involve oral, anal, or vaginal intercourse. For instance, although some form of intercourse was reported in only 5 to 30 percent of the cases in the large-scale studies, they constitute 83 percent of the cases reported by Rimsza and Niggemann (1982), 70 percent of the cases reported by Scherzer and Lala (1980), and 75 percent of the cases reported by Showers and others (1983). This evidence suggests that children and their parents are more likely to report sexual abuse to the authorities when it involves more intense forms of molestation, perhaps to obtain medical assistance for severely abused children. Interestingly, researchers who examined police reports found more contacts with an exhibitionist (50 percent) and fondling (39 percent) (Jaffee, Dynnesson, and ten Bensel, 1975) than intercourse, indicating that the place of initial referral (whether a hospital or a police department) may vary according to the type of sexual activity perpetrated on the child.

Patterns of Abuse. As mentioned previously, studies involving large groups of identified victims allow for an examination of the types of abuse that are commonly reported to authorities. One pattern has already been mentioned, that boys appear to be abused at a younger age than girls. One hypothesis for this pattern is that older boys are more likely than younger boys to repel an abuser physically, requiring abusers to concentrate on younger boys. An analysis of other reports indicates that older children are abused by strangers more often than are younger children (Mian and others, 1986; Rimsza and Niggemann, 1982; Showers and others, 1983; Tilelli, Turek, and Jaffee, 1980). Possibly the greater freedom given older children increases their risk of contacting an abusive stranger. One study found that younger children experienced fondling more often and older children experienced more intercourse (Tilelli, Turek, and Jaffee, 1980), although two other studies found no pattern between age and type of sexual activity (Showers and others, 1983; Spencer and Dunklee, 1986). Older boys experienced more threats or force or both to gain their participation than did younger boys (Showers and others, 1983). Younger boys showed physical trauma more often than did older boys, in large part because of the increased risk of anal trauma in smaller boys (Reinhart, 1987; Tilelli, Turek, and Jaffee, 1980).

Several patterns due to the type of perpetrator have been seen. Strangers generally used more physical force to gain compliance than did those who knew the child (Showers and others, 1983), possibly because those who know the child can use more subtle means. Assaults by strangers also resulted in more nongenital and genital trauma than did assaults by those the child knew (Rimsza and Niggemann, 1982), possibly because children assaulted by strangers were seen in a hospital sooner after the abuse or because of the greater force used by the strangers or because of a combination of these two reasons. In their sample of victims below the age of seven, Mian and others (1986) found that the abuse continued for over a year only in cases of intrafamilial abuse and not in any cases of abuse by friends or acquaintances. These young victims also voluntarily disclosed the abuse more often when it involved perpetrators outside the family than when it involved family members. As for the disposition of cases, more molesters of boys in one study received a jail sentence, 16 percent compared to 1 percent of those who molested girls. The authors suggest that this punishment indicates harsher treatment of homosexual than of heterosexual child molesters (Pierce and Pierce, 1985).

Some patterns due to race have appeared. Black victims were younger than white victims in two studies (Jason, Williams, Burton, and Rochat, 1982; Pierce and Pierce, 1984). White children were more often involved in oral sex, while approximately the same percentages of white and black children were involved in fondling and intercourse. More white children were removed to foster homes than black children, and more white families were referred for counseling or therapy (Pierce and Pierce, 1984).

Summary. Children from samples including only abuse victims are almost always girls and have almost always been abused by someone they know. The average age of the victim is around ten years, and the average age of boy victims is frequently lower than that of girl victims. The abuser is the father more often than is the case in general surveys, although there are also a significant number of teenage perpetrators. The type of sexual activity more often entails some form of intercourse than in other types of surveys. Older children are abused more by strangers than are younger children, and they experience more force to gain their compliance. Younger children often show more physical trauma.

These studies, when compared with studies of general samples, show that children who are reported to authorities have experienced abuse that is not typical. Identified groups of victims as opposed to victims in general surveys are usually younger, experience more serious forms of abuse, and are abused more often by family members. This information will be of use in Chapter Four, when we look at the effects of child sexual abuse and try to ascertain whether certain types of abuse have greater or lesser effects on the victims.

CHAPTER FOUR

Consequences
for Victims

Many clinicians and researchers have described the effects
child sexual abuse has had on victims and their families. In addition, several authors have put forward hypotheses
about the source of these consequences—what it is about the
sexual abuse experience that causes the negative consequences
to appear. Understanding these consequences and their possible
sources is important for all those working with victims and their
families. Much of this information will be useful to those working therapeutically with victims, and we will refer to this chapter when discussing the identification and treatment of both
child and adult victims of child sexual abuse.

We first discuss the limitations to the information that is
currently available about the consequences of child sexual abuse.
These limitations do not render the information that follows
valueless, but they do require that it be used carefully and in appropriate ways. We next summarize the findings of clinical and
empirical reports concerning the consequences. Knowing the
variety of forms of distress that have been seen in victims of
child sexual abuse may help clinicians and others recognize
them in those whom they are working with. This process may
reduce the chance that certain indications of distress will go unnoticed and may increase the likelihood that all important con-

sequences to the victim will be addressed. We then examine the possibility that certain factors of the sexual abuse experience may be used to predict which victims may react most negatively to sexual abuse. This information could be used to identify victims who may have a greater or lesser chance of developing severe symptoms and to identify those who may be in need of more or less therapeutic intervention. Finally, we present several models for understanding what it is about a sexual abuse experience that causes the negative consequences. Because the interventions used with victims and their families should depend to a large degree on the hypothesized source of the consequences, it is important that clinicians and others consider the wide range of possible sources.

Investigations of the Consequences of Child Sexual Abuse

Limitations

Two approaches have been taken to understand the consequences of child sexual abuse. The first involves descriptions of victims seen in clinical settings, and the second involves empirical comparisons of groups of victims and nonvictims. Each approach has strengths and limitations.

Clinical Studies. Clinical samples generally comprise victims who have been seen in a treatment center or by an individual therapist. Because of their intense involvement with the victims, those reporting on clinical samples are often able to provide a more complete description of the effects of the abuse. The personal cost to the individuals of their victimization can be closely observed and described clearly, and the intensity or subtlety of some consequences is not hidden by the statistical analyses and quantitative findings of empirical studies. Also, we would know about an even smaller number of victims than we do without the reporting of clinical samples because most clinicians or mental health agencies do not see enough sexually abused children to allow them to undertake an empirical analysis.

The major drawback to the use of clinical samples is that the intensity of the emotional and behavioral reactions of the victims is seldom contrasted to that of other groups of children and adolescents. Consequently, when problems are reported by victims (such as guilt or problems with relationships), it is not possible to relate the problems specifically to the sexual abuse. As an example of this limitation, if a group of sexually abused adolescent girls complain of feeling uncomfortable when relating to boys, the discomfort may be due to a number of factors, including their sexual abuse and the normal developmental experiences of adolescents. To show that the sexual abuse affected the girls' relations with boys, the amount of discomfort of the sexually abused adolescents would have to be contrasted to that found in an appropriate control group of nonabused girls. Similarly, in order for the sexualized behavior observed in a group of sexually abused boys to be attributed specifically to the sexual abuse rather than to a general reaction to a trauma, their behavior must be contrasted to that of peers who have experienced another trauma.

Another drawback to studies of clinical groups is that they may overinclude those experiencing significantly higher amounts of discomfort than do sexual abuse victims in general. As discussed in Chapter Three, many children do not report abuse experiences, and if they show no signs of disturbance, their parents may believe that there is no reason to seek clinical help for them. Also, parents who discover that their child has been sexually abused yet believe that the child is suffering no negative consequences may choose not to involve the child with the legal or mental health systems. As a consequence of this selective reporting, the use of clinical samples can result in an overestimation of the negative consequences of child sexual abuse if the findings are generalized to all victims. This hypothesis received some support from Herman, Russell, and Trocki (1986), who compared a sample of 53 women in a treatment program for previous abuse with a community sample of 152 women who had never received treatment for a previous sexual abuse experience. The women in treatment had all experienced types of abuse that had caused a higher degree of trauma than others when experienced by women in the community sample.

Empirical Studies. Empirical studies can provide a clearer picture than can clinical studies of the specific effects of child sexual abuse through the comparison of victim groups with others, although the difficulty of quantifying the intensity of the consequences may reduce this ability. They can also examine the effect of a variety of factors involved in the abuse situation and of characteristics of the victim in producing the consequences of the abuse. Some empirical studies also offer the chance to explore the reactions of those who both have and have not previously revealed their abuse. The major drawback of empirical studies is that they often use the average level of a certain characteristic among a group of victims as their basis for comparison. Thus, although the average level of the group can be noted, the reactions of individual victims can be missed.

One important consideration in interpreting empirical investigations is that a sexually abused sample might be different from a control sample not because of the sexual abuse but because of differences present before the sexual abuse occurred. The abused children might come from an environment quite different from that of the control children, and these different environments may be the cause of the differences between the groups. Such considerations highlight the need for the use of an appropriate control group, a problem that plagues research in many areas (Rosenberg and Reppucci, 1983). For instance, in the related area of physical abuse of children, some early studies compared the development of physically abused children to that of nonabused children who were of a higher socioeconomic status. This procedure made it impossible to attribute differences in the physically abused children to the abuse rather than to the stressors associated with coming from a low-income family. Not until equivalent comparison groups were employed were the specific effects of the abuse revealed (Aber, 1982). Similar difficulties can be seen in some studies of the consequences of sexual abuse. Conte and Schuerman (1987), for instance, report on a study in which the behavioral symptoms of sexually abused children were compared with those of children from a comparison group of families that, on the average, had higher incomes, higher parental education, more intact marriages, and fewer overall stressful events. This procedure makes it difficult to attribute the observed differences seen in the two groups of children to the sexual abuse and not to overall living conditions.

Summary. Because of their respective advantages, clinical and empirical investigations each provide information that cannot be obtained from the other. Because of their limitations, one must be careful not to use one type of investigation for information that it cannot accurately provide. Clinical samples provide a detailed illustration of the intensity and subtlety of the symptoms seen in some sexually abused children yet are not useful for attributing the behaviors or emotions of these children specifically to the abuse or for generalizing the findings to all children who have been sexually abused. Empirical studies can be used to understand the unique effects of the sexual abuse or of certain aspects of the abuse but may mask the variability of an individual child's reactions through a reliance on the average reaction of a group of victims. Because of their complementary nature, the use of both types of investigations rather than just one will give a more complete picture of the effects of child sexual abuse.

Reports from Clinical Samples

Emotional Effects. Guilt is an emotional response experienced by many victims (Byrne and Valdiserri, 1982; Fischer, 1983; Gelinas, 1983; Lubell and Soong, 1982; Sturkie, 1983; Summit, 1983). Fischer (1983) and Sturkie (1983) determined that this sense of guilt is felt more often by (a) children who experience abuse over a long period of time, because questions may arise about the willingness of the victim's participation; (b) children abused at an older age, because they and others may believe that they could have stopped the abuse if they had wanted to; and (c) children for whom natural physical responses or the increased attention and warmth from the abuser made the sexual activity pleasurable, because something they enjoyed is labeled as bad. A child abused by a stranger in an area that the child had been instructed to avoid may also feel more guilty than children abused in other situations (Rogers and Terry,

1984). The sense of guilt can be increased if, during the investigation and adjudication stages of the perpetrator's prosecution, the child is portrayed as seductive or as a willing participant (Kirkwood and Mihaila, 1979; Libai, 1969). The guilt felt by a child whose report of incest causes a parent to be incarcerated is often heightened as other members of the family may blame the victim for the family's loss of financial support (Cormier, Kennedy, and Sangowicz, 1962; Giarretto, 1981). The common denominator for feelings of guilt appears to be the victim's sense of responsibility for the abuse or events occurring afterward. These clinical reports suggest that an important area of exploration with a child experiencing high levels of guilt is the child's sense of responsibility. Also, some children may have developed a heightened sense of guilt during their early development (see Erikson, 1967), and this general tendency may increase their guilt about the abuse.

In many victims, a sense of guilt is accompanied by other emotions. Anger or depression is common (Fischer, 1983; Gelinas, 1983). The anger is often pervasive and is directed toward the abuser, other family members, and the social service agencies with which the victims must interact (Lubell and Soong, 1982; Sturkie, 1983). There may be a difference in the direction of anger for boys and girls: Dixon, Arnold, and Calestro (1978) found that boys abused by their fathers were angry at their fathers but did not experience the same amount of anger toward their mothers as did girls who were abused by their fathers. Anxiety is another common emotional reaction. It is often expressed in increased fearfulness, somatic complaints, changes in sleep patterns, and nightmares (Adams-Tucker, 1982; Byrne and Valdiserri, 1982; Gelinas, 1983). Victims often also experience a sense of personal powerlessness. This feeling can arise in response to the victims' inability to stop the repeated invasion of their bodies (Gelinas, 1983; Sturkie, 1983) and to their inability to control events once they begin to interact with social service, mental health, and legal agencies (Lubell and Soong, 1982). A sense of loss is also experienced by many victims: loss of their family if they are placed in foster care or if the family chooses to support the perpetrator rather than the victim, loss of their innocence, and loss of their "normalcy" (James, 1977; Lubell and Soong, 1982).

Burgess, Hartman, McCausland, and Powers (1984a) reviewed the cases of sixty-six children involved in sex groups organized by an adult. They classified the children as either internal or external reactors. The initial reactions of the internal reactors included few overt signs of distress. However, the children reported recurrent frightening memories and dreams, showed signs of increased tension, and had somatic complaints. External reactors often had more nightmares and were observed to fight more often than previously and to participate in dangerous games and activities. Unfortunately, the authors did not hypothesize about the characteristics of the children or abuse situations that made some children react internally and others externally.

Sexual Effects. Several authors have reported heightened sexual activity by victims, both as children and later as adults. DeYoung (1984) reports on four children molested at a young age who acted in sexually provocative ways toward older males. She theorizes that this counterphobic behavior could explain the repeated sexual abuse of some children. Similarly, Yates (1982) reports observing hypersexual behavior in several young, sexually abused children whom she describes as having been "eroticized" by their early sexual experiences. She theorizes that this behavior developed as a way of coping with the inappropriately awakened erotic impulses of the young child (p. 484). Fischer (1983) reports that 46 percent of the twenty-six sexually abused adolescent delinquents she saw engaged in "sexual acting out." James and Nasjleti (1983) and Borgman (1984) report that common behavior of abuse victims in their samples included sexual acting out against adults and simulation of sexual activity with younger children. Kohan, Pothier, and Norbeck (1987) gathered data from 110 inpatient child psychiatric hospitals comparing the behaviors of sexually abused versus other patients. Over 80 percent of the hospitals reported that the sexually abused children were involved in sexual play with others and were seductive with the staff more often than were the other patients.

In a study of forty-four sexually abused boys, Rogers and Terry (1984) found that those who had experienced homosexual abuse displayed confusion and anxiety over their sexual identity. The authors theorize that this confusion stemmed from the boys' concern over both the reasons for their selection as a victim, such as the possibility that latent homosexual qualities were recognized by the abuser, and their inadequate resistance to the abuse. Gundlach (1977) reports that ten of eighteen women abused as girls by strangers, and sixteen of seventeen of those abused by family members, had chosen a homosexual lifestyle. Along similar lines, Bess and Janssen (1982) note that three of the five molested male psychiatric patients whom they interviewed had an ego-dystonic homosexual orientation—that is, homosexuality was not the orientation they wanted. (Ego-syntonic homosexuality, by contrast, is an orientation the person enjoys and wants.) It is curious, however, that sexual experiences with a man might lead both boys and girls to a homosexual orientation later in life. If the mechanism for girls is that they develop a dislike for sexual activity with those of the same sex as their abuser, one would expect that the same mechanism would cause sexually abused boys to develop an even stronger heterosexual orientation than that of the rest of the population. As yet, there is no explanation for this apparent contradiction.

Effects on Interpersonal Behavior. Victims often experience a sense of isolation. Several factors seem to encourage this isolation, including the victim's natural reaction to withdraw from others, actions of social service workers, and the reactions of friends and family. Adolescent victims have isolated themselves from peers, fearing they would be recognized as victims (Sturkie, 1983). Incest victims have also felt isolated from their siblings because of their perception that their siblings resented the increased attention that the victims had received from the perpetrator (Gelinas, 1983). The feelings of isolation are often compounded when a child is removed from an incestuous home and, at the same time, often from all other types of social support. Burgess, Hartman, McCausland, and Powers (1984a) report that children involved in the sex rings they studied were often ridiculed and ostracized by their peers once their involvement was disclosed, that the parents of many other children prohibited them from associating with the victims, and that a number of victims' families moved to new neighborhoods once the involvement was discovered.

Difficulty relating with and trusting others later in life has also been experienced by abuse victims. Six adolescent girls in a group therapy program reported feeling both sexually "damaged" and fearful that the boys they dated might take advantage of them because of their background (Lubell and Soong, 1982). Courtois (1979) surveyed thirty-one self-referred female abuse victims between the ages of twenty-one and fifty. She found that 79 percent showed moderate to severe problems when relating to men and that 40 percent of the victims had never married.

Behavioral Effects. Rogers and Terry (1984) state that the most common behavioral reaction to sexual abuse of the boys in their study was the development of aggressive behavior as a way of reestablishing their masculinity. This behavior often took the form of picking fights or bullying younger children and also included chronic disobedience and antisocial acts. However, a similar heightened level of acting out has been observed in boys experiencing other stress, such as parental marital disruption (Emery, 1982), and thus such behavior may be a response to the stressful, rather than sexual, nature of the abuse.

Bess and Janssen (1982) found that incest and nonincest samples comprising psychiatric patients were distinguished by a higher level of suicidal thoughts and actions in the incest group. High suicidal ideation and behavior among sexually abused children have also been reported by other investigators (Adams-Tucker, 1982; Dixon, Arnold, and Calestro, 1978; Goodwin, 1982a; Herman, 1981). Lindberg and Distad (1985b) found that of twenty-seven adolescents seen in therapy because of previous incest, sixteen had engaged in self-mutilation, such as burning themselves with cigarettes, cutting their wrists or stomachs, or putting their hands through windows. Shapiro (1987) found that six of eleven women incest victims in treatment had engaged in self-mutilation by cutting or burning themselves. Anderson (1981) notes a high rate of both suicidal tendencies and self-mutilation in sexually abused clients. "Feeling depressed and guilty . . . they sought to damage their bodies, which they saw as sullied, or to render their bodies less attractive and therefore less tempting; or they sought to blot out the memory of pleasure with self-inflicted pain" (p. 158).

Effective Coping with Abuse Experiences. Yorukoglu and Kemph (1966) relate two case histories in which an adolescent boy and girl made a positive adjustment to a previous incest experience after an initial difficult adjustment. They add, however, that the adolescents could encounter difficulty in later phases of their development. In a study in the Netherlands, Bernard (1981) studied thirty adults who had sexual contact with a pedophile as a child. He concludes that children can experience such contacts as positive with little evidence of trauma.

In a unique survey, Sandfort (1984) interviewed twenty-five boys age ten to sixteen, each of whom was involved in an ongoing sexual relationship with an adult. The boys were recruited by asking adults involved in pedophile support groups in the Netherlands to provide the names of their child sexual partners. The adult partners indicated that masturbation occurred in each case and fellatio in most cases. Anal penetration occurred in six cases, and most of these involved the child penetrating the adult. The boys were mostly positive about both the physical and emotional relationship. The negative aspects they identified centered on concerns about the reactions of their parents or friends if the relationship was discovered. The author cautions against generalizing the results to all children involved sexually with an adult. He notes that the adults would not be expected to refer the researcher to boys who did not like the relationship. Also, the study involved boys in the Netherlands, and the apparently different attitudes about sex that exist in some European countries may make generalizing the results to boys in the United States problematic.

Summary. The clinical reports indicate clearly that some sexually abused children suffer a variety of negative consequences and that these can last for many years. As noted before, however, the extent to which all child sexual abuse victims experience the same reactions is not known. Emotional consequences include feelings of guilt, anger, depression, and help-lessness. These emotional effects play a major role in the development of many adverse behaviors. Some victims internalize their distress, resulting in somatic complaints, sleep-pattern disturbances, nightmares, and self-destructive behavior. Others externalize their distress, which leads to aggressive behaviors, acting out, and sexual activity with both younger and older individuals. Previous sexual abuse appears to have detrimental effects on the sexuality of older adolescents and adults. However, a few studies have suggested that indications of negative effects do not occur in each case of sexual abuse, and a few researchers have hypothesized that positive outcomes may result in some cases.

Reports from Empirical Studies

Emotional Effects. Gold (1986), contrasting the responses of 103 adult women who had been sexually abused as children and those of 88 nonabused women, found many areas in which the abused women appeared more disturbed. The abused women were more depressed as measured by the Beck Depression Inventory, had more psychiatric symptoms as measured by the Hopkins Symptom Checklist, and had lower self-esteem in social situations as measured by the Texas Social Behavior Inventory. Finding fewer differences than Gold did, Orr and Downes (1985) contrasted a group of twenty sexually abused female adolescents and a control group of acutely ill female adolescents. The abused girls had lower scores on the subscales of "mastery of the external world" and "vocational-educational goals" on the Offer Self-Image Questionnaire than the ill girls, but they showed no difference on several other subscales or on their overall adjustment.

It is difficult to reconcile the differences in the results of these two studies because they used different measures and different control groups. Some speculation can be made, however. The Gold study involved adult women and showed greater effects than did the Orr and Downes study, raising the possibility that abuse experiences may have increasingly dramatic effects on some individuals if not dealt with successfully soon after the abuse. The second possibility concerns the choice of the control group. The Gold study used "average" women as controls, while Orr and Downes used acutely ill adolescents. Gold's finding more differences suggests the possibility that although the specific consequences of sexual abuse may be different from those of other traumas, the total impact of sexual abuse may be similar to that of other forms of childhood trauma such as acute illness.

Sexual Effects. When Gagnon (1965) made an extensive analysis of the Kinsey, Pomeroy, Martin, and Gebhard (1953) data, he compared girls who had experienced ongoing abuse with those who had only one "accidental" abusive contact with a stranger. He found a similar pattern of peer sexual play before the abuse occurred and a higher level of homosexual peer sexual play by the girls experiencing ongoing abuse once it began.

Difficulties in adult sexual adjustment are common in abuse victims. Bess and Janssen (1982) found that 70 percent of their sample of ten psychiatric patients who were abused as children, compared with 18 percent of twenty-two nonabused psychiatric patients, reported adult sexual impairment or variant sexual practices as an adult. The impairments included prostitution, no sex during a marriage, ego-dystonic homosexuality, impotence, and transvestism. Fritz, Stoll, and Wagner (1981) report that 23 percent of the molested women and 10 percent of the molested men in their sample of college students were experiencing problems with sexual adjustment. Unfortunately, they did not report the percentages of nonmolested students experiencing sexual-adjustment problems as a basis for comparison. Gold (1986) found that women abused as children had more symptoms of sexual dysfunction and felt less satisfaction with their current sexual relationships than did a nonabused control group.

Tsai, Feldman-Summers, and Edgar (1979) compared three groups of women: thirty "well-adjusted" women who had been molested as children, thirty nonmolested women, and thirty women who were molested as children and were experiencing enough personal discomfort to request therapy. Those

molested as children who were in therapy had a higher representation in the category of women having more than fifteen consensual sexual partners, were significantly less sexually responsive, and were less satisfied with their current general relations
and sexual relations with men than those in the other two categories. The group of "well-adjusted" women molested as children was not significantly different from the nonabused group
in these areas. This finding illustrates the different responses
that child sexual abuse victims can have. We discuss factors that
can contribute to these different responses in the next section
of this chapter.

Women abused as children appear to be more susceptible
to later sexual violence than are those who were not abused.
Russell (1984) found that former abuse victims were more likely to be raped or physically abused by their husbands than were
women not sexually abused as children. J. Briere (cited in
Browne and Finkelhor, 1986) found a similar pattern; 49 percent of his sexually abused sample of women, compared with
18 percent of the nonabused sample, experienced violence in
the home. Women abused as children may also be more likely
to perpetrate violence than are those who were not abused.
Goodwin, McCarthy, and DiVasto (1981) found a higher percentage of sexually abused women in a group receiving treatment for physically abusing their children than in a control
group of nonabusers.

Behavioral Effects. Gomes-Schwartz, Horowitz, and Sauzier (1985) had the parents of 156 sexually abused children
complete the Louisville Behavior Checklist. Norms for the general population and a clinical population were available for
preschool and school-age children, norms for only a clinical
population were available for adolescents. All three age groups
of victims had a lower frequency of adverse behaviors than the
clinical norms, and the preschool and school-age groups had a
higher frequency of adverse behaviors than the general population norms. The authors state that this intermediate level of
behavioral consequences was due to the occurrence of relatively severe pathology in some victims, which brought the
pathology of the sexually abused group above that of the gen-

eral population, and few signs of pathology in other victims, which kept the group pathology below that of a clinical population. Unfortunately, they did not investigate which factors might have caused the different levels of pathology in the sexual abuse victims.

Friedrich, Urquiza, and Beilke (1986) asked parents of eighty-five sexually abused children between the ages of three and twelve to complete the Child Behavior Checklist (CBCL). Although many studies using the CBCL with other types of clinical samples of children have found that boys more often exhibit externalizing behaviors and girls more often exhibit internalizing behaviors, this pattern was not found with these sexually abused children. Thirty-five percent of the males and 46 percent of the females were elevated on the internalizing scale, and 31 percent of the males and 44 percent of the females were elevated on the externalizing scale (some were elevated on both scales). The amount of externalizing behavior decreased over time, although the authors do not state whether there was a corresponding increase in internalizing behavior. Overall, the younger children had more internalizing behavior, and the older children had more externalizing behavior. A similar pattern was noted by Gomes-Schwartz, Horowitz, and Sauzier (1985), who found that more school-age than preschool children engaged in acting-out behaviors.

Successful Coping with Abuse Experiences. Several empirical studies that detail the negative effects of child sexual abuse also include figures suggesting that, in the particular area being investigated, some subjects were not noticeably affected by the abuse. For instance, although Fritz, Stoll, and Wagner (1981) report that 23 percent of molested women and 10 percent of molested men showed current problems with adult sexual adjustment, apparently 77 percent of the women and 90 percent of the men voiced no concern in this area. Finkelhor (1979) reports that 67 percent of the molested college-age respondents to his survey viewed the experience as negative; that leaves, however, 33 percent of the respondents who viewed the experience as either neutral or positive. Out of the 101 child sexual abuse victims in Haugaard's (1987) retrospective study with college students, eight males and two females rated both their feelings at the time and their current memory of the sexual activity as "very positive." Tsai, Feldman-Summers, and Edgar (1979) report no significant differences on their measures of current sexual functioning between nonabused women and women who had been abused as children yet had not sought therapy for the experience, suggesting that these sexually abused women had either experienced no long-term consequences or had been able to resolve effectively those that did arise without therapeutic assistance.

Symonds, Mendoza, and Harrell (1981) report on 109 respondents to an advertisement in the *Los Angeles Free Press* and other papers, and Nelson (1981) reports on 104 respondents to advertisements in *Psychology Today* and several newspapers asking for volunteers for a study on sexual activity between family members. Although many of the respondents who said that the sexual activity was positive were discussing sexual experiences with siblings, some sexual relations with older relatives were also described as positive. The self-selection of the respondents and the lack of information about the adequacy of their functioning as adults require that the results be viewed with caution.

Constantine (1981) reviewed thirty studies on the impact of childhood incest and sexual encounters with adults. Twenty reported that at least some subjects had no ill effects, thirteen reported no harm to most subjects, and six stated that some subjects had a positive or beneficial experience. Although he acknowledges that the studies have numerous methodological limitations, Constantine concludes that they demonstrate that some children are not detrimentally affected by early sexual experiences with adults or family members. Furthermore, he states that there are legitimate instances of child/adult sex; he defines these as ones "(1) [in which] the child is sexually knowledgeable and fully comprehends the activity; (2) to which he or she freely consents on the basis of that comprehension; (3) that take place in a family and/or social setting that affirms such sexual experiences as appropriate; and (4) that (therefore) do not result in symptoms of dysfunction in the child or the family" (p. 242).

Although a number of exceptions could be taken to all of Constantine's conditions, perhaps the most important ones are the first and last. The question of the child's ability to consent to sexual activity has received considerable comment but no empirical research. Constantine does not state specifically how one can determine that a child has the capacity to consent to sexual activity. Does an eight-year-old have such a capacity? Many would argue that a child of that age does not and therefore that any sexual activity with such a child is exploitative (see Chapter Two). What of a twelve- or fourteen-year-old? Although many would continue to argue that a child of this age cannot legitimately be expected to consent freely to sexual activity with an adult, some research has indicated that children of this age have the capacity to consent to voluntary treatment (Weithorn, 1984), and a recent legal brief by the American Psychological Association asserts that a fourteen-year-old has the capacity to consent to an abortion (Bales, 1987). Although the age of some children may prohibit them from consenting to any sexual activity, all those who have been considered in the definitions of child sexual abuse used by some researchers (which have included children up to seventeen years of age) may not fall into this category. Constantine's fourth point seems to require the ability to forecast the future. He states that child/adult sex is legitimate if no harm comes to the child or family, yet this cannot be known until after the sexual activity. Thus, he does not supply any way to legitimize an adult's approach to a child because the assurance of no harm cannot be assumed in any case.

Summary. Empirical studies, like clinical investigations, indicate that sexual abuse victims suffer emotional, sexual, and behavioral consequences. However, the empirical studies show more clearly than the clinical studies the considerable variability in the magnitude of the negative consequences experienced by abuse victims. Whereas the clinical samples consisted almost exclusively of those suffering relatively serious negative consequences, the empirical samples included some abuse victims who suffered no apparent consequences. Although the apparently unaffected victims may still experience negative consequences, certain types of abuse situations may cause fewer negative consequences, or certain types of abuse victims may be able to deal with their experiences successfully. With our current level of knowledge, it is difficult to understand why some children react with some emotions and behaviors while others react with different ones. Until we have additional information, those intervening with victims are probably well advised to consider the wide range of possible emotional and behavioral reactions that any victim might exhibit, while at the same time being careful not to assume that a victim should be experiencing a particular response.

Factors Influencing the Effects of Child Sexual Abuse

Researchers have now begun to examine systematically the differential effects of various abusive situations. If meaningful relationships between the type of abuse or victim characteristics and the degree or type of consequences can be found, they would provide clinicians with valuable information about the directions for treatment. Unfortunately, as the following review of research shows, few stable relationships have been established. In this section we discuss results of the clinical and empirical research on the differential effects of child characteristics, characteristics of the abuse experience, and occurrences after the abuse experience.

Child Characteristics

Age at Onset of Abuse. Researchers have provided equivocal findings about the influence that the age at which the child is first sexually abused has on later adjustment. Some researchers have found that younger children are more affected than older ones. Meiselman (1978) found a larger percentage of seriously disturbed adult patients among those who had been sexually abused prior to puberty than among those abused after puberty. Courtois (1979) found that women abused before puberty had more difficulty with long-term relationships with men than did women molested after puberty, although she found no differences in their long-term social, psychological, physical, or sexual adjustment. In a small clinical sample, MacVicar (1979) found that adolescents were better able to master the trauma of sexual abuse than were latency-age victims. Gomes-Schwartz, Horowitz, and Sauzier (1985) found that elementary school children were more affected than adolescents and preschool children, suggesting that children during the latency years may be the most affected. Several empirical studies, however, have shown only small and statistically insignificant tendencies for younger children to be more negatively affected by sexual abuse, suggesting few if any differences due to age (Alexander and Lupfer, 1987; Finkelhor, 1979; Russell, 1984; Tsai, Feldman-Summers, and Edgar, 1979; Tufts' New England Medical Center, 1984).

Other researchers have found that older children are more affected by abuse experiences. Sedney and Brooks (1984) report that onset of abuse after puberty was associated with more severe symptoms than was onset before puberty, although they do not state the statistical results to substantiate this claim. Adams-Tucker (1982) reports that of the twenty-eight sexually abused children seen at a child guidance clinic, those abused at younger ages did not receive as serious a diagnosis as did the children abused at older ages.

Prior Emotional Health. A general conclusion of those studies that considered the victim's emotional health prior to the sexual abuse is that those with positive emotional health suffered fewer negative consequences. From a survey of 400 adults and children admitted to an urban sexual assault treatment center, Ruch and Chandler (1982) found that those who had experienced "prior mental health stresses" (not specifically defined) were more traumatized by their sexual assault experiences than were those who did not experience such stresses. Schultz (1973) states that most of the abused children who would be damaged by a court appearance had already indicated personality disturbances before the abuse (although he did not state the specific criteria he used to come to this conclusion). In her clinical sample of abused children, MacVicar (1979) found that the absence of previous emotional difficulties was one of the best predictors of a positive outcome of therapy. Although they did not measure the emotional health of the victim directly,

Conte and Schuerman (1987) found that children from families that exhibited signs of pathological relationships were more adversely affected by their abuse than were children from families not exhibiting such signs.

Characteristics of the Abuse Experience

Duration. Although many assume that long durations of abuse cause greater trauma for the child than short durations, researchers have reported equivocal support for this hypothesis. Adams-Tucker (1982) found no differences in the severity of diagnoses given to older children abused for more than one year and to those abused for less than one year. In the Finkelhor (1979) sample, college students' self-reports of the negative effects of their abuse showed no relationship to duration. Similarly, the Tufts study (1984) found no relationship between duration and the child's current level of distress.

There is some support for the hypothesis that a long duration of abuse produces more negative consequences than does a short duration. Tsai, Feldman-Summers, and Edgar (1979) found that abused women who reported themselves as still being disturbed by their abuse had experienced abuse for a longer period of time (mean, 4.7 years) than did those who did not consider themselves still disturbed by the abuse (mean, 2.5 years). The two broad-based surveys of urban women showed that abuse of longer duration resulted in lower scores on a measure of general well-being (Wyatt, in press) and a higher percentage of victims who rated their experience as having done significant lasting harm (Herman, Russell, and Trocki, 1986).

One important question that has not been investigated specifically concerns those who were abused on just one occasion. Recall from Chapter Three that most victims are abused only once. The consequences felt by these victims might be considerably different from those felt by victims abused several times.

Perpetrator. Some empirical studies have reported that whether the abuse was perpetrated by a family member or a person outside the family did not have a significant effect on the trauma of the abuse (Finkelhor, 1979; Russell, 1984; Tsai, Feldman-Summers, and Edgar, 1979). However, most of the subjects in these studies had never revealed their abuse, thus the total effects in cases where the father is charged with a crime and the victim's family is disrupted may not be reflected in the studies. Ruch and Chandler (1982), however, report that children in their study who experienced incest showed more trauma during their intake interview than did those experiencing non-incest abuse.

Adams-Tucker (1982) and Russell (1983) found that abuse by the father involved greater trauma than did abuse by other family members. In contrast, the Tufts study (1984) found that abuse by the stepfather caused more trauma than did that by the natural father. This result may be explained partially by Russell's (1983) finding that more serious abuse is perpetrated by stepfathers than by fathers. Additional indirect data on the negative effect of abuse by parents come from a study of 365 adults molested as children (Kendall-Tackett and Simon, 1987). In this study, 36 percent of the perpetrators were biological fathers, 3 percent were mothers, and 20 percent were stepfathers. The average time from the end of the molestation to the time that the adults sought therapy was seventeen years, indicating the length of time that incest can affect a victim.

Coercion. Researchers generally agree that the overt use of force by the perpetrator results in more initial and long-term negative consequences for the victim than occur when force is not used. Finkelhor (1979) and Fromuth (1986) found in their college samples that the use of force explained the greatest amount of the victims' negative reactions to the abuse. Russell (1984) found that 71 percent of the victims experiencing the use of force by the perpetrator rated themselves as extremely or considerably traumatized, compared with 47 percent of the victims not exposed to force. Elwell and Ephros (1987) found within a small sample of sexually abused children that those who experienced considerable force had a more negative initial reaction to the abuse than did those who did not experience such force.

Type of Sexual Activity. Reports of the relationship between type of sexual activity and victim reaction also yield contradictory results. Russell (1984) found that women who experienced some sort of vaginal or oral intercourse as girls rated their experiences as being extremely traumatic significantly more often than did women who experienced only the touching of their breasts or genitals. Tsai, Feldman-Summers, and Edgar (1979) state that their clinical group had experienced vaginal intercourse more frequently than their nonclinical molested group. Landis (1956) found that 80 percent of his female subjects who had experienced attempted rape as girls and 50 percent of those who had been approached for intercourse stated that their attitudes toward sexuality had been temporarily or permanently affected versus 28 percent of those who had been fondled and 23 percent of those who had been confronted by an exhibitionist. Finkelhor (1979), however, found no significant differences in the amount of trauma reported due to the type of sexual activity.

Involvement in Pornography. The incidence and consequences of children's involvement in pornography were brought to national attention by the work of the Attorney General's Commission on Pornography (1985–1986). The specific consequences of children's involvement in pornography are difficult to isolate because these children are often involved in other forms of sexual exploitation and have often come from homes where they experienced abuse and neglect (Silbert and Pines, 1984).

Some evidence suggests that involvement in pornography may have specific negative effects. Burgess (1984) examined sixty-two children involved with sex rings and found that those involved for more than one year and those involved in pornography had more negative symptoms than did those involved for less time and not involved in pornography. However, because involvement in pornography was correlated with being in the ring more than one year, the specific consequences of these two aspects of the children's involvement cannot be separated. The children's knowledge that there is a permanent record of their sexual activity may be a cause for a continuing high level of anxiety for many years after their exploitation has stopped

(Mulvey and Haugaard, 1986). Some of the children may have been shown child pornography as a way to entice them into sexual activity or as a way for the adult to show them how much "fun" children can have while their pictures are taken. These children may fear for many years that pictures of them will also appear in these magazines, possibly to be seen by people they know.

Events Subsequent to the Abuse

Reactions of Others. Adams-Tucker (1982), Schultz (1973), Rogers and Terry (1984), and Simrel, Berg, and Thomas (1979) all found that parental response had a major effect on the trauma of the abuse. Schultz goes so far as to say, "It is clear from studies of child sexual victims that it is not the sexual assault that usually creates trauma but the child's parents' behavior upon its discovery" (p. 150). Conte and Schuerman (1987) report that the overall social support available to the child after the abuse and the child's having a supportive parent or sibling lessened the impact of the abuse. The Tufts study (1984), although agreeing that negative responses by mothers tended to worsen the child's trauma, found that positive, supportive reactions did not ameliorate the trauma of the abuse.

Court Appearance. Kirkwood and Mihaila (1979) state that the adversarial approach of the legal system often compounds the traumatic effects of incest. Rogers (1982) argues that the experience of facing their assailants in court can have beneficial outcomes for the children even though the court experience is difficult. None of these authors, however, state the steps by which they come to these conclusions. Nevertheless, the strong assumption is that the effects of a court appearance can be negative on young victims. This assumption has led to numerous changes in legal procedures to lessen these effects. These changes are discussed in Chapter Fifteen.

Some research has begun to challenge this assumption however. Runyan and others (1987) administered the Child Assessment Schedule to 100 victims of incest soon after their abuse was identified and then five months later. They found a reduction of fourteen abnormal behavior responses for children uninvolved with testifying between the two administrations, a reduction of twenty-one responses for those children who had already testified, and a lower decrease (eight responses) for those still waiting to testify. The conduct disorder subscale actually rose for children waiting to testify, while falling for those who did not have to testify. The authors state that the results suggest that it is the anticipation of testifying that is harmful to children and that actually testifying may speed resolution of some children's distress.

Summary

Clearly, there are few unequivocal results in the various studies' attempts to find causes for the different levels of the consequences reported by victims of child sexual abuse. The only agreement that exists is that, on the average, overt use of force by the perpetrator and negative parental response result in more negative consequences, and good prior emotional health in the victim results in fewer negative consequences. The general lack of agreement on other factors may be a result of many of the same definitional and methodological differences that have affected the results in other areas.

Several additional factors also make research in this area difficult and possibly misleading. One problem is the lack of variability among subjects in certain groups. Some of the samples have included only abuse victims in treatment and others have included only college samples. If a general high level of functioning is required to enter college and if several problems are present in those seeking therapy, these samples may include respectively well-functioning and poorly functioning individuals almost exclusively. Thus, the finding of no difference due to a certain factor (such as length of abuse) may be a reflection more of a general lack of difference in functioning in the sample rather than of a lack of difference in the factor being examined. Consequently, samples including a broader cross section of subjects may provide the more valuable information.

A second problem is that the interrelatedness of the char-

acteristics of the abuse make an examination of any one particular characteristic nearly impossible. For instance, one might
wish to determine whether children who have experienced intercourse are more disturbed than other victims. The obvious way
to make this determination would be to compare the reactions
of those who experienced intercourse with those who experienced other forms of abuse. It turns out, though, that experiencing intercourse is related to other aspects of an abuse experience.
Reports from the clinical literature indicate that abuse that
eventually leads to intercourse initially begins with fondling and
other less intense forms of sexual contact. Consequently, one
would probably find that, on the average, those who experienced intercourse had been abused over a longer period of time
than those who did not experience intercourse. Family members
are more often involved in long-term abuse than are nonfamily
members, suggesting that intercourse may be perpetrated more
often by a family member. Also, children who do not tell someone about initial abuse experiences are likely to experience
more abuse, which may eventually lead to intercourse. As a consequence of this combination of factors, if one found that children experiencing intercourse are more disturbed than other
victims, it would not be clear whether the disturbance is due to
the intercourse, the duration of the abuse, the identity of the
perpetrator, or the fact that the child might not have had anyone to whom he or she felt comfortable revealing the abuse. An
effect that is shown by one factor may appear only because it is
related to other factors that do have a meaningful impact on the
child's reaction. In the example just given, length of abuse
might have no effect at all on amount of disturbance, but because it is associated with factors that did cause disturbance
(hypothetically, abuse by a family member and intercourse), it
would appear to have an effect. Researchers can use statistical
procedures to isolate the specific amount of effect of some variables in some cases, but such a procedure is not justified with
the high degree of correlation between the variables that is often
seen in these studies (McDonald, 1985).

   A third problem concerns the way in which the level of
trauma is measured. One method has been merely to ask subjects

experiencing a variety of abuses to rate how traumatic the experience was or the degree to which it was positive or negative. This method presents difficulties when the subjects' responses are then compared. To use a related area as an example, if two children were punished, one by being spanked and one by being beaten almost to unconsciousness, and then they were asked about their reaction to being punished, they might both rate it as being very negative or very traumatic. It would be improper to compare the overall effect of the two punishments by comparing each child's responses to the one he or she received. A comparison by one child who had experienced both a spanking and a beating would be needed. Similarly, in order to compare the effects of types of abuse, only subjects experiencing all the types of abuse being compared should be used for a comparison. Such research has not been undertaken.

These limitations make the comparative studies difficult to interpret, and especially those finding no differences must be interpreted with extreme caution.

Hypotheses Concerning the Source of the Consequences

Now that we have reviewed reports about the consequences of child sexual abuse, we turn to the causes of these consequences. The debate about the source of the consequences of child sexual abuse is not merely an academic exercise. It has important implications for the type of treatment that social service agencies and individual clinicians will offer victims and families. Whether the focus of treatment will be helping the child discuss sexual fantasies evoked by the sexual contact, helping the child avoid seeing himself or herself as a victim, or helping the child develop a healthy relationship with both parents will depend to a large degree on how those intervening with the child and family conceptualize those aspects of the sexual abuse experience that are likely to cause negative consequences.

Currently, no theories are generally accepted as providing the definitive view about the source of the consequences. This lack of acceptance is not surprising because those in the medical and social sciences have not reached agreement about the mechanisms by which any particular event affects an individual's life or personality. Until the unlikely event that the "truth" about the sources of the consequences of child sexual abuse is revealed, we believe that it is important for those working with victims and their families to know about and consider a wide range of possible sources. In this way clinicians will not force the experiences of all victims into a particular framework. The flexibility that is added when a variety of possible sources are considered should help clinicians work successfully with many different types of victims.

Many of the theoretical positions in the literature concentrate on the role of the sexual abuse itself in causing the disturbance seen in a victim. In contrast, we prefer to regard the overall distress exhibited by a child sexual abuse victim and consider that its roots can be traced to three possible areas: the time before the abuse occurred, events surrounding the sexual abuse, and events occurring after the sexual abuse is revealed. In some cases, the source of disturbance in a victim may be traced completely to one of these three time periods, but we suspect that some amount of distress will be found in more than one time period in most cases. Consequently, we believe that it is important to consider the role that the child's life before the abuse may have on the level of his or her disturbance after an abuse experience as well as the impact that events occurring after the abuse may have on the child. In some cases it may be appropriate for the clinician to expend considerable energy exploring issues arising from these two time periods either before, after, or instead of exploring the issues arising directly from the abuse.

Impact of the Child's Life Before the Sexual Abuse

Some sexually abused children come from family environments that have contributed significantly to the distress that they exhibit during or outside of therapy. In some cases, the sexual abuse exacerbates the preexisting distress of the child, and in others the sole source of the distress may be the child's environment other than the sexual abuse. In other words, in some cases the sexual experience may be abusive, but in the context of a myriad of other abuses it may have little additional impact on the child. If we were to conceptualize the level of the child's distress graphically, we might find one of the two patterns in Figure 1 among those children whose environments are the cause of their distress. For each graph, the child's level of distress is indicated on the vertical axis, and time is indicated on the horizontal. At some particular time in the child's life the abuse occurs and is then revealed. (The figures in this chapter merely illustrate a hypothetical change in the level of distress due to the child's environment, the abuse, and its revelation; there is no attempt to quantify the distress or to deal with other factors such as the age of the victim or type of abuse.)

Figure 1. Distress Due to Environmental Conditions.

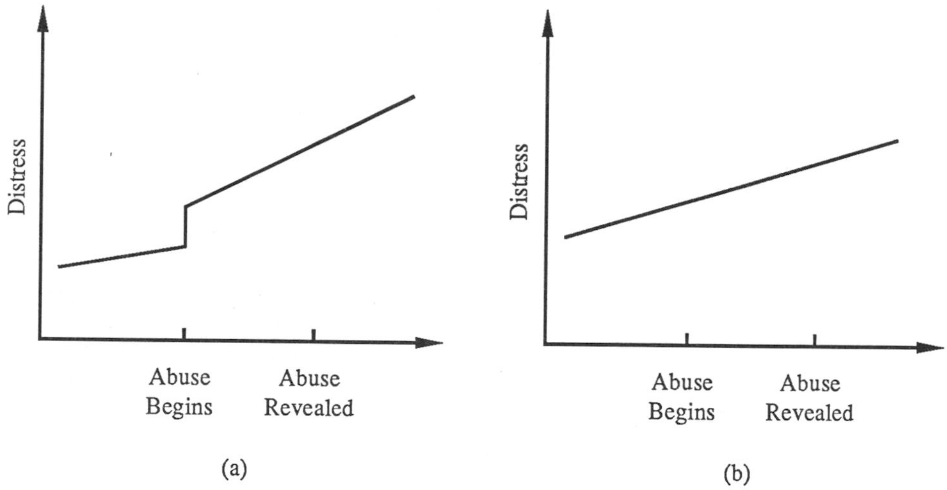

(a)   (b)

Figure 1(a) represents the distress of a child whose family environment causes a steadily increasing level of distress and for whom the abuse adds a significant contribution to the distress. Figure 1(b) represents the distress of a child for whom the sexual abuse does not seem to cause any distress above that already caused by the family environment.

In cases of incest, it may be relatively easy to understand the role that the family environment can have in the distress of the child. Rather than presenting here the specific ways that a child might be affected by each type of incestuous family, we will do so in Chapter Five, where these family types are described. Here, let it suffice to say that a child growing up in any of these families may be adversely affected.

The family environment may also cause significant distress in children experiencing extrafamilial abuse. Consider this case:

> An eight-year-old girl is brought to therapy after it is discovered that two of her mother's boyfriends had fondled her within the past six months. Assessment sessions with the girl and her mother reveal that the mother leads a promiscuous life and has little time for her daughter, who must often fend for herself at home while the mother is out on dates. The boyfriends who fondled the daughter each did so on one or two occasions when the mother had fallen asleep because of excessive drinking. Information from the girl's school indicates that she has been relatively unsuccessful as a student since kindergarten and that she is often withdrawn around peers.

Any distress exhibited by this girl is, to some extent, the result of her family environment. In a less extreme example, a child may be easily seduced by an abuser because the child is searching for emotional closeness that is missing in the home, and this lack of emotional bonding may have a greater effect on the child than the abuse. If a clinician believes that most of the distress exhibited by a sexual abuse victim is due to the child's basic environment, the clinician's interventions may be aimed at increasing the child's general social and emotional development rather than at extensively exploring the sexual abuse experience. A clinician who assumes automatically that the sexual abuse or its aftermath or both are the primary concern of all sexually abused children may miss out on the opportunity to provide meaningful interventions to a child in this type of situation.

Impact of the Sexual Activity Itself

Several clinicians and researchers have put forward theories to explain the consequences that the sexual activity can have on a child. These hypotheses suggest that a sexually abused child's level of distress can be graphed as in Figure 2. Figure 2(a)

Figure 2. Distress Due to Sexual Abuse.

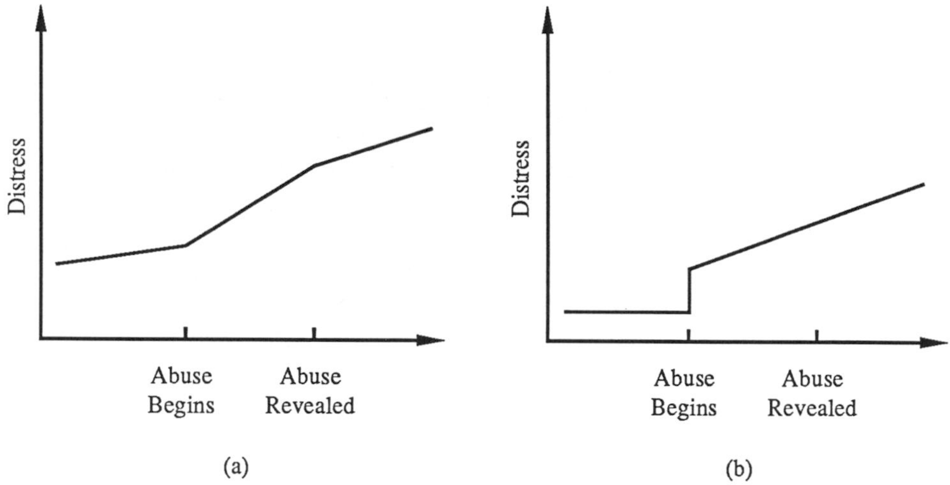

(a)	(b)
Abuse Abuse	Abuse Abuse
Begins Revealed	Begins Revealed

indicates that the negative consequences of a home environment are compounded by a sexual abuse experience, and Figure 2(b) indicates that a child experiencing no abnormal levels of distress due to family environment experiences a marked negative reaction to sexual abuse. We will examine five hypotheses. The first two explain the consequences of the sexual acts from a psychoanalytic and learning perspective. The next two focus on the cognitive and emotional accommodations that a child must make during an abuse experience, and the fifth conceptualizes the abuse as a crisis that produces a post-traumatic stress syndrome in the victim.

Role of Sexual Stimulation. The psychoanalytic view of the effects of child sexual abuse maintains that the sexual stimulation of a child at an inappropriate age causes the negative consequences. Although the mature ego of the adult or older adolescent can manage this stimulation and the unconscious Oedipal conflict that is excited, the immature ego of the young child cannot. Anxiety is caused by this inappropriate sexual stimulation and by the child's concerns about his or her inability to control sexual impulses (Lewis and Sarrel, 1969; Sugar, 1983). A higher level of anxiety is aroused by incestuous than by nonincestuous abuse because of the closeness of the sexual act to the child's Oedipal fantasies. The victim attempts to deal with the anxiety through the development of a number of repetitive, defensive behaviors. Some of the behavioral and interpersonal consequences can be a result of the development of these defensive behaviors. One possible defense is for the victim to identify with the abuser, which may cause the victim to become physically or sexually abusive toward others (Sugar, 1983). Also, the victim's guilt may be a result of identification with the abuser and internalizing the guilt that the abuser feels (Ferenczi, 1949).

Moreover, incest can result in developmental fixation, with an accompanying lack of individuation and development of normal social and sexual relationships (Parsons, 1954). According to psychoanalytic theory, normal development requires the frustration of the Oedipal fantasies, leading to the resolution of the Oedipal conflict and entry into the latency period. Successful entry into the latency period is required for ego advancement and for superego and personality formation. When the Oedipal fantasies are not frustrated, entry into latency is disrupted, and the child's development is adversely affected (Freud, 1981).

With its reliance on the inappropriate stimulation of the young child, the psychoanalytic explanation does not appear to be useful in explaining the consequences of nonincestuous sexual abuse to adolescents. This criticism does not eliminate the usefulness of the psychoanalytic explanation, however, because different mechanisms may conceivably cause the consequences in older and younger victims.

Learning Theory Explanations. A social learning explanation can be used to understand some of the behavioral consequences seen in sexually abused children. A victim who later becomes an abuser may have "learned" from the previous abuse experience that it is an appropriate way to gain warmth, intimacy, sexual release, or power. As such, the victim imitates the previous behavior of a powerful adult when the victim wants to demonstrate power or to achieve warmth or intimacy.

The sexualized behavior and repeated exploitation of some abuse victims can be explained using a classical conditioning paradigm. Some abuse experiences are nonthreatening and provide the child with considerable pleasure, at least initially. If the stimulation of the sexual activity results in physical pleasure for the child, the child may begin to associate physical pleasure and warm feelings with the exploitative situation of the abuse. The victim may encourage his or her own future exploitation because the exploitation has taken on the same properties as the physical pleasure. In psychological terms, the unconditioned response of physical pleasure evoked by the unconditioned stimulus of physical stimulation becomes paired with the conditioned stimulus of an exploitative situation. Eventually, the presence of an exploitative situation alone brings about the physical pleasure.

The classical conditioning paradigm can also be used to explain some of the difficulties with intimacy and sexuality that have been reported by many adolescent and adult victims. If the child feels guilt, anger, powerlessness, or other emotions while being sexually stimulated or in an intimate situation with his or her abuser, these emotions can become associated with intimacy and sexuality. If the association is strong enough, it can remain into adulthood, when sexual or intimate situations will again be accompanied by those emotions. This association can lead the adult to avoid sexual or intimate situations, thus he or she will have little or no opportunity to break the association by experiencing sufficient amounts of nonabusive intimacy or sexuality.

Child Sexual Abuse Accommodation Syndrome. Summit (1983) developed several hypotheses about the consequences of sexual abuse perpetrated by a trusted adult in the child's life. Rather than the sexual activity itself, he suggests that the major cause of negative consequences is the changes that the child must make in his or her self-concept as a result of the atmosphere that surrounds most ongoing sexual abuse. Children do not have an innate sense that sexual activity with an adult is wrong. In fact, many children enjoy the warmth and stimulation that is often associated with the sexual play, especially during the initial phases. However, if the sexual activity continues, the adult must inevitably put pressure on the child to ensure that it is kept secret. From other experiences, children have learned that only prohibited activities must be kept secret for a long time (as opposed to keeping a birthday gift secret until it is given). Thus, the pressure to keep the sexual activity secret gives it a nefarious air. When the perpetrator makes blatant or subtle threats about the consequences to the child, the child's family, or the perpetrator if the child should reveal the abuse, the child is placed in the position of being responsible for the welfare of the family and its members. This inappropriate responsibility to protect those whom the child would normally be protected by places additional stress on the child as the protective value of the family is lessened. The child's inability to stop what has become a negative experience results in the development of a sense of helplessness. Just as a weaker animal cannot lash out against a stronger one, a child is incapable of stopping the abuse and must begin to accept it. The child is confronted with the fact that he or she is engaged in an activity that is considered to be wrong and is powerless to stop it.

In order to live with this ongoing situation, the child must assimilate the abuse into his or her life. In order to do so, the child must accommodate (modify) his or her view of the world and self. The child cannot accept that the abuse is the perpetrator's fault because by doing so the child would have to conclude that a person in whose care he or she is entrusted is bad. Instead, the child begins to change his or her self-concept in the direction of being evil and helpless. This change in the child's self-concept can lead to dramatic changes in behavior. "Much of what is eventually labeled as adolescent or adult psychopathology can be traced to the natural reactions of a healthy child to a profoundly unnatural and unhealthy parental environment" (Summit, 1983, p. 184). Some children try desperately to be good as a way of counterbalancing their negative self-image. Other children overachieve in areas such as school in order to distance themselves from the conflict brought about by the abuse. Others are unable to cope quite as successfully. They become self-destructive or act out against others.

Some support for Summit's hypothesis can be found in the psychoanalytic literature. Barry and Johnson (1958) contrasted several clinical cases of incest in which the children either did or did not feel high levels of guilt and anxiety. Those with low levels had been abused by fathers who felt relatively guilt free about the abuse and whose mothers knew about and condoned the activity. Conceivably, there was less need for secrecy in these relationships. Thus, the children may have been under less pressure to reevaluate themselves in a destructive way in order to assimilate the abuse.

Summit's hypothesis cannot be applied easily to those experiencing abuse by someone who is not a trusted adult. For example, a child may not be required to change his or her self-concept to assimilate abuse by a stranger or neighbor. Summit's conceptualization might be extended to include these types of cases, in that the child's view of others in general might become so negative that the development of social relations would be impaired. It is unclear, however, whether such an extension is justified.

Four Trauma-Causing Factors. Finkelhor and Browne (1985) have developed a paradigm for understanding the negative consequences of child sexual abuse that integrates several perspectives. They postulate that "the experience of sexual abuse can be analyzed in terms of four trauma-causing factors: . . . traumatic sexualization, betrayal, powerlessness, and stigmatization" (p. 530). Although some of the factors appear in other traumas, their combination under one set of circumstances distinguishes sexual abuse from other sources of trauma. Each of these traumagenic factors "alters a child's cognitive or emotional orientation to the world and causes trauma by distorting the child's self-concept, world view, or affective capacities" (Finkelhor, in press). Similar to that of Summit (1983) this conceptualization suggests that the cognitive and affective changes that a child must make cause the consequences of the abuse. Rather than suggesting one path that this accommodation takes, as Summit does, Finkelhor and Browne propose that the child's conceptualization of the world can be affected differently by four aspects of the sexual abuse experience. Each of these aspects can affect a child; their relative strength is determined by the nature of the abuse and the individual characteristics of the child. These variances allow the theory to be used to explain a wide range of sexual abuse experiences.

In this theory, traumatic sexualization is caused by developmentally inappropriate sexual behavior and rewards for that behavior. It affects the child by causing confusion about and aversion to sexuality. Betrayal is caused by the child's feeling manipulated by a person thought to have the child's well-being in mind. Its results are depression, dependency, mistrust, and hostility. Powerlessness is caused by the child's vulnerability to repeated invasion of his or her body and by the child's inability to stop the abuse. It causes anxiety and fear, self-perception as a victim, and identification with the abuser. Stigmatization is caused by the blame forced on the child by the offender, the child's family, the legal system, or the child himself or herself. The result for the child is typically guilt or lowered self-esteem.

Finkelhor and Browne (1985) caution that their conceptualization has not been clinically or empirically tested. In fact, the ability of the theory to explain such a broad range of symptoms may limit its testability. Finkelhor (in press) accounts for many of the consequences of child sexual abuse by logically relating them to one or more of the traumagenic factors. Although this exercise is helpful conceptually, it may be impossible to demonstrate empirically the way in which one of the factors can affect such a wide range of behaviors. For instance, he suggests that powerlessness can account for nightmares, phobias, somatic complaints, flat affect, learning problems, employment difficulties, running away, aggressiveness, and becoming an abuser. It is difficult to imagine an empirical investigation that can relate each of these symptoms to a concept such as powerlessness, which in itself is difficult to define and measure. Consequently, although this model can account for a wide range of symptoms, it must do so on solely a logical basis.

An advantage to this conceptualization is that it takes into account both the complexity of child sexual abuse and of its victims and the idiosyncratic nature of the interplay between each abuse situation and individual victim. In this way it encourages those working with victims and their families to consider a number of sources for the consequences that they see in their clients. This wide view should allow for effective treatment for the greatest range of victims.

Finkelhor (in press) extends the model to take into account events occurring before and after the abuse. He notes that events both before and after the abuse can exacerbate or lessen one or more of the traumagenic factors that are caused by the abuse. Thus, his formulation moves in the direction that we also advocate: viewing sexual abuse within the child's developmental and ecological context.

Post-Traumatic Stress Disorder. As we will discuss in Chapter Ten, several clinicians have described adult victims of child sexual abuse as falling under the disorder defined by the American Psychiatric Association's *Diagnostic and Statistical Manual of Mental Disorders* (1980) as Post-Traumatic Stress Disorder (PTSD). This disorder is characterized by (a) the occurrence of an uncommon, extremely stressful event; (b) reexperiencing of the event through intrusive recurrent thoughts, dreams, or feelings that it will happen again; (c) numbing of responsiveness or interest in one's environment; and (d) at least two of the following: hyperalertness, sleep disturbance, survival guilt, memory impairment or trouble concentrating, avoidance of activities because they trigger memories of the event, or intensification of symptoms when events similar to the stressful event occur. Although PTSD has generally been diagnosed in adults, some authors suggest that it can also affect children who experience stresses such as kidnapping, watching a parent assaulted or killed, or natural disasters (Pynoss and Eth, 1985); and other authors, such as Goodwin (1985), have suggested that it can occur in child victims of incest.

Two conceptualizations for the occurrence of PTSD are of importance to understanding child sexual abuse. The first is derived from Horowitz's (1976) formulation, which attempts to combine the psychoanalytic theories of the repetition compulsion with modern cognitive theories. He hypothesizes that human cognition has an innate "completion tendency," by which experiences are repeatedly worked through in the mind until they can be fit into a person's model of self and the world. They will continue to impinge on the mind until they can be successfully categorized and thus mastered. The painful nature of the memories, however, causes the individual to attempt to reduce their occurrence by withdrawing from the world, especially those parts of the world that might evoke the memories. The attempts to shield oneself from the memories reduce the chance of the mind to work through them, and, consequently, their cyclical intrusion into one's life continues.

In another conceptualization, Janoff-Bulman (1985) suggests that victimization causes one to lose a general sense of invulnerability. One no longer sees the world as a safe place where misfortune occurs to other people but as a frightening, personally unsafe place. Feelings of generalized anxiety and helplessness accompany this suddenly hostile world. One may also make mistaken attributions for one's victimization. For instance, if you have learned that you get what you deserve, you may suddenly have to see yourself as being bad or guilty.

As with the other hypotheses, the PTSD explanation accounts for several of the consequences noted in both child and adult victims of child sexual abuse. Janoff-Bulman's hypotheses provide explanations for many of the emotional consequences, such as anxiety and guilt. Horowitz's hypothesis can account for some of the sexualized behaviors of victims, as they attempt to work through and gain mastery over their abuse. One of the main problems with the PTSD explanation is that it requires an initially extremely stressful event. Some sexual abuse victims have not described the abuse as being stressful at the time and in fact often found a pleasurable quality in it. Thus, the PTSD hypothesis does not seem to fit accurately the experience of many who eventually find their abuse to be a disturbing event in their lives. However, it does fit some victims' experiences and thus may be appropriate to account for some of their symptoms.

Integration of Models. Finkelhor (in press) argues that

the four-traumagenic-factors model hypothesized by Finkelhor and Browne (1985) accounts for more of the consequences observed in victims and thus can be seen as preferable to the PTSD model. We would like to suggest that there might be an appropriate way to combine the models of Finkelhor and Browne (1985), Summit (1983), and Horowitz's (1976) conception of PTSD. Recall that both Summit and Finkelhor and Browne comment on how molestation causes children to reconceptualize, or accommodate, their world in order to assimilate the abuse. These required accommodations in the child's conception of self and world cause the negative consequences to the child. Horowitz's hypothesized source of the recurring intrusion into victims' lives of memories of the victimization and the consequent numbing of their lives is that the abuse experience has not been assimilated and thus is still in the process of being worked through: "As assimilation and accommodation occur, there is a gradual reduction in the intensity, preemptoriness, and frequency of the repeated representations" (Horowitz, 1976, p. 104). The difference in these approaches appears to center on the way that the child handles the abuse emotionally. If he or she denies it and attempts to place its memories out of consciousness, Horowitz suggests that the memories will continue to recur until properly assimilated. Both Summit and Finkelhor and Browne, however, suggest that if the child accommodates his or her view of the world and self in order to assimilate the abuse, then the negative effects of that assimilation will occur. In either case, the child appears to be harmed, but in different ways. These different ways of handling abuse may partially account for some of the differences in symptoms seen in abuse victims. Unfortunately, no hypotheses explain why some children assimilate the experiences and others do not. It may be that learned or inherited personality characteristics or learned methods for dealing with conflict affect which process is employed.

Impact of Events Occurring After the Abuse

Most writers acknowledge that events occurring after sexual abuse is revealed can exacerbate the consequences for the victim. As we pointed out previously in this chapter, reactions of parents and friends may affect the victim's reactions to the abuse. In Chapter Fifteen, we discuss a number of legal changes that have been proposed to ameliorate what is perceived to be the negative consequences of the child's interactions with the legal system once the abuse is revealed. Figure 3(a) demonstrates a sudden increase in a child's level of distress caused by events occurring after the abuse is revealed, with some distress occurring when the abuse begins.

Figure 3. Distress Due to Abuse's Being Revealed.

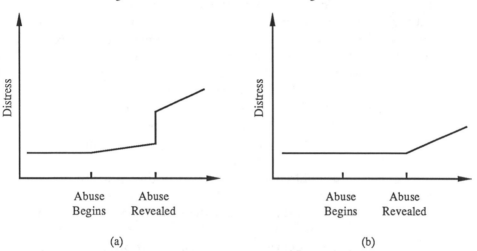

(a)   (b)

Taking a more radical approach than writers who propose this kind of impact, a small group of authors state that nothing is inherently wrong with nonviolent, noncoerced sexual relations between adults and children, and that society's reaction is generally the sole cause of the negative consequences for the children (see, for instance, O'Carroll, 1982). They suggest that the course of the child's distress can be seen as in Figure 3(b), in which no change occurs in the child's distress during the abuse; once the abuse is revealed, the negative consequences begin to appear.

Adherents of this radical position provide examples of children and adolescents who enjoyed and gained emotionally from sexual activity with adults. Such accounts have been attacked by most authors in the field as being both self-serving and not sensitive enough to the possibility of later negative ramifications for the children. In defense of their perspective, these writers indicate that the examples of negative consequences come mainly from children who have become involved in the legal and mental health system, and they point to contrasting examples of children who have not been identified as participants and who have never shown any negative effects.

As respected an investigator as Kinsey conveyed a similar attitude (Kinsey, Pomeroy, Martin, and Gebhard, 1953, p. 121): "It is difficult to understand why a child, except for its cultural conditioning, should be disturbed at seeing the genitalia of other persons or disturbed at even more specific sexual contacts. . . . Some of the more experienced students of juvenile problems have come to believe that the emotional reactions of the parents, police officers, and other adults who discover that the child has had such a contact may disturb the child more seriously than the sexual contacts themselves." Other researchers have also reported from a clinical study (Bender and Blau, 1937) and an empirical one (Ingram, 1981) that the negative consequences to children often did not begin until the abuse was discovered and the children had to face the reactions of others. Ingram (1981) suggests that the loving relationships that the boys in his study experienced with older men were positive for those who were deprived of a loving relationship in their homes.

Admittedly, the basis for this argument does contain a kernel of truth: If our society accepted sexual relations between children and adults in the same way that it accepts sexual relations between consenting men and women, then the negative consequences of adult/child sex might be reduced (although those holding a psychoanalytic or family systems perspective would not agree). The key point, however, is that our society does look negatively on sexual activity between children and adults, and a radical change in this fundamental belief does not appear to be imminent. As a result, the negative consequences for many if not most children who engage in such activity will continue. Large-scale surveys have indicated that negative consequences appear in many individuals who never revealed the abuse; the consequences apparently resulted from the victims' knowledge of the unacceptability of the sexual activity (Finkelhor, 1979; Haugaard, 1987; Russell, 1984). Landis (1956) found that only 5 percent of the girls who told their parents of an abuse experience were more traumatized by their parents' reaction than by the abuse itself. Although the effects of events occurring after the sexual abuse is revealed have been documented by empirical and clinical reports (see, for instance, Kirkwood and Mihaila, 1979; Rogers and Terry, 1984; Tufts' New England Medical Center, 1984), the hypothesis that the reactions of others are generally the principal cause of the negative consequences has not been demonstrated.

Summary and Conclusions

The question remains: What do we know about the consequences of child sexual abuse? From both clinical and empirical studies, we know that most victims are negatively affected by their experience. The extent of the impact that results from the sexual activity, the atmosphere in which it occurs, or the reactions of others when it is discovered is less clear. The different aspects of the entire sexual abuse experience likely have varying effects on the victims for reasons that are not currently understood. Some victims apparently suffer no negative consequences. We do not know what it is about these people or their experiences that protects them from these negative consequences; additional research in this area should provide clinicians with valuable information about treatment. An apparent small minority view their childhood sexual experience with an adult positively. Again, we know little about these individuals and their experiences. Although a number of researchers have looked for variables that might predict whether a victim experiences a more or less intense reaction to sexual abuse, few stable patterns have been found.

A number of theories have been advanced to explain the negative consequences seen in victims. Some of these theories concentrate on the affective component of the abuse, while others hypothesize that the cognitive component of the abuse causes the consequences. Although some attempts have been made to integrate these perspectives, *the* theory has yet to be formulated. As with other aspects of child sexual abuse, we doubt that any one theory will adequately explain the consequences to all victims. This possibility is hardly surprising given the complicated interaction of the variety of sexual abuse circumstances and the individual characteristics of victims and perpetrators. We do not have a theory that adequately explains individuals' reactions to even simpler events than sexual abuse. Perhaps the best strategy is to understand the variety of ways that individuals are affected by sexual abuse so that each individual can be dealt with in the most flexible manner.

Clearly, there is much to learn about the consequences of child sexual abuse. The development of knowledge in this area will provide those treating victims and their families with valuable information and may allow them to develop increasingly effective methods of prevention. Just as with other investigations into human behavior, child sexual abuse researchers have to examine complex issues. Hopefully, the complexity will not frighten them away.

CHAPTER FIVE

Incest and Incestuous Families

F ew if any acts assault the public's sense of propriety more than incest. Some researchers report that incest is abhorred above all other acts except murder and rape (Dietz and Sissman, 1984). A few public figures have suggested that parents convicted of incest be incarcerated for life, without chance of parole. What makes so many people believe that having sexual relations with a son or daughter is worse than stealing the life savings from a retired person, beating someone senseless, or having sexual relations with an unrelated child? In this chapter, we review the development and maintenance of this repulsion toward incestuous relationships, describe various opinions about the reasons for incest, and summarize several descriptions of the parents and children in incestuous families.

The Incest Desire and the Incest Taboo

Many theorists believe that the incest taboo is required because of a strong universal incest desire. The most prominent view of the incest desire comes from the writings of Freud. He believed that an innate incest desire is evident in early childhood and that it continues throughout life in a repressed form (Freud [1933], 1965). Freud interpreted many of his clinical cases as indicating a strong incest desire in children and adults, and more recent clinical writings have also emphasized the presence of a strong incest desire (see Meiselman, 1978).

Not all have developed the same views as Freud. Westermarck (1926) theorized that people living together develop a natural aversion to having sexual relations with each other. He suggests that this natural aversion became accepted as a general custom, and the prohibition of incest became codified without there being a strong incest desire to guard against. Some evidence supports this position. For instance, Fox (1962) found that unrelated children reared together in an Israeli kibbutz seldom had sexual relations with each other. The natural-aversion view has been discounted by others, however, who cite anthropological evidence from some cultures that unrelated children reared together often marry (Bagley, 1969).

The prohibition of incest, or the incest taboo, has been noted across cultures throughout history. Although there have been some isolated exceptions to the taboo, these have been extremely limited and have applied generally to brother/sister marriages within the royal families of certain cultures (Bagley, 1969). The relative strength of the taboo between various family members is also similar across cultures, with the strongest prohibition being against mother/son incest, the next strongest against father/daughter incest, and the relatively weakest against brother/sister incest (Meiselman, 1978).

Development of the Incest Taboo. The origin of this apparently universal taboo has been debated for years. Two general positions have been taken, one emphasizing a strong biological influence, the other a psychological or sociological influence. Theorizing from both these perspectives involves the Darwinian idea of natural selection. According to these theories, when humans were beginning to form societal groups, some of the groups allowed incestuous relationships while others did not. The inclusion of the incest taboo in some social groups was not intentional but happened randomly or for a variety of reasons that may have no relation to group survival. Those groups that did develop the taboo became stronger and survived, and those that allowed incest became weaker and perished.

The biological explanation was popular early in this century, lost its popularity during the mid-century, when environmental explanations of behavior were in vogue, and has made a comeback since then (Meiselman, 1978). The basic hypothesis is that inbreeding causes a decrease in the fitness of the offspring. Two factors could explain the difference in fitness. The first factor is the increased probability that the offspring in an inbred group will be deformed. The increase of deformities is caused by the generally maladaptive recessive genes that can be passed from parents to their children. Sexual relations outside the family heighten the chance that a recessive gene passed from one parent will be paired with a dominant gene from the other, thus masking the effect of the recessive gene. Sexual relations between family members heighten the chance that offspring will receive the recessive gene that each parent inherited from their common ancestor, resulting in the maladaptive trait represented by the recessive gene (Lindzey, 1967). Although there is only a slight chance that recessive genes become paired even in an incestuous family, over numerous generations the increased incidence of infant deformities could have had a noticeable impact on the tenuous survival of any early human group. The second factor is the genetic variability that is found more in outbred than inbred groups. Environmental variation can have more pronounced negative effects on an inbred group. An outbred group has more genetic variability and can adapt more readily to environmental change, thus its chances of survival in a changing world are enhanced. Lindzey (1967) provides a thorough review of the experimental data supporting the negative effects of inbreeding.

Adherents to the social/psychological theory also argue that those societal groups that prohibited incest had a greater chance of survival than those that did not. However, they believe that the causes were more social than biological. The basic hypothesis is that the family unit was weakened in societies that allowed incest and that weakened families caused the weakening of the social group as a whole. For instance, the possessiveness that can accompany a sexual relationship or the jealousy that can arise between possible competitors for the same sexual partner (or both) could cause great rifts in families and create the type of chaotic conditions that would destroy the fabric of the family (Malinowski, 1927). These weakened social groups were likely to dissolve, leaving the individual members vulnerable. Social groups that prohibited incest had a greater chance for survival than did those that did not, and, over the years, only these social units survived.

Freud's theory about the development of the incest taboo is from the social/psychological perspective. Based on what later proved to be incorrect anthropological findings (Arkin, 1984), Freud postulated the idea of the "primal horde" as the origin of the incest taboo (Freud [1933], 1965). According to this theory, the sons in an ancient family unit grew to have parricidal thoughts because they wanted to possess their mother and sisters, who were jealously kept from them by their father. Although the father was able to intimidate the sons while they were young, when they became sufficiently powerful they banded together and killed him. Rather than achieving an outright victory, however, the sons found themselves filled with remorse and guilt because they also revered their father. In addition, they discovered that they were now in competition with each other for the women that they had won. They realized that they might eventually kill each other and end their family through this competition, so they resolved to establish a strong prohibition against incest and require exogamy. The implication of Freud's theory seems to be that those sets of brothers that did not institute the incest taboo eventually did kill each other or were killed by their sons, while those sets that did institute the taboo began families and social groups with a higher chance for survival.

Arkin (1984) agrees with the Freudian notion of the incest taboo and is the only theorist who has postulated an additional innate biological prohibition in women. One of the problems that Arkin finds with most social/psychological theories concerning the incest taboo is that they portray the women as "essentially passive. They stand by and merely grant themselves to the victors" (pp. 375–376). If women were completely passive, they would have to accept incest with their sons, as well.

He theorizes, however, that mothers have an innate mechanism that prohibits them from doing this. As evidence for his hypothesis, Arkin notes that in every culture mothers break the incest taboo far less frequently than fathers, and he also cites several studies of primate behavior in which females were observed to have sexual intercourse indiscriminantly with males of several generations but never with their sons.

Maintenance of the Incest Taboo. Theorizing about the maintenance of the incest taboo is easier than theorizing about its origin because we can observe the benefits of the taboo historically and in modern times. Although the origin of the taboo is generally assumed to have occurred without a conscious effort on the part of social groups, the maintenance of the taboo involves both the realization by those in a particular culture that the taboo is beneficial and the subsequent purposeful decision to continue it. Again, there are two basic types of theories: the biological and the sociological/psychological. Although there are some strict adherents to each perspective, most believe that a mixture best explains the prohibition of incest (for instance, Murdock, 1949).

The biological theory is based on the belief that most societies have recognized that the offspring from those related by blood have a greater chance of being malformed than do offspring from those not related. Evidence for this recognition comes from the myths of many early cultures in which incestuous relations between gods often resulted in malformed offspring (Lindzey, 1967). Modern research has also shown that there is a higher risk of deformed children from incestuous than from nonincestuous relations. One study done in Japan (cited in Lindzey, 1967) found that children of first cousins had a higher rate of deformity than did the general population. Seemanova (1971) studied 161 Czechoslovakian mothers who had a child from both an incestuous relationship and a nonincestuous relationship. He found that 20 percent of the children of the incestuous relationships and 5 percent of those from nonincestuous relationships had a congenital deformity, and that 25 percent of the incestuous and none of the nonincestuous unions produced a mentally retarded child.

Theories from the sociological/psychological perspective state that the taboo promotes individual emotional and physical health and effective functioning of families and larger social groups. Parsons (1954) believed that the taboo was critical for the development of both the individual child and society in general. Theorizing from the psychoanalytic perspective on development, he argued that children's incest desires were valuable in the formation of early attachments to parents and in the development of early sex roles. However, the child's development would be retarded if the child's incest desires were fulfilled during adolescence or early adulthood. If an incestuous relationship developed, the child would be kept close to the family of origin during a time when he or she should be looking outside the family for a mate and a place in the larger society. Furthermore, families that allowed incest would become minisocieties within themselves and would isolate themselves from the larger society. This development would cause them to withdraw their contribution from the larger society, and the society would suffer.

Similarly, Schwartzman (1974) writes that the proper development of the child as an individual depends on the incest taboo. Drawing on the work of several family therapists who found high rates of emotional disturbance in children from families with no psychological differentiation between members, Schwartzman theorizes that the incest taboo is an important mechanism by which the relationship between parent and child is kept from becoming too binding. Without the taboo, the sexual component to their relationship would cause children to become too attached to their parents and the children would not be able to individuate—a necessary process for adaptive individuals.

White (1948) stressed the economic and social benefits of the incest taboo. He argued that networks for support and cooperation are extended through interfamily and intergroup marriages. These larger networks are more secure than single-family networks because of their greater diversity, and they increase the chance for the advancement of all those in the network as ideas and goods are exchanged by a growing number of people. Thus, the prohibition of incest serves to increase steadily the size of the networks. A study of incestuous families in Japan (cited in Bagley, 1969) illustrated the value of the incest taboo in promoting the establishment of a large network by showing how incestuous behavior could promote the purposeful narrowing of an outside network. One of the principal values of incest in these Japanese families was to stop the family wealth from being dispersed to a larger network. White's theory also provides a possible reason for the extension of the incest taboo to extended family members because, in order to promote the widest network possible, marriages to those completely outside the family group would be best.

Legal Perspective. Although we provided legal definitions of incest in Chapter Two, it is worth noting again how changes in incest statutes reflect changes in beliefs about the reasons for maintaining the incest taboo. Initial incest laws in the United States were designed to protect against the risk of deformed children. As such, the statutes did not prohibit sexual activity initiated by a stepparent, uncle, or aunt (although these people often could be prosecuted under other statutes). More recently, a number of states have expanded the scope of incest laws to include stepparents and other relatives. The rationale for these new statutes appears to be concern about the effects that these sexual relationships can have on the family and the child; thus they represent a shift to the sociological/psychological perspective (Wulkan and Bulkley, 1985).

Conclusions. The universality and continued strength of the incest taboo suggest that there is a strong incest desire. The origin and maintenance of the taboo are explained to some extent by all the perspectives stated here—biological, social, psychological, and economic. It seems futile, and it probably is misleading, to try to determine which of the reasons is the true one.

Although each perspective is logical, these theories do not seem to explain fully our strong repulsion to the act of incest. Therapists working with incestuous families have often spoken of the difficulty they have managing their feelings of anger and disgust toward the perpetrator and feelings of pity for and protectiveness toward the victim. People describing an incestuous dream involving their mother or father often report intense negative reactions to it. It is difficult to imagine that the intensity of these reactions can be explained by knowledge of the heightened chance for a deformed baby or by knowledge that the economic position of society might be worsened because of incestuous behavior. This deeply rooted emotional reaction to incest is difficult to explain entirely with the various biological or sociological theories. Whether this emotional reaction is a result of repressed incest desires, an innate aversion to incest, or some other aspect of the human psyche is not known. But the reality is that something clearly drives most of us to avoid not only incest experiences but also incestuous thoughts.

Breaking the Incest Taboo

Despite this seemingly strong taboo against incest, evidence indicates that it occurs with surprising frequency (see, for instance, Fromuth, 1986; Russell, 1984). Epidemiological studies have shown that approximately 1 percent of children in the United States today (or about one-half to one million children) are involved in an incestuous relationship with a parent or parent figure, and many believe that this is an underestimation (Finkelhor, 1979; Sedney and Brooks, 1984; Wyatt, 1985). Explanations for the occurrence of incest can be grouped into four general categories: the functional explanation, the feminist explanation, the chaotic explanation, and the individual-pathology explanation. Examples of incestuous families fitting these categories can be found in historical accounts, and each of the categories forms the foundation for one of the current theoretical explanations for incest.

Functional Explanation. The functional explanation suggests that the act of incest serves some purpose. The function usually occurs within the family, although the incest can also serve a more general function in larger societal units or in a family's interactions with society. This is not to say that the function is beneficial to each member of the family or society or even that it is beneficial for the unit as a whole but simply that it serves some function in maintaining the behavioral patterns of the unit.

Several historical examples illustrate the way in which incest has served a function. Riemer (1940) described fifty-eight cases of incest in rural Swedish families in the 1930s. Each of these families lived in an isolated area, and they were described as being generally accepting of sexual indulgence. When the wife became unavailable as a sexual partner because of illness or injury, the husband turned to the daughter as a substitute. Riemer suggested that these isolated farms became "micro-societies" and that within each society incest became morally sanctioned. The function of the incest appears to be that it kept the family running smoothly because the most powerful member of the family, the husband, remained relatively happy. The effects of her new role on the daughter were not discussed, and it may be that the functioning of the entire family was kept smooth at the expense of the daughter.

Another example of the functional aspect of incest came from Japanese researchers in the 1950s (cited in Bagley, 1969). From a group of incestuous families, twenty-three that had no other apparent pathology were investigated. The function of the incest in these families was to keep the family and its property together by providing sexual partners for family members from within the extended family. Many of the families reported that the incestuous activity was praiseworthy.

Another historical example comes from a custom of Mormons in the 1800s. A man who married a widow was also allowed to marry his stepdaughters when they came of age (Schroeder, 1915). The function of this type of incest was to keep the larger society of the Church together. The Mormons had been persecuted for many years, and this practice helped consolidate the community and keep it isolated. Assuming the validity of one of the sociological reasons for the origin and maintenance of the incest taboo (that it allowed for the dispersing of families and the development of larger social networks), it is not surprising that a relatively small society that wished to remain isolated could sanction incest.

The family systems theory on incest has its roots in the functional explanation and is currently the most widely accepted theory in the mental health field. Rather than viewing the incest as the cause of the problems that are almost always associated with incestuous families, this theory sees incest as a symptom of an already dysfunctional family system. By their nature as a set of interacting individuals, families develop rules of behavior that govern the functioning of each individual and the family as a whole. Within some family systems, behaviors that are defined by society as abnormal occur in order to keep their system and rules of behavior consistent. As such, behaviors of individuals are not viewed as reflecting individual pathology but rather as attempts by the system to maintain its balance of behavior. Much as in other families a child might become anorexic or a parent might become alcoholic, in incestuous families, the incest maintains the rules and boundaries to which the family has become accustomed.

A common behavioral pattern noted in incestuous families seen in therapy is that the father turns his sexual and emotional attention to his daughter in order to distance himself from his wife and reduce tension that has arisen within the parental relationship. Some see the mother as the cornerstone in this process (Lustig, Dresser, Spellman, and Murray, 1966; Machotka, Pittman, and Flomenhaft, 1967). In order to reduce her involvement with the father, she encourages the incest by consciously or unconsciously pushing the daughter toward the father and distancing herself from the daughter. The increasing role of the daughter in the father's life allows the mother to decrease her role with the father, and the result is a reduction of the tension that has arisen between the parents. This process may stabilize a marital situation that the parents fear might lead to the breakup of the family. The price for this stabilization paid by individual family members, especially the child, may be quite great.

Incest may also serve other functions, as this example shows:

> A father is released from jail, where he has been serving time after pleading guilty to having intercourse with his teenage daughter, with the stipulation that he receive therapy. The daughter has been

in several foster homes and institutions since the incest was revealed but desires to return home. The mother is ambivalent about the daughter's returning home. Father and mother attend therapy for several sessions but stop once the judicial order for therapy is lifted. Social services, child protective services, and the probation department all spend considerable time monitoring the family and the father. Once the daughter is returned home, rumors escalate that she and the father are sleeping together openly, but no one in the family will confirm this. The incest is apparently allowing the father, or both the father and daughter, to demonstrate independence from and contempt for the system.

From the family systems perspective, corrective intervention with an incestuous family eventually involves restructuring the rules by which the family functions so that incest or other unacceptable behaviors are not needed to maintain the family's balance. It may also be important to assess whether the incest has had a function for the family's interactions with its community or for the community as a whole, as the proper intervention in these cases may focus not so much on the inner workings of the individual family as on the family's interactions with those outside.

Feminist Explanation. The feminist explanation for incest provides a different interpretation of much of the historical and modern data on which the functional perspective is based. Rather than conceptualizing incest as serving a function, the feminist explanation sees incest as another example of the basic inequality between the sexes that has been perpetrated throughout history by the patriarchal social system. Most men are taught openly or subtly that they have the right to have their sexual urges satisfied. The social system reinforces both this belief and the obligation of other family members to keep the father content. Incest occurs because the father feels justified in turning to his daughter for sex if it is unavailable from his wife.

Furthermore, the rules and relationship patterns of society have made the mother and children dependent on the father for economic survival. As a consequence, it is often impossible for them to confront the father's behavior. In order to survive financially, the mother and children are trapped by the structure of the family and society into allowing the father to behave in any way he desires (McIntyre, 1981).

Of central concern to adherents to the feminist perspective is the role assigned to the mother in an incestuous family by those endorsing the family systems perspective. Once again, the mother is seen as the one who must bear the responsibility for another family member's behavior. This view can be encouraged by the patriarchal nature of society, which has a tendency to see incest from the father's perspective (Taubman, 1984). "The father rapes, abuses, brutalizes, and assaults the children and the mother, but somehow it is the mother's or child's fault" (Wattenberg, 1985, p. 206). This perspective is illustrated by the following case:

> After questioning by her teacher, a fourteen-year-old girl reveals that her father has been molesting her for several years. Father runs the home with an iron hand, physically attacking those who do not immediately accede to his wishes. Several years ago, he began to turn his sexual attention away from his wife, who had become progressively depressed and withdrawn, and he now has sex almost exclusively with his daughter. If the daughter does not perform to his expectations, he beats her or her mother or both of them.

According to feminist theorists, the most effective interventions are those aimed at both society and individual perpetrators. Efforts at the societal level include activities to change the basic inequalities of men and women in society and to alleviate the dependence of women. Individual interventions should be aimed at the perpetrator. Although the mother and children of an incestuous family may need economic and emotional support once the incest is discovered, the family is not seen as needing the reorganization that would be brought about by family therapy. The perpetrator is the one who has erred; when the entire family is involved in therapy, the responsibility for the incest becomes incorrectly shared by all its members (McIntyre, 1981; Wattenberg, 1985).

Chaotic Explanation. A few historical studies have found an apparently high incidence of incest in communities that are undergoing tremendous change and that as a consequence do not have a solid sense of community standards. Two such instances cited by Bagley (1969) are some urban areas of Chicago in the first decade of the 1900s, when there was a mass influx of new people from a variety of cultures, and Germany after World War II, where overcrowded and disorganized conditions prevailed. Bagley describes both these societies as having few if any defined behavioral expectations and the individuals as having little sense of belonging to a community or social group. As a consequence, there were few external controls on members' behavior.

A similar lack of external control is postulated as the cause of incest in some families today (Will, 1983). The descriptions of these chaotic families are similar to those of the chaotic societies. There are few family rules, little control of individuals' behavior, and few if any emotional or physical boundaries between members. The families are often isolated—socially if not also physically—from their community, and the members do not appear to respond to any external standards. Sexual relations often occur between nuclear and extended family members both within the same generation and across generations.

No reports describe specific therapeutic interventions being used successfully with chaotic incestuous families. These families appear to be relatively rare, and enough of them may not be available to one agency or clinician to allow for the development of a systematic therapeutic plan. The families are probably also likely to terminate therapy before much therapeutic work can be accomplished. Nonincestuous chaotic families have been described as being among the most difficult to treat. Intervening with incestuous chaotic families may be viewed so pessimistically that few mental health professionals have pursued therapy with them aggressively.

Individual-Pathology Explanation. Much of the early theorizing about those who broke the incest taboo postulated that they were mentally or emotionally disturbed (Meiselman, 1978). One belief was that most of the perpetrators of incest were schizophrenic or were suffering from some other sort of psychosis that put them out of touch with normal societal expectations. This type of individual pathology is currently viewed as explaining only a small minority of incest cases. Empirical research (Finkelhor, 1979; Wyatt, 1985) and clinical studies (Cavallin, 1966) have shown that the perpetrator of incest is often a man or woman who otherwise functions well in society and in whom few other signs of individual disturbance can be found.

However, the individual-pathology explanation is receiving increased attention, and some investigators suggest that the perpetrator of incest can be understood in the same way as other child molesters, except for the choice of victim (Lanyon, 1986). If this suggestion is true, it would have an important impact on the assessment and treatment of both the perpetrator and the family. If less of the cause of the incest was shown to reside in the family or the society and more of it in the individual perpetrator, then treatment programs should be more focused on the perpetrator than on the family or society. Investigations of similarity between incest perpetrators and other child molesters have involved measuring the similarity of their arousal to stimuli involving different-age children and adults. Arousal is gauged by measuring changes, through one of several different types of apparatus, in the volume or diameter of the subject's penis during the presentation of various stimuli (see Quinsey and Marshall, 1983). It is assumed that erectile changes are adequate representations of overall sexual arousal (Marshall, Earls, Segal, and Darke, 1983).

Two studies in this area are the most cited. Although they resulted in different findings, it appears possible to reconcile their differences. Abel, Becker, Murphy, and Flanagan (1981) found that six incest perpetrators had sexual arousal patterns to audiotapes of adult/child and adult/adult sexual encounters similar to the patterns of ten pedophiles who had molested nonrelatives. Of particular interest is a comparison of the description of mutually initiated sex between an adult and a child and the description of a similar act between two adults. The incest perpetrators showed a slightly higher change in penile volume to the adult/child description than to the adult/adult description. Quinsey, Chaplin, and Carrigan (1979), however, found that nine incest perpetrators had a higher reaction to slides of nude adult women than to nude female children, while fifteen other child molesters showed a more similar response to the women and girls.

These discrepant results are difficult to reconcile because they used different stimuli and each came from a small number of subjects (thus increasing the chance that one individual could have a meaningful effect on the group average). However, Abel, Becker, Murphy, and Flanagan (1981) present the results from one of the incest perpetrators, and this information may help reconcile the studies. The individual who was singled out had a much higher response to the adult/child scene and a much lower response to the adult/adult scene than the average of all six incest perpetraiors. This finding suggests that the average of the six incest perpetrators may have been unduly influenced by this individual and that the average of the other five incest perpetrators may have shown a pattern similar to that of the Quinsey, Chaplin, and Carrigan (1979) sample, with a lower response to the adult/child than to the adult/adult scene.

Additional research using this technology is clearly needed. Use of a nonabusing control group would make for an interesting comparison. Some research has shown that nonabusing males show a higher level of arousal to nude pictures of pubescent and younger girls than they do to landscapes or nude pictures of boys (although their arousal to the females increases with the age of the girl) (Freund, McNight, Langevin, and Cibiri, 1972). Other research has shown that intoxicated nonrapists show arousal patterns to violent sexual scenes that are more like those of rapists than of their own when they are not intoxicated (Marshall, Earls, Segal, and Darke, 1983). A nonabusing control group would allow for a comparison of incest perpetrators' arousal patterns with those of both other molesters and nonabusers, resulting in a clearer picture than we now have of any deviance in the incest perpetrators' arousal.

Although the Abel, Becker, Murphy, and Flanagan (1981) study may not show that incest perpetrators in general have arousal patterns similar to those of other child molesters, the arousal pattern of the one incest perpetrator clearly shows that some incestuous fathers may commit the incest because of sexual desire rather than family dynamics. This result suggests that in some cases the main focus of intervention must be the father.

Which Explanation Is Correct? Authors have provided either empirical reports or clinical examples supporting each of the explanations for the occurrence of incest. Kaufman, Peck, and Tagiuri (1954) reviewed eleven cases of incest involving families that appeared quite chaotic. Many of the fathers were alcoholic and had deserted their family at some time. The mothers had also deserted the children at one time or another. Will (1983) describes chaotic families in which incest often occurred between several nuclear and extended family members. The individual-pathology model is supported by research that has found incestuous fathers to be higher than nonincestuous fathers on the psychopathic deviate scale of the Minnesota Multiphasic Personality Inventory (MMPI) (Anderson and Shafer, 1979) and to be sexually aroused by children (Abel, Becker, Murphy, and Flanagan, 1981). Several clinicians have documented that incest served a function in stabilizing families (Hoorwitz, 1983; Machotka, Pittman, and Flomenhaft, 1967; Taylor, 1984). Garrett and Wright (1975) interviewed the wives of seven men convicted of incest and concluded that the incest served a function for the wives by making them feel superior to their husbands and providing them with sympathy from those in their social network. Other researchers have provided evidence indicating that the mothers in incestuous families are often physically and emotionally abused themselves, lending credence to the feminist perspective (Herman, 1981; Truesdell, McNeil, and Deschner, 1986).

These seemingly contradictory reports make the search

for a single, all-encompassing explanation for the cause of incest problematic at best. Even taking into consideration the possibility that individual investigators' results might be influenced by their theoretical positions, the various reports paint quite different pictures of incestuous families. Perhaps the best approach is to conclude that there are several equally valid explanations depending on the family in question and that the search for the ideal explanation for incest may be fruitless. It is also possible, or even probable, that incestuous families may fit a combination of several different descriptions. For instance, many chaotic families are not incestuous, and it may be a combination of the chaotic conditions and individual psychopathology in the father that leads to the incest in one particular family.

Moreover, the search for a single explanation may hamper the treatment of incestuous families. The explanation for the incest held by a professional may have an important influence on the type of intervention provided to the family or its individual members. A professional who is convinced that the family systems perspective is the only way to view incestuous families may provide appropriate treatment to some families but inappropriate treatment to those in which the father has truly terrorized the members into acceding to his sexual demands. Similarly, a professional viewing the incestuous family solely from the feminist perspective may miss the chance to help a mother who has colluded in the incest. Those holding stubbornly to either perspective may not provide needed treatment to a pathological parent.

It is always tempting to reduce complex problems to simple ones. Evaluations and interventions are made much easier when the behavior of individuals and families is simplified to the point where it can be easily understood and categorized. Incest occurs in a wide range of families, however, and is perpetrated by adults of diverse backgrounds and personalities on many different types of children in a wide variety of situations. A good focus, then, would be to acknowledge the complexity of the causes of incest and the concomitant complexity of the interventions that must be applied when it occurs.

The Incestuous Family and Its Members

Several authors have attempted to describe the "typical" incestuous family (for instance, DeYoung, 1982; James and Nasjleti, 1983; Machotka, Pittman, and Flomenhaft, 1967). These descriptions have often come from small clinical samples; for instance the Machotka sample was three families. The variety of descriptions has led other authors to suggest that there is more than one typical type of family (for instance, Hoorwitz, 1983; Will, 1983). Efforts have also been made to describe various risk factors that might lead a family to incest. Finkelhor (1984), for instance, writes of four preconditions that must be met for incest to occur: motivation of the perpetrator to sexually abuse, lack of internal inhibitors, lack of external inhibitors, and lack of resistance on the part of the child or the presence of resistance that can be overcome by the perpetrator. Incest becomes increasingly likely each time one of the preconditions is met. Trepper and Barrett (1986) developed a risk-factor scale that includes the vulnerability of the individual perpetrator and family, the presence of a precipitating event, and the lack of family coping skills. They hypothesized that the more risk factors that are present the higher the likelihood that the family might engage in incest. The risk-factor approach has several advantages: It allows for the consideration of a large number of factors; it acknowledges that certain risk factors can be "overcome" by protective factors that reduce the possibility of incest; and it recognizes that the possibility for incest is increased by the presence of risk factors but that incest is not inevitable even in high-risk families.

The thorough documentation of certain family structures, histories, or risk factors that are often associated with the occurrence of incest would be of great value. Mental health professionals working with children and families would be able to closely investigate the possibility of incest in families that matched a particular profile. Social workers and other mental health professionals could concentrate preventive efforts on families with a high risk for becoming incestuous. Thus, the search for a profile of the incestuous family– its members and its dynamics—is a useful one. Several roadblocks are associated with this search, and the value of the findings may be limited. In this section, we discuss these limitations, outline several descriptions of the incestuous family and its members, and then discuss the value of these descriptions in light of their limitations.

Limitations to the Research

The use of clinical samples as a basis for a description of the incestuous family results in several limitations, and these must be kept in mind so that the descriptions are not considered as absolute guidelines for identifying incestuous families. One major drawback is the inability to discriminate between incestuous and nonincestuous families on the basis of these descriptions. Because there is a lack of systematic empirical research employing groups of nonincestuous control families with which the incestuous families can be compared, it is impossible to assess whether characteristics that are present in an incestuous family are also present in nonincestuous families. Consequently, it is not possible to estimate the extent to which the presence of a particular characteristic can be used to identify an incestuous family. For instance, if withdrawn, dependent mothers are found in many incestuous families and in few other families, then the maternal style could be considered an important factor in identifying incestuous families. If, however, withdrawn, dependent mothers are also present in many nonincestuous families, the value of this characteristic as an indicator of incest, at least by itself, disappears.

A second limitation has already been mentioned in Chapter Four: the extent to which the descriptions obtained from clinical samples can be generalized to all incestuous families. As we noted in Chapter Two, low-income families are often overrepresented in clinical samples because they come to the attention of child protective services and the courts more frequently than do higher-income families. As a result, it is difficult to gauge the extent to which the risk factors or typical patterns that emerge from an examination of clinical cases also pertain to higher-income families. There is also general agreement that only a small minority of incestuous families are discovered. No investigations have examined the families that reveal incest versus those that do not. Thus, we do not know whether those families that reveal incest are typical of the majority that do not and consequently whether the patterns found in families from clinical samples are representative of those found in other families.

A third limitation concerns the improper use of clinical reports to make statements about the cause of incest. For instance, if a mother in an incestuous family is found to be sexually and emotionally withdrawn from the father, some investigators may interpret her withdrawal as one of the causes of the incest. In actuality, it is seldom clear whether the observed withdrawal led to the incest or, on the contrary, whether the incest led to the withdrawal. In other words, rather than being the cause of the incest, the observed withdrawal might have been a consequence. Making a causal statement remains problematic even if the couple maintains that the withdrawal occurred before the incest because a third, undiscovered factor, such as the occurrence of physical abuse or individual pathology in one of the parents, may have caused both the incest and the withdrawal. In this type of case, the incest and the withdrawal are both consequences of something else, even if the consequence of withdrawal occurred before the consequence of incest. Because of the presence of alternate causal models, it is generally impossible to determine accurately, solely on the strength of clinical reports, the cause of incest.

Descriptions of the Incestuous Family

The focus of this section is on families in which father/daughter incest has occurred. Instances of mother/son incest are reported rarely, and instances of father/son and mother/daughter incest appear even less often. A brief description of the members of the other types of incestuous families follows the thorough discussion of the father/daughter incestuous family.

Background of Parents. One important factor that has emerged from many clinical reports is the history of the parents. Investigators have found that many parents who sexually abuse their children, and many parents whose partners sexually abuse their children, were once physically or sexually abused themselves (DeYoung, 1982; Rosenfeld, 1977; Will, 1983), although this pattern does not hold across all studies (Groff and Hubble, 1984). One hypothesis to account for this intergenerational pattern is that the incest is an attempt by a parent to master his or her own abuse by repeating it from a powerful position. Another factor often found in the histories of incest perpetrators is neglect or emotional abandonment by their parents (Justice and Justice, 1979; Meiselman, 1978; Will, 1983). Parker and Parker (1986), for instance, found that fathers incarcerated for incest recalled more maltreatment from their parents than did fathers incarcerated for other crimes. This neglect may raise the risk of parents becoming incestuous because of the inappropriate or incomplete example of parenting that they received as children or because the neglect contributed to a reservoir of anger or tension that is released in the later incest. It is important to emphasize, however, that there is no evidence available concerning the proportion of sexually or physically abused children who later become abusive parents; therefore, it cannot be assumed that a sexually abused child is likely to become an incestuous parent. Recall, for instance, the study by Goodwin, McCarthy, and DiVasto (1981), which showed that although 38 percent of an abusive group of mothers had been sexually abused as children, 24 percent of a control group of nonabusive mothers had also been sexually abused, indicating that quite a few molested children do not grow up to molest their own children.

Personalities of Parents and Victim. The incestuous father has been described in several ways. In one variation, the father is domineering and has a need to keep his wife and children in a helpless position (Herman, 1983; Hoorwitz, 1983). This control is often accomplished through physical abuse (Herman, 1981; Truesdell, McNeil, and Deschner, 1986). Another variant describes the father as sexually frustrated yet demanding, emotionally immature, and dependent on his wife as a mother figure (Furniss, 1983b; Hoorwitz, 1983). In other cases, the fathers appear to have low self-esteem. Some clinical reports have found the incestuous father to be alcoholic or an occasional abuser of alcohol (Dietz and Craft, 1980; Hoorwitz, 1983). Muldoon (1981) found that 65 percent of a sample of perpetrators abused alcohol, although other investigators have found a considerably lower percentage (Groff and Hubble, 1984; Herman, 1981).

In other areas of investigation, Anderson and Shafer (1979) found incestuous fathers to have a significantly higher MMPI psychopathic deviate score than did fathers of daughters being seen for other problems in the same clinic. Scott and Stone (1986b), however, found that a group of sixty-two incestuous fathers had MMPI scores in the normal range. They also report a pattern of scores suggesting that many of the fathers had covert antisocial tendencies that might lead them to take improper risks and be deficient in empathy. This evidence is congruent with that from clinical reports in which the father is categorized as having poor impulse control (Zefran and others, 1982). Other clinical reports have described the father as paranoid, hostile, and having unconscious homosexual tendencies (Cavallin, 1966). In what appears to be the only description of incestuous fathers by their daughters, Buskirk and Cole (1983) report that eight women in therapy described their fathers as "independent, active, competitive, self-confident, emotionally cold, tenacious, and decisive" (p. 148), descriptions that may be as positive as they are negative.

From clinical samples, mothers are often described as meek, withdrawn, and submissive to and dependent on their husbands (DeYoung, 1982; Herman, 1983). Herman (1981) notes a high rate of debilitating physical or mental problems in mothers from incestuous families, and Finkelhor (1979) found that girls who rated their mothers as emotionally distant or frequently ill were at higher risk for sexual abuse than were girls who did not rate their mothers this way. These factors may increase the risk of incest as the father turns from the withdrawn mother for sexual activity. However, two studies contradict the picture of the mother as an emotionally or physically withdrawn parent. Borgman (1984) interviewed sixteen girl victims of sexual abuse and found that the majority consistently felt close emotional bonds to their mothers: "Nine of the sixteen girls identified their mothers exclusively as the person they wished to be like, who treated them the best, and with whom they most liked to associate" (p. 183). Zefran and others (1982) describe mothers from fifty-five incestuous families, clustering them into one of five categories: passive, dominant, absent, disabled, or nurturing. As with other investigators, they found that the passive category was predominant. However, the second largest category was nurturing. Scott and Stone (1986b) found that a group of forty-four nonparticipating mothers from incestuous families had MMPI depression and anxiety scores in the normal range. They comment that this result was strange given the recent disclosure of the incest and consequent family disruption. They hypothesize that the mothers were prone to use disassociation as a way of avoiding feelings about the incest.

Little work has focused on the reasons a particular child in a family becomes the victim of incest. In DeYoung's (1982) clinical sample of sixty incest female victims, 83 percent were the oldest daughters and 5 percent were only children, suggesting the vulnerability of the oldest daughter. DeYoung also notes that some have theorized that a daughter who looks like her mother is more vulnerable to incest than a daughter who does not, but she cites no studies to substantiate this claim. Meiselman (1978) found little relationship between physical attractiveness and vulnerability to being a victim of incest.

Although some of Freud's theorizing about the incest desire would suggest that the personality of the victim may place her at a higher risk than her sisters, we cannot find any reports examining this possibility. One reason for this lack of attention may be the assumption that if investigators find that certain personal characteristics of a child place her at risk for abuse, this information could be used to put some of the responsibility for the abuse on the child. It would be unfortunate if research in this area was being discouraged because of a fear of the possible results. Systematic investigations into victims' beliefs or behaviors might indicate that they place certain children at higher risk for incest. Even if this were so, we are not suggesting that the child be held responsible for the incest; the parent is the family member responsible for interactions between the parent and the child. However, if certain actions or personality variables of victims could be identified, then interventions aimed at helping victims understand these factors might help protect them from being victimized again.

Structure of Family. The early experiences of the parents of an incestuous family affect not only their personalities but also the structure of the families that they form as parents. Early experiences help form expectations and needs that are played out later in the choice of a mate and in the formation of family rules and structure. One dynamic of the incestuous couple appears in many clinical descriptions: a marked difference in the authority of one parent over the other and a resulting blurring of role boundaries as the nonpowerful parent aligns more with the children than with the other parent.

One family pattern has been described as representing a "pathological exaggeration of generally accepted patriarchal norms" (Herman, 1983, p. 83). It involves a dominant, often physically abusive father who is in clear command of the home and a submissive mother who is usually withdrawn because of a physical or emotional disability and who acts and is treated much like one of the children (Browning and Boatman, 1977; Finkelhor, 1979; Herman, 1981). Some empirical evidence supports this conceptualization of the exaggerated traditional family. Alexander and Lupfer (1987) surveyed 586 female undergraduates and reported that those who experienced incest rated the family structure more often as having traditional male/female and parent/child relationships than did either those abused by someone outside the family or those who had not been abused.

Another pattern is, in many ways, the mirror image of this one. The mother is described as angry, dominant, and hostile, and the father as passive and dependent. The mother nurtures not only the children but also the father (Greene, 1977). Families with either of these structures appear to be at greater risk for incest than are those with different structures because of the overinvolvement of a parent with the child subsystem. This overinvolvement blurs the boundaries between the two subsystems, making it easy for the sexual boundary to be blurred also. In addition, one parent is left alone in the parent subsystem and this increases the chance that a child will be taken into the parental subsystem to fill the void.

A role reversal between the mother and a daughter has been described in incestuous families with a passive mother. The structure of the family encourages the daughter to take over many of the household and emotional responsibilities of the mother, and eventually the daughter may take over the sexual responsibility as well. Support for this type of father/mother/daughter relationship is provided by Serrano, Zuelzer, Howe, and Reposa (1979) in their comparison of seventy incestuous with seventy nonincestuous families. They found a higher degree of involvement between the father and daughter and a lower degree of involvement between the mother and daughter in the incestuous families. In an incestuous family with a dominant mother and dependent father, the role of the father changes and he becomes more of a sibling than a father to the daughter. This new role can increase the likelihood of incest because sexual activity between siblings is viewed with less condemnation than is that between a parent and child.

Kaufman, Peck, and Tagiuri (1954) provided a psychodynamic transgenerational interpretation for the role reversal between mother and daughter. They suggested that the mother in an incestuous family feels great resentment toward her own mother for abandoning her. In order to reach some mastery over these feelings, the mother begins to establish one of her daughters as a replica of her mother by giving the daughter special treatment and adult responsibilities. This process then allows the mother to place herself in the role of the daughter vis-à-vis her own daughter and provides the mother with the opportunity to symbolically relive and master her relationship with her own mother. In some families, the maternal role of the daughter is expanded to include the sexual role.

As noted previously, one typical family pattern with its foundation in the functional explanation is for the father in a family where the parents are alienated from each other to turn to the daughter to fulfill his sexual needs (Taylor, 1984; Will, 1983). Although a number of clinical samples have shown these dynamics, some studies have indicated that sexual or emotional estrangement between husband and wife is not present in all incestuous families. Herman (1983) states that many fathers in her sample still had sexual relations "on demand" with their wives during the period of the incest. Kroth (1979) reports intake counselors' impressions of what led to the incest in 156 families. Only 16 percent of the cases primarily involved emotional alienation between the parents, and in only 15 percent was sexual alienation listed as the cause. DeYoung (1982) found that only 43 percent of her clinical sample of couples from incestuous families stated that they experienced sexual alienation from each other. Apparently, then, estrangement between husband and wife occurs in some incestuous families but is not present in all of them.

Almost all descriptions of the incestuous family note their isolation. In some cases this isolation is physical. For instance, Finkelhor (1980a) found that children living on farms had a higher chance of being molested than did nonfarm children. Generally the isolation is more social than physical. One hypothesized cause of this isolation is the parents' fear, brought with them since childhood, of family disintegration. In order to avoid the possibility of a family breakup, all family members are required to rely only on each other and are not allowed, physically or emotionally or both, to stray far from the family (Larson and Maddock, 1985). In the absence of sexual relations with the mother, the father does not seek sexual or emotional support outside the family because he fears that by doing so he will cause the disintegration of his family and destroy his image as a competent patriarch. Similarly, the wife may collude in the incest by not "noticing" it because of her fear that it will cause the disintegration of the family if brought out into the open. Once the incest begins, the family becomes further isolated as the father attempts to restrict the activity of the other family members in order to keep the incest secret (Herman, 1983; Hoorwitz, 1983; Will, 1983; Zefran and others, 1982).

Summary. Giarretto (1978) notes that "despite or because of" the large number of incestuous families that he had treated, he had not been able to arrive at a psychological profile of any member of the family (p. 68). As this review of personality and historical factors has shown, we are, in the field as a whole, in the same position. Although few suggest that individuals with "healthy" personalities or families with healthy patterns of functioning engage in incest, the specific "unhealthy" factors that encourage incest have not been outlined clearly. We may lack these explanations because we have been searching for the wrong factors, because we have failed to see the common denominators of what appear to be disparate factors, or because the entire process of looking for these common factors is fruitless.

Although descriptions of the typical incestuous family vary, they have some factors in common. One or both of the parents may have been sexually or physically abused when they were children or may come from families in which they were abandoned or otherwise neglected. This early experience increases the risk of a person's becoming incestuous through the example set by his or her own parents, through identification with the parents, or through the building of a reservoir of anger that is released upon the person's children. The relationship between the parents in an incestuous family is often characterized by a marked difference in power and prestige, although it may be either of the parents who is the more powerful. The less powerful parent is often identified with the child subsystem, which raises the risk of incest as the boundaries within the family are blurred. The incestuous family is often isolated from its community, with a subsequent lessening of external prohibitions against the incest.

Other Forms of Parent/Child Incest

Father/Son Incest. Few reports of father/son incest are found in the literature, thus it is difficult to find any patterns within such relationships (Mrazek, 1981). Dixon, Arnold, and Calestro (1978) describe six father/son relationships. In each, the father was brutal and domineering in the family and was sexually promiscuous. He often had ongoing sexual relations with the mother during the same time as the incest, as well as sexual relations with other sons and daughters. The mothers were often aware of the incest but felt unable to intercede because of their financial dependence on, or fear of, the father (see also Pierce, 1987). The chaotic or feminist explanations for incest appear to be most appropriate for these families. The one example of father/son incest that was described by Langsley, Schwartz, and Fairbairn (1968) involved a father who had grown up in an atmosphere in which sex was condemned as dirty, who had had an earlier homosexual relationship with an uncle, and who appeared to have a bisexual orientation. Thus the etiology of the incest in this family seems less tied to family dynamics than to the pathology of the father.

Mother/Son Incest. As noted previously in this chapter, theory suggests that mother/son incest would be exceedingly rare because of the greater taboo against such behavior than against father/daughter incest. Experience also indicates that this is true. There are few clinical reports of mother/son incest, and large-scale surveys have found no instances of mother/son incest in their samples (Finkelhor, 1979; Haugaard, 1987). The few clinical reports available describe the mother as a woman who is promiscuous and who often has problems with alcohol. The sons are usually past puberty at the time of the incest and seem to have had a strong symbiotic relationship with their mother. The father is absent from the home, and the son has often observed the mother having sexual relations with several men. The son essentially becomes the sexual partner of the mother, often with strong ambivalent feelings about the relationship. Chasnoff and others (1986) and Finch (1973) describe women who fondled or had oral sex with their infants (or both). These women were often single and lonely, and were frequently diagnosed as Borderline Personality Disorder (as defined in the American Psychiatric Association's *Diagnostic and Statistical Manual of Mental Disorders,* 1980). Many of them had withdrawn from active social and sexual lives with the birth of their babies, and appeared to be using the babies to satisfy their sexual desires.

Mother/Daughter Incest. This form of incest appears to be exceedingly rare. Only a few instances have been reported in the literature. Russell (1984) found that only one woman in her sample of 930 had been abused by her mother; no victims of mother/daughter incest were found in the Haugaard (1987) or Wyatt (1985) samples. Clinical reports have shown that these relationships usually involve a lonely and promiscuous mother who was often a victim of sexual or physical abuse as a child and who becomes involved in fondling her young daughter (McCarthy, 1986; Mrazek, 1981).

Summary. Incest other than that between father and daughter is rare. The perpetrator in these incestuous relationships is often described as having many character and emotional problems. The effect on the child victim found in these clinical examples is usually negative. One cannot help but notice the parallel between the current descriptions of the perpetrator and victim in these types of incest and the descriptions of the typical father and daughter of several decades ago. One can speculate about whether these other forms of incest are actually occurring more often than reported and whether we currently have reports only about those who are the most disturbed by it. Additional victims of these types of incest may be discovered during the next few years, and we may begin to develop a new portrait of the perpetrator of these forms of incest.

Value of Descriptions

The chief value of the descriptions of incestuous families is that they help mental health professionals and others understand the dynamics of incest, and aid those involved in the prevention of incest or the treatment of incestuous families. The first step in prevention or treatment is understanding the phenomenon that one is dealing with. With an understanding of the dynamics of incest and of the development of incestuous behavior, prevention can be aimed at those at greatest risk for incest, and treatment programs can be developed to change the individual or family problems that contributed to the onset of the incest. Clinicians may be able to recognize certain patterns in families that cause them to question the possibility of incestuous behavior. They may then be able to stop ongoing incest or to have prior incest revealed so that its consequences can be dealt with in therapy. However, our inability to state that incest has been caused by the factors observed in incestuous families requires that clinicians not assume that by changing certain patterns of behavior they will eliminate the risk of incest in a family or even reduce it.

Great care must be taken not to assume that certain families are (or are not) incestuous merely because of their resemblance (or lack of resemblance) to the "typical" incestuous families that have been described. As we have seen, several different individual personalities and family dynamics have been associated with incest. There may be many more that we have not discovered yet or that appear so rarely that they have not become typical. We also do not know the probability that a family meeting a description of a typical incestuous family is actually incestuous. There may be many nonincestuous families with the dynamics of an incestuous family. Because the clinical samples that are discussed in the literature are often not representative of the general population, we cannot assume that the families described in them are typical of all incestuous families.

Overall, then, the descriptions of incestuous families provide some information to mental health professionals that may allow them to form hypotheses about whether a family is incestuous. The descriptions may also provide information about the forces behind the incest in a family and thus give some guidelines as to needed clinical interventions. The value of the descriptions is circumscribed however. Additional research is needed to increase the value of the descriptions that have been established by early work.

Part 2

IDENTIFYING VICTIMS
OF CHILD SEXUAL ABUSE

*I*n the second part of this book, we discuss the issue of identifying victims of child sexual abuse. We examine two general situations. In Chapter Six we examine the value and process of identifying clients who come to therapy for some other problem and who have been sexually abused previously or who are currently experiencing abuse. We outline a number of indicators that researchers and clinicians have suggested to identify these apparent nonvictims. In Chapter Seven we discuss a task that increasing numbers of clinicians are being asked to perform: assessing whether a child who claims to have been sexually abused is telling the truth. We outline the process that several clinicians have used in making these assessments and the signs that may indicate whether children are or are not accurately recounting what has happened to them.

We present this material separately from the information on interventions, which constitutes Part Three, even though identifying whether a child has been sexually abused may be an important component of an intervention. This separation is used to highlight the differences between the assessment and the intervention processes. Many clinicians are beginning to recognize the importance of keeping these two processes separate (see Goldstein, Freud, Solnit, and Goldstein, 1986; White, Santilli, and Quinn, 1987) either by having them performed with the same child or family by different clinicians whenever possible or by having the clinician keep the two functions separate in his or her own mind when having to perform them both with one client.

We would like to suggest from the outset that this identification or assessment process is inexact and usually must rest on the judgment of a clinician after consideration of often conflicting evidence. Although some writers seem to indicate that the identification process is reasonably straightforward and can be done reliably by a trained clinician, we are not so confident. It may be relatively easy in some cases; however, in a number of situations the correct identification of a victim may be difficult, and in others the clinician must admit to inconclusive findings. We attempt to elucidate these difficult situations and discuss the merits of various methods for identifying victims.

CHAPTER SIX

Diagnosing Sexual Abuse in Therapy

*A*s noted in Chapter Three, research has repeatedly shown that many sexually abused children never reveal their experiences (see, for instance, Committee on Sexual Offenses Against Children and Youth, 1984; Finkelhor, 1979). Some of these children enter therapy because of the emotional or behavioral consequences of the sexual abuse or other aspects of their lives. Other victims seek therapy as adults and do not reveal their previous abuse experiences. Clients may not reveal these experiences for several reasons. The same forces that caused them not to reveal the abuse before may also affect whether they reveal it in therapy. The threats made to some children to keep them from revealing the abuse or their feelings of guilt or shame may discourage them. Both child and adult victims may find their experiences too difficult to discuss, especially in the early stages of therapy. Some of these clients may not know how to approach the subject and may actually be hoping that the clinician broaches it. Also, some clients may believe that their previous sexual abuse is not related to their current problems.

The identification of these victims may be an important component of therapy. In some cases, a clinician may be able to stop ongoing sexual abuse. Some children who are afraid to reveal their abuse may be consciously or unconsciously engaging in the behaviors that prompted their referral to therapy in an attempt to draw attention to ongoing abuse or because of their emotional reactions to the abuse. Some young children may not yet realize that they are being abused because of a lack of knowledge about sexual abuse or sexuality.

In a general sense, the identification of victims can be important to the overall therapeutic process. Because sexual abuse has far-reaching consequences for some victims, a resolution of its aftermath can be critical to the well-being of the client. Failing to deal with the abuse may leave a major emotional issue unaddressed, resulting in an overall reduction in the value of therapy.

Because victims may not spontaneously reveal sexual abuse experiences, the clinician must decide whom to question about them. Decisions must also be made concerning the timing of such an inquiry, the approach that will be taken, and the extent to which the inquiry will be pursued in the face of an initial denial. Some clinicians advocate asking every child or adult who comes into therapy about sexual abuse experiences. Others prefer to question only those who display emotions or behaviors suggesting that they have been sexually abused. As with many decisions that a clinician must make regarding child sexual abuse cases, there are advantages and disadvantages to each approach. In this chapter we examine these advantages and disadvantages, and assess the value of the behavioral and emotional indicators used by clinicians to determine which clients might have experienced sexual abuse. A vignette illustrates the clinician's dilemma:

> A clinician is assigned a family that has recently and somewhat reluctantly asked for family therapy. The family consists of a mother, a twelve-year-old daughter, a ten-year-old son, and a stepfather who married the mother six months ago. The children visit their natural father every other weekend. The mother reports that her daughter recently has been more withdrawn at home and at school, and that her son has begun to act out more

at school. The children have become increasingly ambivalent about their relationship with both their natural father and stepfather, and have begun to ask not to be sent to their natural father's for the weekend. Aware of the number of child sexual abuse cases that enter therapy, the clinician wonders whether one or both of the children might be experiencing abuse. The clinician ponders whether to raise the question of sexual abuse with the children or parents and how to proceed if the initial response is that none has occurred.

Asking Each Client About Child Sexual Abuse

If all sexually abused children or adults had similar behavioral and emotional responses to their experience, it would be possible to ask only those exhibiting these signs about sexual abuse. A selective inquiry such as this is not possible, however, because victims of child sexual abuse do not respond in a uniform manner (see Chapter Four for examples of the wide range of consequences). Those who advocate asking each client about possible sexual abuse experiences believe that the clinician needs to question each client in order to identify as many victims as possible. Another advantage to asking each client is that even if some sexually abused clients do not reveal their abuse in response to initial questioning, the willingness of the clinician to introduce the topic may encourage these clients to reveal such abuse later in therapy.

Some clinicians prefer to ask about child sexual abuse during the first or second therapy session in the same matter-of-fact way that they ask about other life experiences. In this way, the inquiry does not take on an aura of special significance, yet allows the client the opportunity to reveal the abuse. The question to a child might be, "Has anyone ever touched you in a way that made you feel uncomfortable?" Renshaw (1987, p. 266) suggests, "Boys and girls learn about their private sexual parts of their body. Have you? Who helped you? How?" This somewhat indirect approach, without any mention of abuse, may also help to avoid frightening a child. Topper and Aldridge (1981) suggest that thorough probing can be important—for example, "asking directly, depending upon the age of the child, whether he or she has been sexually assaulted and repeating this at intervals by asking more specifically detailed questions about sexual activity" (p. 115). Although the authors do not detail the extent to which they would pursue such an inquiry or the methods for doing so, one guideline seems to be that the presence of behaviors similar to those reported for identified victims should encourage the clinician to pursue such an inquiry with greater vigor than in cases where no such behaviors are present. In general, however, guidelines for determining the extent to which an initial denial of sexual abuse should be followed by detailed questions have not been discussed in the literature.

Negative consequences may arise from asking each client about child sexual abuse experiences, and these should be considered before deciding on such a strategy. One concern is that individuals or families may be driven away from the benefits of therapy by initial questioning about sexual abuse. For instance, the possibility exists that a nonabusive family that has reluctantly agreed to enter family therapy may bolt from therapy or may proceed only with great caution and reluctance if they are confronted initially with the suggestion that the parents are involved sexually with their children. A similar situation may also arise with individual adult or child clients. Another concern is that because no evidence indicates that a reluctant client will reveal abuse when asked, questioning about sexual abuse might put some previously abused clients on the defensive, and others might be put in the position of starting the therapeutic relationship by lying to the clinician.

Asking about child sexual abuse experiences in family therapy may provide an even more difficult challenge than with individual clients, especially if the concern is incest. Although some children may respond to such questioning by revealing ongoing or previous incest, the environment of collusion and secrecy that has often been reported in incestuous families implies that such an admission is unlikely, especially when all members of the family are seen together. A possible strategy to encourage the revelation of child sexual abuse is to question each member of the family individually during the initial family sessions, although such a tactic can be criticized as promoting secrets between family members and thus being detrimental to the overall process of family therapy.

Asking Selected Clients About Child Sexual Abuse

Rather than asking each client about sexual abuse experiences, some clinicians prefer to ask only those who they suspect might be victims. This suspicion usually arises when the child or family displays emotions or behaviors similar to those of identified victims and their families. Several of the indicators that have been noted both in and out of therapy are summarized in this section. An advantage to this selective approach is that the clinician can avoid beginning the therapeutic relationship on a possibly negative note with some clients. The principal disadvantage is that because the behaviors of all abuse victims do not fit a consistent pattern, even a detailed knowledge of the typical behaviors of identified abuse victims will not provide firm guidelines for deciding whom to suspect as a victim. Consequently, some sexually abused clients who would reveal their abuse if given the opportunity may never do so because they are not asked.

Child Behaviors Outside of Therapy. As detailed in Chapter Four, a number of authors have described the behavioral responses of child sexual abuse victims. These behaviors include aggressiveness, antisocial behavior, sexually aggressive behavior with other children, running away from home, and high rates of suicidal or other self-destructive thoughts and actions. Other possible indicators are fear of being left alone with adults, a fear of bathrooms or showers, or refusal to change clothes for physical education classes.

Burgess, Groth, and McCausland (1981) report four clusters of symptoms. In the physical cluster are stomachaches, headaches, urinary-tract infections, and lack of appetite. The psychological cluster includes difficulty sleeping, nightmares, and minor mood swings. In the social cluster are changes in school behavior such as declining grades or erratic attendance, increases in fighting or stealing or both, and refusal to attend social activities. The behavioral cluster includes withdrawal and inappropriate sexually focused behavior.

A few authors note developmental differences in the behaviors of sexually abused children. Young children have exhibited regressed behavior such as thumb sucking, bed wetting, baby talk, difficulty with toileting, sleep disturbances, fear of men, and excessive clinging to their mothers (Goodwin and Owen, 1982; Mayhall and Norgard, 1983; Simrel, Berg, and Thomas, 1979). School-age children have had nightmares, exhibited aggressive or withdrawn behavior, or become school phobic (Simrel, Berg, and Thomas, 1979). Adolescent victims have run away from home, have been promiscuous, and have been suicidal (sometimes in combination) (Goodwin and Owen, 1982; Mayhall and Norgard, 1983; Will, 1983).

Sebold (1987) surveyed twenty therapists from residential treatment centers about behaviors they felt indicated that a child had been sexually abused. As well as the behaviors just mentioned, the therapists noted two behaviors that were gender specific. They found that fire setting was often an indicator for boys but not girls and that running away was an indicator for girls but seldom for boys. Homophobic behavior was often noted in boys abused by males.

Sgroi, Porter, and Blick (1982, p. 40) list twenty behaviors that could indicate that a child had experienced sexual abuse: "overly compliant behavior; acting-out, aggressive behavior; pseudomature behavior; hints about sexual activity; persistent and inappropriate sexual play with peers or toys or with themselves, or sexually aggressive behavior with others; detailed and age-inappropriate understanding of sexual behavior (especially by young children); arriving early at school and leaving late with few, if any, absences; poor peer relationships or inability to make friends; lack of trust, particularly with significant others; nonparticipation in school and social activities; inability to concentrate in school; sudden drop in school performance; extraordinary fears of males (in cases of male perpetrator and female victim); seductive behavior with males (in cases of male perpetrator and female victim); running away from home; sleep disturbances; regressive behavior; withdrawal; clinical depression; suicidal feelings."

Although Sgroi, Porter, and Blick (1982) relate examples of each of these behaviors being exhibited by children in treatment for sexual abuse, they do not indicate which ones might be more reliable than others as indicators of sexual abuse. They state that any child displaying these symptoms should be questioned about possible abuse experiences. It is not clear, however, whether they mean that the display of any one of the symptoms requires questions about abuse, whether only a combination of several of these symptoms should prompt such questioning, or whether certain indicators, such as inappropriate sexual knowledge or behaviors, should be weighed more heavily than others. Because it is difficult to imagine a child brought to therapy who does not have at least one of these symptoms, if a clinician were to question each child displaying even one of these signs about sexual abuse, the clinician would be questioning every child.

Child Behaviors in Therapy. A few clinicians have described the behaviors of sexually abused children during therapy sessions. The occurrence of these behaviors may also prompt a clinician to ask a child client about sexual abuse. Krieger, Rosenfeld, Gordon, and Bennett (1980) describe seven children who had been involved in long-term sexual relationships with parent figures. During initial therapy sessions, all the children showed compliant behavior and were concerned about pleasing the therapist. Angry, hostile behavior toward the therapist emerged as the sessions progressed. (The specific compliant and angry behaviors are not described.) The five- and six-year-old children were "clearly seductive" initially, rubbing their bodies against the therapist and speaking coyly of sexual matters. Similar seductive behaviors by children have been described by Mrazek (1981) and Yates (1982).

Family Behaviors Outside of Therapy. As discussed in Chapter Five, a number of authors have written about patterns of behavior in incestuous families from clinical samples. A clinician may be inclined to investigate the possibility of incest in families approximating these descriptions. Briefly, many incestuous families have been described as quite chaotic or very isolated or both. The parental relationship is often characterized by a marked difference in level of authority. In some families the father is dominant and the mother is submissive, while in other families the reverse is observed. Often the father is overprotective of and overinvolved with the abused child. The mothers often have a debilitating psychological or physical problem.

Family Behaviors in Therapy. A family may provide clues that they are incestuous by their behaviors in family sessions. Herman (1981) notes that although the incestuous father may be dominant at home, he is often docile and cooperative during therapy sessions. His quiet behavior may be the result of concern that the incest will be revealed in the session. He may believe that not upsetting anyone in the session will reduce the chance that his wife or child will reveal the abuse or, if they do, that the therapist will believe them. Also, his behavior in therapy may indicate a general pattern of submission to authority outside the family, which is compensated for by authoritarian behavior while at home. The mother may be withdrawn in therapy sessions, and the daughter may have a more powerful position than the mother, reflecting a role reversal that may also occur at home. Patterns of collusion or overinvolvement (or both) between the father and abused child may be apparent, again reflecting the pattern that occurs outside of therapy. Mayhall and Norgard (1983) comment that favoritism of one parent for a particular child or a parent's overprotection of one child may indicate incest. They state that sibling incest can be indicated by a brother and sister acting like a boyfriend and girlfriend, or by one child's being afraid to be left alone with a sibling.

Will (1983) suggests that when a clinician suspects that incest has occurred, the parents should be told outright of the therapist's suspicions and that "the response of the parents is virtually diagnostic" (p. 238). An innocent parent will react with shock, while a guilty parent will react with defensive anger. However, this hypothesis has not been explored systematically; innocent parents may also respond with anger. Sgroi (1978) disagrees with the wisdom of confronting the parents. She states that if incest is occurring, confronting the parents with little proof is putting the child in danger of further harm. She believes that the therapist should avoid such a confrontation unless willing and able to separate the child and other members of the family "via arrest of the suspected perpetrator" (p. 137).

Both Will and Sgroi make important points. As Will notes, the response of an abusing parent may be diagnostic; however, as Sgroi points out, the clinician who suspects child sexual abuse may have a difficult time convincing social service or legal agencies that they should intervene in the family solely on the strength of the clinician's impressions. If a child protective agency is unwilling or unable to intervene in a truly incestuous family, the child can be placed in greater danger and the abusive family can mobilize even greater defenses against revealing the abuse. Unfortunately, little guidance is available regarding the delicate issue of when to confront a parent or set of parents about a clinician's suspicions. This issue is not one for which general admonitions to the clinician about the appropriate way to proceed seem reasonable. The clinician must balance the possible harm to the child of letting the suspected abuse continue against the harm that might occur if the parents are accused of abuse. Clearly, careful consideration must be given to the circumstances of each case before a decision about appropriate action is made. Consultation with other clinicians or with child protective or social service agencies may prove to be of great value in these situations. Child protective workers may be able to tell the clinician what they could or would be able to do given a certain set of circumstances, and this information may help the clinician decide whether to confront parents at a particular time.

Use of These Indicators. DeYoung (1986) cautions about the dangers of using behavior and emotion indicator lists such as those just mentioned. She notes that different authors used diverse methodologies and samples of abused children to establish the lists and the lists often are contradictory or describe symptoms seen in children who experienced a wide range of stressors. "The net effect is a kind of mélange– a veritable grab bag of indicators that potentially lends itself to much abuse and most certainly to false positive identifications" (p. 555). DeYoung makes a valuable contribution by indicating the extent to which the reactions of sexually abused children may parallel those of children experiencing other traumas.

It is possible to conceptualize how each of the behaviors could indicate that a child is a victim. The emotional conflicts experienced by many children, especially those incestuously abused, can lead to high levels of anxiety, and this anxiety can be expressed through angry or withdrawn emotional responses or physical symptoms. Changes in social or academic performance can be caused by the victim's emotional state, and these symptoms, as well as those such as refusing to change clothes for physical education classes, can be caused by the victim's concern that other children may discover the abuse. Victims who run away or become self-destructive may be using the only means that they believe are available to escape the abuse. A social learning explanation can be used to understand the sexual or seductive behaviors of the victims, and identification with the abuser can explain some of the sexually aggressive behaviors.

However, several equally valid explanations may exist for each of these behaviors and emotions. Other forms of stress may cause anxiety in nonsexually abused children, resulting in emotional or somatic responses similar to those seen in sexually abused children. Children can learn to be aggressive or withdrawn without being sexually abused. Changes in school behavior may result from nonabusive peer or family influences or normal developmental changes. Sexualized behavior may be harder than other behaviors to explain from a different perspective, but it could be caused by the child's extensive viewing of sexual behavior in movies or on television with or without parental knowledge. The literature concerning other areas of stress to children contains examples in children's behavior that parallel the changes reported for sexually abused children but which appear to be caused by these other stressors. For instance, Emery (1982) reports on a wide variety of children's behavioral changes associated with parental discord and divorce. Block, Silbert, and Perry (1956) found that some young children whose town had been partially destroyed by a tornado regressed in toilet training, engaged in autoerotic activity, and abandoned some previously learned skills. Burke and others (1982) found that school-age children became more aggressive and showed higher levels of anxiety than usual after a severe winter blizzard engulfed their town.

Because of these other possible explanations for a child's or family's behavior, we agree with DeYoung that symptom lists must be used with extreme care. Although they may provide the clinician with a basis for hypothesizing about sexual abuse, such hypotheses warrant confirmation by other means. Use of the lists or descriptions alone could result in a clinician's believing that many nonabused children are victims, with the concomitant result that the therapy could be adversely affected if its course is inappropriately changed by the clinician's assumption. The opposite could also happen. Conte and Schuerman (1987) found that social workers noted that 21 percent of children whose abuse had been confirmed displayed none of the behaviors supposedly common among victims. This finding indicates that one should not assume that a child is not a sexual abuse victim because of a lack of these behaviors.

An Important Ethical Concern

Renshaw (1987) brings up the important ethical question of whether a child can give informed consent to answer questions about sexual history. This in turn raises the issue of whether a clinician has the responsibility to inform any child who is going to be questioned about possible sexual abuse (which for some clinicians is every child they see) about the clinician's actions if the child were to answer that he or she has been abused. Because the clinician knows that a positive response from the child to questions about any type of abuse will result in the clinician's reporting the child to protective services and that this reporting will subsequently result in an intrusion of some sort by the protective service into the child's family life, it would appear to be unethical for the clinician not to inform every client of this result before asking about abuse. Although this requirement may well stop children from revealing abuse, it seems required by the ethics of disclosing the limits of confidentiality in the clinician/client relationship. Informing young children of the clinician's responsibility to report any abuse may be especially difficult because of the child's limited understanding. We are not suggesting that the child must be informed immediately before questions about abuse or each time the subject is raised, but some discussion of the limits of confidentiality before asking about abuse seems required.

Failure to inform a child of the clinician's required actions if abuse is occurring may result in damaging the clinician/child relationship, especially with older children. The child who reveals abuse without knowing of the consequences and then is surprisedly caught up in social service and legal proceedings may have learned the lesson that confiding in a clinician can bring unexpected and negative consequences. The ability of this child to gain anything from future therapy (one of the reasons for having the child reveal the abuse in the first place) may be destroyed.

Many clinicians do not obey the reporting laws, a prosecutable offense, because of this issue and because of concerns about the efficacy of protective services. For example, Kalichman and Craig (1987) found that 25 percent of a sample of nonlicensed mental health professionals would not report a confirmed case of incestuous abuse because of concerns about the protection of the child and feelings that treatment would be disrupted if they reported. Alfaro (1985) found that clinicians in New York City were reluctant to report suspected child sexual abuse cases because unnecessary negative consequences were often viewed as outweighing possible benefits.

Identifying Women Who Were Molested as Children

As we saw in Chapter Three, although estimates vary, it is clear that a sizeable number of women experienced sexual abuse as children. Most of these women did not receive any therapeutic help as children, and many did not tell anyone of the abuse. Some of these women enter therapy as adults for a variety of concerns. Although their abuse may have an important bearing on their current concerns, some will not reveal it because they have forgotten it, because they are embarrassed, or because they do not believe it has a bearing on the problem that brought them to therapy. Although indications that a woman experienced abuse as a child are described far less than are indications of current or recent sexual abuse of children, some information can be gleaned from the literature by examining patterns of behavior in women identified as child victims. As with children, this information can be a way of identifying those women for whom extensive questioning about possible early abuse experiences might be valuable (although the limitations of using the descriptions also apply).

McGuire and Wagner (1978, p. 12) describe a characteristic pattern of sexual dysfunction in sixty women who had been sexually abused as children: "The women often are easily orgasmic, particularly through intercourse or often only through intercourse; they experience little sexual appetite before having contact or minimal arousal during contact; they rarely initiate love making; they have great difficulty in touching and caressing their partner or being caressed; they experience feelings of disgust and revulsion about their own and partner's body; they enjoy sexual contact only when penetration has been effected and, in fact, often develop a sexual style restricted to intercourse alone." McGuire and Wagner express surprise at the number of "coitally orgasmic" women discovered. One explanation may have to do with the type of molestation experienced by the women. Recall from Chapter Three that most cases of child sexual abuse involve only some sort of fondling and that few cases of actual intercourse are reported. It may be that the specific areas of the women's bodies that did or did not give them pleasure as an adult were the areas that were or were not stimulated during the previous abuse. Unfortunately, the authors do not state the type of abuse suffered by the women, so this is simply speculation.

Other authors have reported that women molested as children often have difficulty with sexual and nonsexual relations with men. For instance, Tsai, Feldman-Summers, and Edgar

(1979) found that molested women in therapy had had more consensual sexual partners but were less sexually responsive and were less satisfied with their sexual activity than were non-molested women. However, they also found that molested women who had not requested therapy were no different than a group of nonmolested women in these areas. Thus, lack of sexual difficulties cannot be taken as a sign that a woman has not experienced previous abuse. Russell (1984) and Briere (cited in Browne and Finkelhor, 1986) found that molested women were more likely than nonmolested women to experience sexual aggression by their husbands.

McGuire and Wagner (1978) found that molested women often entered treatment two to four years after a marriage, as their dissatisfaction with their sexual response became salient. Goodwin and Owen (1982) note that molested women in their sample often entered treatment when facing childbirth because of concerns that they or their husbands might become physically or sexually abusive toward the child.

Summary and Conclusions

It is difficult to decide whether the arguments for or the arguments against asking each client about child sexual abuse are more persuasive. The arguments for asking each client are that discovering abuse experiences is important for successful therapy and that it is not possible to determine accurately which clients to ask selectively. The arguments against asking each client are that by doing so the clinician may irreparably harm the process of therapy with some clients and that few clients who are reluctant to reveal their abuse will do so when asked during the initial stages of therapy. As with many other aspects of the treatment of child sexual abuse, our current level of knowledge makes firm statements for or against asking each client prematurely. Unfortunately, no investigations have been made of the effects on the therapeutic relationship of asking clients about sexual abuse experiences. Therefore, clinicians are left with little other than their own intuition and experience on which to base their decisions about this issue.

Those who prefer not to ask all clients can be guided by similarities between the behaviors and emotions of their clients and those of identified victims. Some clinicians may want to continue to entertain the hypothesis that clients have experienced child sexual abuse if their behaviors match those of identified victims, and clinicians may then pursue the topic later in therapy. In such cases, understanding the indicators that suggest that a client has experienced sexual abuse can be useful. However, sole reliance on these indicators for the identification of sexual abuse victims is not supported by the current research. The use of these indicators to confirm that a child is or is not a victim, the subject to which we turn in the next chapter, is especially dangerous. Regardless of the approach taken, all clinicians must properly inform children and families of the limits of confidentiality before asking questions about abuse.

CHAPTER SEVEN

Evaluating Accusations of Child Sexual Abuse

B enedek and Schetky (1986) note that a "cottage industry/ profession" has developed among some psychiatrists, pediatricians, and mental health professionals who claim to be specialists in the assessment of alleged child sexual abuse victims. The call for these assessments has grown rapidly with both the increased reporting of child sexual abuse and the concern that not all allegations are true. Most cases of alleged sexual abuse involve a child's accusation against a parent or other adult; others, such as the highly publicized Jordan, Minnesota, and Manhattan Beach, California, cases, involve children who are suspected victims but who initially deny that they are. In this chapter we outline the procedures employed by a number of clinicians for determining whether an accusation of sexual abuse is accurate. We describe both the physical examinations and the clinical interviews that are used in the assessment process, and we highlight the different processes of assessing and confirming whether sexual abuse occurred.

The difficulty of making these assessments is matched by the harm that may be caused by an incorrect one. Consider two examples in which an incorrect assessment resulted in negative consequences, in one case for the victim and in the other for the alleged perpetrator.

A ten-year-old girl was evaluated by several physicians for recurrent abdominal pain, sleep problems, and decreased school performance over the previous six months. No specific cause was found for her problems; however, she told a school counselor that her father had been attempting intercourse with her. When she and her parents were questioned further, she retracted her claim of sexual abuse. A month later, while hospitalized for a suicide attempt, she again spoke of her father's sexual abuse. This time her mother came forward and confirmed the child's story (DeJong, 1985, p. 511).

One mother went so far as to threaten her seven-year-old son with never seeing his father again, never being able to ride his bike, and having to go to the hospital where they would stick needles in him if he didn't tell his mother that his father had "put his finger in his tushy." After a series of relentless threats and endless interrogations, the child told his mother what she wanted to hear and repeated this story to the authorities. This taped conversation was admitted as evidence in court, and the father was sentenced to life in prison [Benedek and Schetky, 1986, p. 14].

Interesting shifts have occurred over time in the acceptance of children's reports of sexual abuse. Until the 1960s, most reports that were denied by the alleged perpetrator were believed to be an expression of the child's fantasies of sexual involvement with an adult, especially if the alleged perpetrator was a parent. Cases in which a child was believed in the face of an adult denial were rare, probably in large part because of the acceptance of the Freudian theory that neurosis in women resulted from a daughter's fantasies of incest with her father (Freud, [1933] 1965). During the 1960s and 1970s, the pendulum shifted, and it was generally assumed that children almost never reported sexual abuse unless it had occurred. Cases in which an adult's denial was believed in the face of a child's accusation were scarce. (The believability of the adult should not be equated with the percentage of cases that are successfully prosecuted because a successful prosecution involves much more than the mere belief by those in mental health or legal agencies that the child is being truthful.) Recently there has been a swing in sentiment again, although a noticeably smaller one. A growing number of clinicians have reported cases in which a child's accusation of sexual abuse was later determined to be false. The most accepted belief now is that a great majority of children's accusations of sexual abuse are accurate but in some instances an accusation needs to be more critically examined than in others. Although some authors have made statements concerning the percentage of accusations that are not true (Mann, 1985, for instance, states that less than 2 percent of children lie about sexual abuse), no reliable evidence supports these statements.

The latest shift in opinion appears to be due in large part to the use of child sexual abuse accusations by one parent against another to obtain sole custody, to terminate visitation or parental rights, or to harass a noncustodial parent (Benedek and Schetky, 1985). A growing number of false accusations coming from discordant parental relationships are being documented, specifically when the custody of a child is in dispute. Although it was "fashionable" at one point for a divorcing parent to accuse the other of adultery, some individuals have found that today an accusation of child sexual abuse works well to defame the character of a partner (Benedek and Schetky, 1986). Also, even when one parent does not set out to accuse the other falsely, statements or behaviors of a child may be misinterpreted by one parent and result in an accusation of child sexual abuse, especially when the parental relationship is characterized by animosity and suspicion (Bresee, Stearns, Bess, and Packer, 1986). Thus, children may be no more likely to make up stories of abuse on their own than they were before, but the pressures from a parent for a child to construct such a story may be greater. As an illustration of this trend, Lacayo (1987) reports that sexual abuse charges in the state of Michigan in 1986 are a component of 30 percent of contested custody cases, up from 5 percent in 1980. Spiegel (1987) maintains that the increased determination by authorities to uncover child sexual abuse has caused an overabundance of false charges that devastate the lives of those accused. In Spiegel's case, although he was finally acquitted of charges that he had sexually abused his two-and-a-half-year-old daughter and was awarded joint custody, during the two-year legal process he was denied contact with his daughter, lost most of his practice as a clinical psychologist, and incurred legal fees in excess of $70,000.

Assessment of the credibility of an accusation of child sexual abuse is difficult because there is seldom any physical evidence or witnesses other than the child. Sgroi, Porter, and Blick (1982) state, "Determining the validity of an allegation of child sexual abuse is first and foremost a matter of belief. You either believe the child's story or you do not. If you require that there be corroboration of the child's story by physical evidence, witnesses, or a confession by the perpetrator, you will turn many cases into 'noncases' " (p. 69). What is unclear from this statement is the amount of evidence needed before a clinician justifiably can believe that sexual abuse has occurred. In the following sections we review three methods for developing a belief in a child's accusation of sexual abuse: physical examinations, observation of the child's emotions and behaviors, and testing and interviews.

Physical Indicators

A physical examination can provide valuable information about the possibility of abuse in some cases. Physical trauma or injury has been found in 20 to 35 percent of suspected child sexual abuse cases (DeJong, 1985). The percentage is low both because the most prevalent form of child sexual abuse, fondling, often leaves no physical indications and because children experiencing more invasive forms of sexual activity often do not report the abuse until long after it has occurred, at which time conclusive physical indications are often no longer present.

Even though physical indicators are present in only a minority of sexual abuse cases, most clinicians and physicians recommend that a physical examination be completed with each suspected victim. In some cases a child may be willing to admit to less intense forms of sexual activity but feels too embarrassed to say that other types of sexual activity, such as intercourse, occurred. For this reason, some physicians have recommended that the possibility of all forms of sexual abuse be investigated during the physical exam, regardless of the initial complaint of the child (Enos, Conrath, and Byer, 1986; Sanfilippo and Schikler, 1986). In these instances, the results of a physical exam may encourage the child to discuss the other sexual activity. Also, even if no physical evidence is found, the finding of no physical harm will be a relief to both the child and the parents (Sgroi, Porter, and Blick, 1982).

Preparing the Child. As will be seen in the description that follows, the physical examination is often a thorough and generally invasive procedure, and has the potential of being traumatic to any child. The risk of a negative reaction to the physical exam may be even higher in a child who has recently been sexually abused than in a child abused previously. The child not only must discuss with the physician the details of the abuse but also must allow the physician to handle the parts of his or her body that were once manipulated by the perpetrator. Because of the potential for trauma, great care must be taken during the examination. The examination should take place in as supportive an environment as possible and be conducted by a physician who is sensitive to the emotional state of the child. When a clinician suggests that a child receive a physical examination, it is advisable for the clinician to outline the examination process with the child and parent, and discuss the reasons for each procedure. Recent research has shown that involving the parents in the child's preparation and working to calm the parents have helped to relieve the child's anxiety before surgery, and a similar procedure may be valuable for sexual abuse examinations (Tedesco and Schnell, 1987). Some children may find the presence of a parent or other supportive adult during the examination reassuring, while others may wish to be examined in private.

Sgroi (1978) suggests that the examination be done with the full cooperation of the child whenever possible and that the preparation of the child for the exam is a crucial aspect of the process. When the child is initially uncooperative, a proper introduction may often result in the child's agreeing to the examination. This introduction may include the reasons for specific procedures, the fact that a supportive adult will be nearby, and assurance that the child can ask for a break in the examination when desired. Sgroi also advises waiting a day or so before examining some children who are unwilling to participate. In some cases physical evidence can be obtained several days later (for instance, evidence of injury to the genitalia); however, in cases such as those in which semen is believed to be present on the child's skin, an immediate physical examination may be required.

Although it would be wrong to force a completely uncooperative child to have a physical exam, when a child is reluctant to be examined, concerns about losing valuable evidence of the abuse must be weighed against the possible beneficial effects of allowing the child to return at a later time. Obtaining sufficient physical evidence may mean that the child will have to spend less time as a witness in a future court proceeding or may not have to appear at all. Thus, trauma caused by the medical examination may be outweighed by a reduction in the trauma that the child would have to face in a courtroom. As with most other aspects of dealing with victims of child sexual abuse, whether to examine a reluctant child is a thorny question that must be handled thoughtfully, with consideration given to what is best for the child overall. Both aspects of the decision—obtaining physical evidence and the consequences to the emotional state of the child of obtaining the evidence—must be considered on a case-by-case basis in consultation between the physician, clinician, child protective worker, and parent and child when appropriate.

The Physical Examination. The physical examination generally includes a thorough medical history taken from the parents and child. "Constipation, rectal fissures, hematochezia, vaginal discharge, or recurrent urinary tract infections" can be indications of child sexual abuse (Sanfilippo and Schikler, 1986, p. 622). A detailed account of the sexual abuse and when it last occurred can also provide important information because certain aspects of the physical examination may take on increased importance depending on the type and recency of the sexual activity.

Enos, Conrath, and Byer (1986) suggest that the examination begin with the least invasive procedures. If the sexual activity was recent, their routine begins with an inspection of the hair and head for dried semen. Smears taken inside the mouth and on the lips with a moistened swab are used to detect semen and to provide cultures for detection of venereal disease. The mouth can be rinsed with a saline solution and the solution centrifuged for signs of sperm. Inspection of the male genitals for trauma should be accompanied by a swab of the urethral area for detection of venereal disease. Likewise, females are examined for trauma to the external genitalia. A photographic record may be made of any observed trauma in male and female victims, but photographs ought to be taken only after careful discussion with the child and parents. Some sexually abused children may have been photographed by their abuser, and even those who have not may find the idea of having their genitalia photographed disturbing.

With females the hymen is inspected, with its intactness and condition carefully noted (for more detailed information and pictures see Emans, Woods, Flagg, and Freeman, 1987; Enos, Conrath, and Byer, 1986). The location of hymenal tears may distinguish between digital or penile penetration (Sanfilippo and Schikler, 1986). The application of toluidine blue dye to the area just below the vaginal opening can increase the detection of fourchette lacerations in both young and adolescent girls. The presence of these lacerations has often been accepted as evidence of penile penetration (McCauley, Gorman, and Guzinski, 1986). Swabs are inserted in the vagina and left for one minute to absorb vaginal material. The swabs can be inspected later for the presence of sperm and venereal disease. When appropriate, a test for pregnancy should also be given.

Physical examination of the rectal area includes notation and photographing of any trauma. Separating the buttocks laterally normally results in a contraction of the anal sphincter, while in recently sodomized individuals the result is a relaxation of the sphincter. Likewise, stroking the perianal skin normally causes contraction of the sphincter, and this reaction is also lost in recently sodomized individuals (Sanfilippo and Schikler, 1986). Swabs can be inserted in the anus to provide specimens for detection of sperm and venereal disease.

The child's general physical health should also be investigated. Neglected children who have been sexually abused may have a number of physical ailments, and these should be identified and treated. As noted in Chapter Five, a number of incestuous fathers are also physically abuse. Because of this possibility, signs of physical abuse such as bruises, concussions, perforated eardrums, and burns should be carefully investigated and treated.

Examining the Siblings of a Sexually Abused Child. One question that has received little attention is the appropriateness of requiring or requesting that the siblings of a sexual abuse victim be examined. As we reported in Chapter Five, a number of incestuous fathers abuse more than one child, and some cases have been cited in which the father begins with the oldest child and abuses the other children as they reach a certain age. Although some incestuous fathers may sexually abuse only one child, they may physically abuse others. As Burgess (1984) notes, some perpetrators of extrafamilial abuse form sex rings, which enable them to attract and abuse more than one child in a family. For these reasons, it may be prudent to examine the siblings of a sexual abuse victim. If other victims are discovered, they can receive needed attention, and if no other victims are discovered, parents should feel reassured. Such a procedure presents some difficulties however. As noted, the physical examination can be quite invasive, and it may be inappropriate to require some children to endure it if there is no indication that they have been molested. Some siblings who have not been abused may view a physical examination as an indication that their parents do not believe them when they say that they have not been abused. Some siblings may blame the victim for making it necessary that they undergo the physical examination, in-

creasing the stress on the victim. Thus, although physical examinations of siblings may produce valuable information, they
must be approached carefully and be done only after consultation with those involved in each case.

   A Cautionary Note. Unfortunately, as with most other
areas of child sexual abuse, unequivocal answers about the occurrence of abuse cannot always be obtained even from a physical examination soon after the sexual activity. For instance,
Emans, Woods, Flagg, and Freeman (1987) found that only 44
percent of their sample of 119 sexually abused girls had irregu-
larities in the vaginal area and that the percentage of irregulari-
ties among nonabused girls who presented with vaginal infections or other problems was similar to the percentage of those
who had been sexually abused. Enos, Conrath, and Byer (1986)
note that in criminal prosecutions the jury, not the physician, is
charged with the responsibility for determining the occurrence
of abuse. They suggest that rather than the physician's merely
asserting that physical signs are or are not indications of sexual
abuse, the physician should first state the specific findings, then
state the way or ways that the findings can be interpreted, and
finally state the strength of his or her opinion that sexual abuse
has occurred. This procedure not only provides the jury with
the most complete information but also places the physician in
the role of investigator rather than advocate.

Emotional and Behavioral Indicators

   Because conclusive physical evidence of child sexual abuse
is available in a minority of cases, the clinician must usually
base his or her judgment about the credibility of an accusation
on statements, emotions, and behaviors of the child and the
child's family. This method of assessment is less reliable than
using physical indicators, and the assessing clinician must often
weigh conflicting statements and evidence. Suggestions concerning the process of the assessment are reviewed here. Throughout
the interview process, the clinician searches for indications that
the sexual abuse either did or did not occur. Child and family
behaviors occurring outside of or during the assessment sessions

that authors claim may indicate that sexual abuse has occurred were reviewed in Chapter Six.

Basic Interview Process

Interviewing the Child Who Accuses a Parent or Other Adult. The predominant view among clinicians is that it is best to interview suspected victims by themselves or with a supportive adult if the child will not be seen alone (see, for instance, Conerly, 1986; Sgroi, Porter, and Blick, 1982). Interviewing the child alone is often regarded as optimal because even supportive adults may inhibit the child if they give concerned or horrified looks as the child begins to describe the abuse. It may be helpful to have the mother present during the first part of an initial interview (providing that she was not involved with the abuse) in order for her to "give permission" to the child to discuss the abuse situation with the clinician (Mrazek, 1980).

When a child accuses a parent, some authors suggest that each member of the family, including the siblings, be interviewed separately and, if their stories do not agree, that each family member be asked to comment on the lack of similarity (Goodwin, Sahd, and Rada, 1978). In contrast, other clinicians suggest that when the suspected abuser is a parent, the child be interviewed alone and then with the parents. Mrazek (1980), for instance, suggests that the child be interviewed with each parent separately, and then with the entire family. This procedure provides a valuable view of family dynamics and the dynamics between the child and each parent. If one parent is being accused by the other, the interactions between the parents and the child while in the same room may strengthen or weaken the accusation. Fearful or seductive behavior toward a parent suspected of abusing the child strengthens the accusation. However, if the child appears to be "checking" his or her answers with the accusing parent and appears emotionally close to the accused parent, the accusation is weakened (Green, 1986).

As these different views suggest, the clinician may choose from a number of methods for the interview. The advantage of interviewing additional family members, such as siblings, is that confirmatory information may be gathered. However, it may be difficult to reconcile conflicting interview results, and such a process has the potential of alienating the victim from other family members. Interviewing the victim with the parents may provide information about family dynamics, but the clinician should also consider that interviewing a child with an abusive parent may be quite traumatic for the child. Careful consideration of the situation surrounding each case—including the needs of the law-enforcement agency and the needs and emotional state of the child and the family—rather than adherence to a specific process with all cases is the best way to proceed.

When the entire family is interviewed, the location is usually the office of the clinician. This location allows space for some family members to wait while others are being interviewed and may be the most convenient if the interviews are videotaped. When the child is to be interviewed alone, the interview may also take place at school, in a park, or at another location that is familiar to the child as a way of lessening the child's anxiety (Sgroi, Porter, and Blick, 1982). Interviewing the child or family in their home is generally seen as undesirable, especially in cases of incest. The child's concerns about the possibility that a family member might be listening or the resurgence of upsetting emotions that might occur if the abuse took place in the house can lower the child's candor.

A clinician can involve a shy or frightened child in the interview in a number of ways. The development of rapport with the child can be critical to the entire assessment process, and it should be fostered carefully. Several methods are available for children to express what they experienced. Some children feel comfortable making drawings. Others prefer to re-create the abuse scene using anatomically correct dolls. Others can simply describe what happened in words. Often, the assessment interview involves basic clinical skills of rapport building and assisting the child to tell his or her story. For this reason, the general steps for this interview are not described here. For detailed accounts of the assessment process used by various clinicians, the reader is referred to Burgess and Holstrom (1978), Jones and McQuiston (1985), Mrazek (1980), and Sgroi, Porter, and Blick

(1982). A discussion of specific techniques to use with a preschool child can be found in MacFarlane and others (1986).

The use of anatomically correct dolls has become widespread and controversial, and deserves special mention. (Although referred to as anatomically correct dolls, the more appropriate description would be anatomically detailed because the proportions of the various body parts are not usually correct.) In general, these dolls are used by the child to re-create the abuse situation. The dolls should be viewed as a means for children to clarify their verbalizations through demonstration and not as a "test" for sexual abuse (Melton and Limber, 1987). Using dolls may be easier for some children than describing the abuse because of a limited vocabulary or difficulty speaking directly of the abuse. MacFarlane and Krebs (1986a) note that the courts are beginning to examine critically the use of these dolls, mainly because of a concern that the sexual play of an alleged victim may be in response to the sexual nature of the dolls and not to any previous abuse. At issue is whether nonabused children will normally engage in sexual play because of the genitalia of the dolls. Some preliminary investigations have shown that nonabused children generally do not, although a small percentage of apparently nonabused children do. The sexual or aggressive play of this small group with the dolls may reflect their actually having had experienced some abuse, or it may be a natural reaction of a minority of nonabused children (Boat, 1987; Sivan, 1987). However, having even a small percentage of nonabused children engage in behaviors most commonly found in abused children may be problematic because the defense lawyer in a trial can then argue that the child in question is one of that small minority.

MacFarlane and Krebs (1986a) discuss some precautions for the clinician to take when using the dolls. These include having more dolls than those representing the child and the alleged perpetrator, having the child select the dolls to play with rather than having them handed to him or her by the clinician, and having the child rather than the clinician undress the dolls. By using these procedures, the clinician may be able to assert with more confidence that the child's play was a reflection of previous abuse rather than a result of the environment fostered by the clinician in the assessment interviews. MacFarlane and Krebs also note that some clinicians prefer to have the child discuss the abuse before the dolls are introduced in order to avoid the possibility that the dolls caused the child to talk about sexual matters. Clearly, care must be taken while using these dolls. Their proper use can help a child explain an abuse experience, while their improper use may lead the child to respond to the clinician in a certain manner. (This topic is discussed in the section on assessing or confirming abuse later in this chapter.)

DeYoung (1986) notes the importance of determining the extent of other stressors in the child's life during the assessment process. She states that stresses experienced by non-abused children, such as the parents' divorce, may cause some of their behaviors to resemble those of sexually abused children. DeYoung astutely observes that a child who has been coerced to lie about a sexual abuse experience also experiences significant stress. She states that the manifestations of this type of stress would be different from those of sexual abuse, although she gives no reasons for these differences. Although her assertion is not very convincing, her emphasis on multiple sources of stress that may evoke the types of behaviors seen in sexually abused children is well placed.

Interviewing the Child Who Initially Denies Being a Victim. Assessing the validity of a child's confirmation of sexual abuse after an initial denial was brought to national attention by the cases involving the preschool teachers at the McMartin Day Care Center in Manhattan Beach, California, and a group of parents in Jordan, Minnesota. In both cases, some children who were interviewed by clinicians over several sessions initially said that they had not been sexually abused and then later changed their stories to say that they had been. Those who believed the children's later statements (which generally included the clinicians involved in the investigations) contended that the children were understandably afraid of talking about their abuse when the investigation began and that only after the development of rapport with the clinicians as the sessions progressed did the children begin to feel safe enough to reveal the abuse. Those who believed the children's initial statements about not being abused contended that the children changed their stories simply to please the clinician or their parents (or both).

At issue is whether it is appropriate for a clinician to continue to question a child about sexual abuse if the child has stated once or several times that he or she is not a victim, and an accompanying concern is the relative weight that should be given to the child's initial and subsequent statements about the abuse. MacFarlane, who was one of the primary investigative clinicians in the McMartin case, contends that it is important for the legal system to realize that child sexual abuse cases cannot be investigated in the same way other cases can (MacFarlane and others, 1986). She notes that child victims often experience physical and mental pressure to gain their participation in the sexual activity, are often threatened with dire consequences if they reveal the abuse, and are often embarrassed about the sexual abuse or feel responsible for it. For these reasons, many children are afraid to reveal the abuse, especially to a clinician who is a stranger when the investigation begins. She claims that it is not reasonable to expect that these children will respond as if their memory about some nonemotional event were being tested. Because of this possibility, development of rapport with the clinician and repeated, supportive questioning about the abuse in the face of an initial denial are viewed as essential to assessing the child's actual involvement.

Those who oppose this process with alleged victims (many of whom have been involved in the defense of accused perpetrators) suggest that the following sequence may occur in some cases: The child initially provides an accurate rendition by denying that abuse has occurred. Under the pressure of repeated questioning by the investigating clinicians, the child believes that the initial story is unacceptable and in a desire to please the clinicians changes the story in some random way (which may account for the many differences in children's abuse statements during the course of an investigation). At some point, the child gives a story that is acceptable to the investigators, and when the investigators appear to be satisfied with that story, the child incorporates it as the truth in order to avoid a continuation of the investigation.

It appears to us that the appropriateness of the continued

questioning of an alleged victim must be decided on a case-by-case basis. The danger, we believe, comes when one perspective about the continued questioning is held dogmatically (as appears to happen in some instances). In some cases a child will be understandably reticent to admit to abuse initially and will later give a more accurate account of his or her experiences with the abuser. For this reason, the continued questioning of a child may well be appropriate. However, it is conceivable that some children will change their stories in the face of repeated questioning simply to please interviewers or someone else. This suggests the danger inherent in such a course. Thus, it appears that repeated questioning should be done by a clinician who makes a concerted effort to be alert to the possibility that the form of the questions or the manner of the questioning may begin to influence the child's answers inappropriately. As we discuss later in this chapter, videotaping of all sessions may provide the only material for assessing the clinician's method of investigation and may be the only way for the clinician to show that repeated questioning was appropriate and was done correctly (or for others to show the opposite).

Given the fact that a child's story has changed after repeated questioning, some will assume the change indicates that the interviewer was finally able to make the child feel safe enough to tell about the abuse, while others will assume that the child has been coerced into changing the initial true story into a false one. Both of these assumptions are just that—assumptions. The clinician who automatically assumes that a child is finally telling the truth when he or she admits to being a victim may miss important indicators that the child has been coerced into changing the story. However, if the child's initial denial of abuse is automatically accepted or if a change in the story is dismissed without consideration, cases in which a child has been abused may be missed. As noted throughout this chapter, the assessment of a charge of child sexual abuse is often an inexact process. A change in a child's story should be taken as an additional piece of information, not as an infallible indication of either abuse or a conspiracy on the part of the investigating clinician to railroad the alleged perpetrator.

Assessment Versus Confirmation. There appear to be two basic processes that a clinician can follow during an interview— assessing whether the alleged sexual abuse occurred or getting the child to confirm the clinician's belief that abuse occurred. Certain attitudes and behaviors seem to distinguish clinicians involved in these two processes. Those interested in confirming that abuse has occurred are able to justify more intrusive methods for getting such a confession. Occasionally these methods become extreme. Wilcox (1987) reports a case in which a frustrated clinician finally said to a child who steadfastly refused to say that abuse had occurred, "You are lying to me and I know it; you had better stop lying or you will go to hell." Eberle and Eberle (1986) report a case in which one child in an investigation was told, "Johnny said that this happened to him. Johnny is a smart boy. Don't you want to be as smart as Johnny and tell me that it happened to you too."

The justification for using these types of techniques appears to be that it is in the child's best interest to admit the abuse. The child's admission may ensure the perpetrator's conviction; the child may feel safe if the perpetrator is sent to prison, and the child may have increased faith in the fairness of the social system. Also, the admission may increase the possibility of enrolling the child in therapy in order to lessen the effects of the abuse. We wonder, though, whether the best interest of a child victim is served when the child experiences high levels of coercion to admit the abuse. The child's admission may cause him or her to become involved in a long legal process and eventually to be asked to testify in court, a process that can be terrifying for some. The child may receive some therapy, but the child's reaction to future clinicians may be adversely affected by feelings of being manipulated by the investigating clinician. Also, if the coercive process of the interview is revealed during the trial, a guilty perpetrator may be released because of the clinician's style of investigation. Matters will probably be even worse if the child has been convinced to admit to abuse that never occurred. The child may have to go through the same procedures but with the requirement that the child maintain a false story.

The process of assessing whether abuse has occurred is

quite different from confirming its occurrence. White, Santilli, and Quinn (1987) describe the ideal type of assessment interview. They suggest that the interviewing clinician be unaware of the alleged circumstances of the abuse so that the clinician cannot suggest these facts to the child. This procedure helps the clinician be free of "external contamination"—material that may predispose the clinician to suspect that a certain type of abuse occurred or that it was perpetrated by a certain person. If the clinician determines that abuse did occur by a certain perpetrator after an interview free of external contamination, the information clearly came from the victim and not from the assumptions of others. The clinician should also strive to eliminate "internal contamination"—a predisposition to believe that the child has been abused simply because he or she is present at an evaluative interview. Although the clinician gives the child ample time to become comfortable and reassures the child that it is all right to change his or her story as the interviews progress, the clinician gives no indication about the type of story desired and does not immediately end the assessment when a story about abuse tentatively begins to emerge.

Avoiding contamination of the interview is a difficult and often subtle process. For instance, while using anatomically correct dolls with alleged victims, Shamroy (1987) suggests that the clinician present the dolls to the child and say, " 'Let's pretend that this is you.' If the child does not name the adult dolls, the [clinician] can say, 'Let's pretend that this is mommy' (or daddy, or whoever), and suggest a situation, such as bedtime. . . . Any information about where the sexual abuse took place or the suspected offender can be included in the 'let's pretend' situation" (p. 165). White, Santilli, and Quinn (1987), however, suggest that the child not be given any directions about what to name the dolls or which situation to put them in. They argue that doing so may suggest incorrect information to the child, inappropriately direct the interview in one direction, and reduce the chance that some other type of abuse that the child has experienced will be revealed.

White, Santilli, and Quinn (1987) remind us that the judge or jury is charged with determining the guilt or innocence of an accused perpetrator and that the clinician should provide accurate information so that this decision can be made. Often information in addition to the facts provided by the assessing clinician must be weighed by the legal system when reaching a decision. Consider the following case (discussed by Yates, 1987, p. 478):

> A forty-year-old single father of a five-year-old boy practiced holistic health by bathing nude in a spa with the child and massaging the child's back, feet, legs, and inguinal lymph nodes (those located in the groin). During a custody dispute the child's mother accused the father of sexual molestation.

It is easy to imagine how an investigating clinician could influence the child's description of this situation and of the father's intentions. Although the clinician would want to gain as full a picture as possible of the child's experience, including, perhaps, the child's view of the intent of the father, it is up to the jury, not the clinician, to decide the ultimate issue of the father's intentions.

Additional Assessment Issues

Videotaping. The clinician may wish to audiotape or videotape the assessment sessions. Although such videotapes are seldom admissible in a trial (in contrast to videotaped testimony, which is described in Chapter Fifteen), they may be allowed during some courtroom procedures: (a) if a clinician is called as an expert witness to testify about the emotional state of the child during the interview, a videotape may be allowed as corroborating evidence for the clinician's opinion; (b) when special motions are made during a trial, for example, for the exclusion of those not essential to the case (such as the public or the press) while the child testifies, a videotape may be used to demonstrate the difficulty the child has when describing the abuse; and (c) in cases where a child retracts the accusation of abuse on the witness stand, the videotape may be called by the prosecutor to impeach the testimony of the child (MacFarlane, 1985).

The advantages and disadvantages to videotaping are insightfully outlined by MacFarlane (1985) and MacFarlane and Krebs (1986b). One significant advantage of videotaping is that it reduces the number of times a child has to repeat the abuse description. A number of negative consequences can occur if a child must repeat the story of the abuse to police, prosecutors, clinicians, physicians, and child protective workers, and then finally during a preliminary hearing and trial. After many repetitions, the child may begin to relate the experience in a non-emotional, rote fashion, which may give the impression that the child is not describing an upsetting event. The child may also begin to incorporate adult language into the description of the abuse, making it appear that the description was suggested to the child by adults. Finally, the child may become so upset by having to repeat the story that he or she merely stops doing so and refuses to participate any further in the investigation. The negative effects of repeated questioning are supported by the empirical investigation of Tedesco and Schnell (1987). Responses from forty-eight child victims indicated that they were interviewed from one to forty times, with the average being seven. The greater the number of interviews, the more negative reaction the children had to the entire investigative process.

Rather than having the child repeat the story to many investigators, interviews with one investigator can be videotaped, and these can be made available to other investigators. To make full use of this advantage, all the questions that are of importance to the various agencies have to be asked during the videotaped sessions. Consequently, careful coordination among agencies that will be involved with the child is required. Participants should be informed of the taping, and their consent, if needed, should be secured.

Another advantage of videotaping is that the tapes can be used to support the actions of an investigating clinician if a child initially states that no abuse occurred and then changes his or her story as the investigation proceeds. In some cases, the videotape may clearly show that the clinician did not encourage the child to change the story. In other cases, the clinician's actions may be controversial and open to interpretation. Even in cases that are not clear, however, a record of the investigation can be viewed by the judge and others involved in the case. If the videotapes are to be used in this manner, all sessions with the child must be taped. The practice of some clinicians of "priming" the child during initial untaped interviews and then taping a final interview may produce a pleasing tape from the perspective of having the child appear to be completely sure of what happened, but the tape is not an accurate representation of the clinician's interactions with the child. Clinicians who choose to videotape only selected sessions may be required to defend their decision in any court proceeding in which the tapes are used.

The videotape may also be of benefit therapeutically. If the child begins therapy with a new clinician once the investigation stage is complete, the clinician can learn about the abuse and the experience that the child went through during the investigation by watching the videotape. Nonoffending parents can also watch the videotape in order to gain further understanding of the effects of the abuse on the child.

There are disadvantages to videotaping, and these should be carefully considered before a videotape is made. When charges are filed against any individual, the defendant and his or her attorney have a right to all the evidence related to the case. If interviews with the alleged victim are videotaped, the defendant may have a right to view them and possibly obtain copies of them. Thus, the record of an interview that was initially thought to be confidential may eventually become public knowledge if "leaked" by a defendant or shown in a public court hearing. Because the clinician may not know before the interview whether a videotape of it will become public knowledge, the parents and child must be carefully warned about the possible lack of confidentiality. Given the proper warnings, a number of victims and their parents may refuse to participate in an assessment that is being videotaped.

Another disadvantage concerns the changes that may naturally occur in many children's stories as the investigation proceeds. If a videotape of such a process is viewed by the defendant, the defense attorney may find it advantageous to question the child about the change in his or her answers over time. One of the principal weapons of any attorney hoping to reduce the value of the testimony of a witness is to show inconsistencies in the witness's answers. Thus, a defense attorney could ask, " 'At first you said that nothing happened, now you say it did—when were you lying, then or now? Do you lie a lot? Why did you lie to the interviewer? How do we know that you're still not lying?' " (MacFarlane, 1985, p. 133). Such questioning may harm the prosecution's case in the eyes of the jury by casting doubt on the reliability of the key witness against the defendant, although in some cases an expert witness can testify that this is often the normal way that an abused child reveals the experience.

MacFarlane points out that the current state of affairs puts the clinician and victim in a difficult position. By not videotaping, the victim may be required to go through the grueling process of repeatedly describing the abuse. If a videotape is made, the clinician cannot guarantee that the assessment will not become public knowledge, and the natural course of the assessment may be used to impugn the reliability of the victim. At this time there does not appear to be any general solution to this dilemma. As a result, the clinician must examine each case individually and decide, as best as can be done before the interview, whether the advantage of videotaping outweighs the possible problems that may occur. Consultation with legal and protective service professionals is often valuable in these situations.

It does appear to us, however, that videotaping is an integral part of presenting to child protective agencies or the courts the most accurate representation of the assessment interviews. Those clinicians who are assessing rather than confirming that sexual abuse has occurred will want to place accuracy above all else in these cases. In some situations being accurate may result in a guilty perpetrator's not being charged or convicted, but in others it may prevent an innocent person from being falsely convicted. The fallibility of the judicial system, however, does not seem to be a satisfactory reason for clinicians' presenting just that part of the interview they believe should be presented.

Confidentiality. The issue of confidentiality is an important one and should be addressed early in the assessment process. This issue can be of greater importance in small towns or

rural communities where "everyone knows everyone else" because of repercussions against a family or child that reveals sexual abuse (Long, 1986; Topper and Aldridge, 1981). As the investigation begins, the clinician should acknowledge to the child
that his or her description of the abuse will eventually be related to the parents and others (Mrazek, 1980). Although this
acknowledgment may stifle some of the child's descriptions,
the clinician is not setting the child up for feeling invaded and
mistrustful, which may harm later investigatory and therapeutic
efforts. The clinician should also describe to the parents, and to
the child in an age-appropriate fashion, the extent to which information gathered during the assessment process will or might
become known by the legal system or the general public.

Language. Letting children describe anatomy and the sexual acts in their own words can facilitate a discussion of the
abuse (Adams-Tucker, 1984; Sgroi, Porter, and Blick, 1982).
For instance, Conerly (1986) relates that a young child claimed
that her father had hurt her "potty" with "a stick with a nail in
it" (p. 42). Only after careful and patient questioning was the
clinician able to ascertain that the "stick" was the father's finger (along with his fingernail), which felt like a stick when he
inserted it in the child's anus. One way the child's language can
be clarified is by having the child label the parts of a drawing of
a human figure or an anatomically correct doll (MacFarlane and
Krebs, 1986a). Bauer (1983) suggests that the clinician use the
vocabulary of older children or adolescents initially and then
begin to help the children substitute conventional terms so that
they appear competent when testifying. Some clinicians disagree with Bauer, however, and suggest that such assistance is
tampering with the child's testimony.

Great care must be taken when using the child's own language because miscommunication can result, and the credibility
of an entire assessment may be jeopardized if it is later revealed
that the clinician misunderstood a critical part of the child's
conversation. The clinician and child must form a mutual understanding of each term early in the assessment, and the clinician
should check with the child during the course of the evaluation
to ensure that the meaning of the terms has not changed. For

instance, *having sex* or *making love* may mean quite different things to children of diverse backgrounds and ages. The use of common terms like *masturbate* may be a problem even with older children if they are unwilling to acknowledge a lack of understanding of the terms and if the clinician has not asked them specifically about the meaning. The clinician must discover whether a young child uses a term solely for one particular activity or body part. For instance, it would be important to know whether a child who called her vagina her "pookie" also used that term for other parts of her anatomy (for instance, her anus). Care must also be taken with a child who uses nonspecific terms. As an example, a young child who uses the term *his thing* for her father's penis as well as for other objects for which she does not have a name may later mean that he put some other "thing," such as his thumb, in her mouth.

Sequence and Wording of Questions. Most writers suggest that once rapport has been established, the assessing clinician begin by asking general questions about the alleged sexual abuse. These general questions allow the child to tell the story without any clues from the clinician about what "should" be said. The clinician's questions can become gradually specific as the child needs increased structure in order to describe the incident accurately or as the clinician needs detailed information about what happened. This pattern of general-to-specific questioning helps to ensure that the clinician does not suggest information to the child and is often the pattern children use naturally when disclosing abuse.

MacFarlane (1985) suggests that the clinician review with the child the various ways that each question can be answered. By being clear with the child, the clinician can reduce the chance that the child will give misleading information. MacFarlane begins by telling the child that it is permissible to answer either yes or no to any question. Although this may seem rather obvious, some children may not feel that they have the right to answer no to some questions, and if they always answer yes, the value of their accurate positive answers is reduced. MacFarlane also cautions each child that, when appropriate, it is better to say that he or she does not want to answer a question than to say no to it. This caution lets the children know that they do not have to give an incorrect answer to avoid a difficult question. Along similar lines, the child is told that it is proper to say that a question has not been understood rather than to guess an answer to it. Some clinicians have found it valuable to insert occasionally a question to which the obvious answer is no to ensure that the child has not developed a pattern of always answering in the positive. Such assurance may be especially valuable during videotaped interviews.

Children's testimony has traditionally been viewed as unreliable in part because of concern over their suggestibility—that is, the extent to which information given during questioning can subsequently become part of their stories. For instance, after a child says that her father touched her in a private place, a suggestive question would be: "Were your pants off when your father touched you between your legs?" In this case, the clinician is assuming that "private place" is the same for the child as her crotch. If this question is asked many times, the child may begin to incorporate into her story the "fact" that her father touched her in the crotch, even if she initially meant something else by "private place." Research on the suggestibility of children has provided equivocal results (an elaboration of this issue can be found in Chapter Fourteen). As a consequence, the extent to which false information may be inadvertently picked up by the child through questioning is not known. Because of the concerns about children's suggestibility, the use of suggestive questions may result in the testimony of both the clinician and the child being excluded from the trial of the perpetrator. Because of these dangers, the clinician must carefully construct each question and the sequence of questions to ensure that both the entire experience of the child is revealed and that no incorrect facts are suggested to the child during the course of the interview.

Objective and Projective Tests with Children and Parents. Results from objective and projective tests can provide the clinician with additional information to use in judging whether sexual abuse has occurred. However, there is no evidence that a certain type of response to objective or projective tests or that a certain type of drawing clearly indicates that a child has been sexually abused. As a result, such tests must be interpreted with caution. Although they may be used as a way of increasing or decreasing the confidence that a clinician has in his or her assessment of the accuracy of an accusation, reliance on them to substantiate abuse is inappropriate at this time. There is a potential for wider use of these tests in the assessment of sexual abuse, but further investigations of the differences between sexually abused and nonabused children's responses must be completed before the potential can be realized.

Behavior checklists can be completed by those who are familiar with the child, and the behaviors of the child can then be compared with those of identified victims. Some caution must be used with these checklists however. In another area of research, it was found that when divorcing parents were asked about the behavioral reactions of their children to the divorce, a pattern emerged in which the parent who initiated the divorce rated the children as having few behavioral problems, while the parent who did not initiate the divorce rated the same children as having several behavioral problems (Wallerstein and Kelly, 1980). A similar pattern may develop in cases of sexual abuse. Consequently, the reports of an accusing parent may provide as much of an evaluation of the parent as of the child. Teachers have often been found to be more accurate in their descriptions of children's behaviors than are parents. However, asking the child's teacher to complete a behavior checklist may involve telling the teacher of the investigation, and the child may experience negative consequences as a result of being identified as a victim even before the investigation is completed. If the child is removed from the home, a foster parent may complete the checklist, although in this case the child's behaviors may be a reflection of his or her removal from home as much as, if not more than, of the alleged abuse.

Intelligence testing has been suggested for both assessing the validity of the child's report and providing guidance in planning later intervention. Projective tests such as the Rorschach or Thematic Apperception Test may reveal areas of emotional conflict (Mrazek, 1980). Although the need for interpretation of the projective tests may lower their reliability, their value stems from the fact that they ask the child to do more than repeat his or her story about the alleged abuse.

Drawings may also provide additional information. If a child can draw an abuse scene, the clinician's doubts that the child has merely memorized a description suggested by a parent may be reduced. The emotional response to drawing the perpetrator or the abuse scene may also be diagnostic (Goodwin, Sahd, and Rada, 1978). Kelley (1985) suggests that abused children often make self-portraits or other human-figure drawings that include genitalia or sexual themes. In an initial investigation of this hypothesis, Yates, Beutler, and Crago (1985) had eighteen sexually abused children and seventeen nonabused children in treatment for other emotional problems complete a drawing of a human figure. There were no differences in the hypersexuality of the pictures between the groups, although the abused group was more variable in the amount of genitalia included than the nonabused group, with some victims including detailed secondary sexual characteristics and others appearing to avoid them completely. Additional investigations must be undertaken before the value of such drawings for assessing sexual abuse can be ascertained. If human-figure drawings are used, it may be important to have the child draw a self-portrait before being asked to draw any pictures of the sexual abuse in order to eliminate the chance that just drawing the alleged sexual abuse scene would suggest that a sexual theme should be added to a self-portrait.

When the accusation of child sexual abuse has been made against one parent by the other, evaluation of each parent can be an important step in the overall assessment and should include a detailed sexual and childhood history and projective tests (Green, 1986). Objective personality measures such as the MMPI can provide some information that may be useful in judging the personality traits and parenting abilities of each parent (Bresee, Stearns, Bess, and Packer, 1986). When the accusing parent appears to be more disturbed than the accused parent, a question about the accusation can be raised and added to other information from the case. As a caution, however, Bresee,

Stearns, Bess, and Packer (1986) note that even a significantly disturbed parent may discover that genuine sexual abuse is occurring. Also, recall from Chapter Five that some incestuous families are characterized by a mother who has withdrawn from the father because of physical or emotional problems. This possibility provides another reason for not automatically discounting a report of child sexual abuse that comes from an apparently disturbed parent.

Indicators of the Truth or Falsehood of an Accusation. Several authors discuss indicators occurring during an assessment that they have found valuable in determining the accuracy of an accusation of child sexual abuse; these indicators are summarized here (Benedek and Schetky, 1986; Bresee, Stearns, Bess, and Packer, 1986; DeJong, 1985; Green, 1986; Mann, 1985; Schuman, 1986; Sgroi, Porter, and Blick, 1982). Child behaviors that may be indicative of sexual abuse were presented in Chapter Six and are not reported again. Some of the indicators pertain only to cases where a parent is accused, while others are potentially useful in all cases. Although many alleged cases may involve indicators that the accusation both is and is not true, they may be of value in determining the relative strength of the accusation. However, no evidence clearly associates these indicators with true or false accusations, and no evidence suggests the likelihood that a child or parent exhibiting one or more of the indicators is or is not making a true accusation.

Indicators that the accusation is true include these situations:

1. The child has a difficult time disclosing or talking about the abuse.
2. The child makes several half-hearted retractions and subsequent reconfirmations of the abuse.
3. The disclosure is accompanied by depressed or anxious affect.
4. The child has difficulty confronting the alleged abuser.
5. The child is anxious or seductive in the alleged abuser's presence.
6. The child describes the sexual activity in age-appropriate

language and can give a detailed description of the specific activities that took place.

7. If attempted or completed intercourse is alleged, the intensity of the sexual activity grew gradually over time.
8. The accusing parent is ambivalent about involving the child in the investigation.
9. The accusing parent indicates remorse for not recognizing previous signs of the abuse and for not sufficiently protecting the child.

As will be discussed in Chapter Ten, many children who are sexually abused by a trusted adult have ambivalent feelings about both the abuser and the sexual activity. This ambivalence, as well as threats that may have been made to the child to ensure his or her silence, can contribute to the first five indicators. In a number of cases, however, the child has only negative feelings about an abuser, resulting in a straightforward, angry accusation. Consequently, these five indicators cannot be expected in all cases. A child who is pressured to make a false accusation, however, may also show signs of anxiety, may be upset, and may have difficulty confronting the alleged perpetrator. Differentiating between these two sources of anxiety may be difficult in some cases and impossible in others. If the child describes the abuse in age-appropriate language, the suspicion that the child is being coached by an adult is diminished. However, an adult can coach a child to use age-appropriate language. Empirical research, such as that reviewed in Chapter Three, has indicated that most reported cases of incest initially involved less intense forms of sexual behavior and gradually grew to include intercourse. Such a pattern should not be expected to happen in every case, especially those that involve strangers.

Indicators that the accusation is false include these situations:

1. The disclosure is made easily and is not accompanied by noticeable affect.
2. The child uses adult sexual language and is unable to provide specific descriptions of the sexual activity.

3. It appears that it is easy for the child to confront the accused parent.
4. There is a discrepancy between the child's accusations and his or her comfort with the accused parent.
5. It appears that the child is being prompted by the accusing parent.
6. Very intense incestuous sexual activity is described as beginning almost at once.
7. The parents are involved in a custody dispute or there are other signs of high levels of marital discord.
8. The accusing parent is eager for the child to testify at all costs and insists on being present when the child is interviewed.
9. The accusing parent gives only vague responses when asked about the development of his or her suspicion that abuse was occurring.
10. An older accusing child appears to be seeking revenge against a parent.

The first four indicators reflect the belief that making the accusation or describing the abuse is a difficult process for the victim. As noted in the previous discussion of videotaping, though, the child's affect during the initial description of the sexual activity will in all probability be quite different from that during the tenth description. When the child is required to repeat the story many times, it may eventually sound like a rote description of a nonemotional event. The fifth, eighth, and ninth indicators are based on the assumption that many parents who falsely accuse their spouses of sexual abuse are angry at the spouse, and that anger overshadows their concerns about the child. It is possible, however, a parent's anger over an actual case of sexual abuse may make him or her less considerate than usual of the child's well-being. On the one hand, as discussed previously, a number of false accusations come from divorcing parents or parents who have a discordant relationship. On the other hand, as noted in Chapter Five, stressful parental relationships may encourage incest in some cases, so the presence of such a relationship should not automatically reduce the strength of an accusation. The tenth indicator suggests that a child may use an accusation against a parent. However, a child who has endured abuse by a parent for a long time may finally reveal it once the parent does something else to anger the child—for example, refusing to let a daughter date. Consequently, a child in a conflictual relationship with a parent cannot be assumed to be making a false accusation against that parent.

As can be seen from the listing and discussion of these indicators, they are not infallible guidelines. Therefore, it is important that they be used to generate hypotheses about the accuracy of an accusation and not to confirm hypotheses. Additional empirical research must be completed before we know the extent to which they can accurately indicate which child has been sexually abused. However, even if it should be discovered later that a certain indicator occurs in 95 percent of the cases of false accusations, a clinician cannot say for sure that any particular case is not one of the 5 percent for which the indicator is invalid. We are not suggesting that these indicators be ignored; they can play a role in a clinician's assessment especially if many indicators are present. However, the clinician should not base an assessment of the credibility of an accusation solely on the indicators.

Two Additional Unresolved Issues

Using a Syndrome of Emotions and Behaviors to Identify Victims. It has been asserted in several legal cases that the presence of a particular set of emotional responses and behaviors should be allowed as evidence to indicate that sexual abuse occurred to a particular child and that it was perpetrated by someone emotionally close to the child (see Chapter Fourteen). This syndrome of emotions and behaviors has often been referred to as a Child Sexual Abuse Syndrome or the Child Sexual Abuse Accommodation Syndrome in response to the work of Summit (1983). As summarized in Chapter Four, Summit asserts that the reactions of children to ongoing abuse by someone close to them cause a certain pattern of emotions and behaviors as they accommodate their lives to include the abuse.

We believe, however, that there is not a sufficient accumulation of evidence to support this assertion. The principal flaw with the notion of a specific syndrome is that no evidence indicates that it can discriminate between sexually abused children and those who have experienced other trauma. Because the task of a court is to make such discriminations, this flaw is fatal. In order for a syndrome to have discriminant ability, not only must it appear regularly in a group of children with a certain experience, but it also must not appear in other groups of children who have not had that experience. Although clinical reports have indicated that many sexually abused children exhibit certain combinations of emotional and behavioral reactions, no evidence indicates that these combinations are not also present in groups of children experiencing other sorts of trauma, and, as noted previously, some evidence exists that they are present after a variety of traumas. As a result, one cannot reliably say that a child exhibiting a certain combination of behaviors has been sexually abused rather than, for instance, physically abused, neglected, or brought up by psychotic or antisocial parents. Although future research may support identification of victims by their behaviors, such identification is currently not possible.

The presence of a particular combination of behaviors in a child may increase the likelihood that some sexual abuse has occurred, and the clinician may feel confident in stating that the presence of this pattern was used as one of the ways of arriving at the final assessment. To assert further that the behavioral and emotional pattern clearly indicates that the child has been sexually abused is not sufficiently supported by available research.

Retraction of the Child's Accusation. In some instances, the child retracts an accusation of sexual abuse. Assessments would be facilitated if one could assume that a retraction indicates that the child made a false accusation initially. The experience of many clinicians has shown, though, that such an assumption should not be made. Many children experience intense pressure from themselves, their families, and the perpetrator to retract their statements about the abuse. If it appears that the family is disintegrating because the perpetrator has been required to leave, if the perpetrator appears headed for jail, or if the child has had negative experiences with mental health, social service, and legal agencies, he or she may decide that the best course is to take the blame for making up a story and let the matter rest, even without pressure from others.

Consequently, correctly assessing the accuracy of a retraction may be just as important, and just as difficult, as assessing the initial accusation. Some authors appear to believe that nearly every retraction is false and has been made under pressure, while others are inclined to see the retraction as an indication that the child had been pressured into making a false accusation in the first place. As with other aspects of child sexual abuse, the middle ground is probably the most accurate. The assessing clinician would probably be wise to take a retraction and the atmosphere in which it has been made as one additional piece of data in the overall assessment. Discussions with the child, away from all other adults, may give clues as to the motivation behind the retraction, and this information should be crucial in assessing its accuracy.

Summary and Conclusions

The assessment of the credibility of an accusation of child sexual abuse is a complicated and inexact process. It appears that absolutely conclusive statements cannot be made unless the alleged perpetrator admits to the abuse, there are witnesses to the abuse, or there is unimpeachable physical evidence. Clinicians asked to evaluate an accusation of child sexual abuse are thus in a difficult position. This position is similar to that of clinicians who are asked to assess the sanity of a criminal defendant or the dangerousness of a patient in a mental hospital: Harm may be done to someone if an incorrect assessment is made in either direction. As in all these cases, the assessing clinician must form an opinion after careful review of all the available evidence. A number of clinicians and researchers provide descriptions of victim and parent behaviors and emotions that they say can be used to assess whether the accusation is accurate. We contend that although an accumulation of these indicators can raise or lower a clinician's confidence in an assessment of the accusation, the lack of infallible indicators means that in each disputed case the clinician's opinion is just that–an opinion.

Benedek and Schetky (1986) note that some clinicians develop reputations for either always seeing or never seeing sexual abuse. They advise that a clinician examine each case with no preconceived ideas and, when explaining conclusions, acknowledge the weaknesses inherent in each conclusion. This procedure, they say, will enhance the reputation not only of that particular clinician but also of all those who are involved in the difficult task of assessing possible victims. In many instances, the conclusion that there are insufficient data or reasonable doubts as to whether the abuse occurred may be the most accurate one (although often unsatisfying). Goodwin, Sahd, and Rada (1978) stress the importance of differentiating between a case where there are clear indications that the abuse did not occur and a case where there is not enough information on which to form an opinion. Without this delineation, a finding that there is not sufficient evidence to assert that sexual abuse definitely occurred can be misconstrued as indicating that it did not occur.

Because absolute proof can seldom be obtained in a disputed case of child sexual abuse, an assessing clinician may be tempted to slant an assessment in one direction or the other, depending on the clinician's own beliefs. Those who believe it is more important for the good of the child to err in the direction of finding sexual abuse are more likely to find abuse, while those who believe that it is more important to err in the direction of not convicting a defendant unless there is incontrovertible proof are likely to find sexual abuse much less frequently. We agree with Judge David Bazelon (1982) that such a determination by a clinician is improper and usurps the function that is assigned by our legal system to the judge and jury. Rather than making conclusive judgments based on inadequate data, assessing clinicians should outline all their findings, suggest what each finding indicates to them, outline which findings indicate clearly one conclusion or another and which are equivocal, and then rely on the judge or jury to make the final determination. Although the results in some cases may not please the clinician, such a policy ensures that the clinician remains a source of viable information in the legal process.

Part *3*

HELPING VICTIMS
AND FAMILIES

T he third part of this book focuses on therapeutic interventions for victims of child sexual abuse and their families.
Since the 1970s, many clinicians have described their own interventions in books and journals. We bring these often diverse
styles together so that the reader can gain the widest possible
picture of the treatment of victims and families. In each chapter
we consider a specific aspect of treatment, although in practice
some of these aspects will need to be considered concurrently
during the course of treatment. For each type of treatment, we
discuss several therapeutic issues and the ways that they have
been approached by various clinicians. We also discuss issues
that have received little attention and thus represent gaps in our
knowledge of treating child sexual abuse cases. We believe that
pointing out these gaps is as important as pointing out the current wisdom of the field because by recognizing and beginning
to fill in the gaps we can expand our expertise.

We begin in Chapter Eight with a discussion of several
therapeutic issues that are pertinent to all forms of treatment
and that should be considered by anyone dealing with child sexual abuse victims and their families. The four chapters that follow outline the types of interventions that can be used. Chapter
Nine deals with the concerns of the clinician who first encounters a family after a case of sexual abuse is revealed: crisis inter-

vention and treatment planning. Chapters Ten, Eleven, and Twelve focus on specific treatments that can be employed: individual, group, and family. Finally, Chapter Thirteen details efforts to design and evaluate child sexual abuse prevention programs.

As we reviewed the literature and reflected on our own experience, it became apparent that there were many ways of resolving the various issues that arise when deciding on the best form of treatment for victims and families. Other authors describe the ways that they have found to be most effective in handling these issues. We, however, describe the differences of opinion and the rationale for each position so that the reader can gain an understanding of the variety of ways that have been found useful when treating victims and families. When there are disagreements, we avoid making judgments about the relative correctness of each position because we believe that there seldom is only one correct position for all clinicians in all situations. Our aim is to present the diverse opinions in such a way that the reader will be able to understand the various arguments and so that those involved in the treatment of victims and families can make initial judgments about the best ways to proceed with their particular cases. Rather than describing our resolution of an issue, we describe the various factors that we considered while pondering which resolution would be best. In the short run our presentation may be frustrating because it does not provide a specific "recipe" for curing the trauma that can be caused by child sexual abuse. We believe, however, that in the long run individual clinicians will need to grapple with the variety of approaches before finding the one that is best for them, and we hope to encourage this process.

We describe a few treatment programs in detail in order to provide a fuller flavor of some of the methods currently in use. We also provide references so that the interested reader can study other interventions in detail. Within each chapter, we discuss several therapeutic issues that have yet to be resolved or to be addressed. By presenting these issues, we hope to encourage their consideration by clinicians and to stimulate empirical research where appropriate so that information contributing to their resolution can begin to be gathered.

Throughout this part of the book, we also concentrate on techniques that have been used specifically with sexual abuse cases. We do not discuss the basic clinical or counseling skills that are common to all types of treatment. For instance, we do not discuss methods for developing basic rapport with a sexually abused child, except to point out reasons why such rapport may be particularly difficult to establish with sexual abuse victims, or reasons a given technique may differ from normative strategies. We trust that those readers who will be providing direct services to abuse victims and their families already have the basic skills or will develop them through the use of other sources.

In Part One we were able to draw from clinical and empirical studies in order to understand child sexual abuse. As mentioned there, both clinical and empirical studies have advantages and limitations; therefore, using the studies in concert yielded the most information. Unfortunately, we cannot continue with this pattern in these chapters because empirical work on the treatment of child sexual abuse is almost nonexistent. As a result we are unable to draw on empirical studies in our attempt to understand the benefits of the diverse types of interventions. Although we can be guided by the wisdom of those who have developed and refined various clinical interventions, there is a need for increased empirical work, and this need will be apparent as we discuss a number of therapeutic issues. To cite just one example, some therapists prefer to have a male/female team provide therapy to groups of sexual abuse victims, while others prefer to have a female/female team. Those with each perspective give logical, convincing arguments about the wisdom of their approach. Nevertheless, a mental health professional who is forming a group therapy program for sexual abuse victims has only his or her judgment about the arguments and perhaps some personal experience with which to evaluate the type of team that would be the most advantageous. Empirical research documenting the reactions of group members of different ages to the two types of teams would add valuable information.

The lack of empirical evidence regarding the treatment of sexual abuse is not surprising. Many roadblocks exist to carrying out valid outcome research with most types of therapies; see the special issue of *American Psychologist* (VandenBos, 1986) for a review of these issues. Also, as Conte (1984a) notes, interest in the treatment of child sexual abuse has increased dramatically only since the 1970s; thus, expectations of extensive intervention research are probably unwarranted.

Ethical issues and the conflicts between the needs of researchers and of interveners have also led to the dearth of empirical research (Coulter, Runyan, Everson, and Edelsohn, 1985). Many clinicians and researchers assume that it is unethical to provide therapy to some victims and place others on a waiting list in order to assess the value of the therapy, especially when it is perceived that the child faces high levels of manipulation from an incestuous family. The basis for this assumption is the belief that therapy will be valuable to all sexual abuse victims. However, this belief may not necessarily be correct. Although there are no data directly related to this issue in child sexual abuse cases, two relatively sophisticated evaluations in the area of juvenile delinquency may give us pause. Klein and his colleagues (Klein, 1979; Lincoln, Teilmann, Klein, and Labin, 1977) achieved random assignment of juvenile offenders to release without referral and treatment; community referral and treatment; and court petition (processing through the juvenile court system). A twenty-seven-month follow-up revealed significantly lower recidivism rates for the nonreferred, released offenders than for either of the other groups. McCord's (1978) thirty-year follow-up of 506 individuals who as adolescents were judged to be delinquency prone and who were assigned to either a preventively oriented counseling program or a no-treatment control group provided the extraordinary finding that all significant differences favored the no-treatment controls. Similarly, treatment may not be beneficial to all child sexual abuse victims, and consideration of delaying treatment for some victims in order to test this hypothesis may be appropriate.

It may also be unethical to place victims in certain types of therapy randomly if it is believed that some victims can benefit more from one type than from another. However, decisions about the best form of therapy are usually based on clinical judgments, and, as will be seen throughout these chapters, clinicians often differ in their judgment. These differences of opinion within the professional community may make such random assignment less problematic than is generally assumed. It is less clear whether it would be unethical to investigate small issues—for instance, by randomly assigning some victims to a group co-led by a male and female team and others to a group co-led by two females in order to observe the differences in the groups. Although it will be difficult to accomplish, empirical research is needed if we are to continue to improve the interventions available to sexual abuse victims and their families.

Another gap in information that is apparent in this part of the book arises from the fact that most of the authors who write about therapy in sexual abuse cases have been involved primarily with the treatment of incestuous families. Consequently, there is little information on treatment of nonincestuous cases. Although many of the treatment issues raised in cases of incest are also of importance to those working with victims of extrafamilial abuse, there may be important differences. For instance, treating a child who has been sexually abused one time by a neighbor may require an approach different from that used to treat a child involved with incest. Wherever possible, we indicate when a treatment appears to be aimed at a victim of a particular type of sexual abuse.

We also use a circumscribed definition of incest here. As delineated in Chapter Two, the legal definition of incest varies from state to state and often includes sexual abuse by relatives such as grandparents, uncles, and aunts. Many empirical studies of the epidemiology of incestuous sexual abuse also include abuse by members of the child's extended family. Most clinical cases of incest, however, involve the child's parent or parent figure. Consequently, in these chapters we use this circumscribed definition. Thus, an incest perpetrator could be a natural parent, a stepparent, or a foster parent but not a more distant relative or a person temporarily living with one of the child's parents and having little or no emotional tie to the child. Sexual abuse by someone other than a parent figure will be referred to as extrafamilial abuse or nonincestuous abuse, even though the perpetrator may be in the child's extended family.

CHAPTER EIGHT

Basic Issues
in Treatment

A number of issues should be considered by anyone working
with child sexual abuse victims and their families. These
issues are discussed in this separate chapter because they are
pertinent to all types of therapeutic situations. Consideration of
these issues by clinicians and others before actual interventions
begin may result in the avoidance of situations potentially harmful to the outcome of therapy.

Reactions to Working with Victims and Families

A psychology intern had been having a particularly
hard time developing a close connection with a sexually abused girl whom she had been seeing for
about a month. During a supervisory session, the
intern's supervisor commented that whenever the
girl began to talk about the positive feelings she
sometimes had during the physical contact, the intern diverted the child's attention to the negative
aspects of the abuse. The intern revealed that she
had been fondled by a neighbor when she was a
child and that she felt a continuing repulsion to the
experience. Over subsequent supervision sessions

187

the supervisor and intern were able to discuss how the intern's experiences might be affecting her style in therapy sessions. The intern's relationship with the child improved significantly.

Several countertransference issues face the clinician working with sexually abused children and their families. In general, countertransference reactions are evoked by the interplay of the client's behaviors and the beliefs and emotions of the clinician. The process is often out of the consciousness of the clinician and consequently may result in behaviors by the clinician that are later evaluated as having been countertherapeutic and for which the clinician has no explanation. For example, in cases of child sexual abuse a clinician may react unconsciously to the sexualized behavior of a victim by withdrawing from the child or to the victimized behavior of the child by becoming overly protective. Countertransference reactions can be beneficial when they are recognized because they can provide the clinician with information about how others may react to the client's behavior. In general, awareness of the possibility of countertransference reactions and of the steps that are possible to reduce the negative and enhance the positive effects of these reactions seems an important component in the often emotionally charged cases involving child sexual abuse.

Because a clinician often has difficulty discovering countertransference reactions, careful evaluation of the clinician's reactions to clients is required. Observing videotapes of therapy sessions can allow clinicians to evaluate their behaviors that might otherwise go unnoticed. Some clinicians have found cotherapy valuable if one clinician feels free to confront the other about behaviors in therapy (Nichols, 1984). Consultation with supervisors or other clinicians may also reduce the chance of negative countertransference effects. Many clinicians, especially those working in agencies, have found using a team of clinicians useful in cases of child sexual abuse. The primary clinician is observed by other clinicians or has tapes of the sessions reviewed by other team members. Among other benefits, this procedure allows for concerns about countertransference to be raised.

The data presented in Chapter Three indicated that sexual abuse happens to many children at all social and economic levels. Thus, it can probably be safely assumed that some clinicians who work with such cases have experienced child sexual abuse themselves. The countertransference reactions of clinicians who are previous victims may be especially strong. It may be especially important for these clinicians to engage in some type of supervision so that they can regularly explore ways that their previous abuse may be affecting their current therapeutic work.

Feelings Evoked by the Victim. As noted in Chapter Six, some sexually abused children have displayed sexualized behavior toward the clinician while in therapy. Children may ask about the clinician's sexual habits, disrobe, masturbate, or rub their bodies against the clinician (Mrazek, 1981; Yates, 1982). This behavior may occur because some victims have learned that such behavior is an appropriate way to interact with adults. Other victims may be comparing the responses of the clinician and the abuser as a way of testing the sincerity of the clinician and gauging the safety of the therapeutic situation. These behaviors can be quite disturbing, and clinicians have reported being physically aroused by and irritated with the child during the therapy hour (Kohan, Pothier, and Norbeck, 1987; Krieger, Rosenfeld, Gordon, and Bennett, 1980).

A clinician can make several responses to a child's sexualized behavior. Because such behavior can be somewhat unnerving to any clinician, planning a general response strategy before seeing a victim in therapy may better enable the clinician to react purposefully. Krieger, Rosenfeld, Gordon, and Bennett (1980) suggest that the best tactic is to establish clear guidelines about behavior in therapy and then to remain predictable and consistent if the child breaks the rules. (Establishing rules about sexualized and aggressive behavior is discussed in Chapter Ten.) Lamb (1986) notes that ignoring the obvious attempts of the child to engage the clinician through seductive behavior will lead the child to view the clinician as unrealistic or phony. She suggests that the clinician conceptualize the behaviors as inappropriate attempts by the child to relate to the clinician. The clinician can give such an interpretation to the child and appropriate ways to relate can be explored. Jones (1986) suggests that the child may have come to associate the presence of sexual feelings with warmth and trust. If the clinician suspects that this association is the cause of the child's behavior, the clinician can reflect to the child the possible reasons for the sexualized behavior and assert that the child does not have to act in a sexual fashion in all situations involving warmth or trust. These statements can result in a discussion of the appropriate and inappropriate times for sexualized behavior. Another tactic when children attempt inappropriate physical contact is for clinicians to say that such contact makes them feel uncomfortable and that they do not want to participate in such activity (Friedrich and Reams, in press). By reacting in this way, clinicians model the type of self-protective behavior that it is hoped the children will develop.

Furniss (1983a) notes that after an initial period of anger and hatred toward her father the incestuously abused girl often begins to experience and express feelings of closeness and love for him; these feelings are often difficult for the clinician to accept. If the clinician attempts to discourage these loving feelings during therapy, the child may come to believe that only certain emotions are acceptable. This perception may reduce the child's genuine expression of emotions in therapy or in her life outside of therapy.

Another countertransference concern is that the clinician may treat the child as a helpless victim because of the child's victimized behavior. This treatment may encourage the child's development of a general pattern of victimized behavior. The clinician may also feel the need to rescue the child from an incestuous family and thus subvert what may be realistic plans for eventual family reunification (Webb-Woodard and Woodard, 1982). This possibility is of special concern to a clinician who is working primarily with the victim.

Ganzarian and Buchele (1986) raise a possible countertransference issue when the victim is seen simultaneously by more than one clinician (although they write specifically about adult victims of child sexual abuse, the same concern may apply to child victims). They suggest that clinicians can engage in competition over who will have control of the case and who is offering the most effective treatment. They note that some incestuously abused children occupy a privileged place in their families and that the subsequent behaviors of these children can encourage clinicians to see them as "special patients." This perception may encourage competition among the clinicians treating them.

Feelings Evoked by the Perpetrator and Family. In many cases, the clinician may discover personal feelings of anger or hatred toward the perpetrator and other members of the victim's family. In cases of extrafamilial abuse, the clinician may believe that the family did not provide the child with sufficient protection from a potentially abusive situation or that a careless choice of a caretaker for the victim was made. The feelings arising from these beliefs may make it difficult for the clinician to interact effectively with the family and promote the type of family environment that can protect the victim and other children in the family.

Feelings toward an incestuous family may be even more intense than toward the family of a victim of extrafamilial abuse. As Giarretto (1981) points out, "Despite their schooling, members of the helping professions are not entirely free of punitive emotional reactions to abusive parents. The image of a five-year-old girl performing fellatio on her father in submission to his parental authority does not engender compassion for the parents. Instead, the images evoke spontaneous feelings of revulsion and hatred that shatter any reason and capacity to perform as a therapist" (p. 188). Such negative feelings may be sensed easily by the family members. Many incestuous families have relationships that are tangled and confused, and thus they are carefully attuned to nuances indicating judgmental or rejecting views on the part of the clinician (Krieger, Rosenfeld, Gordon, and Bennett, 1980; Lamb, 1986; Topper and Aldridge, 1981). A clinician's condemning attitude can influence the reactions of the family members to the clinician and can consciously or unconsciously influence the clinician's actions. One way to avoid a deleterious attitude is for the clinician to understand the strengths of the perpetrator and other family members that may lead to eventual family reunification as well as the weaknesses that led to the incest (Giarretto, 1981).

Solin (1986) discusses the displacement of anger by members of an incestuous family. She notes that members of some incestuous families have highly ambivalent emotions toward the father. They want to support the father while feeling anger at and repulsion to his acts. Solin theorizes that this ambivalence is often handled by displacing the anger onto the social service agency and clinicians involved in the case. This anger may evoke similar emotions in the clinician or the clinician may give in to the family in order to mollify the anger.

In some cases, the mother may develop a sense of hostility toward the clinician as the child forms an attachment to the clinician (Goodwin and Owen, 1982). This hostility may develop in any case of child sexual abuse, although it may be more likely in incestuous than in nonincestuous cases. Recall from Chapter Five that one of the theories of the etiology of incest is that it is encouraged by the isolation of a family and that this isolation is often caused by the parents' fears of loss of each other and other family members. A mother from such a family may be especially prone to view the child's attachment to the clinician as a threat to the child's attachment to her. The clinician may begin to have negative feelings toward a mother who is being subtly or overtly hostile. The result can be further estrangement of the child from the mother and the rest of the family or competition between the clinician and the mother for the loyalty of the child.

Responsibility for Child Sexual Abuse

Responsibility of the Child and the Adult. Early conceptualizations of the responsibility for sexual abuse often placed some or most of the blame on the seductiveness of some children, especially of adolescents (for instance, Bender and Blau, 1937). Some modern authors expand on this theme. Their writings include case examples to illustrate that sexual activity is justified in some cases because the children have encouraged adults to be sexual with them (Ingram, 1981; O'Carroll, 1982).

Ingram obtained his descriptions of boys' apparent seductive behaviors from the adults with whom they had been provocative. However, although some of the descriptions may indicate the possibility that the boys had been seductive ("boys offering the man to show his genitals or masturbate"), others appear to indicate the ease with which adults can misinterpret the actions of some children ("boys with long legs and little, round bottoms wearing short, tight pants; boys using obscene language and sexy conversation; . . . boys seeking affection") (p. 185).

Some clinicians suggest that not all children are helpless victims; they make a distinction between responsibility for the abuse (which is always attributed solely to the adult) and participation in the sexual activity. For instance, Furniss (1983a) acknowledges that the parent is always responsible for incest because of children's dependence on adults, yet adds: "In all the cases I've seen so far, the daughter herself did at one point play an active role. In my experience, long-term incest does not exist without the active participation of the child, in one form or another" (p. 267). MacVicar (1979) classifies victims into "accidental victims" and "participating victims," with victims who experienced the abuse over a period of time being classified as participating.

The current predominant attitude among clinicians and researchers is that the total legal and moral responsibility for any sexual behavior between an adult and a child is the adult's. Even if a child is seductive toward an adult (and there is not any agreement on how frequently, if at all, this occurs), it is the responsibility of the adult not to respond to the child. They believe that subtle or overt pressure from the adult causes the child to act in a way that appears to indicate willing participation. The relative power of an adult and a child often requires that the child accede to the adult's wishes, including perhaps the wish that the child enjoy and actively participate in the sexual activity. In more general terms, the literature on operant conditioning is filled with examples of the actions of one individual meaningfully influencing the actions of another without the other's knowledge.

As noted in Chapter Four, many victims feel responsible

for their abuse. The sources of this guilt may be internal or external to the child. Some children's internal sense of guilt may be mobilized. This guilt is probably due to inappropriately gratified sexual wishes or to young children's grandiose tendency to see themselves as responsible for everything that happens in their world. The child's sense of guilt may also be exacerbated by the actions of others. For instance, family or friends may suggest that because the abuse was not immediately reported, the child must have enjoyed it, or the lawyers for the accused perpetrator may attempt to portray the child as seductive. In some cases, these external forces may be the only cause of a child's guilt.

Clinicians have often attempted to counteract this guilt by repeatedly assuring children that they are not responsible for the abuse. In cases of incest, many treatment programs require that the perpetrator, and other family members when appropriate, tell the child that the adults were totally responsible for the abuse. Pioneer clinicians in the field had to oppose vigorously the tendency of offenders and often the legal system to blame the child and in the process developed the style of repeatedly reassuring the children that the abuse was not their fault. However, even in the face of repeated reassurances by clinicians, many children continue to express concern about their own responsibility for the abuse. Some clinicians have begun to discuss the possible negative effects of dealing with the children's perception of their own responsibility merely by reiterating that children are not responsible. It may be important to distinguish between legal guilt and psychological guilt for incest. Legally, the adult is completely responsible for any sexual activity that occurs; however, psychologically, the child may continue to feel some responsibility regardless of the clinician's repeated insistence to the contrary. It may be necessary to explore actively the child's sense of psychological responsibility. Although the clinician should continue to maintain to the child that the adult is responsible for the sexual behavior, the clinician should also promote an atmosphere in which a discussion of the child's sense of responsibility, and the feelings associated with that responsibility, can take place.

Lamb (1986) cautions that repeatedly telling victims that they are not at all responsible for the sexual activity may provide short-term solace, but it may also reinforce the children in their role as victims and therefore be counterproductive in the long term. Rather than seeing the child victim as having been helplessly swept along by the desires of the adult, Lamb sees the child as having faced and made several choices during the course of the abuse. Although the child may have had no choice about whether to participate, he or she may have made choices about ways to try to avoid the perpetrator and about whether to tell about the abuse. Even if many of the choices were greatly influenced by the actions of the perpetrator, they were still choices made by the child. Lamb believes that the child should be helped to understand that choices were made as well as to understand the factors that may have extremely limited those choices in some cases. The child should also be helped to develop other ways for handling difficult choices in the future. By helping the child in this way, the clinician is acknowledging both the child's vulnerability and self-efficacy in the world; the child can then use the abuse experience to learn to manage the world more effectively.

Some support for Lamb's perspective comes from other studies of victims' behaviors. Janoff-Bulman (1985) hypothesizes that a victim of any negative event can employ two types of self-blame: "characterological self-blame," in which the victim blames his or her personality characteristics for the victimization, and "behavioral self-blame," in which the victim believes that an improper choice of behaviors led to the victimization. She suggests that when behavioral self-blame exists without characterological self-blame, it can be adaptive— " 'I did a stupid thing but I'm not a stupid person' " (p. 29). She continues by citing studies of accident victims, cancer victims, and victims of the Three Mile Island technological disaster in which those who exhibited behavioral self-blame were able to cope with the experience more successfully than were those who exhibited characterological self-blame or those who exhibited no form of self-blame.

The extent to which children should be encouraged to

discuss their feelings of responsibility or their correct and incorrect choices during their abuse remains unspecified. Lamb's perspective appears to be the minority view at this time. Many important factors should be considered when deciding on the way to handle the child's sense of responsibility—for example, the child's age, the child's cognitive ability, the identity of the perpetrator, and other characteristics of the abuse experience. Younger children may have a difficult time understanding how they might have had responsibility for some decisions but not for the abuse as a whole. It is also not clear whether a child who does not express concerns about responsibility should be encouraged to do so if the clinician believes that the feeling may be present.

Responsibility of the Mother and Father. As noted in Chapter Five, adherents to the feminist perspective emphatically state that the father is totally responsible for any incest. However, the family systems perspective on the amount of responsibility that should be borne by each parent is not as clear. Family systems therapists agree that the father must admit total responsibility for the incest in order for any treatment to be effective, but they also generally agree that the mother must admit her share of the responsibility for the family atmosphere that allowed the incest to occur.

Machotka, Pittman, and Flomenhaft (1967) state that the mother is often the cornerstone of the incestuous family. While discussing themes that generally appear in therapy with a mother from an incestuous family, Sgroi and Dana (1982) make this assertion: "Most mothers of incest victims have failed in their responsibility to maintain appropriate limits between themselves, their husbands, and their children. This is not to say that mothers must accept responsibility for their husband's incestuous behavior. However, the women must acknowledge their own failure to prevent the incestuous behavior by contributing to and permitting the blurring of role boundaries among family members. It is difficult for most women to be held accountable in this fashion. For the mother, it is far more palatable to blame the husband entirely for the incestuous behavior and to perceive herself totally as an additional victim" (p. 199). We find this statement confusing. The mother is not to be required to accept any responsibility *for* the incest but she must accept her share of responsibility *for not preventing* it. The authors seem to say that the mother should not be allowed to blame the father entirely for the incestuous behavior, yet she is not at all responsible for it. Although this confusion may be discounted as semantic, the conceptualization of the responsibility for the incest may adversely affect treatment if not handled carefully. For instance, an incestuous father who is told at one point that he should accept total responsibility for the incest and then listens as his wife is encouraged to take responsibility for the atmosphere that allowed it to occur may leave treatment not clearly understanding his level of responsibility. The chance of recurrence of the incest may be increased if each parent leaves therapy believing that a recurrence will be the fault of the other.

Summary. Clearly, one can conceptualize the responsibility for child sexual abuse in a number of ways. Currently, the legal responsibility for any sexual abuse always rests with the adult, regardless of the child's behavior. However, taking the position that no child ever has any part to play in the abuse situation may be just as unwise as taking the position that nearly all abused children have been seductive. Approaching each case without preconceived notions about the roles played by the victim, perpetrator, and family, or about the responsibility that the child and adults perceive they have seems to be the best strategy. By taking this approach, the clinician will not impose on one victim or family the beliefs that the clinician has developed from working on previous cases. This should increase the chance that the clinician will be able to understand the dynamics of each case and consequently provide the most effective treatment to each client by exploring all the emotions that the client is experiencing.

Legal Coercion to Participate in Treatment

Incestuous Families. With legal agencies involved in most if not all reported cases of incest, some form of legal process is often available to coerce the perpetrator and family to participate in treatment. The predominant view in the literature is that because of the extreme reluctance of many incestuous families to attend treatment, a specific legal requirement to remain in treatment is essential for it to be effective (Furniss, 1983a; Giarretto, 1981; Herman, 1983; Hoorwitz, 1983; Ryan, 1986; Sgroi, 1978). For the family, the short-term benefits of adhering to this requirement may be that the father stays out of prison or that the child either remains in the home or is able to return home after the completion of therapy. A long-term benefit is that an effective course of treatment may enable the family to function better than they did previously.

Clinicians who believe that treatment is preferable to incarcerating the offender cite several reasons. Incarceration usually puts tremendous financial strain on the family, thereby punishing the entire family for the incest. The loss of the father and the change in the mother's role caused by financial concerns may disrupt the functioning of the family, reducing the benefits of family life for all the members. In some cases, the victim may be blamed for the incarceration of the father and the breakup of the family, making incarceration as much a punishment for the victim as for the father. In addition, the father who has been incarcerated may have no incentive to receive treatment, as he may believe that his debt to society has already been paid (MacFarlane, 1983). Many clinicians treating incestuous families also believe that a successful course of therapy will greatly diminish the likelihood of a recurrence of the incest and that merely jailing the offender may not reduce the chance of recidivism once the offender is released and returned to the family. Some families may need to be coerced into treatment initially because of their fears about therapy, but they will later discover that it is beneficial and opt to continue. Consequently, the initial coercion of the family into treatment may be an important step in the family's recovery from the incest.

The implementation of, and reliance on, legal coercion presents several problems, however. Most clinicians dealing with a wide range of clinical problems assume that voluntary involvement is required for therapy to be successful in the long term (see Monahan, 1980). Moreover, although clinical impressions do exist, no data substantiate the claim that coerced treatment of the offender and the family is more likely to stop recurrence of the incest and rehabilitate the family than is incarceration of the father or no action at all. Similarly, no evidence indicates that the behaviors of the perpetrator and family while in therapy are continued once therapy has been declared successful and is terminated. This type of data should be gathered if coerced treatment is to be continued. A study by Wolfe, Aragona, Kaufman, and Sandler (1980) supplied data from a related area—the physical abuse of children—although the extent to which similar results would be obtained from sexually abusive families is not known. Of the seventy-one families studied, those that were required by the courts to attend treatment sessions in order to have the children returned to their homes were five times more likely to complete therapy successfully than were those not required to do so. The success of the therapy was evaluated only by observing family interactions soon after the end of therapy and only for those families that completed therapy. Therefore the long-term changes made by those families required and not required to attend therapy are not known. Similar but more extensive studies could be undertaken with incestuous families.

Little has been written about requiring the mother or victim or both to attend treatment when the father has been incarcerated and there is no desire to reunite the family. Friedrich and Reams (in press) found that the quality of the adjustment made by the child involved in an incestuous relationship was often similar to the quality of the adjustment made by the mother. A number of mothers in the study refused to involve themselves or their children in therapy even though therapy was strongly recommended. Would it be appropriate to insist that these mothers receive some type of therapy? An argument for requiring the mother and victim to enter therapy may be that doing so would be in their ultimate best interest. However, ethical concerns exist about requiring nonperpetrators to enter therapy as well as about the benefit that a hostile mother would gain from therapy. Data substantiating benefits of required therapy in these types of cases would be of great value.

Little has been written about the special situation that a clinician faces when working with a family that has been coerced into therapy. Mrazek (1981) notes that these families present the clinician with a more difficult challenge than do those entering voluntarily and that extra work is required on the part of the clinician to engage the family in therapy. She suggests that clinicians need to be honest with families about the recommendations they make to the court and need to be alert to the resistance of the family, which may include appearing to change when they have not.

Extrafamilial Abuse. Although there has been limited discussion about coercing the incestuous family into treatment, there has been no discussion about coercing the victim or other family members into treatment when a child is abused by someone outside the nuclear family. In some cases it may appear that the abuse took place because the family was negligent in supervising the child. Should the child and parents be required to attend treatment? Many of the same questions can be raised about coercion in these cases as in cases where the perpetrator has been incarcerated.

Interagency Cooperation

Work with sexually abused children and their families is often a combined effort by individuals from legal, social service, and mental health agencies. Work with incestuous families may involve even more agencies. One mental health agency may be evaluating the incestuous father and another the wife and victim; the child protective agency may be seeking a particular way of handling the victim; and the district attorney and defense lawyers may be making their own demands. If not well coordinated, the interaction of so many agencies and individuals may result in a lowering of the effectiveness of each of them and of the "system" as a whole.

A few examples of poor interagency cooperation demonstrate the effect that it can have in individual cases. Furniss (1983b) cites a case in which he hypothesizes that the dynamics of an incestuous family were duplicated by the agencies working with it: The police were trying to protect the daughter by removing her from the parents' home; the mental health workers were attempting to keep the family together by protecting the position of the father within the family; and the mother was being pulled in two directions by the conflict. In another example, Webb-Woodard and Woodard (1982) warn about problems that can occur when more than one clinician is involved in the treatment of an incestuous family. They cite a case in which the clinician providing individual treatment for the child began to usurp the role of the parents after the family had been reunited by continuing to ignore the parents when decisions about the child were made. As a result, when the child was unhappy with the directives of the parents, she would threaten to call her clinician, and the parents felt obligated to let the child have her way in order to avoid trouble with the child protection system. The result was a delay in the eventual re-formation of the family into a unit with the parents in an appropriate position of control, the goal of a second clinician working with the family unit. The authors conclude that these actions occurred because the child's clinician had not been involved in the family treatment and consequently had narrowed her focus to only the apparent needs of the child.

A number of factors can make interagency cooperation difficult to achieve. The different functions of the agencies that deal with sexual abuse cases can result in the development of different languages, goals, and methods. Recall from Chapter Two that the same words may have different meanings for different groups of professionals, making communication between agencies problematic. In addition, the various agencies working on a particular case may have different mandates. The actions taken by one agency to meet its mandate can impede the progress of another agency toward meeting its mandate, and this situation can exacerbate the difficulties that the agencies may have working together. For instance, although they may be concerned about the alleged victim, the police are interested in apprehending the perpetrator and are also concerned with the litigation that may arise if they arrest someone because of a false accusation of sexual abuse. Consequently, they thoroughly in-

vestigate the accuracy of a child's story before arresting the perpetrator and may find that the actions of a clinician impede
their ability to form a case against the person they arrest. The
primary concern of the clinician who is therapist for the victim
is the child's immediate and long-term well-being. As a consequence, a clinician may see the repeated questioning of the
child or a delay in pressing charges against the perpetrator as inappropriate actions by the police (Bander, Fein, and Bishop,
1982).

In addition, professional personnel may consider other
agencies as not being effective. For example, Alfaro (1985) surveyed 243 school, hospital, and law-enforcement professionals
mandated by New York State law to report possible incidents
of child maltreatment. Alfaro found that 40 percent of the
school personnel and 8 percent of the police acknowledged instances of nonreporting, mainly because of a combination of
fear of reprisal against the child and doubts about the efficacy
of child protective services.

The difficult process of interagency cooperation can be
further inhibited by the ability of some incestuous families to
play one agency against another. Anderson and Shafer (1979)
characterize the incestuous family as being similar to a charac-
ter-disordered individual. The family is self-centered, and the
powerful members will use whatever methods are available to
promote what they think is in their immediate best interest.
The family is adept at using a lack of communication between
agencies to its advantage as a way of avoiding change.

In order to provide effective service to child sexual abuse
victims and their families, agencies and individuals within those
agencies who have seldom needed to cooperate on an ongoing
basis must learn to do so. To foster this cooperation, meetings
and negotiations can take place at both the agency and individual case levels. Each agency must develop an understanding of
and appreciation for the goals of and problems faced by the
other agencies with which it is involved. This process can be encouraged by holding meetings to discuss the goals and methods
of each agency as well as the ways in which these goals can be
furthered or impeded by other agencies. In addition, the agencies

may need to draft agreements concerning the specific functions that will be performed by each one. Specific procedures can be developed for each agency to provide feedback to the others concerning the handling of cases in general or of one case in particular. A process for ongoing review of interagency cooperation can also be developed.

Similar steps can be taken on a case-by-case basis. Meetings can be held by the individuals from each agency that will be directly involved in a particular case. The basic ground rules for determining which agency will perform specific functions can be reviewed, and applications of those ground rules to the particular case can be discussed. In general, getting to know individuals from the other agencies may facilitate questioning their actions, asking for help on a certain issue, and developing an ongoing sense of cooperation. Webb-Woodard and Woodard (1982) suggest that occasional inclusion of members of one agency in the interactions of another agency with a victim or family can also encourage this cooperation.

Role of the Clinician

Clinicians who become involved in child sexual abuse cases may find themselves with one or more of a variety of roles. In nonincest cases, these roles may include investigating whether the sexual abuse occurred, assessing the condition of the victim and family in order to plan treatment, or providing therapy. Working with incestuous families provides a further complication. Clinicians may be asked to assess or provide individual therapy to the victim, perpetrator or another family member, or to participate in group or family treatment. When therapy has been ordered by a court, clinicians may be expected to report nonattendance, or to testify in court about the condition of a family member or the progress that a client or family has made in therapy.

Because of these many roles and responsibilities, it is important for clinicians to have a clear understanding of their specific role in each case of child sexual abuse and to communicate the requirements of the role to the client or family (Goldstein,

Freud, Solnit, and Goldstein, 1986; Hoorwitz, 1983; James and Nasjleti, 1983). Unless this understanding is reached, clinicians may find that promises made to clients early in therapy regarding an issue such as confidentiality cannot be kept (Melton and Limber, 1987). In such a case, the possible positive impact that the clinician can have with the client may be reduced, and the ability of the client to trust any clinician may be endangered.

Some debate the appropriateness of a clinician's playing more than one role with a victim or family. Jones (1986) writes that the clinician may be able to take on more than one role and that in some cases this dual role can be beneficial to the client. He notes that it is appropriate for a clinician to testify in a court hearing about a child seen as a therapy client even if the clinician's recommendations run counter to the preferences of the child. Such a disagreement can be a source of "reality-based" play and discussion between the clinician and the child. It is unclear, however, whether Jones is speaking of all child clients or those of a particular age. The effect of such disagreements may be different with young children and with adolescents; conceivably the therapeutic relationship with an adolescent would be more negatively affected by such a disagreement. In contrast, Sgroi (1982b) and Sesan, Freeark, and Murphy (1986) suggest that it is valuable for the family and the victim to have regular contact with a clinician who is not involved in the legal investigation, a process that often runs concurrently with the initial stages of therapy. They note that the exploration of feelings and concerns that arise during the investigation is often an important component of the early stages of therapy and that clients may not be as open about their concerns and feelings with a clinician who is involved in the investigation.

Goldstein, Freud, Solnit, and Goldstein (1986) forcefully argue that clinicians and legal professionals should have only one role at a time with a particular client. They pose the questions: If court appointed, is the clinician responsible for reporting any disclosures the child makes in the course of a therapy session? Should the clinician serve an investigative or neutral role? Is it possible to serve as both a court-appointed investigator and a therapist and still promote the best interest of the child? They conclude: "Our clinical experience suggests that a professional person generally cannot effectively perform such dual roles. Potentially conflicting loyalties tend to prevent either assignment from being faithfully discharged. Therefore we believe that the operative presumption for legislature, agency, and court ought to be against the assignment of dual professional roles. And the presumption of professional participation ought to be against accepting or assuming such roles" (p. 80).

Tester (1986) provides a relevant example of the problem of assuming dual roles. In the Jordan, Minnesota, child sexual abuse cases, in which charges against twenty-one citizens were eventually dropped, many clinicians who were appointed by the court were confused about the roles they were expected to play and where their loyalties should lie. For example, one clinician was court appointed to examine ten children and report her impressions of their credibility and of the validity of their accusations. This same clinician had the children in therapy and served as guardian *ad litem* for them. She felt she was violating the children's confidentiality by reporting to the court what they told her in therapy but felt obligated to give the court names of adults whom the children implicated during the course of therapy. One result of the dual role played by therapists in this case was that several children felt betrayed and abandoned by their therapists. Tester reports, "One therapist said that the biggest mistake she made was telling the children that 'everything would be fine' if they told the truth; when she then turned to the police with information the children had given her and the cases got dismissed, . . . the children became resentful and bitter, and the treatment process was set back dramatically" (p. 15).

One possibly effective way for a clinician to maintain consistency in a case of child sexual abuse is to have a clear understanding initially of who the clinician's client is and to avoid changing clients midway though the case. In some cases the client will be the court, as when the clinician is asked to investigate whether the abuse occurred; in others, it will be a social service agency that is asking about the best placement for an abused child; and in still other cases it will be the child who comes to the clinician for therapy. In any case a clinician may perform a number of functions and the identity of the client distinguishes how those functions are carried out. For instance, a clinician may act as an investigator in many cases, but the way that the investigatory role is pursued depends on the client. If the client is the court, the clinician will develop rapport with the child and then investigate in a straightforward manner the possibility that abuse occurred. If the clinician is providing therapy to the child (and thus has the child for a client), some investigation of what happened to the child will undoubtedly take place, but the form that this investigation takes may be quite different, perhaps emerging slowly throughout the course of therapy. In sum, the clinician's actions can be dictated best by the requirements of the client. Although the clinician may occasionally be required to take two roles, as when a child in therapy reveals abuse and the clinician becomes involved with a protective service agency, a prearranged understanding with all concerned as to who the clinician's client is can reduce the number of times that the clinician has to take on dual roles.

Communication Among Clinicians

Along with deciding about communication among agencies, a clinician must also decide about communicating with other clinicians who are involved in the same case. The question that must be addressed is the extent to which details about the process and content of therapy sessions are to be shared. Although this issue can arise at any time when more than one clinician is involved with a family, such as in cases of extrafamilial abuse when one clinician sees the parents and another sees the child in therapy, it arises more with incestuous families because several family members may be in therapy with different clinicians and family members may have contradictory needs. The question also arises when a therapy team is formed to provide services to a family. Is it appropriate for the mother's or father's clinician to view sessions with the victim? How might one clinician's ability to deal effectively with a client be affected by a detailed knowledge of what other family members are or are not saying?

Some clinicians (Anderson and Shafer, 1979; Furniss,

1983b) advocate extensive sharing of information gathered in individual, dyadic, or family sessions by all clinicians working on a case. This procedure is viewed as especially important with incestuous families because of the hypothesis that the individuals in many incestuous families pursue their needs covertly and that direct communication between family members is often absent. The clinician may inadvertently collude with one family member against the others unless there is careful communication among all clinicians working with the family. By keeping all information out in the open, the clinicians are able to model an open style of communication for the family, avoid inadvertently colluding with one family member against the others, and avoid becoming drawn into the established patterns of communication and goal seeking of the family.

This close between-clinician communication in child sexual abuse cases seems to go against the usual standards of confidentiality between therapist and client. When more than one clinician is involved with other families, it is often assumed that they will speak in general terms with each other about those they are seeing but that the specific content of the therapy sessions will remain confidential between each clinician and the individual client. The notion behind this approach is that successful therapy is more likely to occur when the client is open with the clinician and that this openness is encouraged when the client knows that all sessions are confidential. When a client knows that what is said will be repeated to clinicians treating other members of the family, the tendency of the client to be forthright and honest may be decreased. This lack of honesty may cause the overall process of therapy to be less effective than it would be if sessions were confidential. If one member of a therapy team becomes inappropriately affected (possibly through countertransference reactions) by watching the sessions of another family member, the clinician may become less effective with his or her own client. In incestuous families, clients may believe that they can communicate with other family members through the clinicians, and this belief may also affect their responses.

There are no reports available to guide clinicians about the appropriate amount of communication among those working on a sexual abuse case. Clearly though, there are both advantages and disadvantages to regular communication among clinicians about the content of therapy sessions. At this time, it appears to us that the best decision can be made only by weighing the advantages and disadvantages of such communication on the outcome of each case and by mutual agreement of each clinician and client involved. Clinicians who decide to communicate openly with other clinicians involved with a particular case should discuss this decision with their clients. In such instances, the clinician should be aware that the client may be less forthright and may tend to give more socially desirable responses than if the sessions were confidential. Clinicians who choose not to communicate to such an extent with other clinicians should be aware of the dangers of beginning to see the entire case from the perspective of their client only and of the possibility that they may begin to advocate for their client at the expense of the total case.

Bander, Fein, and Bishop (1982) sound a caution for those clinicians working with an incestuous family who freely share information among themselves. They write that a therapeutic system employing close communication can result in "maximal positive impact or maximal confusion" (p. 186). In their experience, when communication between clinicians was consistent, crises could be handled effectively, relevant issues could be addressed with each member simultaneously, and the responsibility for decision making about and management of the family could be shared, reducing the burden on any one clinician. When communication broke down, as when clinicians were unable to meet on a regular basis, this breakdown appeared to reinforce the poor interactions and communication patterns of the family, resulting in a more difficult case for all involved.

Conclusions

Clearly, many issues must be confronted by those working with child sexual abuse victims and their families. For each issue several authors have suggested resolutions, and these resolutions are often at odds with each other. The number of issues that each professional confronts makes working on these types of cases demanding and filled with conflict. The easy way out is either to ignore the issues or to accept dogmatically certain authors' conceptualizations of how to handle them. The individual who takes this easy way, however, risks establishing such a narrow view of child sexual abuse and its victims that he or she will be able to provide meaningful services to only a narrow group of victims and families. The ongoing debate about and confusion over these issues is a healthy and essential part of their resolution.

CHAPTER NINE

Crisis Intervention and Treatment Planning

*T*he initial steps that are taken in the treatment of sexual abuse victims and their families are outlined in this chapter—protecting the victim, providing crisis intervention, and planning further treatment. Although in practice these three tasks are generally performed simultaneously, we have divided them here for clarity and to help the reader consider the specific issues connected to each function.

Protection of the Victim

The first priority for those involved with the victim is to ensure that the sexual abuse has ceased and that the victim is protected from its immediate recurrence. Not only is a cessation of the abuse important for the child's well-being, but, as Peters (1976) notes, children not protected from recurring abuse will not develop faith in the power of "the system" or the clinician, and the development of a trusting relationship between the child and clinician may be irreparably harmed. In some cases, protective measures will already have been taken by social service or child protective agencies; however, the clinician should consult with these agencies to ensure that the victim remains protected. The victim may experience renewed abuse if each agency assumes that another agency is protecting the child. Although the victim and family will be encouraged to take on the protective role in the future, most clinicians believe that these responsibilities belong to the clinician and others outside the family when the abuse is first revealed because the added stress of having sexual abuse revealed may further reduce the effectiveness of a family that is perhaps already dysfunctional. The clinician's assumption of the protective function is important until the family gains the strength to provide it. In order to provide protection, the clinician may need to become an active, authoritative advocate for the child.

In most extrafamilial sexual abuse cases, the child can be allowed to remain in the home, although in some cases the child may need to be placed in a temporary foster home. In cases of incestuous abuse, there are three basic ways to protect the victim: removing the victim from the home, having the perpetrator leave the home voluntarily or through a court order, or keeping the family together under supervision. Each method of protecting the victim has advantages and disadvantages. We will outline these methods and then discuss the criteria used by various clinicians to determine the best protective measures for a specific case. Because nearly every reported case of incest involves the father as the perpetrator, we refer to the father when speaking of the perpetrator.

Extrafamilial Sexual Abuse

Little has been written about the best methods for protecting the victim of extrafamilial sexual abuse, perhaps because clinicians generally assume that alerting the victim's family to the abuse and to the identity of the perpetrator, if known, will suffice. However, two authors question the adequacy of this form of protection in all cases. Sgroi (1982a) writes that when deciding on actions to protect the victim, the clinician should assess the amount of responsibility that should be attributed to the victim's family for initially failing to protect the child. For instance, the family may have shown poor judgment in choosing a babysitter or may not have supervised the child's outside activities sufficiently, thus increasing the child's vulnerability. In some of these cases the child's protection may be in question, and close work with the family may be necessary to decrease the child's vulnerability to future abuse.

Mrazek (1980) hypothesizes that when a family responds to the discovery of the sexual abuse with indifference, the child faces an increased risk of the abuse's recurring. If the family is resistant to any change and if the child appears vulnerable to continuing abuse, other measures to protect the child should be considered, such as temporary removal from the home. However, Mrazek does not state the extent to which the family is required to change before the child is allowed to return.

Although removing the child from the home should not be ruled out automatically, most clinicians suggest that this rather drastic solution be considered only in extreme cases. Removing the child makes a clear statement to the family about their perceived inability to protect the child and perhaps increases the chance that the child will not experience further abuse. These benefits must be weighed against the negative consequences of removing the child (which are reviewed in detail in the section on removing children from incestuous families) as well as the possibility of making the family and child so angry at the protection agency or clinician that they will refuse future attempts to treat them.

Another strategy for protecting the victim is to work directly with the victim to encourage self-protective skills. The need for these skills may be great for children from families that offer little protection. Some treatment programs for victims (see Sturkie, 1983) allocate time specifically to help victims learn self-protective skills, and it may be appropriate to encourage all victims to take this type of training even if they do not receive other forms of therapy. The format for teaching these skills can be similar to that used by sexual abuse prevention programs (see Chapter Thirteen).

Incestuous Sexual Abuse

Removal of the Child. Removal of the child from the incestuous home provides the greatest assurance that abuse by the previous perpetrator will not continue, especially if the perpetrator is not incarcerated (Anderson and Shafer, 1979). This solution is the intervention least advocated by all professionals, however (Atteberry-Bennett, 1987). There are, moreover, several case reports of victims being sexually abused by the foster parents or other children in a temporary foster home, so the child's protection from all sexual abuse cannot be assumed merely because the child is removed from the home. For this reason, the clinician may want to give the child who is removed explicit instructions about what to do if sexually abused again or if fearful that abuse will occur again. Another possible advantage of removing the child from the home is that the child is taken from an environment in which great pressure may be exerted to convince the victim to retract the accusation of abuse. Experiencing this pressure can be stressful to the child; and if it alienates the child from other family members, it may be more detrimental to the child's long-term relationship with the family than temporary removal (James and Nasjleti, 1983; Topper and Aldridge, 1981). In some cases, the child may prefer removal, although the age of the child and the family situation may be considered when determining the weight that the child's wishes should carry.

Several authors outline drawbacks to removing the child from the home. Many therapeutic efforts hinge on the assumption by the child and family that the adult perpetrator is completely responsible for the abuse (see Giarretto, 1982; Sgroi, 1982b). Both the child and other family members may view the child's removal as an indication by the child protective or social service agency that the child was partially or fully responsible for the abuse, despite repeated statements to the contrary; consequently, removing the child may make subsequent therapy more difficult. Removing the child may reinforce the tendency of some parents to band together against the child. Mothers often report feeling pulled in two directions by their allegiance to the father and the victim, and the pull away from the victim may be stronger if the victim is not present. Also, the child may perceive the removal as punishment, with a subsequent increase of guilt feelings (Anderson and Shafer, 1979; Herman, 1983; Hoorwitz, 1983). Some children who are removed also experience the added stress of the loss of a caring mother during a time when such support could be of great comfort (MacVicar, 1979).

Removal of the Father. Removing the father is a clear indication that the legal and social service systems believe that the responsibility for the abuse lies with him. It also allows the victim to lead as normal a life as possible during an often traumatic time (O'Connell, 1986). The bond between the mother and child may be strengthened if they are left together, a process that many clinicians believe is essential for the eventual reunification of the family (see Herman, 1983). In some incestuous families, the father abuses more than one child; consequently, removing the father may protect the other children in the family from sexual involvement with him once the previous victim is removed (Meiselman, 1978). Removing the father may also reduce the vulnerability of some families to physical abuse. A number of incestuous fathers are also physically abusive (Herman, 1983), and the possibility of physical abuse may be increased as the father faces the stress of involvement with the legal system. Furthermore, removal may place pressure on the father to attend treatment in order to gain reunification with the family.

There can be negative consequences to removing the father in some cases. If he is forced to leave, other family members may become quite angry with the victim, who is viewed as causing his removal (Mrazek, 1980). Such a situation may be likely in a family that suffers financially from the removal of the father or one in which the victim is held in low regard. If a negative reaction occurs, it may be more stressful to the child and other family members than the child's temporary removal.

In some cases the father will voluntarily remove himself from the home. Topper and Aldridge (1981) note that such fathers may have one of two motives. The first is a genuine concern for the welfare of the child and the family. In this case, the prognosis for the eventual reunification of the family is enhanced. An alternative motive is a desire to manipulate the opinion of the agencies involved with the case, in which case the possibility of family reunification is weakened. The authors caution that if clinicians suspect that the father is being manipulative, they must take care to ensure that he is not remaining with the family while appearing to be living separately. Unfortunately, the authors provide no guidelines for distinguishing fathers having each motive, and such a determination would appear to be quite difficult. Clues may be found in the father's behavior. For instance, some fathers who leave home to gain an advantage in legal proceedings may repeatedly refer to their sacrifice and suggest that it be matched by other family members.

If the father leaves the home, the extent to which contact with the family or victim will be allowed must be determined. Topper and Aldridge (1981) suggest that such a decision should be based on the attitude of the victim toward such a visit and that, if visits are allowed, they should take place in a controlled setting to reduce the chance that the experience will become detrimental to the victim. It appears to us, however, that the wisdom of placing any or all of the responsibility for permitting the visits on the victim is debatable. If pressure is put on the victim either to allow or not to allow visits, the victim has to balance the conflicting demands of family members; this responsibility may have been part of the original dynamics contributing to the abuse. Even without pressure from others, the victim's own ambivalent feelings about visits may be difficult to reconcile. To avoid this added pressure on the victim, the clinician or child protective worker may need to take full responsibility initially for the decision about visitation. In some situations, the age or stability of the daughter may indicate that an important component in the decision will be the daughter's feelings about visits, especially if they are negative, while in other situations it may be unfairly stressful to a young or ambivalent daughter even to request her input.

Leaving the Family Intact. A few authors note that a third option for protecting the victim is to allow the family to remain together while under close scrutiny of the appropriate child protective agency (Mrazek, 1980). Hoorwitz (1983) notes that in such cases each family member should be informed clearly of the steps that must be taken if the abuse recurs and that changes in sleeping or child-care arrangements may be required. The advantage to this solution is that the disadvantages of having either the child or the perpetrator leave the house are avoided. One disadvantage to this approach may be that children lose confidence that they will be protected from further abuse. However, a nonresident perpetrator may still visit the home regularly with or without the mother's encouragement, and no research indicates that keeping the family intact results in increasing levels of recidivism. Another disadvantage is that the family may believe that the maintenance of the status quo indicates that the clinician or the legal system or both consider the previous sexual abuse of little importance.

Deciding on the Appropriate Course of Action

In cases of extrafamilial abuse, determining the ability of the family and child to protect the child from further abuse is important when deciding whether to remove the child from the home. The age of the child and the reactions of the child and other family members to the possibility of the child's removal should also be considered, but little guidance is available in the literature on the weight that these factors should be given. As mentioned, all authors appear to favor allowing the child to remain in the home except under extraordinary circumstances.

In cases of incest, the opinion of most authors is that removal of the father from the home is preferable. No systematic investigations of the differential effects of removing the father, removing the victim, or leaving the family intact have been made. All the information available comes from case studies, and the amount of consideration that should be given to variables such as the age of the victim, the quality of the victim/ mother and perpetrator/mother relationships, and the extent or type of sexual abuse has not been investigated. Greene (1977) writes that the reactions of the mother may be central, especially in incestuous families. She suggests that the child remain in the home unless the mother is clearly more supportive of the perpetrator than of the child. Sgroi (1982b) suggests that the child remain in the home if a strong adult ally for the child can be found and activated; although this adult most commonly would be a nonoffending mother, a grandparent or grown sibling might also be appropriate. According to Sgroi, if no adult ally can be found, removal of the child is probably indicated. Thus, an important influence on the decision about whom to remove from the home, if a move is to take place, is the state of loyalties within the family. Even though in many situations it may seem unfair to remove a victim, especially if the victim is young, leaving a child in a hostile family environment may add to the overall negative impact of the abuse.

Crisis Intervention

Goals

The clinician who first sees a sexually abused child or the child's family is likely to be involved in a crisis situation. An important part of the clinician's work at this point is to resolve the crisis so that the victim and family can begin to take steps to repair any damage done by the abuse.

In general, a crisis occurs when a person or family is unable to solve a problem with the coping strategies that they have developed in the past (Aguilera and Messick, 1982). Few families or individuals who are faced with sexual abuse have ever had to resolve a situation with similar emotional and legal consequences. Consequently, most people have not developed coping strategies that can be used when the sexual abuse is revealed, and, not knowing in which direction to turn, they are often frozen into inaction.

The general goal of crisis intervention is to return the person or family to their level of functioning before the crisis developed. Once the family is out of crisis and relatively stable, other forms of therapy can be employed more effectively and the family can begin to mobilize other resources. In some cases crisis intervention may increase the level of functioning over that present before the crisis, but this outcome is not essential for the crisis intervention to be considered successful. Crisis intervention is not a reflective type of therapy; the clinician frequently takes an active and directive role with clients in order to assist them through the crisis period (Aguilera and Messick, 1982).

A mother contacts a crisis intervention center and reports that her eleven-year-old daughter has just revealed that the mother's live-in boyfriend has been fondling her for several months. When the mother confronted the boyfriend, he denied the abuse took place, but he has moved out of the house and away from the area. The mother says that the boyfriend was the family's only source of income, that her daughter is so embarrassed about the abuse that she is threatening to run away, and that the girl's two older brothers are also embarrassed and are encouraging the girl to leave home. The mother is unsure how to support the daughter and how to make the upcoming rent payment.

Sesan, Freeark, and Murphy (1986) state the following goals for crisis intervention with sexually abused children and their families: giving "permission" for the family to discuss the abuse, exposing previously unexpressed fears, allowing ventilation of feelings, putting the abuse and the effects of the abuse into proper perspective, exploring the reasons for the child's vulnerability to sexual abuse and beginning to lessen the vulnerability, and planning future therapeutic work. Indications that the crisis intervention has been successful include: The family has an accurate perception of what occurred and of the possible effects on the child and family; the affect is being properly managed in that individuals are aware of their feelings and these feelings are being discharged appropriately; and the family is seeking and using the help that is available (Simrel, Berg, and Thomas, 1979). As can be seen from these descriptions, restructuring the family system, gaining insight into various members' behavior, and inducing personality changes are not attempted during the crisis intervention stage. Rather, the clinician works to stabilize the family and to have its members begin to explore the abuse in an appropriate manner so that these long-term goals can be effectively pursued. In some cases the family may be handling the abuse situation well, and little time will need to be spent on crisis intervention. Other families may need considerable directive intervention before other forms of therapy are appropriate.

Because crisis intervention is aimed at ameliorating the effects of a specific crisis, determining which event precipitated the crisis should be the clinician's first objective. The events precipitating the crisis may be quite different in cases involving incestuous and nonincestuous abuse, and a different aspect of the total abuse situation may have precipitated a crisis for various members of a particular family. For instance, if a child is sexually assaulted one time by a stranger, the precipitating event for all members of the family may be the assault, and the crisis intervention would then focus on the family members' reaction to the assault and its aftermath. In the case of a long-term sexual involvement between a child and a neighbor, the precipitating event for the mother and father may be the revelation of the sexual abuse and their consequent perception that they have failed as parents, while the precipitating event for the victim may be the fact that parents and friends have discovered the sexual activity and the fear of being expelled from the family. When a case of long-standing incest is revealed, the loss of the father's income may be the precipitating event for a mother who was unaware of the father/child relationship, while the sudden intrusion of the criminal justice system into his life may be the precipitating event for the father.

When family members are experiencing different crises, it is important to address each crisis, otherwise an unresolved crisis for one member may impede work with the entire family. In some situations concerns can be addressed individually, as when dealing with the perpetrator's interactions with the legal system. In other situations it may be valuable to deal with an individual crisis—for instance, a victim's fears of abandonment by the family—in a family session as a way of alerting all family members to the concerns of one member.

Because of the variety of crises that a clinician can face in sexual abuse cases, we do not believe it possible to outline specific steps that should be taken with each individual or family. Instead, in the following sections we summarize the themes that frequently arise in these cases. Awareness of these themes may facilitate the clinicians noticing them if they begin to emerge in treatment. For an outline of a generic form of crisis intervention, the reader is referred to Aguilera and Messick (1982).

General Process and Techniques

Although some of the crisis intervention process in cases of extrafamilial abuse involves individual counseling with the victim, Sesan, Freeark, and Murphy (1986) write that a significant portion of crisis intervention should be done with the family as a whole. In this way, other family members can be encouraged to join together and show support for the victim.

Helping the Victim. Two of the important goals of crisis intervention with victims are protecting the child from self-induced harm or harmful actions by others and encouraging the child to begin a discussion of the abuse and his or her reactions to it. An important first step with the victim is to reduce the possibility that self-induced harm will occur. Recall from Chapter Four that many victims contemplate or attempt suicide and other self-destructive behaviors. The suicide potential of the child should be carefully probed; hospitalization may be required if the potential is high (Anderson and Shafer, 1979). Because the victim may be contemplating running away, this possibility should also be investigated.

In some cases of abuse, the perpetrator may have encouraged the child's silence by detailing dire consequences if the child revealed the abuse. Some of these consequences may have occurred, such as the jailing of the perpetrator or the parents' blaming the child for the abuse, which may make a fear of the other threatened consequences intense. By asking about any threats made by the perpetrator, the clinician may be able to understand the extent of the child's concerns about them.

Some authors suggest that children be reassured that they will be protected from further abuse and any actions that perpetrators may have threatened. Some caution may be advisable in this regard however. Despite all efforts, no clinician is able to guarantee either that the child will not be abused again or that other consequences, such as being rejected by family members, will not occur. Promises that eventually are not kept may reduce the value of the child's therapeutic involvement with the clinician. It may be best to outline the steps that the clinician and others have and will take for the safety of the child, discuss the ways in which these steps are designed to protect the child, and encourage the child to discuss any situations arising in the future that cause the child to feel unsafe.

Another important task with the child is to encourage a discussion of the abuse experience and the feelings that surrounded it. Children may believe that discussing the sexual aspects of the abuse is not proper; beginning such a discussion in the supportive environment of therapy can encourage its appropriate continuation with parents. The clinician can also encourage the child to identify and understand feelings and to reconcile ambivalent feelings. Depending on the age and preferences of the child, exploration of feelings can be accomplished by talking, through the use of dolls, or by drawing (Sesan, Freeark, and Murphy, 1986; Simrel, Berg, and Thomas, 1979). Older children may have fears about the effects that the sexual abuse will have on them, such as whether they will become homosexual or promiscuous. These fears may be probed for, although not in a way that suggests them to the child. Other fears about the reactions of parents and friends can be discussed, and methods for dealing with these people and their reactions can be discussed and practiced through role play.

In an age-appropriate way, clinicians can discuss with victims the need for and the process of any upcoming medical procedures. In this way, clinicians can help children understand the procedures and can reduce their sense of being helpless participants in a series of confusing events. Feelings about these upcoming events or about procedures that have already occurred should be explored (Sesan, Freeark, and Murphy, 1986). The implications of any medical reports should be reviewed at an appropriate level with each child.

Helping the Parents. Authors who have written about crisis intervention in cases of extrafamilial abuse have generally outlined a greater number of procedures to use with the parents than with the child (see Sesan, Freeark, and Murphy, 1986; Simrel, Berg, and Thomas, 1979). These authors appear to be suggesting that effective crisis intervention with the parents is of great importance for the well-being of the victim. Through crisis intervention with the parents, the clinician can affect the reactions of the child by influencing both the parents' reactions to the abuse and the ways in which the parents interact with the child while helping the child cope with the abuse. Sesan, Freeark, and Murphy (1986) and Simrel, Berg, and Thomas (1979) note that some time should be set aside for work with the parents alone during the crisis intervention process. This procedure allows for the ventilation of feelings that the parents do not feel comfortable exhibiting in front of the child and permits the parents to explore fears about the effects of the abuse without frightening the victim.

To help ensure the safety of the child, the clinician can discuss with the parents methods both to protect the child and to make the child feel safe from future abuse or harm that might have been threatened by the perpetrator. If the parents are concerned for the physical safety of themselves or their child, appropriate referrals to police or child protective agencies can be made, or other methods for avoiding harm can be discussed. Sgroi (1978) notes that because child sexual abuse situations may be volatile, the clinician should probe for the possibility of parental violence toward the child or the perpetrator.

During work with the parents, their feelings about the abuse can be explored. Through this process, the clinician indicates the importance of revealing and discussing feelings rather than keeping them secret and models methods for encouraging such discussions with the child. Some parents may blame themselves for the abuse or they may be blamed by members of their extended family, and the appropriateness of this blame can be explored. The chance that rage against the abuser has been displaced to other family members can be discussed (DeVoss and Newlon, 1986). By asking about some of the parents' fears, the clinician can help the parents view them realistically. For instance, the parents may have fears about the consequences for their child, such as future homosexuality or promiscuity

(MacVicar, 1979; Simrel, Berg, and Thomas, 1979). As discussed in Chapter Four, these problems do occur with abuse victims, but most victims do not experience long-lasting devastating effects.

A number of authors suggest that the parents be encouraged to return their family life to normal as soon as possible to provide the victim with a sense of security and a sense that the abuse need not permanently affect his or her life. The clinician may want to encourage the parents to talk with their child about the abuse and can model nonthreatening ways of doing so. Some parents may need assistance in developing ways to discuss the abuse with the victim's siblings or other family members. Strategies for helping their child deal with the reactions of others can be outlined and practiced through role play. Some parents may become overprotective, isolating the child from peers and adults in an attempt to eliminate the chance of any further abuse. The tendency to overprotect the child can be explored with the parents, and appropriate levels and styles of protective behaviors can be discussed (DeVoss and Newlon, 1986).

As was done with the child, the reasons for and process of medical or legal procedures should be reviewed, and the parents' concerns about these procedures can be explored. The results and implications of any medical tests should be discussed as they become available. This process can help to give the parents a realistic perception of the physical effects of the abuse. It may reduce the fears of some parents and may help to raise the concerns of some parents who may be viewing a relatively serious case of abuse nonchalantly.

Special Concerns in Cases of Incest

Most of the crisis intervention strategies that are useful in cases of extrafamilial sexual abuse are also appropriate in cases of incest. However, the incestuous family almost always is faced with a more complicated legal, financial, and emotional situation than is the family of a child abused by someone outside the family. In this section we suggest additional areas that the clinician may want to explore with incestuous families. Many authors believe that the same fear that may have kept many families from revealing the incest initially, the destruction of the family, is the precipitating event of their crisis. To reduce the strength of these fears the clinician "must be seen as a person in a position of authority who can help resolve the situation" (Topper and Aldridge, 1981, p. 122).

Ryan (1986) notes the importance of clinicians' not making promises about matters that are out of their control. Specifically, he notes that some clinicians are prone to reassure the family at this stage that the legal system will show leniency if all is revealed when, in fact, the clinician has no control over the charges that are brought against the father or the treatment he will receive in court. If the clinician's promises are not kept, the family may begin to view the father as the victim, a situation that can greatly impede any subsequent therapy.

Helping the Victim. Hoorwitz (1983) and James and Nasjleti (1983) suggest that it is critical for the victim of incest to feel that the clinician will be able to function as a powerful adult ally, especially when the perpetrator and mother appear to have joined against the child. An adult ally can provide the child with the necessary emotional support to endure what is often a difficult legal and therapeutic process. If the child has been removed from the home, concerns about the removal and the problems that may have arisen in the child's adjustment should be addressed. If the child is unable to see the family at all, some form of communication between family members through the clinician may be advisable. Where appropriate, this communication can provide the child with the sense that he or she has not been abandoned by the entire family and may facilitate the family's eventual reunification.

The child may feel pressure from a number of sources to retract the accusation. Herman (1983) states that in order to counteract this pressure, the child should continue to receive support from the clinician for revealing the abuse and for not retracting the accusation. One method Herman suggests is to tell the child that most victims feel pressure to retract the accusation and to state that if the child feels the need to do so, the clinician will provide the support needed to resist. However, encouragement for the child to resist the temptation to withdraw the accusation may be dependent on the clinician's belief that the accusation is accurate. As noted in Chapter Seven, in a small but perhaps increasing number of instances, children have been encouraged by one parent to make a false accusation of incest against the other. The appropriate actions when the child's therapist suspects that the child's accusation is false are unclear. Encouraging the child to continue with the accusation may place increased pressure on the child to harm a parent that the child is attached to. However, it would be presumptuous for a clinician to encourage a child to withdraw an accusation based only on the clinician's suspicion of its accuracy. Such a situation places the clinician in an ethical and moral dilemma.

It may be appropriate for a clinician to tell the child that the clinician is available to discuss feelings about retracting the accusation and that, before a retraction is made, such a discussion would be desirable. The clinician can then gain an understanding of the child's reasons for considering a retraction and can determine the extent to which the child should be encouraged to maintain the accusation. Emotional support of the child is just as important in cases where a false accusation is being made. Consequently, the clinician should be able to provide nonjudgmental support to the child regardless of the truth or falsehood of the accusation.

Another difficult situation can arise when a clinician assigned by the court to investigate an accusation of incest believes that the accusation is false, while a clinician who is the therapist for the child believes that it is true. A similar situation may occur if one clinician involved with the child or family believes that it is in the child's best interest to retract an accusation, while another clinician believes that it should be maintained. Without close cooperation between these clinicians and care in the way they interact with the child, the child may experience subtle or overt pressure from each clinician to act in a certain way. This pressure has the potential for greatly increasing the stress on the child. Suggestions of methods that have been used by clinicians to resolve these dilemmas would be valuable additions to the literature.

Helping the Mother. The victim's mother may have grave

concerns about financial issues if the family is dependent on the perpetrator, and these concerns may take precedence early in the crisis intervention process. Resolving these concerns can provide the family with a stable environment and allow the mother to deal with her own emotional concerns and those of her children. In some cases, a mother can be guided to appropriate social service agencies for assistance, although such a solution may embroil mothers in a bureaucracy that they are unwilling or unable to cope with without additional support from the clinician. In some situations, assistance and support to a mother moving into a less expensive apartment or trying to find a part-time job may be an important clinical function. Some mothers may need specific step-by-step instructions or direct assistance from the clinician. Therefore, a clinician working in these types of crisis situations must have an accurate knowledge of the various types of support available within the community. Communities that intend to deal effectively with child sexual abuse must directly address the issue of providing support for families that need it in order to continue functioning as a unit.

The suicide potential of the mother should be assessed. Recall that mothers in incestuous families have often been described as depressed, and the revelation of the incest and the concomitant increase in stress may push a depressed mother further along the road to suicide.

Many mothers will feel ambivalent about whether to support the victim or the perpetrator. If the mother supports the father, she may risk alienating her daughter; if she supports the daughter, she may risk losing financial and emotional support from the father. Even if the mother supports the victim initially, she may feel increasing pressure to support the father as the case continues. Several authors believe that the clinician should help the mother explore these feelings and should assist the mother in maintaining her support of the victim (Herman, 1983; Hoorwitz, 1983; James and Nasjleti, 1983).

The issue of the mother's responsibility should probably be addressed at this time. Many mothers may struggle with the question of whether society (possibly as embodied by the clinician) blames them for the abuse (for instance, by assuming that if they had provided sufficient sexual stimulation to their husbands, the abuse would not have occurred). To avoid the un-known reactions of society, the mother may be propelled to withdraw from society and therapy. Even a mother who re-mains in therapy may avoid discussing any feelings of responsi-bility, although her unspoken concerns may continue to bother her and impede therapy.

Helping the Father. The incestuous father may find him-self with no place to live, no job, and no support system once the incest is revealed, and he will usually find himself in the middle of a legal process about which he may have little under-standing. Consequently, as with the mother, assistance with tasks such as finding a job, setting up independent housekeep-ing, and dealing with the police or probation department may be a priority during the crisis intervention process (Webb-Wood-ard and Woodard, 1982). During this time the father may also need the emotional support of a clinician. Although providing such support may be difficult for many clinicians, it is possible to do so without condoning the sexual abuse (Hoorwitz, 1983). Helping the father may facilitate family reunification in cases where it is desired, which may benefit all family members in-cluding the victim. The suicide potential of the father should also be assessed, as well as his potential for violence toward the victim or the mother (Sgroi, 1978).

Helping Siblings. Although one research study showed that the siblings of the victim were the most disturbed family members one year after the incest had been revealed (Kroth, cited in Goodwin, 1982a), there is almost no mention in the lit-erature of the concerns of the siblings in an incestuous family or of how they should be dealt with during the crisis intervention process. James and Nasjleti (1983) mention that the siblings may be just as confused as the mother about whether to sup-port the victim or the perpetrator once the incest is revealed. Because the siblings are a potential source of support for the victim, an exploration of these feelings with the siblings may be beneficial to both them and the victim. The siblings may also need the opportunity to express their fears about the dissolu-tion of the family and about their own safety and the reactions of their friends if the incest becomes public knowledge.

As noted in Chapter Five, in some incestuous families the

father sexually or physically abuses several children. These other children may have had ambivalent feelings about revealing the abuse, and now that they see the reactions of those around them to the accusation of the identified victim, these feelings may be intensified. It may be beneficial for the siblings to discuss their feelings about revealing such abuse because dealing with these feelings may be difficult. An important question for the clinician is whether to pressure a sibling to reveal suspected previous abuse. Revealing the abuse of a sibling may help the prosecution of the perpetrator, but it may also embroil another child in the legal aspects of the case. Although the clinician is generally required to report suspected sexual abuse of a sibling, the extent to which the clinician should probe for this information is another dilemma.

Treatment Planning

During the course of crisis intervention, the clinician should be forming hypotheses about whether treatment for the victim or family will be needed once the crisis has been resolved and, if so, what the most appropriate form will be. In some cases the clinician may be the one to provide further therapy, and a gradual shift from the directive, crisis intervention mode of therapy to a form of longer-term therapy will occur. In other cases the clinician will recommend that the client or family begin treatment with another clinician known to be expert in a certain type or types of therapy. Several factors can be considered when planning future treatment. It is most appropriate to consider questions about future treatment in the following order: Should additional treatment be given? If further treatment is appropriate, what should the focus of the treatment be? And, finally, what treatment mode is best suited for the needs of the victim or the family or both?

Should Treatment Be Given? Consider the following case:

> A parent calls a friend who is a clinician to ask her advice. The parent's eight-year-old child has just revealed, almost casually, that she had been fondled

on two occasions by a counselor while at a day camp the previous summer. The child does not seem to be bothered by the incident and has shown no negative behaviors since the incident six months ago. Nevertheless, the parent is concerned that the child may have been adversely affected but does not want to upset the child by making too much of the incident. The parent asks the clinician to recommend whether the child should be taken for some therapy.

The assumption in most of the treatment literature appears to be that victims of nearly all forms of child sexual abuse would benefit from some form of therapy after any initial crisis is resolved. Although there is some debate about the type of therapy that is most appropriate for certain types of cases, there is limited debate about whether some sort of therapy should be provided. One probable reason for this recommendation is that it is based on treatment programs described in the literature, most of which have dealt with children traumatized by relatively long-term incest. Recall from Chapter Three, however, that children who are brought to treatment are a small and generally unrepresentative sample of sexual abuse victims. Therefore, assuming that all victims of child sexual abuse need treatment because of the disturbed nature of those whose treatment has been described might be erroneous.

A few authors question the need of all victims for treatment. Conte (1984a) hypothesizes that mental health professionals, as well as those in the legal and social service fields, may cause harm to victims through "system-induced trauma"—through requiring children or adults to relive sexual abuse experiences that they have adequately dealt with previously. "It seems important for the therapist to be open to the idea that the client may have resolved the experience and be ready to live life as an individual—not as a member of mental health 'victims' " (Conte, 1984a, p. 260). Conte's caution may be best applied to instances where the sexual abuse occurred considerably before it was revealed, but research has shown that this type of delayed reporting often occurs. Mrazek (1980) doubts that providing trial psychotherapy to sexually abused children who show every indication of handling the situation well is valuable. He believes that there should be some indication that therapy is needed before it is begun.

One indicator of the need for therapy used by clinicians is the identity of the perpetrator. Several authors state that abuse that is nonviolent and does not involve a family member can often be dealt with successfully by using crisis intervention techniques with the victim and parents (MacVicar, 1979; Sgroi, 1978). Cases involving an extended family member or a trusted adult in the child's life may require therapy, depending on the length and type of abuse, but often the therapy can be short term (Sgroi, 1978). Some believe that cases involving a nuclear family member may take several years to resolve because of the many emotions aroused and the inappropriate family behavior patterns that have become entrenched (Porter, Blick, and Sgroi, 1982).

The amount and quality of support that is available to the victim from within the family and through other networks may also influence the clinician's decision about the need for therapy. Victims with greater levels of support from family members or friends may need less therapeutic support from a clinician (Porter, Blick, and Sgroi, 1982). This hypothesis has received some empirical support. Conte and Schuerman (1987) found that children with higher levels of social support reacted less negatively to an abuse experience.

Three other factors that can be considered also come from the empirical research on the consequences of child sexual abuse. Recall from Chapter Four that the only factors that consistently predicted the amount of distress to the victim were physical coercion during the abuse, presence of negative parental reaction, and prior mental health of the victim. These studies indicate that abuse involving physical violence or abuse to which the child's parents have reacted in a condemning manner is usually more detrimental to the child and thus may require a longer course of therapy, and that abuse experienced by a child with good prior emotional health may require less treatment.

Although these indicators have been discussed in the literature, methods for evaluating whether some form of treatment is or is not needed have not been clearly outlined at this time. The current strategy of many clinicians appears to be to provide more extensive therapy to children who have experienced abuse that has been traumatic for other children, even if the children display no symptoms. The assumption behind this strategy appears to be that the risk of providing therapy to a child who does not need it is outweighed by the benefit of providing it to children who do need it but show no overt sign of needing it. This is, however, an assumption. There may be negative aspects to providing therapy to some children– for example, they may assume that something must be wrong with them because "you do not go to the doctor unless you are sick." An important aspect of therapy with these children may be to examine their belief about the meaning of their involvement in therapy as a way of counteracting any misconceptions.

Choosing the Focus of Additional Treatment. If the clinician chooses to recommend some form of therapy past the crisis intervention stage, the next important decision concerns the initial focus of the therapy. Although this focus may change through the course of treatment, deciding on the best initial focus may be an important task, especially with children who may not be allowed to remain in therapy for a long period of time. One decision is whether to focus on the sexual abuse or on the client's current behaviors. Several factors may affect this decision, including the amount of time since the abuse ended and the clinician's theoretical perspective on the course that therapy should take. Borgman (1984), for instance, writes that his experiences with sixteen sexually abused adolescent girls in group treatment homes indicated that addressing the previous sexual abuse in depth during therapy would have been counterproductive because doing so would have allowed the girls to avoid dealing directly with the behavioral problems that they were exhibiting at the time. Other clinicians may believe that the previous abuse is the most meaningful cause of the client's current behavior and thus choose to concentrate on the sexual abuse experience.

When treating child victims, the clinician must also choose the time of the child's life on which to focus. Recall the discussion of the source of the negative consequences of child sexual abuse in Chapter Four. We asserted that, theoretically, the principal source of trauma seen in the child could be associated with the child's life before the abuse began, the abuse itself, or the events occurring after the abuse. The clinician can use this model to hypothesize about the chief source of the child's disturbance. During the early phase of treatment, a thorough history of the sexual abuse should be taken, and a developmental assessment of the victim and his or her family should be made. In the case of incest, the assessment of the relationships within the family are of increased importance. Once the assessment is made, the clinician can use information about the abuse, victim, and family to make initial treatment recommendations. It may be apparent that the family atmosphere has produced deficits in all of the children and that the victim exhibited symptoms of distress before the abuse began. This situation might call for interventions aimed at helping the child achieve missed emotional development, with relatively less emphasis initially placed on exploring the abuse. In other situations it may be clear that the child's disturbance coincided with the onset of the abuse, and in still others, with the revelation of the abuse. The focus of treatment might be on the abuse and its aftermath for these children.

Another important consideration in determining the focus of treatment is the apparent amount of time that the child will be involved in therapy. Although this amount will often be difficult to judge, in some situations a court order or parental interest may make it likely that the child will attend therapy for a long period of time, while those situations in which the parents or the child or both are ambivalent may make a long course of therapy doubtful. If it appears that the child will be in therapy for only a short period of time, beginning an exploration of ambivalent feelings about the abuse or trying to restructure the child's role in the family may be inappropriate because volatile issues may only be brought to the surface and not resolved. In these cases, work to help the child develop assertive and self-protective skills may be the most beneficial.

Choosing Methods for Exploring the Abuse. If the clinician decides that an in-depth exploration of the sexual abuse experience should be undertaken, a number of treatment modalities can be employed. Unfortunately, the choice of treatment is sometimes dictated solely by the orientation of available clinicians or by the space available in certain treatment programs. In other cases a wide range of treatment is available. Most clinicians prefer to involve a victim in individual counseling first, seeing it as the most effective way to engage the child and begin work on issues of specific interest to the child. Hazzard, King, and Webb (1986) hypothesize that it may be especially important for sexually abused adolescents with severe psychopathology to receive individual therapy. Although they give no reasons for this position, it may be that severely disturbed adolescents need individualized therapy or that they are unable to join a group emotionally and their presence would have negative implications for both them and the other members of the group. Other individual factors of the client may also be important to consider when making a treatment choice. For instance, Mrazek (1980) suggests that children who are withdrawn from their peer group benefit from early placement in group treatment, while those who continue to show signs of internalized unresolved conflicts or high levels of anxiety should remain in individual treatment for a longer period of time.

Some clinicians argue that group therapy can be superior to individual therapy once any initial crisis has been resolved. For instance, James and Nasjleti (1983) note that because of the face-to-face nature of individual therapy, the child may feel pressure to engage in a possibly painful discussion of the abuse. In a group setting, the child may be able to discuss the abuse at a comfortable pace. Children who have trouble expressing emotions about their abuse in individual therapy may be able to express emotions in reaction to the experiences of other group members. Individual therapy may also reinforce the notion of sexual abuse as the child's secret because what is said is generally held to be confidential between the child and the therapist. Steward and others (1986) note that group therapy is appropriate even for victims who appear most disturbed. They suggest that the undivided attention that the clinician gives to the child in individual therapy may be the cause of the apparent disturbance in some cases, especially if the clinician is of the same gender as the child's abuser.

A central issue in treatment planning for an incestuous family is whether the eventual goal of therapy is the reunification of the family. When it is, a number of treatment programs may be followed (these are described in Chapter Twelve). (When reunification is not desirable, most clinicians suggest individual or group therapy or both for the perpetrator, mother, and victim.) Authors generally stress that both parents must be willing to commit themselves to a possibly long and difficult process in order to achieve eventual reunification (Mrazek, 1980; Topper and Aldridge, 1981). Goodwin and Owen (1982) state that reunification is seldom desirable for a family in which the father has attempted or completed intercourse with a child under the age of seven because the father is almost always psychopathic. Interestingly, in general there is little mention of the advantages and disadvantages of assessing the victim's reaction to family reunification, although this may be an important factor, especially with an adolescent victim.

Another potentially useful way to plan treatment for a particular incestuous family is to assess the reason for the occurrence of incest in that family. Recall that in Chapter Five four different theories for the occurrence of incest were described: functional, feminist, chaotic, and individual psychopathology. Those conceptualizing incest from each of these perspectives also suggest therapeutic interventions. For instance, a family that resembles the typical incestuous family described from the family systems perspective may be a prime candidate for family therapy and eventual reunification. A family terrorized by an uncaring father may need protection from the father and financial support from social service agencies. A chaotic family may need the services of a social worker, and a family with a perpetrator with psychopathology may need to receive financial and emotional support while the perpetrator receives intensive psychotherapy or is incarcerated (or both).

Summary

The clinician who first comes into contact with a child sexual abuse victim and family faces three important tasks–protecting the victim from further abuse, providing crisis intervention to the victim and family, and planning further treatment. Most clinicians recommend that protecting the victim from further abuse be done by consulting with the family in cases of extrafamilial abuse and by removing the father from the home in cases of incest. When the clinician believes that the victim faces a hostile family environment or is in danger of further abuse, removal of the victim to a temporary foster home or shelter may be appropriate.

Many victims and families are in crisis when the abuse is first revealed because of a lack of coping strategies for handling such situations. The clinician should help those in crisis ventilate their emotions and in an active, directive manner guide them in successfully coping with the many changes that the revelation of the abuse may cause for the family and each member.

When planning future treatment, the clinician should first consider whether further treatment is indicated. The clinician should then determine the focus of therapy and the treatment mode that best suits the idiosyncratic nature of each case.

CHAPTER TEN

Individual Treatment

I ndividual treatment may be employed solely for crisis intervention in some cases, and in others it will continue to be used after the crisis has been resolved and long-term therapy is begun. Individual therapy is valuable as either the main form of treatment or as an initial part of the therapeutic process because it can be (a) the least threatening form of treatment, especially during the early stages of therapy, (b) most easily tailored to the specific needs of the client, and (c) used to prepare the client for other forms of treatment. If the client later begins group or family therapy, concurrent individual treatment can help the client explore issues that arise during these sessions or work through issues that the client does not yet feel able to reveal in the other settings.

Although we outline here some of the techniques of individual treatment that have been used with child victims and parents, we assume that the general form of treatment will be guided mainly by the individual clinician's theoretical orientation and therapeutic style. Consequently, we do not outline specific intervention styles that have been used in cases of child sexual abuse. We are not sure that there is an ideal way to provide individual therapy to sexual abuse victims and their families; at any rate, the superiority of one form of therapy over another has not yet been demonstrated.

This chapter focuses on the themes that clinicians have found to be of importance with victims and their parents. Many of these themes also appear in group and family treatment. By referring to Chapter Four, the reader can obtain additional information on important treatment themes by understanding the consequences that have been observed in many victims. Not all these themes or therapy issues will occur with each victim. However, by being aware of the issues found in other cases of child sexual abuse, the clinician can develop possible strategies for dealing with them should they arise. Also, by being aware of the themes that have occurred with other clients, the clinician can explore for their presence with his or her clients, reducing the risk that an important theme will go unnoticed.

Treating the Victim

Development of Rapport. As is the case with therapy in general, developing rapport and an alliance with the sexually abused child is an important goal early in the therapeutic relationship. A number of factors may make this task even more difficult with sexually abused children than with other children in therapy. Burgess and Holstrom (1978) note that the children initially may be reluctant clients for several reasons. They may not realize why they are being brought to therapy and may believe that it is either some sort of punishment (as when a child who misbehaves in school is taken to the principal) or an indication that something is wrong with them (as when a child is taken to a physician when physically ill). The authors state that it is important, therefore, for the clinician to determine the child's beliefs about the reason for therapy and to correct any misconceptions early in therapy. Another hindrance to rapport building is that the child may not understand the difference between a previous investigation and the current therapy, and may believe that the clinician has the same role as those who investigated the possibility that the child had made a false accusation

(Jones, 1986). A child who had a negative experience during the investigation may be especially reluctant to deal with the clinician. In order to reduce the interference that previous investigations may have on therapy, clinicians can discuss their role with the children and contrast it to the role of previous investigators.

Another factor that may contribute to the difficulty of building rapport is the similarity of the relationship that clinicians may tell children they can have in therapy and the relationship that the children had with abusers. Clinicians may tell children that they will have a special relationship in which what they say and do will remain confidential. To a young child, this may appear to be the same sort of secret relationship fostered and then insisted upon by the abuser. Clinicians may allow children to play freely during therapy, and abusers may have allowed the same sort of freedom while seducing the children. Therapy may include a good deal of sexually oriented play or discussion of sexual matters, and such play or discussions may also have occurred with the abuser. We are not raising these parallels to discourage clinicians from using confidentiality, free play, or discussions of sexual matters in therapy; rather, we mention them to alert clinicians to the effect that these actions may have on some children. Being aware of these possibilities should encourage clinicians to make considerable efforts to ensure that their role is clear to the children. Children abused by trusted adults may be hesitant to place their trust in the clinician, especially if trust between the perpetrator and child was used by the perpetrator to keep the child from revealing the abuse. The clinician with such a child for a client may have to expect that only through a long, gradual process will the child be able to develop a sense of trust in the therapeutic relationship.

General Themes. Clinicians report that some of their sexually abused child clients exhibit sexualized behavior toward them during therapy; others exhibit anger through aggression toward them or by breaking dolls or other toys in the therapy room. Although these sexualized or aggressive behaviors do not appear to occur regularly in therapy with sexually abused children, it seems wise for the clinician to make some preliminary plans about whether the behaviors will be allowed, whether they will be stopped if they appear, or whether limitations should be put on behavior at the beginning of therapy. Jones (1986) notes that setting limits initially can be helpful in reducing the anxiety that a child can develop if given free rein to act in any way during therapy. Initial limitations may also forestall the clinician from having to require that a child stop certain behaviors. A disadvantage to initial limit setting may be that in some cases the child will receive the message that only certain thoughts or emotions can be expressed in therapy. Limits may also prohibit the clinician from experiencing the sexualized behaviors that the child may be engaging in with others, denying the clinician the opportunity to discuss these behaviors with the child. Clearly, the advantages and disadvantages of initial limit setting must be carefully considered in each case. The child's behavior in previous therapeutic or assessment sessions or parents' reports of the child's behavior may be useful. If the clinician decides not to set initial limits, an assessment of how much of each behavior will be accepted and of methods for stopping excessive angry or sexualized behavior should be made.

Regardless of the type of abuse, children may need to work through concerns about trust and safety. These issues may be most salient to children abused by a trusted adult, although young children or children who have been taught that all adults are trustworthy may find it difficult to develop trust in any adult after the abuse, even if it was perpetrated by a stranger.

Anger is an important emotion to explore with victims. Again, those abused by a trusted adult, especially by a parent, may have even more intense feelings of anger. Children may also be angry at parents, police, child protective or social service workers, or mental health professionals for their treatment after the abuse was revealed. Guilt is another frequent emotional response that can be caused by children's perceived responsibility for the sexual activity or for the changes that have occurred in the family. These two emotional responses regularly occur during therapy with victims (see Chapter Four). Because these emotional responses may lead to the development of poor self-esteem (Gelinas, 1983), interpersonal difficulties (Courtois, 1979), and adverse behaviors (Gomes-Schwartz, Horowitz, and Sauzier,

1985), their exploration and resolution should be important components of therapy.

Sexually abused children may also experience considerable fear (Jones, 1986; Porter, Blick, and Sgroi, 1982). This fear may be heightened if the perpetrator is not incarcerated or if the perpetrator had threatened to harm the child if the abuse was revealed. Resolution of the ways in which this fear is expressed (such as fear of sleeping in one's own bedroom) may be an important step in allowing the child to resume a normal life (Goodwin and Owen, 1982). Resolution of fears may be accomplished by exploring the child's fearful emotions and/or by instituting specific steps that will make the child feel safe, perhaps with the parents' cooperation, such as putting additional locks on doors or windows.

Another important way to help children resume a normal life is to aid them in reestablishing normal attendance and performance at school (Goodwin and Owen, 1982; MacVicar, 1979). School is an essential ingredient in both the intellectual and social development of children, but the sexually abused child may be reluctant to attend, especially if the abuse has become public knowledge. Methods for coping with reactions of friends and possible taunts by others can be discussed and practiced with both the child and parents, although care should be taken not to encourage the child or parents to overestimate or overreact to the responses of others. Tutoring or special academic help may be advisable if the child has had to miss school or has performed poorly because of the abuse or the subsequent investigation. In some exceptional cases, reassignment to another school may be an option worth considering.

Children may have concerns about why they were "chosen" to be abused, and they may need some guidance in understanding the perpetrator's motivation for choosing them as victims. Some children may view the abuse as punishment for previous misdeeds and thus believe themselves to be evil. This view may contribute to the feelings of responsibility for the abuse that many victims express (Gelinas, 1983). Others may view the abuse as a sadistic attack (MacVicar, 1979). Concerns about being chosen may be especially great for a boy abused by a man because he may wonder whether his own unrecognized homosexual tendencies were responsible for attracting the perpetrator to him (Nasjleti, 1980; Rogers and Terry, 1984). One way to deal with these concerns may be to emphasize to the child that abusers often molest many children and do not seem to pick victims because of unusual characteristics (for instance, Abel, Becker, Murphy, and Flanagan, 1981, found that subjects from a group of homosexual pedophiles had averaged thirty-one victims each, and heterosexual pedophiles had averaged sixty-two victims each).

Porter, Blick, and Sgroi (1982) suggest that sexually abused children suffer from a "damaged goods syndrome"—that is, they become concerned that they will be permanently damaged physically, socially, or morally by the abuse. The reactions of parents or others in the child's life may exacerbate these concerns. A complete physical examination and thoughtful review of the findings should help to quell concerns about permanent physical harm. Helping the child to view the abuse as a painful experience but one that does not have to have permanent negative consequences can aid in the elimination of fears about other forms of damage. Detailed sex education, concentrating on the physical and emotional effects of abuse on later sexual functioning, may be of value for adolescents. Close work with the child's family about these concerns may play an even greater role in reducing fears than work with the child because the unaddressed fears of the parents may continue to affect the victim long after therapy has ended.

As noted in Chapter Four, Finkelhor and Browne (1985) have developed an interesting paradigm for understanding the various consequences of child sexual abuse and developing appropriate targets for intervention. They postulate that "the experience of sexual abuse can be analyzed in terms of four trauma-causing factors: . . . traumatic sexualization, betrayal, powerlessness, and stigmatization" (p. 530). These factors and their effects are described in Chapter Four. Here we will discuss the ways these factors manifest themselves. Traumatic sexualization is manifested behaviorally through preoccupation with sexual behavior, sexual dysfunction, or phobic reactions to intimacy. Stigmatization is often manifested in isolation, drug use, criminal activity, or self-destructive behavior. Betrayal is manifested in isolation, vulnerability to other abuse, aggressive behavior, or delinquency. Powerlessness is manifested in somatic or sleep complaints, school problems, phobias, or delinquency. This conceptualization can help the clinician by suggesting specific targets for interventions with a victim. By noticing the child's behaviors or the aspects of the abuse that the child seems most concerned about, the clinician can begin to hypothesize about the aspects of the abuse that are having the greatest impact on each child and make preliminary decisions about the initial focus of therapy. Finkelhor and Browne caution that their conceptualization has not been clinically or empirically tested and, thus, should be viewed only as a general guide for treatment planning. However, it may prove to be a useful tool in deciding on the direction for treatment.

Clinicians must also decide the extent to which their treatment will involve working directly to modify the child's behaviors outside therapy. The child's behavior at home or at school may be affected by the abuse, and some behaviors, such as sexual aggression, may be causing the child great difficulties. If a child is displaying improper behaviors in various settings, the clinician needs to decide whether programs to modify the behaviors are called for and whether other individuals, such as the child's teacher, should be informed of the abuse. If the child is having behavior problems at school, the clinician may be able to contact the teacher and outline a behavior modification plan without mentioning why the child is in therapy. Discussing the abuse may be appropriate in other situations, especially if there are rumors about the source of the child's problems. The potential problems for the child who is labeled as a sexual abuse victim within the school must be considered when deciding whom to inform about the abuse.

A final function of individual treatment may be preparing a victim who will be required to testify in court. Bauer (1983) and Benedek (1982) suggest that a detailed description of courtroom procedures, a visit to the court building, and, if possible, meetings with the prosecuting attorney and the judge are valuable. Bauer suggests other preparation procedures based on the age of the child. For instance, for latency-age children, a role play including questions that will probably be asked in court is often useful. During these role plays, the child's own anatomical vocabulary can be used, although Bauer suggests that the vocabulary that will be used in court should be introduced gradually during this process so that the child will appear competent in court. However, encouraging children to develop a complete technical vocabulary may reduce the value of their testimony by making it appear that they were extensively coached by adults (see Chapter Seven for a discussion of this issue). Adolescent victims should be apprised of the fact that they will be questioned in court and that the value of their testimony will be judged in large part by the consistency of their statements. Tedesco and Schnell (1987) note that those involved in preparing children for surgery have found that including the parents in the process reduces the children's stress. The inclusion of parents in the children's preparation for court testimony may have a similar effect.

Special Concerns of the Incestuously Molested Child. The anger of the victim of incest may be much greater than that of other victims. Several clinicians note that incest victims may be especially angry at their mothers for failing to protect them, whether or not the mothers were consciously aware of the abuse (for instance, Giarretto, 1981; Hoorwitz, 1983). Young children may still view their parents as omnipotent and consequently are likely to believe that their mother knew about the abuse even when it is clear to the clinician that she did not. Helping children to understand the noninvolvement of their mothers may be an important step in therapy, although some hypotheses about children's cognitive development suggest that only with age will children be able to understand this concept. Helping a child to deal with anger may be a difficult process. Kroth (1979), for instance, found that victims nearing the end of treatment had a reduced level of anger toward their incestuous fathers but no reduction in the level of anger toward their nonparticipating mothers.

Victims may be confused about the appropriate roles that

children and parents should have within the family. This confusion may be strongest in a family where the child gradually replaced the mother in the maternal role. Helping the child to understand the roles that children and parents should have within a family through discussion and role play can be important not only for the child at the time but also for the child as a future parent (Hoorwitz, 1983; Porter, Blick, and Sgroi, 1982).

Zefran and others (1982) discuss salient treatment themes for the child according to the type of family situation that resulted after the abuse was revealed: family without abuser, in which the child remains with the mother and other children and the perpetrator permanently leaves the home; family together, in which the long-term goal of treatment is family reunification; and victim without family, in which the family is unable or unwilling to allow the victim to return, and permanent placement outside of the home is sought for the victim. In the family-without-abuser situation, helping the victim and mother communicate their feelings about the abuse is an important step in strengthening their bond. The victim may also need to be able to "say good-bye" and let go of any attachments to the perpetrator, especially if warm feelings were exchanged during the abuse (Goodwin and Owen, 1982). Individual work with the child whose family hopes to reunite may include exploration of the child's feelings about reunification (which may be quite ambivalent and confusing), and preparation of the child for therapy sessions and meetings with the perpetrator or other family members. When it appears that the child will be permanently removed from the home, treatment may cover three themes: the sexual abuse, rejection by the family, and difficulties adjusting to a new living situation. Because the child may be removed from not only parents but all other forms of social support, continuity of contact with the clinician may be especially important in these cases. The child may have no one else with whom to discuss strong feelings of anger and resentment toward family members and no one else from whom to get guidance concerning adjustment to a new home and school and the development of a new system of social support. The clinician may also be the only person available to offer ongoing support during any court proceedings in which the child must participate. In this conceptualization, the sexual abuse receives the greatest emphasis when the family is to remain together, probably because of the salience of the abuse as the victim and family reunite with the perpetrator. Although attention is paid to the sexual abuse in the other two situations, more emphasis is placed on the effect that the change in the family structure will have on the victim.

Use of Drawings and Play with Anatomically Correct Dolls. The use of art and play has been recognized as valuable in therapy with children presenting a wide range of problems. Play and drawing are natural activities of most children, and through them they can often express inner conflicts or concerns with greater ease than by talking. Having sexually abused children draw the abuse scene can provide valuable information that young children may not be able to verbalize because of their emotional state or limited vocabulary and language skills (Kelley, 1985). However, Goodwin (1982b) found that many children had as much difficulty drawing the abuse scene as they had talking about it. Children who will not draw the abuse scene may find other types of drawing easier. For instance, victims can also be asked to draw pictures of themselves or the perpetrators. Kelley (1985) notes that a child who draws sexual anatomy on a self-portrait may be expressing sexual concerns, and a child including the opposite sex's genitalia on a self-portrait may be indicating sex-role confusion. Furthermore, progress in therapy can be hypothesized if these themes disappear from later drawings. Having the victim make a Kinetic Family Drawing or a drawing of his or her house can provide the clinician with a view of the child's world and can act as a stimulus for discussion about the child's family and home. Older children who are reluctant to draw can be asked to make a floor plan of their house as a stimulus for discussion (Goodwin, 1982b).

The use of anatomically correct dolls has increased dramatically since the 1970s. Clinicians can now purchase these expensive dolls from a number of distributors. With these dolls, the child is able to re-create the abuse for the clinician. It may be easier for the child to do this than to describe the scene in words, especially if the child's vocabulary or language skills are limited. The child can also ventilate emotions toward the perpetrator or other family members through the dolls, a procedure that may be far less threatening than directly discussing the child's feelings toward these people. Some clinicians have used the dolls as a way of allowing the child to re-create the abuse many times over the course of therapy. One of the goals of this therapeutic approach is to have the child express, become aware of, and discharge feelings resulting from the abuse. Thus, the dolls play an important role in the overall therapeutic process (Friedrich and Reams, in press).

Jones (1986) prefers merely to have the dolls available and does not encourage the child to use them. He suggests that the use of the dolls in therapy may cause the child to confuse therapy and a previous investigation in which the dolls were used. He also believes that in some cases their use may artificially slant the therapy toward sexual themes and away from concerns that are of more importance to the child. Jones's point is an interesting one. Although it is true that the dolls can be used in nonsexually oriented play and the clinician does not have to encourage the child to use them to act out sexual themes, the child may assume that the dolls are used only for sexual themes if that is how they were used during a previous investigation. In some cases this assumption may direct the child's and clinician's attention away from other pressing therapeutic themes. Consequently, the clinician who uses them should be aware that anatomically correct dolls may have a meaningful effect on the direction of therapy.

Treating Parents from Nonincestuous Families

Much of the therapeutic work with parents of a child who has experienced extrafamilial sexual abuse can be done during the crisis intervention stage. In some situations the clinician may recommend that one or both parents receive additional treatment either as a couple or as individuals. In other cases, the parents may request additional treatment.

The abuse of a child may rouse dormant feelings caused

by the previous sexual or physical abuse of a parent (Sgroi and Dana, 1982). The emergence of these memories and feelings may be traumatic for parents and may interfere with their ability to help their own child. Exploration of the feelings that the parent experienced during the abuse and those that remain, as well as the effect that these feelings have had on interactions with the child, can be beneficial as a way of understanding both personal feelings and the emotions that the child may be experiencing (Gomes-Schwartz, Horowitz, and Sauzier, 1985). DeVoss and Newlon (1986) suggest that parents may be helped to channel their anger constructively by advocating for victims in public policy matters.

Other parents need help in other areas. They may need assistance in developing a protective home environment in which the chance for recurrence of the abuse is minimized. Individual or couple therapy also may be useful to help some parents develop their parenting skills. Other parents may need ongoing guidance to handle the changing emotional and behavioral responses of their child to the abuse (DeVoss and Newlon, 1986; Lyon and Cassady, 1986).

Treating Parents from Incestuous Families

Each of the themes that can be raised with parents from nonincestuous families may be of equal importance to parents of incestuous families. Parents from incestuous families may also face a number of other issues, though; these are discussed in this section.

Nonparticipating Mother

The amount and type of individual treatment for the mother will be influenced by (a) her current emotional state, (b) the assessment that the clinician makes about the mother's role in the family and in the incest, (c) the current structure of and future plans for the family, and (d) the mother's inclination and ability to be a source of support for the victim. Based on these factors the clinician may feel several areas are important topics for the initial focus of treatment: the mother's executive function in the family, the mother's relations with the daughter, and the mother's emotional state and reaction to the abuse and its aftermath.

If the perpetrator leaves the home, the mother needs to take control of the emotional and financial concerns of the family. This may be a new experience for many mothers, especially dependent women from the type of incestuous family described as exaggerating traditional family roles (see Chapter Five). Even if the perpetrator remains out of jail and continues to contribute to the family financially, his salary must now also be used to maintain his separate residence, thus reducing the amount available to the family. This change in finances can place a great strain on a family, regardless of income, because their style of living will probably undergo a marked decline. Also, the mother may have depended to some extent on guidance from the father to set the direction for the family, and she must now set this direction and provide support for the children on her own. These changes, disruptive enough by themselves, may be exacerbated by the accompanying intrusion of legal and social service agencies into the family. Mothers may need concrete, ongoing guidance to conduct the affairs of the family successfully, and just as in the crisis intervention stage this guidance may take priority during the early stages of therapy (Sgroi and Dana, 1982). If the perpetrator has left the home permanently, long- and short-term plans may need to be developed to assist the mother in establishing an independent household. Helping the mother in these ways may also enhance the development of a close therapeutic alliance with the clinician, and this alliance can be helpful in later therapeutic work.

An important decision that must be made by the mother at some point is whether she wishes to be reunited with the father. O'Connell (1986) writes that the clinician needs to help the mother become aware of both the advantages and disadvantages to reunification. Discussion of the mother's motives for pursuing or not pursuing reunification is an important aspect of this process, as it may give the clinician useful information about the mother's relations with other family members and her level of dependence on the father.

The relationship between the mother and victim may be quite strained at this time. The mother may have a strange mixture of ambivalent feelings, including concern for the child's well-being, anger at the child, and a sense of being let down by the child (Hoorwitz, 1983; Giarretto, 1981). Contributing to these feelings may be the mother's guilt over the incest, the child's anger toward her, and similar ambivalent feelings toward the father. In some cases, this alienation is a significant emotional burden for the mother, and it interferes with her ability to provide the victim with the emotional support that may be important for the child's recovery. It may also prevent the mother from providing appropriate structure and discipline for the child, and this lack of structure may reduce the child's sense of security in the family. Ryan (1986) cautions against expecting the mother to support the victim soon after disclosure, believing that forcing the alliance may alienate the mother and cause her to leave or ignore treatment. He suggests that the mother be viewed as in the grief process during initial treatment and that she be offered the same type of emotional support as that given to a grieving widow. The mother may also need guidance in setting and maintaining reasonable limits for the victim and the other children in the family as a way of helping her to take concrete steps to improve her position within the family structure and to provide the children with emotional and physical stability (MacVicar, 1979; Sgroi and Dana, 1982).

The mother may have a number of emotions that need exploration—for example, a need for nurturance (Hoorwitz, 1983), an inability to trust, an impaired self-image, unassertiveness, and anger toward the perpetrator and victim (Sgroi and Dana, 1982). Helping the mother with these issues may enable her to feel better about herself and to provide more effective parenting for all of the children in her family. Another important function for the clinician may be to help the mother establish a social network that can provide her with long-term support. One source of this support is a therapy group in which she can interact with and receive support from other mothers from incestuous families. One caution however: Although such a group may be used to develop an initial support network, the clinician may want to encourage the mother to develop a diverse network as her treatment progresses, in order to lessen the possibility that she will begin to identify herself mainly as the mother in an incestuous family. The clinician can encourage the mother to find a support system outside of therapy, or the mother can join a general therapy group where she can interact with mothers from diverse types of families.

The clinician may also help the mother to confront her own conscious or unconscious complicity in the incest. The way that this issue is approached depends on both the clinician's theoretical understanding about the development of incest within a family and the clinician's assessment of the dynamics of the family in question. Some authors believe that confronting the mother with her role in the incest is an important therapeutic process (for example, Giarretto, 1981; Machotka, Pittman, and Flomenhaft, 1967; Sgroi, 1978). Others believe that such a confrontation further victimizes the mother (for example, Wattenberg, 1985). Little guidance is available to clinicians on this mostly theoretical issue.

Perpetrator

Assessment. Incest perpetrators have been found to have a variety of family and social backgrounds; they have several different types of personalities; and some of them have various additional problems. Consequently, a thorough assessment of the father and of the reasons for the occurrence of the incest is vital. Not only will the results of the assessment be used as a guide for the father's treatment, but they can also provide some guidelines about the appropriateness of family reunification and thus may have an impact on the treatment strategies for the mother, victim, and family.

Recall from Chapter Five that several theories attempt to explain the etiology of incest. Supporters of these theories argue that incest is caused by dysfunctional family systems, lack of societal standards, inequality between the sexes, or the preexisting psychopathology of the father. We argue that each of these explanations appears to account adequately for incest in some families and not in others. Thus, an important component of the assessment process is for the clinician to hypothesize about the cause of the incest. Groth's (1978) paradigm of child molesters as either regressed or fixated can provide a valuable guide in this regard. Regressed molesters are defined as those who generally derive sexual gratification from adult heterosexual partners but who seek sexual gratification with children during specific times, such as periods of high stress. For these perpetrators either the family systems or feminist explanations for incest are probably most appropriate. In contrast, fixated molesters have a lifetime pattern of deriving sexual gratification from children. Although they may also have sexual relations with adults, as in a marriage, their primary sexual focus is with children. The individual-psychopathology explanation seems most relevant for these perpetrators. Determining which theoretical category best describes an incest perpetrator will provide information about the type of treatment that he requires and may indicate the prognosis for eventual reunification of the family.

Obtaining a thorough sexual and relationship history from the perpetrator is one part of the assessment process. Because of the increasing concern about the percentage of incestuous fathers who have a primary sexual orientation toward children, questions about the development of sexual awareness, targets of early sexual arousal, and sexual history are crucial. Of central concern are any other sexual contacts that the father had with children when he was an adolescent or adult. Information about his general relationships and his comfort in social situations is also important, as the father may have turned to children for emotional support because of an inability to relate to adults. Specific questions about the circumstances surrounding the onset of the incest as well as about his initial sexual and emotional reactions to the incest may provide clues about the function of the incest for the father and, consequently, about the extent to which the incest was caused by family dynamics. Assessing the extent to which alcohol or other drugs played a part in the incest also provides direction for treatment.

Some authors advocate laboratory assessment of the sexual arousal patterns of incestuous fathers because of the perception that some fathers may not be honest about their sexual preference and because research has shown that child molesters in general report higher arousal to adults and lower arousal to children than their physical responses indicate they have (Abel, Becker, Murphy, and Flanagan, 1981). Laboratory assessment is usually accomplished by having the subject place one of several types of devices around his penis to measure changes in either its diameter or volume during arousal. A measurement is taken with the penis flaccid, and then the man is directed to masturbate to a full erection for another measurement. Arousal is usually measured by the percentage of full erection that the man achieves during the presentation of various stimuli (see Earls and Marshall, 1982). These stimuli usually are either pictures of nude children of various ages and of nude adults or audiotapes describing a variety of sexual and nonsexual encounters between adults and children or adults and other adults. Marshall, Earls, Segal, and Darke (1983) stress the importance of including descriptions of sexual encounters between adults and children that involve varying levels of force (from mutually consenting sex to scenes where the adult brutalizes the child even though the child accedes to his demands) as a way of assessing the extent to which violence or sexuality is a source of the father's arousal.

Although they provide numbers that appear scientific, interpretations of the results of laboratory assessments are subject to debate. Additional research on both normal and sexually deviant individuals' responses to the stimuli is needed. Research by Freund, McNight, Langevin, and Cibiri (1972) showed that twenty normal male college students had higher arousal to pictures of young girls (age six to eight) than to landscapes or to nude young boys. The students' arousal increased with the age of the females and was highest for women the age of the students. The reasons for the students' arousal to the young girls are unclear. They may have been aroused by the girls themselves; the nude pictures may have caused an arousal by reminding them of nude pictures of older females; or their memories or fantasies of sexual encounters with peers may have been activated by the pictures. Research of this type indicates the importance of not merely assessing arousal to a specific stimulus (such as a young girl) but rather of comparing arousal to the deviant stimuli with arousal to normal stimuli (Quinsey and Marshall, 1983).

The results of the laboratory assessment may be combined with the father's history to guide the decision about the appropriateness of therapy designed to reduce his sexual arousal to children. The reason for such therapy is the belief that fathers with high sexual arousal to children will be more inclined to repeat the incest or to abuse children outside the family (Quinsey and Marshall, 1983). However, this hypothesis does not have overwhelming empirical support. Some evidence indicates that arousal patterns match actual sexual practices, but little research specifically examining incest and sexual arousal has been completed.

Treatment. Individual treatment is usually the first of a number of treatment modes in which the perpetrator will be asked to participate. Some treatment programs for the perpetrator may last three years or more, and individual therapy may be continued during the entire course of treatment (Taylor, 1986). Both behaviorally oriented therapies to reduce the father's arousal to children and insight therapies to assist the father in understanding the role of the incest have been used with success. In this section we describe some general treatment themes and then the behaviorally oriented treatments. The insight treatments are often done in a group setting, and they are described in Chapter Eleven; however, many of the themes in these group treatment programs are also meaningful in individual therapy with the perpetrator.

The development of rapport with the perpetrator may be a difficult task. He may believe that everyone who knows of his actions automatically condemns him and thus may enter therapy with a negative attitude toward the clinician or a feeling that the clinician will be unable or unwilling to understand his feelings and beliefs. Also, he may equate the clinician with those from the legal agencies who investigated the case, especially if his treatment has been court ordered, and this perception may increase his defensiveness. As was discussed in detail in Chapter

Eight, the clinician may also have a number of emotional reactions to the perpetrator, and these may be a roadblock to the development of a therapeutic alliance. Clinicians' emotional reactions may be heightened if they have treated the victim or if they experienced sexual abuse as children.

If the clinician's assessment suggests that alcohol or other drugs contributed to the atmosphere in which the incest took place, then substance abuse treatment may be indicated. The clinician may provide this treatment or may refer the perpetrator to a substance abuse program and monitor his progress (Anderson and Shafer, 1979).

According to many clinicians, one of the prerequisites to reuniting the family is the father's assumption of full responsibility for the incest. Rather than taking only the legal responsibility for the abuse, he must also accept the emotional consequences of admitting to the incest (Giarretto, 1982; Sgroi, 1978). If the abuse has been going on for a long time, the perpetrator may have constructed strong defenses against the negative emotions he felt when the abuse began. These defenses will undoubtedly make the uncovering of these painful emotions a difficult therapeutic task for the clinician, and their exploration a difficult task for the father. If the father has convinced himself that his child enjoyed the abuse, that the child had no feelings one way or the other, or that the child's feelings do not need to be considered, he must develop an appreciation of the feelings of others and ways for ascertaining accurately what those feelings are. As part of this overall process, the father should be helped to develop impulse control, which may involve exploring the way in which alcohol or other substances reduce his control (Sgroi, 1978; Taylor, 1986). Anger toward his wife may hinder the development of an empathic attitude toward her or other family members, in which case this anger should be explored (Hoorwitz, 1983).

Sexual relations with his child may have served as an outlet for the father's frustration and anger, as a way of reducing stress, or as a way of gaining emotional support or intimacy. Helping the father to discover the function or functions that the incest served and then finding alternate ways of fulfilling the needs that the incest once fulfilled are important steps in reducing the chance of recidivism.

If the clinician determines that alteration of the father's sexual-arousal patterns is needed, several methods are available. However, although these methods have been shown to alter a man's arousal pattern to stimuli pictures or stories, whether his actual arousal to children and adults is meaningfully altered has not been shown. Also, it has not been demonstrated that even successful altering of arousal patterns has an effect on recidivism of incest. As a result, altering arousal patterns alone cannot be assumed to lower the chance of recidivism (Kelly, 1982).

One altering technique involves pairing aversive experiences with fantasy or pictorial representations of inappropriate sexual stimuli, such as verbal descriptions of sex between an adult and a child or pictures of nude children, and thereafter presenting appropriate sexual stimuli, such as pictures of adult nude women, with no aversive consequences. Hypothetically, the aversive pairing will weaken the rewarding nature of the inappropriate stimuli, and the nonaversive, appropriate stimuli will become rewarding. Generally, clinicians use an overt aversive stimulus, such as an electric shock, or a covert aversive stimulus, such as having the individual imagine himself in prison or being beaten up. In some cases, the man's penile responses are monitored and indicated to him, and when a certain level of arousal is present, an electric shock is given. In this case, the man can avoid the shock by keeping his arousal low (Quinsey, Chaplin, and Carrigan, 1980).

Abel, Becker, and Skinner (1987) report on a process called masturbatory satiation. The man is instructed to reach orgasm through masturbation as quickly as possible using appropriate sexual fantasies. Once he has ejaculated, he is to switch his fantasies to images involving children and continue to masturbate until the total masturbation time is one hour. The individual verbalizes and audiotapes his fantasies throughout the hour session. Taping the appropriate and inappropriate fantasies allows a clinician to review them and suggest changes and also allows the abuser to complete the exercises at home. The authors hypothesize that this technique reinforces the appropriate fantasies through the pleasurable feelings of orgasm and diminishes the fantasies involving children, because they are associated with the relatively nonpleasurable masturbation that occurs after ejaculation. It is assumed that changing the relative strength of the fantasies will alter the man's sexual behavior.

A procedure that can be used with or in place of those just mentioned involves increasing the man's arousal to socially acceptable sexual stimuli. Generally, the man is asked to masturbate regularly to appropriate fantasies or to appropriate sexual stimuli (Marshall, Earls, Segal, and Darke, 1983). As with the masturbatory-satiation program just described, the authors assume that the physical pleasure experienced with appropriate fantasies will reinforce the use of these fantasies and affect the individual's arousal patterns.

Treating Women Who Were Molested as Children

Less has been written about the treatment of women who were molested as children than about the treatment of victims whose abuse is discovered while they are still children, although a few authors describe specific treatment programs for women. Possibly most women abused as children are treated much as a client suffering from another childhood trauma would be.

Lindberg and Distad (1985a) describe seventeen women twenty-two to forty-four years old who were in individual therapy for a variety of concerns. All of them had experienced childhood incest, and all met the criteria for a diagnosis of Post-Traumatic Stress Disorder in that they had experienced "intrusive imagery of the incest, feelings of detachment or constricted affect, sleep disturbance, guilt, and intensification of symptoms when exposed to events resembling the incest trauma" (p. 329). Each woman viewed the sexual abuse as the most psychologically damaging event of her childhood, although many of them had not connected it to their current complaint. The women all lacked close emotional bonds with other people. Lindberg and Distad treated all the women with individual insight therapy. Therapy goals included expressing feelings about and relinquishing responsibility for the incest, understanding their family dynamics, and exploring how their experiences had led to current self-defeating behavior.

McGuire and Wagner (1978) provided individual and couple therapy to women abused as children who complained of sexual dysfunction. These women generally were able to enjoy the actual coital act but felt repulsed by other sensual and sexual acts (they are described in detail in Chapter Six). The treatment was traditional sensate-focus sex therapy: The couples became involved in increasingly intense forms of sensual touching and fondling. The authors note that several important issues arose during therapy. The women often experienced intense rage as the sensate focus progressed. The authors found that it was important to help a woman to direct this anger toward the memory of her abuser in order to keep it from interfering in the sensual work with her current partner. Throughout the course of treatment, it was important to give the woman control over the initiation and extent of the sensual activity, something that she did not have during her previous abuse. As treatment progressed, the women experienced guilt as they began to enjoy the sexual and sensual pleasure. Again, the authors found that helping the women to distinguish between their previous and their current sexual feelings was critical.

In what appears to be the only report of the use of implosive therapy with an incest victim, Rychtarik, Silverman, Landingham, and Prue (1984b) describe their treatment of a woman who experienced fondling by and intercourse with her father between the ages of twelve and fifteen. They had initially seen the woman at age twenty-two in a treatment program for alcohol abuse and later learned of symptoms associated with the incest. Her symptoms were recurrent, intrusive memories of the abuse, anxiety that her fiancé and others would find out about the incest and reject her, and intrusive, angry thoughts about her mother. After admitting her as an inpatient, the authors conducted ninety-minute implosive therapy sessions with her on five consecutive afternoons to reduce the intensity of the memories and feelings. Through imagery, she experienced three scenes: the initial abuse scene with her father, a scene in which her fiancé and others find out about the incest and are disgusted and reject her, and a scene in which she becomes angry with her mother. The authors had the woman complete a state-anxiety questionnaire after each session and monitored her electro-dermal activity as a physiological sign of anxiety.

During each imagery session, the woman experienced high levels of anxiety, although her anxiety steadily decreased during the periods immediately following the imagery as the sessions progressed. At the end of the sessions, in a six-month follow-up, and in a one-year follow-up, the woman said that she was no longer bothered by thoughts about the incest and felt that the treatment had been beneficial. At the one-year follow-up, the woman had experienced a relapse of her drinking, yet she attributed this relapse to her husband's drinking and not to the incest.

Kilpatrick and Best (1984) express concerns over several aspects of the treatment provided by Rychtarik and colleagues: The treatment might have been improperly aimed at desensitizing the woman to sexual abuse or sexual attack; the nature of the implosive therapy might have increased the possibility that the woman would quit treatment; and the focus of the treatment was too narrow. Rychtarik, Silverman, Landingham, and Prue (1984a) respond that the focus of the treatment had been to desensitize the woman not to sexual abuse but to the recurrent intrusions of the incest memory. They note that no research has shown that clients who are properly briefed on implosive therapy and have formed a therapeutic alliance with the clinician are more likely to leave therapy than are other clients, and some research indicates that they may complete therapy more often than other clients. The authors also maintain that the return of the woman's drinking problem could be attributed to factors besides the incest, and they believe they effectively minimized the effects of the memories of the incest on the woman's life.

An evaluation of this treatment method cannot be made solely on the basis of one case study. Future controlled studies of this or other behaviorally oriented therapies should indicate their value in the treatment of women molested as children. It is worthwhile noting again that the authors had admitted the woman as an inpatient before the imagery was begun, an important step that allows the patient to be closely monitored during the intense therapy.

Summary

Individual therapy is often used as the first step in the therapeutic process with victims and their parents. Through individual therapy, the client can be introduced to the therapeutic process, issues of immediate concern can be addressed, and the client can be prepared for subsequent forms of therapy. If the client becomes involved in group or family therapy, individual therapy may be continued as a way of supporting the client during the other phases of treatment, although the amount of individual therapy may diminish as the client becomes involved in the other forms of therapy.

Clinicians need to keep various themes in mind when providing individual treatment. The development of rapport between the clinician and family members may be problematic. The clinician may want to set some limits on the child's exhibition of sexualized or aggressive behaviors. Emotions to explore with the child victim include anger, fear, guilt, and lack of trust. Helping the child to resume as normal a life as possible at home and at school can also be an important task. Incestuously abused children may also need help detaching from the offender and developing an appropriate sense of role boundaries within the family. Individual work with parents may include helping them to understand the child's emotions and behaviors and to provide appropriate family structure and discipline. Parents who experienced sexual abuse as children may need to explore the issues arising from that abuse. Mothers in incestuous families may need considerable help in managing the affairs of the family if the perpetrator has left the home. They may also need to explore feelings about their daughter and husband. Assessment of the reasons for the incest is important in order to design appropriate interventions for the perpetrator. The perpetrator needs to admit responsibility for the abuse and begin to explore his emotional responses to the abuse. He also needs to begin to discover alternate ways of meeting the same needs he once met through the incest. Behaviorally oriented therapy to change the father's pattern of sexual arousal may be called for, as may therapy to reduce abuse of alcohol or other drugs. Treatment of women abused as children has included procedures to help with sexual dysfunction and a controversial use of implosion therapy.

CHAPTER ELEVEN

Group Treatment

Group therapy is a common treatment form for victims of child sexual abuse and for the offending parent, non-offending parent, and the parents as a couple in cases of incest. In a survey of thirty-six incest-treatment professionals and programs, Forseth and Brown (1981) found that group therapy was cited most often as the preferred method of treatment for the victim and the abuser. The average time spent in group therapy was thirty-nine hours for the victim, fifteen hours for the abusing parent (almost always the father or father figure), and thirty-two hours for the nonabusing parent. Group therapy can take place at the same time as or subsequent to individual treatment and can be concurrent with family treatment.

In this chapter, following a short summary of the advantages and disadvantages of group treatment, two different group treatment programs for victims are reviewed. The reader is referred to Blick and Porter (1982), Delson and Clark (1981), Fowler, Burns, and Roehl (1983), Furniss, Bingley-Miller, and van Elburg (in press), McFarlane and others (1986), Hazzard, King, and Webb (1986), and Wayne and Weeks (1984) for descriptions of other treatment programs. We then describe groups for parents and for adults abused as children. Throughout, we focus on therapist and group-process issues that have manifested themselves in group treatment programs.

Advantages and Disadvantages

A vignette illustrates some of the advantages group treat-ment can have:

> A nine-year-old girl was repeatedly molested by her uncle. Although she has made some progress during individual therapy in expressing and understanding her reactions to the abuse, she remains withdrawn from her peers at school and has not made much progress in understanding that her experiences are not unique. A place in an ongoing group treatment program of sexually abused girls becomes avail-able, and she reluctantly joins. She interacts little during the first few sessions but listens intently to the experiences of the girls who have been in the group for a while. She gradually begins to interact in the group and makes friends with some of the other members. She begins to involve herself with her peers at school and attributes this interaction to her realization that other sexually abused chil-dren appear normal to her and that they are able to keep their friends in school.

Group treatment can provide victims with experiences not available in individual or family treatment and can thus be a valuable complement to other forms of therapy. By meeting and talking with others who have been molested, victims can discover that their abuse experiences have not made them unique. By discussing their experiences in an accepting environ-ment and hearing the experiences of others being discussed in a straightforward manner, group members learn that their experi-ences do not have to be kept secret (Delson and Clark, 1981; Fowler, Burns, and Roehl, 1983). The group can also be a place for members to form meaningful peer relations, which can re-duce the sense of isolation and alienation from peers reported by many victims (Knittle and Tuana, 1980; Lubell and Soong, 1982). Within the group, victims are able to plan for their future with the support and guidance of the therapists and other group members (Fowler, Burns, and Roehl, 1983). Interpersonal behavior within the group can be observed and related to past or present experiences when appropriate, and the members and therapists can give each other growth-producing feedback. Members are able to experiment with new behaviors outside the group and get feedback on their experiences from group members (Lubell and Soong, 1982; Wayne and Weeks, 1984).

Giarretto (1981) states that group therapy can provide the mother and perpetrator from an incestuous family with many benefits. It is often easier for an adult to dismiss the confrontation provided by a clinician than to dismiss that provided by another adult who has had similar experiences. Also, the peer interaction helps increase a sense of self-responsibility and self-efficacy, and decreases the reliance of parents on authority figures to "cure" them.

In a practical vein, group treatment may be more cost effective than individual therapy. In areas where there are not enough qualified therapists to see victims individually, public mental health agencies may be forced to choose between providing group therapy or no therapy at all. Even in areas in which this extreme condition does not exist, many of the issues that must be dealt with by victims and their families may be dealt with just as easily in group therapy as in individual therapy, allowing time for clinicians to provide individual therapy where it is crucial.

A few authors comment on negative aspects of group treatment. Blick and Porter (1982) note that when the girls in their group began to share more in the group, they began to share less with their individual therapists. This decrease in sharing created a problem for the individual therapists unless they were in close communication with the group therapists. The effect of the changed pattern of sharing on the client was not discussed. Webb-Woodard and Woodard (1982) disagree that group treatment is the treatment of choice in cases of incest. They suggest that family members develop identities and learn unique sets of skills within their groups, and that if these identities and skills are different for each member, the subsequent reconstitution of the family is difficult. Such a concern seems justified in some cases. Communication between group and family therapists about the goals and methods of their respective programs may help to reduce the chance that the two processes will work against each other.

Another concern about group therapy is that it may "suggest" symptoms or concerns to some group members. For instance, in Sturkie's (1983) group treatment program, which is described in the next section, eight themes are presented to each group. One is the children's feelings of responsibility for the abuse. If some children do not feel responsible for the abuse (as opposed to those who feel responsible but cannot talk about it), they may begin to believe that they should feel responsible as they hear other children discuss their feelings of responsibility. Investigations in social psychology have shown the strong drive toward conformity within a group (Asch, 1972). Other investigations have shown that people who publicly state that they feel a certain way will have their attitude changed in that direction by their statements (Festinger, 1972). These findings suggest the possibility that in order to appear the same as the other children in a group of victims, some children may state that they feel a certain way (although it is not true), and this statement may cause them to actually begin to feel that way. Clinicians leading groups should be aware of this possibility. A method for reducing this possibility is for clinicians to indicate regularly that some emotions may be experienced by all group members while others are experienced by selected members. Examples of how some children are frightened by one movie or made happy by another, while others do not experience the same emotions, may help to reduce any concern by members experiencing an emotion not experienced by all group members.

Programs for Victims

In this section we describe two group treatment programs for victims. Selecting the two programs from the literature was not an easy task, and their selection should not be taken to indicate that we believe they are better than the others. The two programs we include were described in detail, and not all the other programs were. In our opinion, both program descriptions were different enough from each other and from the descriptions of group therapy with children in general to provide the reader with an idea of the ways in which group treatment programs can function.

Two Different Approaches

Lubell and Soong (1982) describe a group therapy program typical of many except that it was shorter than a number of others. The program was designed for sexually abused thirteen- and fourteen-year-old girls, all of whom had been molested by their father or father figure. All the girls were in a foster home, and all their fathers had remained in the family home. Thus, along with the incest, the girls faced a number of issues about removal from their home. The abuse had been identified during the six months prior to the beginning of group sessions, and crisis intervention work had been completed through individual counseling. The group met for one and a half hours each week for nineteen sessions. It was co-led by a male and a female therapist, with the male therapist taking a planned one-month vacation mid-way through the therapy. The sessions were videotaped, and the unseen male video technician occasionally became an important "other presence." The group work was offered to help the girls adjust to their experiences and their changed lives, to improve their self-concept, to develop or improve social skills, and to reconnect with peers. The authors do not state whether they determined prior to the group that these issues would be addressed or whether they were addressed in reaction to the needs of the members as the group progressed.

The authors found that a sense of trust was difficult to establish within the group. One hypothesized cause was the girls' fear of becoming involved in another trusting relationship. The authors write that the problem was exacerbated because the members were not initially told why each of them was in the group. Suspecting that this was a problem, the clinicians clearly stated during the third session that each girl was there because of previous abuse experience, with the result being that the girls immediately became more open than they had been. As the group progressed, a developing sense of trust allowed for a progressively freer sharing of experiences and feelings among members.

Several themes arose during the course of treatment. As the group began, the girls' feelings of isolation were important. Many felt isolated from their mothers because they perceived that their mothers had sided with their father against them. The girls had isolated themselves from old friends because of concerns about the friends' reactions to the abuse, and they were afraid to form new friendships because they feared having to reveal their abuse experiences to new friends in the normal course of becoming acquainted. During the middle stage of the group, sadness over the girls' many losses became a dominant theme for the group. After discussing these losses, the girls were able to help each other begin to rebuild their lives. Anger, a theme present throughout treatment, became intense during the middle stage. Initially the anger was directed at the girls' parents and social service agencies. Later, the anger became directed at group members. Resolving the issues that had led to the anger within the group became a priority, and the recognition and resolution of the anger helped the girls identify the impact that their anger had on their lives outside the group. As the group moved toward its termination phase, previous themes were reviewed but from a more hopeful perspective than previously. Each girl began planning for her future with help from the group.

At the end of the group experience, all the girls stated that the group had been beneficial: They reported that their living situations had improved; they felt better about themselves than they had; their anger and sadness were less intense than before; and they felt more hopeful about the future than they had previously. Individual and family therapists with whom the girls had contact during the group experience also reported that the girls' self-esteem and social functioning had improved. However, the girls' concurrent involvement in other forms of therapy does not allow for a specific assessment of the value of the group program.

In contrast to the group therapy described by Lubell and Soong (1982), Sturkie (1983) describes a structured group treatment that covered eight themes. Each of the groups consisted of four to eight girls between the ages of seven and twelve. Girls who had experienced various types of abuse, from incest to abuse by a stranger, and those who had experienced abuse lasting varying lengths of time, from a single time to years, were included in the same groups. The groups met in eight-week cycles, with each one-and-a-half-hour session devoted to a specific topic. The children could enter the cycle at any point and remain in the program for as many cycles as desired.

Sturkie reports that after initial experimenting with various themes, exercises, and formats, the project staff decided that the structured format was advantageous for several reasons: Because the children's time within the group could be dictated by parents or others, the format allowed all important themes to be covered in as short a time as possible; because most of the group facilitators were graduate students, the format made for easier training in group process and caused little disruption when facilitators were changed; and the predictability of the format made it easy to include meaningful experiential activities.

The eight treatment themes were: believability, guilt and responsibility, body integrity and protection, secrecy and sharing, anger, powerlessness, other life crises and tasks, and court attendance. The theme of believability was included because a number of children are not believed when they initially report abuse. Through discussion, reasons for a parent's believing or not believing such a report were aired, and through role play the children experimented with various ways to make a report of sexual abuse. Covering themes of guilt and responsibility acknowledged the fact that children often feel responsible for their abuse because of their egocentric nature or the actions of others. These themes were dealt with in several ways: The adult's sole responsibility for the abuse was repeatedly stressed by the group facilitators; the children were encouraged to discuss their feelings of guilt; and, to reassure those who felt some physical pleasure during the abuse, the children were informed of the automatic physical responses that occur during sexual stimulation. Throughout this session, the children were encouraged to "externalize" their feelings of guilt and "redefine" them as anger. During the session on body integrity and protection, the children first did drawings of the human body as a form of sex education and later practiced ways of protecting themselves by yelling no and by asking someone not to touch them. The theme of secrecy and sharing was included to reinforce the children for revealing the abuse and to identify appropriate ways to share their experiences with others if they chose to do so.

Although the facilitators found that anger was present during all the sessions, a specific session was set aside for its expression. The children were encouraged to express anger toward the abuser and if appropriate toward their other parent by screaming what they would have liked to say to them or by beating on pillows or both. The theme of powerlessness was included because many of the children had been put in an exploited, powerless position by a trusted adult. The children were encouraged to discuss areas of their lives over which they had control. Inappropriate ways that the children used to maintain power in their lives, such as being manipulative or deceptive, were also explored. Because abused children's lives are often disrupted by events such as foster-care placement and change of schools, strategies for successfully dealing with these changes were discussed during the session on other life changes. During the session on court appearances, the children were encouraged to discuss their anxiety about future court appearances and their feelings about previous ones. Through role play, the children were introduced to the functions of various court personnel and to the basic procedure for court testimony.

During the first year of the program, twenty-four children participated in the group and in individual or family therapy or both. The average length of participation was not noted. Also, the relative benefit to children who participated for more than one cycle was not mentioned. Sturkie notes that it was impossible to assess clearly the specific effects of the group treatment, but he does report that there was no recurrence of the abuse among families in the treatment program and that all seventeen children who were required to testify in court were able to do so successfully. Specific information concerning the children's functioning after the group is not included in the report.

Therapeutic Issues

Purpose of the Group. Perhaps the key issue, and one on which many other issues depend, is the proposed goal of the group experience. Some groups may be intended to help members with the resolution of the sexual abuse experience only, while others may be designed to aid the members in their personal growth. Some groups may be seen as a component of the victim's therapy, and others may provide most or all of the therapy that its members will receive. Because of the many functions that a group can serve, the purpose of the group must be clearly defined by all those who will take part in its formation and implementation. This initial decision provides some of the framework for the other decisions that must be made as the treatment program is formed. For instance, the duration and membership of the group may be affected by whether the group will focus on the sexual abuse or also cover other aspects of the children's lives. A short duration may be possible if the focus is strictly on the sexual abuse, and having members at the same developmental level may be desirable if the members' general functioning will also be a focus.

Time and Place of Meetings. Most groups described in the literature met in a room at the sponsoring agency. Such an environment is new for each group member and consequently will not evoke painful memories, as might happen if the meetings were held at a member's school or home (Blick and Porter, 1982). Meeting at the offices of the child protective agency that is involved in the investigation may be difficult for those members who had a negative experience during the investigation (Hazzard, King, and Webb, 1986). Discussion-oriented groups need a space large enough to allow for role play. For play groups, materials for acting out various themes are needed. Materials used in these groups include a furnished playhouse and figures of people, a police station with police officers, materials that can be used to construct a courtroom scene, puppets, art materials, and mats and pillows. Some treatment programs use foam bats to allow the children to express anger physically (Delson and Clark, 1981; Sturkie, 1983), and some therapists for younger children have found that "baby" materials such as bottles and blankets are useful (Delson and Clark, 1981; Fowler, Burns, and Roehl, 1983; Steward and others, 1986).

Most groups met for one and a half hours weekly, although some clinicians had hour-long meetings both for twelve- to fifteen-year-old girls (Furniss, Bingley-Miller, and van Elburg, in press) and for children from two and a half to six years old (Steward and others, 1986). Some clinicians served juice during a period of reacquaintance at the beginning of each session or had a snack break at the end while reviewing the session and allowing the children to calm down before leaving. The serving of food was generally seen as a nice symbol of group nurturance. Blick and Porter (1982) write that meeting early in the week was advantageous because it gave the members a chance to discuss matters that arose during the group session with their individual therapists before the weekend. Early evening was the preferred time to meet, especially when the members relied on parents for transportation.

Group Membership. One issue that should be considered before a group is formed is the desired amount of heterogeneity among the members. The composition of the group will probably depend in part on the number of children in an area that need group treatment. Those in small communities may find that if a group is to be formed at all, it must be relatively heterogeneous. Other communities may have the option of forming heterogeneous or homogeneous groups. Groups can be heterogeneous in a number of different ways. They can include a wide variety of children with diverse sexual abuse experiences; or they can comprise many children with a certain characteristic and a few different children (mostly incest victims and a few victims of extrafamilial abuse, for example); or they can comprise relatively equal subgroups of children with certain characteristics (half boys and half girls). Currently, however, it is unclear how these types of heterogeneous groups may differ in process or outcome (or both) from each other or from homogeneous groups. The issue of whether to include boys in a group composed mostly of girls is also salient, as this vignette illustrates:

> At a monthly review of ongoing child sexual abuse cases, the clinicians in a particular agency identify eleven early-adolescent girls and two early-adolescent boys who are currently in individual treatment and who they believe would benefit from group treatment. It is proposed that two groups be formed. Debate centers on whether the two boys should be put together in one of the groups, should be separated, or should not be included in either group. Those arguing in favor of including the boys say that the group experience would be valuable for them and would enhance individual treatment. Those concerned about including the boys question the benefits that they would receive from being in a group of girls and suggest that the girls may not be willing to discuss sexual matters with boys present. Whether it would be essential to have a male therapist if the boys were included and what effect a male therapist might have on the girls are also debated issues.

Most authors state that their groups comprised girls only, presumably because many more girls than boys are in treatment for child sexual abuse. Although some boys were involved in a group treatment program, it is unclear whether they were included in groups with girls or joined a separate group for boys (Delson and Clark, 1981). Writing about children's groups in general, Gumaer (1984) suggests that if boys and girls are both included, they should be in roughly equal proportion. He hypothesizes that otherwise the clinician risks having those in the minority become progressively less active. Even if a relatively equal number of boys and girls were available for a group, there may be some hazards because the presence of those of the opposite sex may inhibit some members from discussing sexual topics, especially in groups of older children (Berliner and Ernst, 1984).

Several authors state that only incest victims were included in their groups, apparently because incest victims more often than other abuse victims receive treatment past the crisis intervention stage and not because the authors were concerned about combining incest and other victims in the same group. Some clinicians have combined incest and nonincest victims. Sturkie (1983) had both types of victims, although the highly structured nature of his program may have facilitated working with both types. Hazzard, King, and Webb (1986) found that the issues faced by incest and nonincest victims were "more similar than dissimilar, particularly with regard to short-term issues," and they experienced no problems combining both types of victims in the same group (p. 219). It may be especially easy to combine incest victims with victims abused by other trusted adults in their lives. It may not be effective, however, to combine those abused on a long-term basis by a trusted adult and those abused once by a less familiar adult.

Groups have usually been organized around age ranges of under seven, seven to twelve, and thirteen and older. Steward and others (1986) note that they found it best to have children of the same developmental level in their groups of children under seven years of age. They also found that a mixture of active and withdrawn children was beneficial. Berliner and Ernst (1984) write that, in general, including one or two children of a different developmental level from the rest of the group was unwise because it could exacerbate any feelings of being different that were caused by the abuse. They note that in some cases the inclusion of an immature child in a younger group or a precocious child in an older group is appropriate.

Blick and Porter (1982) are the only authors who state that they screened the children before the beginning of the group in order to determine their appropriateness for group treatment. They do not specify the factors that made the children either appropriate or inappropriate but do give one example of a girl who was inappropriate. They characterize her as "immature" and note that she was quite disruptive during the one group meeting that she attended on a trial basis. Rather than including her in the group, they provided her with individual treatment. Gumaer (1984) suggests that, in general, children should be voluntary members of a group whenever possible. He interviewed children before their entry into a group to ascertain their feelings about joining the group and referred those who were unwilling to other forms of treatment. Although few authors have discussed screening children from group treatment, such a tactic may be beneficial both to the child screened into another form of therapy and to those in the group. If more descriptions of children who have and have not done well in group treatment were available, the process of selecting suitable and unsuitable candidates might be aided.

Treatment Themes. As was shown in Chapter Four, child sexual abuse victims exhibit a wide range of behavioral and emotional consequences. Clinicians have addressed these consequences in group treatment by exploring a number of treatment themes. Because a clinician is able to guide discussion toward or away from topics even in relatively unstructured groups, a clinician who understands the themes that have been important in other groups can at least be sure that those themes are introduced. This may increase the chance that themes of importance to all group members will have some airing.

A few treatment themes were reported by many authors —the development of trust within the group, the expression of anger, and providing sex education. Sturkie (1983) states that the eight themes covered in his structured group treatment program—believability, guilt and responsibility, body integrity and protection, secrecy and sharing, anger, powerlessness, other life crises, and court attendance—were determined by examining themes that had arisen naturally during previous, less structured groups, suggesting that they might be important themes for any group. Steward and others (1986) note seven treatment goals for their groups with young children: helping the children translate their thoughts and feelings into words so that they can express themselves and their preferences, supporting the children's ability to say no and ask for help, allowing the children to experience a relationship with caring adults, limiting the children's assumptions of their own ability to evoke violence in others as a way of relieving their sense of responsibility for the abuse, supporting the development of peer-interaction skills, supporting an increased sense of self-worth, and encouraging the attainment of appropriate developmental milestones. Hazzard, King, and Webb (1986) had the following treatment themes for their groups of early-adolescent girls: dealing with their emotional reactions to the abuse and with the reactions of others to both the abuse and the victims, preparing themselves for court appearances, exploring ambivalent feelings about the perpetrator and family members (when appropriate), learning age-appropriate peer-interaction skills and gaining the courage to use them, learning about their own sexuality, and developing higher levels of self-esteem and assertiveness.

Berliner and Ernst (1984) note that many abused children are curious about the adult's motivation for the abuse. They suggest that clinicians be aware of the various theories about the etiology of abusive behavior and be able to relate these in appropriate language to the group members. Caution may be needed in this area however. One hypothesis about the etiology of abusive behavior is that being a victim of abuse as a child contributes to abusive behavior as an adult. Given in an inappropriate manner, this hypothesis may suggest to some group members that they are destined to become abusive adults. This belief may both add significantly to their current level of distress and raise the chance that they will become abusive as adults. Although many abusive adults have a history of being abused as children, many abused children do not become abusive adults (see Goodwin, McCarthy, and DiVasto, 1981), and no generally accepted theory explains why. It may be that receiving therapy as a child reduces the chance of later abusive behavior, and this hypothesis may be of comfort to children concerned about their future behavior.

Gender of Therapists. Although descriptions in the literature tell us that most groups for sexually abused children are co-led by a team of two clinicians, few of the descriptions include information about the gender of the clinicians. Lack of attention to this specific issue may reflect a belief that either the gender of the clinician is of little importance to the overall functioning of the group or that other factors—for instance, the skill levels of the clinicians available—are of greater importance. However, other factors being equal, the gender of the clinicians may make a difference.

A few authors have described the reasoning behind their selection of a specific type of clinician team. Lubell and Soong (1982) used a male/female team in their treatment program for girls. They believed that some of the girls' feelings about men would be more accessible with a male clinician present than with only a female clinician. They found that the girls' behavior was different toward each of the two clinicians, although they note that other variables (for example, therapist style and personality) could have also accounted for the girls' behavior. The girls were more curious about the male clinician's life outside the group, they made more comments about his clothes and personal attributes, and they seemed more concerned about his reaction to them. Furniss, Bingley-Miller, and van Elburg (in press) also found that the girls treated the male and female clinicians differently. The members were initially frightened of the male clinician and expressed anger or were sexually provocative toward him. They would often try to split the alliance of the clinicians by siding with one against the other. The girls also acted as if the female clinician were a rival for the male clinician's attention. This attitude changed slowly, and eventually the girls wanted maternal attention from the female clinician.

Others have used male/female teams to model appropriate roles. Gottlieb and Dean (1981) used such a team in their group treatment of twelve- to fourteen-year-old girls. They felt that the girls would benefit from the role model set by the clinicians, who acted as equals when solving problems that arose between them and who discussed sensitive topics with each other. Goodwin and Owen (1982) found that a male/female team allowed group members to explore their beliefs about a healthy male/female relationship and that it served as a model for a healthy parental relationship.

In contrast, Blick and Porter (1982) chose to use two female cotherapists. They feared that the inclusion of a male clinician in the early stages of therapy would cause the girls to be inhibited and would produce a threatening environment for them. Hazzard, King, and Webb (1986) also felt that the selection of two female clinicians would make the girls more comfortable initially; they suggested that the girls could later become involved in an "advanced" group with a male/female team.

No systematic investigations have explored the advantages and disadvantages of including a male clinician in groups of sexually abused children. The only information available comes from Lubell and Soong (1982), who describe the difference in group atmosphere during the vacation of the male clinician. They note that during his vacation, as opposed to when he was present, the girls dressed in a more feminine fashion, felt freer to discuss sexual issues, and talked about their relationships with their fathers in more detail. At the same time, the girls became increasingly aware of the unseen video technician, occasionally flirting with him through the studio window. Overall, the girls discussed more intimate issues during the male clinician's absence than they did in his presence. The difficulty of generalizing from this one case should be noted, however, because the change in behavior could have been caused by other factors, such as a developing sense of trust in the group.

Lubell and Soong's description seems to provide limited support for Blick and Porter's belief that girls would be more inhibited with a male clinician. It may be, however, that the apparent disadvantages of having a male clinician—such as the girls' feeling inhibited and developing seductive behavior toward the male—present the group with important issues that can result in growth for the members. Dealing with the members' inhibitions and sexualized behavior may add to the benefits they get from the group, and they may not be able to deal with these aspects as effectively without a male clinician. The suggestion of Hazzard, King, and Webb (1986) that the use of a female/female team may be best initially, with the members later graduating into a group with a male/female team, is interesting. Using a female/female rather than a female/male team at first may make the initial experience easier for the girls; they can then confront the more difficult issues that may be raised with a male clinician later in therapy.

All this information on therapist gender has come exclusively from descriptions of group treatment programs for girls. Different factors may be salient in decisions about including a male clinician in a group with some or all boys. A male clinician may provide the boys with a positive gender model, or the boys may find it easier to describe the sexual acts they experienced to a male clinician than to a female clinician. However, because most boys are abused by older males, they may have more difficulty discussing the experience with a male than with a female. A group of both boys and girls may benefit from including a male therapist, especially if the boys are a distinct minority; the male therapist would be an apparent advocate for the boys, and his presence would indicate that the conversation was not just going to be "girls' talk."

Duration of Therapy. Little has been reported about the effect of the number of meetings on the group experience. Wayne and Weeks (1984) state that they began to curtail their group meetings in the fifth year because of members' sporadic attendance. Their girls continued to live in what the authors describe as dysfunctional families during their group treatment, which may have encouraged such a long course of therapy. An interesting observation from this group was that the girls' behavior was cooperative and calm during the initial ten weeks of therapy, but it became angry and disruptive afterward. This observation may suggest that victims' negative affect may not begin to show until they are familiar with the group and its members.

Other time limits have been tried. Blick and Porter (1982) required a commitment of six months from prospective members before they were admitted into the group; they felt that this was the minimum amount of time necessary for meaningful progress to be made. They also believed that the girls benefited the most from the group after they had been members for at least a year. Other authors write of groups with much shorter durations—Lubell and Soong (1982) for nineteen weeks, Hazzard, King, and Webb (1986) for twelve weeks, and Sturkie (1983) for eight weeks—and these clinicians believe that the members benefited from treatment of this length.

The optimal duration of a group treatment program probably depends on a number of factors, such as the children's current living situations, the types of abuse they experienced, whether they are or have been involved in other types of therapy, and the clinician's conceptualization of the group's goals. Some programs, such as Sturkie's (1983), seem to be more oriented to crisis intervention than others. Each of the important themes was presented in his groups in such a manner that the children could quickly assimilate the information. These shorter groups may be most effective with children who are functioning relatively well in most areas of their lives and who need help in dealing effectively with their abuse experience. A group where relatively longer participation is required, such as the one described by Blick and Porter (1982), appears to be oriented toward also providing help in general personal growth. As such, they may be appropriate for victims coming from pervasively disrupted environments.

An advantage to groups that continue for a long period of time is that the members are given the opportunity to improve several areas of their lives. A possible disadvantage is that the members' regular involvement in a group comprised solely of other victims may encourage them to begin to assimilate the role of sexual abuse victim into their personalities. One way for countering this possibility is for victims to join generic groups once some group work on the sexual abuse is completed.

Family Involvement. Family involvement is usually an important component of successful group treatment if for no other reason than that the child generally depends on family members for transportation to meetings. Family resistance to a child's participation in therapy can be caused by a number of factors, including the parents' desire to put the experience behind them by ignoring it and their distress over any initial negative changes in the child's behavior as the abuse experience is explored. Resistance by parents in cases of incest may be particularly high. They may be concerned that the information the child gives during treatment will jeopardize the perpetrator or other family members in court, and they may be generally resistant to any form of therapy mandated by a court. Two general strategies for dealing with family resistance are described in the literature: actively attempting to involve family members in treatment and assisting children whose parents try to discourage their participation.

Berliner and Ernst (1984) found that a group meeting with (nonoffending) parents before the initial meeting of the children's group was useful. Parents could be told about the general functioning of the group and could ask about specific concerns that they had. It may also be helpful for the clinician to predict to the parents that they will have some negative reactions to their children's behavior changes and to their children's participation in therapy. This caution may help them realize that their resistance is natural, and they may be less likely to act on it than if they had not been warned (Blick and Porter, 1982; Hazzard, King, and Webb, 1986). Another method found useful for reducing parents' resistance is to encourage them to become involved in some treatment of their own. During their own treatment, they may discover the benefits of therapy and want their child to have the same benefits, or they may be able to explore their resistance to therapy for their child (or both of these results may occur).

Some clinicians have attempted to involve parents throughout their children's treatment. Delson and Clark (1981) write that they were relatively unsuccessful in securing the parents' cooperation however. They scheduled meetings with parents to discuss the children's regressive behavior at home and ways to handle it but felt that the parents were not receptive to the assistance they offered. Steward and others (1986) attempted to engage the children's caretakers (parents, foster parents, or another adult) in treatment. They believed that they were fairly successful in this process, even though the caretaker/therapist relationship was difficult at first. They scheduled meetings with each child's caretaker every two months in order to discuss the child's progress and offer assistance with managing the child at home. One possible reason for the difference in success reported by the authors is that the children in the groups led by Delson and Clark engaged in considerable regressive behavior. This behavior may have carried over into their home lives, increasing the resistance of their parents.

Even when the clinician makes extensive efforts to mollify the family, the family's resistance may still make it difficult for the child to attend treatment. In these cases, an agency may choose to provide transportation for the victim as the only way to allow for continued participation in treatment (Blick and Porter, 1982; Giarretto, 1981). Those taking this approach indicate their belief in the value of therapy for the child in spite of parental objection. It is possible, however, that this approach may require the child to choose between going to therapy and siding with a parent by resisting therapy. Making this choice may further damage an already tenuous parent/child relationship. Accordingly, it may be important for agencies to consider carefully whether transporting a child in the face of parental resistance or putting other forms of overt or covert pressure on the child to continue treatment is a reasonable resolution.

Outcome Research. Although research has been directed at understanding group process in general, no systematic investigations have studied the benefits of group therapy for sexual abuse victims. As a consequence, those designing comprehensive treatment programs for victims and families have no empirical evidence on which to base decisions such as whether to provide group treatment, when treatment should occur, and how the treatment groups should be formed. No studies have utilized before and after measures; consequently, we have only the subjective opinions of the clinicians and the group members as to the benefit of the group. Clearly, we need a body of research. It may be possible, for instance, to determine that certain types of children receive the most benefit from groups that are formed a certain way or that use a particular type of group process. It may also be possible to document differences between children who participate in group therapy and those who participate only in individual treatment.

Programs for Parents from Incestuous Families

There are fewer descriptions of group treatment programs aimed at the parents of an incestuous family than of programs for the victim. Several treatment programs for incestuous families that have as their ultimate goal the reuniting of the family have instituted group treatment for each member of the family and for the parents as a couple. In this section we examine some of these programs briefly.

Nonparticipating Mothers. As noted in Chapter Ten, a mother from a family in which incest has recently been revealed may face a number of difficult tasks. She must deal with her own, the victim's, and other family members' emotional reactions, and need to assume the management of the household and family. Incestuous families are often physically and socially isolated from the community; consequently, the mothers may have few if any people to turn to. Group involvement can help the mother deal with her immediate problems and can also help her begin to form a support system by developing friendships with other women in the group. In this way, a group for mothers can be a personal growth group, in which dealing with incest is an important but not exclusive issue. This double role for the group may explain why Forseth and Brown (1981) found in a survey of thirty-six treatment programs that the mother typically spent twice as much time in group therapy as the abusing father and almost as much time as the victim.

Sgroi and Dana (1982) describe a mothers' group. They encouraged the mothers to join soon after the abuse was revealed because they found that if they waited until the crisis had passed, the mothers were reluctant to join. The group met for one and a half hours a week and was co-led by two female clinicians. While they attended the group, the mothers continued individual therapy with one of the cotherapists. When new members arrived in the group they were often in crisis, with their concerns focused exclusively on the incest and the effect that it was having on them and their family. Themes at this time included the ventilation and examination of emotions such as anger and fear, exploration of their previous sexual abuse experiences (if any), getting specific assistance to help the family survive financially and emotionally, and understanding the social service or legal process. As the crisis of the incest passed, the mothers began to focus on general issues such as building self-esteem. Other topics included identifying unreasonable expectations that the mother had of both her children and men in general, developing the ability to set and maintain appropriate limits for her children, and improving social and assertiveness skills.

Abusing Fathers. Perpetrators can benefit from group treatment, as this vignette shows:

> As part of a court order, a father who steadfastly refused to admit that he molested his young daughter entered a group treatment program for incestuous fathers. After several sessions, he admitted to his wife that he had molested his daughter, and arrangements were made for him to apologize to his daughter during a later family session. He claimed that it was listening to the other fathers discuss their situation and hearing the support that they got from each other that gave him the strength to admit the abuse.

Emphasis is now placed on intensive treatment for fathers outside the family context before family treatment is begun or reunification is considered. As discussed in Chapter Ten, this treatment may include behaviorally oriented programs for reconditioning arousal patterns. Another aspect of treatment is insight therapy, during which fathers discover and explore beliefs and interpersonal relationship patterns that may have led to or encouraged the incest. Group treatment is often used in this process because clinicians working with incestuous fathers believe that the confrontation and support each father can receive and give during group treatment are valuable and are more easily achieved during group treatment than in individual therapy (although many of these treatment themes are useful during individual therapy with the offender also). Many fathers' groups follow a pattern similar to those for alcoholics and other addicts: initial acknowledgment by the father that he cannot control his own behavior and his consequent submission to external control along with gradual acceptance of responsibility for his own behavior (Herman, 1983).

Groth (1983) developed a treatment program for incarcerated sexual offenders. Many of the themes Groth covers are also useful in therapy for incest offenders either in or out of prison. Treatment is based on the hypothesis that sexual assault "is the product of defects in development and deficits in life-management skills. It is the long-term consequence of trauma and maltreatment . . . during the formative years, which have interfered with the psychological maturation of the individual" (p. 163). Groth considers sexual offense an acting-out of unresolved developmental issues and believes that an individual's assaultive inclinations will never be cured—they are too ingrained in the personality—but can be successfully restrained and controlled, providing the offender is willing to expend considerable effort. The purpose of the treatment program is to provide the man with the insight and skills needed to gain control over his assaultive behavior, an essential step before reunification of the family is attempted. This control is achieved by helping him to understand the role that the assaults have had in his life and to develop the capacity for normal meaningful relationships.

It is important to recognize that those with a family systems perspective may see fewer incest perpetrators as having ingrained patterns caused by their personality development. Extensive individual treatment for the offender, both in individual therapy (as described in Chapter Ten) and in groups, is founded on the belief that the primary cause of incest resides in the offender not in the family system. Programs based on other hypotheses about the etiology of incest stress extensive individual therapy for the offender less than do programs such as Groth's.

There are three treatment themes in Groth's program, each having three components. The first theme is reeducation, which comprises sex education, understanding sexual assault, and personalizing the victim. Observations have indicated that adult sexuality is often frightening for sexual assaulters. Sex education is provided to help each man gain an understanding of both the physical and emotional components of sexuality as a way of helping to reduce his fear. Helping the man understand sexual assault is "aimed at dispelling the self-deceptions, rationalizations, and projections of responsibility that sex offenders use to avoid recognizing their problems and to diminish their responsibility for their offenses" (Groth, 1983, p. 170). Many incarcerated child molesters believe that their victims often enjoyed and gained from the sexual experiences; the offenders have little sense that there were negative consequences for the victim. Such beliefs can easily lead to justification for recidivism. Consequently, considerable effort is expended in helping sexual offenders understand the consequences to victims.

Resocialization is the second general theme; sessions are planned to help the offender improve interpersonal relations, management of aggression, and parenting skills. A number of sexual offenders show a lack of interpersonal skills, which is hypothesized to contribute to their tendency to form abusive relationships. As the perpetrators feel increasingly comfortable in social situations, it is assumed that their need to control others through abusive relationships is lowered. Offenders are helped to improve their relationship-forming skills, their sex-role expectations, and their general comfort with others. The ways that aggression leads to sexual assault and outlets for the stress or frustration that may lead to the aggression are also explored. Because of the hypothesis that neglect and abuse during the perpetrator's life led to the abusive behavior, the poor examples of parenting that the perpetrator's parents provided are counteracted through education about appropriate parenting skills.

The first aspect of the counseling theme is an exploration of the dynamics of each perpetrator's offense, the factors that contributed to the offense, and the early warning signs that indicate that abusive behavior may recur. Understanding these aspects of the offense are seen as essential to reducing recidivism. The neglect and abuse that the offenders experienced during their childhood are detailed, and the emotional reactions to them are explored. This review may help the offender to understand both his own behavior and the effect of the abuse on his victims. Finally, as a way of restitution, offenders are encouraged to speak to law enforcement and child protective workers about such topics as the ways that they engaged their victims in order to help officials reduce the occurrence of sexual assault and protect other children.

Fowler, Burns, and Roehl (1983) describe a treatment group designed specifically for incestuous fathers. The group met for twenty-four weekly sessions of three to four hours each. In order to qualify for admission, each father had to have admitted abusing his child, although the initial admission could have been as vague as acknowledging the possibility that he might have committed incest. He also had to contract not to engage in any aggressive behavior toward himself or others. During the first sessions, each member described his sexual offenses. Those who claimed that they could not remember what happened were told directly that they were suppressing the details and that they could remember them if they tried hard enough. The authors note that eventually each member was able to describe the abuse in detail.

The remaining sessions were divided into discussion of five issues. The first was the fathers' early sexual experiences. Any fixation on sexual activity with children was explored. The second, related issue was the fathers' current sexuality. Emphasis was placed on developing behaviors that would enable them to have normal sexual relationships with their wives or other women. The third topic was the fathers' aggressive behavior and the relationship of the incest to aggression. The goal was to aid the fathers in developing self-control and management of their impulses. Substance abuse was the fourth issue. The extent to which the fathers had used alcohol or other drugs to repress painful realities or to provide themselves with an excuse for the incest was explored, and other methods for fulfilling needs were developed. The fifth issue was the self-esteem of the fathers. An additional session was a meeting with a therapy group of women who were victims of incest as children. Those in each group shared their experiences and attempted to develop an understanding of the reason for and impact of incest.

Couples. In some treatment programs for incestuous families, one of the prerequisites for family therapy is marital therapy. Giarretto (1981) writes that such therapy is a key component of the overall therapeutic process if the family is to be reunited. Although some of this therapy may be done with individual couples, couples' groups have also been found to be important.

Taylor (1984) describes a couples' group treatment program that was part of a larger treatment regimen for incestuous families. He notes four prerequisites for a couple to be accepted into the group: Both parents had to agree that the father was completely responsible for the abuse and that it was harmful; the father had to have a period of separation from the family as a way of promoting the couple's willingness to confront and solve their problems; the mother had to establish herself above the daughter in the family hierarchy while at the same time establishing closer emotional bonds with the daughter; and the couple had to express a willingness to confront each other and work within the group. The groups met for ten weekly, semi-structured sessions. All the couples began a group together in order to promote a sense of trust and group unity. The groups were led by two cotherapists, although Taylor does not mention whether a specific gender combination was used.

The groups focused on four themes. The first theme was conflict. Ways in which conflict can be handled in a healthy, open way were contrasted with ways in which conflict can be harmful if handled in a covert manner. The second topic was the development of communication skills between the spouses. The third theme was mutuality; each individual learned that the effort put into a relationship is important but that one spouse cannot control the behavior of the other or the outcome of their interactions as a couple. The fourth theme was sexuality, with the couples discussing the "beliefs, rules, fears, and rights of a person in a sexual relationship" (p. 201). This topic, assumed to be the most delicate, was discussed at the end of the group and was approached forthrightly yet sensitively by the clinicians.

Programs for Adults Molested as Children

Increasing attention is being paid to the needs of adults who were molested as children, with group therapy a popular form of treatment. Before describing these treatment programs, we need to discuss an important issue that might arise in some groups: the possibility that a group member may admit that he or she has sexually abused a child as an adult. As discussed in Chapter Four, some researchers and clinicians hypothesize that being molested as a child increases the possibility that the individual will become an abusive adult. Most states require that a clinician report to the authorities any client who is suspected of sexually abusing a child. The issue is whether the clinician, during the initial meeting of the group, should discuss the steps that must be taken if a member admits to sexually abusing a child. Although such a discussion would seem to be required in the interest of fairness, it may cause clinicians to be seen as representatives of the court or police and thus may dampen any discussion within the group. There are no easy resolutions to this issue, but those involved in group treatment with adults should carefully consider the ways in which this information is to be given to group members before beginning treatment.

Women Molested as Children. Goodman and Nowak-Scibelli (1985), Herman and Schatzow (1984), and Tsai and Wagner (1978) describe group treatment programs for women molested as children. The women who participated in the different programs and the format that the sessions followed differed in several respects.

Each program had different criteria for selecting members. Herman and Schatzow selected thirty women from fifty who had been referred. The women met three criteria: expression of positive feelings about being in the group, reasonable functioning in daily lives, and an appropriate ongoing relationship with an individual therapist. Goodman and Nowak-Scibelli also screened potential members. Because of the intense nature of the group experience, they did not feel it wise to include women who were already feeling overwhelmed by their experience. They excluded women who appeared psychotic, suicidal, or showed other signs of high instability. Tsai and Wagner did no screening and accepted all women who applied. Although Goodman and Nowak-Scibelli expressed concern about including very disturbed women, the other authors found that the group experience was valuable for women experiencing considerable difficulties. Herman and Schatzow report that ambivalence about being in the group was the greatest hindrance to successful group completion and that one woman with an "apparent thought disorder" and two borderline women were able to complete the group successfully. Tsai and Wagner found that two women with psychotic histories were able to complete the group with special support; they expressed no concerns about members' ambivalence and stated that all women who wished to participate would continue to be admitted.

Each of the groups met for a prearranged number of sessions. The Tsai and Wagner groups met for four sessions with one follow-up session three months later; those of Herman and Schatzow met for ten sessions, with one follow-up meeting six months later; and the Goodman and Nowak-Scibelli groups met for twelve sessions. The time was prearranged so that the emotional trauma that the members were expected to experience would be limited and they could get on with their lives and so that the focus would be on the incest itself and not on interpersonal conflicts within the group. Goodman and Nowak-Scibelli felt that twelve sessions were the minimum necessary for the dynamics of the abuse to arise and be resolved, although the other clinicians believed that their groups of shorter duration were valuable for the members.

The Tsai and Wagner groups were co-led by a male and a female therapist, and the groups of Goodman and Nowak-Scibelli were co-led by two female therapists. Tsai and Wagner do not provide a reason for using a male/female team; Goodman and Nowak-Scibelli state that they would have liked to experiment with a male/female team but could not find a male therapist willing to participate. Herman and Schatzow do not state who led their groups.

Each of the groups spent much time discussing the specific experiences of each woman and exploring the emotional and behavioral consequences that the sexual abuse had had on her life. One important difference between the groups was the timing of the discussion of the members' abuse experiences. Both Herman and Schatzow and Goodman and Nowak-Scibelli waited until a feeling of trust developed within the group and introduced the idea of sharing incest experiences during the third or fourth session. Tsai and Wagner, however, asked each member to share her incest experience during the first session and felt that a sense of trust within the group was facilitated by this sharing (this tactic may also have been required by the short duration of the group). Each pair of authors felt that their approach was beneficial to the group members, and because none of them varied the timing of these discussions between the groups that they led, comparisons of the two approaches are not available.

An important theme in the two groups that met for a longer period of time was preparation and support for sharing the molestation experience with someone else or confronting the perpetrator or other family members. The authors describe this sharing as a task that the participants faced with high anxiety and for which they needed much encouragement. Those who were able to confront their family about the abuse successfully often felt considerable relief.

All the authors describe the termination of the group as a difficult time, with members reluctant to end their contacts with each other. Goodman and Nowak-Scibelli note that termination brought up feelings of abandonment for many group members and that expressions of anger toward the therapists were not uncommon during this phase. Tsai and Wagner encouraged those women who were most unwilling to end the group to meet without the therapists, although they do not comment on whether the women did.

Six months after termination, both Tsai and Wagner and Herman and Schatzow sent questionnaires about their experiences in the group to all members who completed treatment. Herman and Schatzow report that members consistently felt less ashamed and guilty, less isolated, better able to protect themselves, and had higher self-esteem than they had before. They found that the amount of change in general and in sexual relationships varied considerably among the members. Tsai and Wagner report that members consistently felt less guilty and had better general and sexual relationships than they had previously. Members of both programs rated the most valuable aspect of the group experience as the chance to share feelings with women with similar experiences and suggested that the number of group sessions be increased.

The differences in the groups make it difficult to determine which variables led to the differences in postgroup functioning reported by the authors. At any rate, the reported outcomes appear to indicate the value of a limited number of group therapy sessions. Although it cannot be determined whether members would have experienced further growth with added sessions, the members' enthusiasm for such sessions clearly suggests that the experience was positive and supportive.

A self-help treatment group for women molested as children was sponsored by the Child Sexual Abuse Treatment Program (CSATP) (Giarretto, 1981, 1982), which is described in detail in Chapter Twelve. Many of the women were involved with other aspects of the CSATP program, such as individual or couples' treatment, while in the group. The women met with a clinician on a weekly basis for group therapy. One advantage to this program was that the women benefited from participation in other groups sponsored by the CSATP. For instance, after being in the women's group for a while, members were encouraged to join the program's "orientation group," the first group that parents of incestuous families joined after entering the treatment program. In this group, the women were able to learn about and begin to understand the parents of incestuous families. This experience turned out to be an important source of growth for many of the molested women. Some women also became involved in the groups for molested children, extending understanding to the children and feeling the therapeutic value of offering help to someone else. As with the groups described previously, Giarretto notes that an important goal for the molested women was confronting either their mother or father or both about the incest. Methods for discussing the incest were practiced during group meetings through role play. Giarretto found that the women who were able to confront their parents benefited the most from the group treatment.

Men Molested as Children. Bruckner and Johnson (1987) provide what appears to be the only description of groups for men molested as children. They describe two groups that they held for men, each lasting for six sessions of two and a half hours each. Employing a male/female cotherapist team, they found that the men had no trouble disclosing their abuse to a female clinician and that it was helpful for them to be able to practice disclosure with those from both sexes.

In general, the authors found that the same themes that arose in groups they had organized for women molested as children were important in the men's groups. There were, however, certain differences. The men feared becoming sexually abusive toward children, a theme seldom found in women's groups. Through group discussion, the members were able to see that they had not exploited children, and they were able to gain a realistic picture of the possibility of their doing so in the future. Several members disclosed that they had been sexually aggressive as adolescents. Group members "appropriately condemned the act" and were able to empathize with the guilt experienced by the aggressor.

Reporting other differences, the authors state that the men were able to reveal their abuse more easily than were the women in previous groups. They were more open about what had happened and showed more interest than the women in making their own abuse public as a way of educating others about the dangers of child sexual abuse. The men were also more likely to confront their abuser than were the women. A number of the men personally confronted their abusers relatively soon after the start of the group, while women in similar groups spent many weeks drafting and redrafting letters to their abusers. The men seldom became socially engaged with other men in the group outside of group sessions, while this phenomenon was relatively common within the women's groups.

Although the authors caution that these differences occurred in only two groups of men and thus may not be typical reactions, the differences suggest that the directions set by clinicians for therapy groups of men and women abused as children may be different in some regards. They also suggest that effective therapeutic efforts with boys and girls may also require different directions and methods. As additional work describing differences between boys' and girls' and men's and women's reactions to their abuse and to therapy is reported, we will gain an understanding of any differences in therapy that should be considered.

Summary and Conclusions

The relatively large amount of literature on group treatment programs (and consequently the length of this chapter) indicates the popularity of group treatment for victims of child sexual abuse and their families. Group treatment offers group members a chance to interact with other abuse victims, reducing each member's sense of being the only one to have suffered abuse and offering members the opportunity to understand how others have reacted to and handled their abuse. In addition, more victims can receive clinical services than might be possible using individual therapy. One concern about group therapy is the possibility that some group members will develop symptoms or beliefs because other members have them, and this possibility must be considered by those organizing and facilitating these groups.

A number of issues concerning the organization and functioning of group treatment programs remain undecided, such as whether to form heterogeneous or homogeneous groups of victims, the gender of the clinicians, the length of the program, and the best ways to involve the victims' families. Although it may be impossible to ever resolve these issues, we can begin to understand them clearly only through reports by a wide range of clinicians about the relative successes and failures of various ways these aspects of group treatment can be handled. Many clinicians believe that group treatment has been shown to be an effective way of providing help to abuse victims. As we begin to refine the group process based on the published experience of many clinicians, group treatment should become even more effective than it now is.

CHAPTER TWELVE

Family Treatment

P roviding family treatment in cases of child sexual abuse, especially incestuous abuse, has been increasingly advocated. The emphasis on family therapy comes from clinicians who view incest as a symptom of a dysfunctional family rather than an indication of individual pathology. Their belief is that making basic changes in the structure and functioning of the family is the most effective way of eliminating the recurrence of incest and reducing the chance of the development of other inappropriate behaviors. However, not everyone agrees that family therapy is beneficial in cases of incest. For instance, some advocates of the feminist perspective suggest that family therapy may be harmful because it can indicate that the family, rather than the perpetrator, is responsible for the incest (Wattenberg, 1985). Recent concerns over some fathers' sexual preference for children suggest that family therapy may be appropriate only after considerable individual and group therapy for the father. Despite these dissenting viewpoints, the family systems conceptualization of incest is predominant among clinicians today. As a result, many treatment programs place an emphasis on restructuring the family.

Nonincestuous Families

Sgroi (1982a, 1982b) is one of the few authors who has written about the importance of family treatment in all sexual abuse cases, even when the abuser is a stranger. Sgroi found that the natural inclination of many families was to avoid dealing with the abuse once it was revealed, as a way of putting it behind them. The overall goal of her family treatment model is to do just the opposite: open a discussion of the family's concerns about the abuse. This goal is based on the belief that when concerns are verbalized, the chance that they can be resolved is increased.

Treatment in these cases may involve the parents primarily, but at least one family session with parents, victim, and other siblings is important. Sgroi hypothesizes that each family has contributed in some way if sexual abuse occurs. Consequently, the family treatment is begun by assessing the extent to which actions or inactions by family members contributed to the abuse. For instance, the victim may have been given inadequate supervision, or an inappropriate choice of a surrogate caretaker may have been made. In such cases, the clinician can help family members accept their share of the responsibility for the abuse and take steps to reduce the risk of further abuse for the victim and other children in the family. The parents may feel guilty about the child's abuse, especially if it was perpetrated by a surrogate caretaker, and these feelings can be explored.

During at least one family session, the specifics of the abuse and the victim's reaction to it are discussed in order to minimize any misconceptions about the abuse that other family members have. Family members' feelings about the abuse and their perceptions of the victim can also be explored. Some family members may believe that the victim has been permanently changed or damaged by the abuse, and this perception can increase the negative impact of the abuse on the victim. Furthermore, the family can be educated about the typical consequences of child sexual abuse and about the role that each family member may play in either increasing or decreasing the magnitude of the consequences.

Sgroi's assertions about the responsibility of the family are based on her observations and those of her colleagues rather than on empirical evidence. Although the actions of some families may have played a role in the molestation of one of the children, other families may be free of responsibility. For instance, if a child is molested while playing in a neighborhood park in which she and her friends have played for years without problems, it is questionable whether the parents contributed to the abuse because of insufficient supervision. Parents in this type of situation may react to an intervention designed to have them discuss and remedy their supervision with increased guilt, which may not be helpful to them or the child, or with increased anger, which may lead them to take the child away from any possibly beneficial therapy. It may be wise for a clinician to explore the possibility that a particular family had a role in the molestation of a child but not to assume that it had.

Incestuous Families That Do Not Reunite

Family therapy is often the final step in the therapeutic process with incestuous families hoping to reunite, and several authors describe programs for these families. In comparison, there has been little discussion in the literature on the utility of family therapy with incestuous families in which either the perpetrator or the victim is not expected to return home. Such a state of affairs is curious because family therapy may be valuable with these families also.

In cases where the perpetrator has permanently left the home, some authors describe the value of dyadic therapy with the mother and victim as well as group or individual therapy (or both) for each of them (see, for instance, James and Nasjleti, 1983; MacFarlane and others, 1986; Zefran and others, 1982). As is generally true in the literature on the treatment of child sexual abuse, little attention is paid to the possible effects of the abuse on the siblings of the victim. There may be some advantages to including the siblings, victim, and mother in family treatment in order to explore each member's feelings about the new family constellation and the loss of the perpetrator. Any inclinations of family members to blame the victim for the breakup of the family can be brought into the open and discussed rather than being allowed to remain unspoken. In addition, family treatment can provide an opportunity to begin an appropriate realignment of roles and power within the newly formed family. Recall from Chapter Five that clinical reports indicate that mothers in many incestuous families have little power and occasionally have less power than one or more of the children. Left unchanged, this situation may prohibit a mother from assuming the role of family leader.

Clinicians have also seldom considered family therapy in cases where the victim may not be returning to the family within the foreseeable future. In some cases it may be appropriate to have family therapy that includes the victim, although the sessions may become quite stormy. For some family members, the victim may continue to be present in the family emotionally if not physically, and a discussion of such feelings may be comforting to the victim and provide an opportunity for family members to deal openly rather than covertly with the issue of the victim's leaving. The victim may be able to express ambivalent feelings about the family and the requirement that she leave it. This type of therapy may be appropriate in only a few cases. Joining his or her family in therapy may make it harder for the victim to separate, and many angry feelings may surface without a chance for resolution. Whether to have family sessions with these families is clearly a decision that must be weighed carefully by the clinician.

Family therapy may be appropriate for the remaining family members when the victim has left, especially when other siblings continue to live at home. If the perpetrator remains in the home, these other siblings may face abuse themselves, even if the family is being supervised by a child protection agency. Clinical intervention may provide the children and mother with skills to prevent the abuse, and the perpetrator may be less likely than he would otherwise be to attempt further abuse during or after treatment. In an optimistic vein, the removal of the victim may have had a sufficiently disruptive effect on the structure of the family to allow for a restructuring of the family along healthy lines.

Reuniting Incestuous Families

Prerequisites for Therapy

Even with families that are working toward reunification, most clinicians have found that a number of steps must be taken before family therapy can be effectively started. When Giarretto (1982) started the Child Sexual Abuse Treatment Program (described later in this chapter), family therapy was begun as soon as a family entered treatment. This procedure was soon seen as a mistake. By the time the incestuous families reached treatment, they had been badly fragmented by events before and during the incest, by the revelation of the incest, and by their subsequent treatment by legal authorities. This fragmentation required considerable work with the victim and parents as individuals and dyads before family therapy was effective. Other clinicians have also stated that work with individuals, then with the mother/father and mother/victim dyad, and finally with the father/victim dyad is a prerequisite for family treatment (see Anderson and Shafer, 1979; Furniss, 1983a; Hoorwitz, 1983).

After initial individual treatment, work with the mother/victim dyad encourages sharing feelings and strengthening the bond between them, a critical process for the eventual success of family therapy according to some authors (for instance, Herman, 1983). Similarly, Giarretto (1982) considers work with the mother/father dyad an essential treatment element because it helps them explore their emotional reactions to each other, especially the anger that occurred both before and after the incest (see also Hoorwitz, 1983), and facilitates strengthening the marital bond and the parental role. The father/victim session or sessions, which usually occur just prior to the beginning of family therapy, allow the father to apologize to his child (Hoorwitz, 1983). Giarretto and others often work with families in which incest has been a long-term pattern. It may be that avoidance of family work early in the therapeutic process is not appropriate for families in which incest occurred only once or twice before it was discovered. As with other issues, we suggest that various authors' beliefs about the timing of family therapy be used to raise possibilities for handling a particular case—not to provide inviolate guidelines.

Few specific guidelines have been suggested for deciding when a family is ready to begin treatment together. The comfort of the victim with family meetings, as well as the progress made in individual and dyadic sessions, is an important criterion for determining readiness for family therapy. Hoorwitz (1983) writes that beginning family therapy as soon as feasible is important because the mother may choose to remain in group or individual therapy and avoid family therapy if the family work is not begun quickly. His position, however, has not been echoed by other clinicians.

O'Connell (1986) found that having the father write a letter to his daughter, with the assistance of his therapist, is useful for the father and provides good initial contact between the father and daughter before they meet in therapy. In the letter the father accepts full responsibility for the abuse and indicates an understanding of the difficult position in which he has placed his daughter. The letter does not include a plea for forgiveness by the father or anything that would make him appear pitiable, because it is assumed that the daughter cannot be expected to forgive or pity her father at this point.

Basic Process of Therapy

With considerable therapeutic work usually occurring before family treatment, the family therapy described by most authors includes the exploration of many nonincest issues. Some discussion of the incest and its role within the family is needed; otherwise it may appear that the clinician is avoiding the issue or has decided that it is unimportant. However, if the incest is a result of a dysfunctional family system, other areas of family life will have been affected. Working with and changing family patterns in a range of areas is an important process and may take most of the therapeutic time once issues associated with the incest have been explored. Key therapeutic goals include reestablishment of a strong parental coalition, development of a clear hierarchy of authority with the parents at the top, and establishment of firm boundaries between the parents and children (Reposa and Zuelzer, 1983; Webb-Woodard and Woodard, 1982).

The average time taken by families for the entire therapeutic process varies considerably in different programs. To use the two treatments described later in this chapter as examples: Giarretto (1981) states that the average time a family is in treatment in his program is nine months; in contrast, James and Nasjleti (1983) state that the average time in treatment is eighteen to twenty-four months and that ideally it should be two to three years. Although the overall time in treatment depends on the state of each family, it also appears to depend considerably on the treatment philosophy of the clinician.

Two Different Approaches

Two treatment models are outlined here in order to provide a clear idea of the components of a treatment program. The reader interested in descriptions of additional programs is referred to Anderson and Shafer (1979), Furniss (1983a), Herman (1983), Hoorwitz (1983), Sgroi (1982a, 1982b), and Taylor (1984).

Giarretto (1978, 1981, 1982) founded the Child Sexual Abuse Treatment Program (CSATP) in Santa Clara County, California. It has become a model for numerous other incest treatment programs across the country. Giarretto states that the character of the program was derived from the principles of humanistic psychology and from the belief that each member of an incestuous family is a victim. The program works only with those who are or have been involved with the legal process. One advantage of involvement in the CSATP is that offenders are often given suspended or short prison sentences, allowing them to support their families financially and to attend treatment sooner than they otherwise would. (It should be acknowledged that short or suspended sentences are seen as an advantage by those supporting this type of program; others may view the punishment of the perpetrator as more important.) One of the critical elements of the program is the close cooperation of legal and social service agencies, the courts, and the treatment program.

Giarretto (1978) outlines the goals of the program: "Productive case management of the molested child and her family calls for procedures that alleviate the emotional stresses of the experience and of punitive action by the community, enhance the processes of self-awareness and self-management, promote family unity and growth, and engender a sense of responsibility to society. The purpose is not to extinguish or modify dysfunctional behavior by external devices or to cure 'mental diseases.' Rather, we try to help each client develop the habit of self-awareness (the foundation of self-esteem) and the ability to direct one's own behavior and life-style" (p. 67).

The treatment professionals of a newly formed CSATP are drawn initially from the local agencies that handle child sexual abuse cases, adding to the interagency nature of the program. As programs grow, other professionals may be hired. In the Santa Clara program, much of the clinical work is done by graduate student interns who are supervised by licensed professionals. Undergraduate interns and community volunteers assist with administrative tasks, giving the program a community base.

The pattern of clinical interventions is: individual counseling, especially for the child; mother/child counseling; mother/father counseling, which is viewed as the cornerstone of successful family reunification; father/child counseling; and family counseling. Throughout this therapeutic process, three themes are stressed: self-assessment and confrontation, self-identification, and self-management; exploration of all three often occurs simultaneously. Through self-assessment and confrontation, clients work to understand their own characteristics and the characteristics of the family. Initially, positive aspects of the family are examined as a way of convincing members that the family is worth working to save. Eventually, painful aspects are discussed, and feelings about the incestuous behavior are explored in depth. Work on self-identification encourages clients to develop a strong identity, a prerequisite for developing positive self-esteem. Work on self-management helps family members understand that each of them has the power to control the way that he or she lives.

Throughout this process, all family members are encouraged to acknowledge responsibility for their actions. The father's feelings are listened to with compassion, yet the incestuous behavior is not condoned in any way. It is crucial that he eventually admit total responsibility for his behavior, both to himself and to his wife and daughter. The mother is helped to confront the problems in her relationships with both husband and daughter, and to understand that she contributed to the underlying causes of the incest. The mother is encouraged to tell the daughter that she has been poorly parented by both the mother and father in order to relieve the daughter of self-blame for the incest. The daughter is encouraged to understand that she was not entirely a helpless victim, although responsibility is not switched from the father (or parents) to the daughter (the exact process by which this seemingly difficult maneuver is accomplished is not detailed).

An integral part of the entire treatment process is involvement in the self-help groups of Parents United and Sons and Daughters United. Parents United includes groups for men and women as well as mixed groups and groups for couples. Sons and Daughters United has groups for preadolescents and adolescents, with boys' and girls' and mixed groups for both ages. The CSATP apparently makes much greater use of these self-help groups than does any other program. In some cases, Parents United members accompany police officers when they arrest an alleged perpetrator and immediately begin to offer the perpetrator and mother assistance. Parents and children may remain as group members long after formal therapy. Thus, a family's association with the self-help groups may begin as soon as their involvement in the legal process, and it may end years later.

The main purpose of Parents United is to provide group therapy. At weekly sessions, all members meet together initially and then break into small groups for therapy co-led by a clinician and a trained member of Parents United. The groups take on many other functions as well. As just mentioned, members provide support to other incestuous families who are just entering the legal process. Members may help each other find jobs or supply babysitting and transportation if it is needed. The Santa Clara group even has a form letter that it sends to perpetrators' lawyers if it believes they are taking advantage of the vulnerability of perpetrators and charging excessive fees. The group suggests an appropriate fee and the actions that will be taken if the lawyer is not willing to adjust the fee. Members also speak to community and school groups as a way of encouraging other incestuous families to come forward and receive help.

Daughters and Sons United is an adjunct to Parents United and comprises children five to eighteen years of age. As with Parents United, the primary function is providing group therapy. Other activities such as group outings help members develop a sense of belonging.

Kroth (1979) analyzed several aspects of the effectiveness of the CSATP, although he notes that a number of constraints made the evaluation less than ideal. Because of the ethical concerns that we discussed in the introduction to Part Three, it was determined that treatment for some families and not others would be unethical, and thus it was impossible to have an untreated control group. Consequently, the possibility remains that the changes seen in the CSATP families might have occurred naturally over time after the incest was revealed, without any therapeutic involvement. Also, a six-month time limit that was set for the analysis precluded any long-term evaluation of the effects of the treatment program. No other programs appear to have attempted such analysis, however, and despite the methodological limitations the attempts at self-evaluation by the CSATP are commendable and deserve to be emulated by other programs.

One part of the analysis involved comparing the amount of "deterioration" experienced by the members of three groups of twenty-three victims each. The members of each group were matched on several variables such as age, relation to perpetrator, and length of abuse. One group had just entered treatment; one was judged to be about mid-way through treatment; and the third was judged to be nearing termination. It was assumed that without treatment identified victims would increasingly feel negative consequences of the abuse over time and thus "deteriorate." Group comparisons revealed no statistically significant differences in behaviors that might indicate deterioration, such as running away, truancy, and use of drugs. Those nearing the end of treatment were no worse off in this regard than those just entering.

Kroth notes that these results can be viewed as indicating either the ineffectiveness of the treatment, because the termination group was no better than those just entering treatment, or the effectiveness of the treatment, because those in treatment longer had not deteriorated as one might expect they would have had they not been in treatment. Kroth chose the second explanation, although it is unclear why he did so. Most of the reports of the deterioration of sexual abuse victims come from cases where a child has deteriorated sufficiently to require some therapy, and no reports indicate the amount or pattern of deterioration that occurs in victims who are not given treatment once the abuse ceases. To judge the effectiveness of a program on a lack of deterioration when the typical pattern of such deterioration has not been described may be misleading.

In another area of investigation, Kroth found a clear indication of growth in family members. The victims who had been in treatment the longest had the best self-reported relations with the perpetrator and peers. Interestingly, there was no statistically significant corresponding improvement of relations with the mother. Comparisons of the parents of the children in the three groups indicated an increase in positive emotional relationships and increasingly frequent and satisfying sexual relationships between the offender and spouse as the family progressed through treatment.

Other aspects of the program were also evaluated. Daughters who were removed from the homes of families in the CSATP by child protective workers were returned sooner than were daughters in other communities without a similar treatment program. As of 1982, there was no recurrence of incest in any of the families that had completed therapy. Giarretto (1981) places great emphasis on evaluating the effectiveness of the CSATP by the number of new referrals it receives each year. Between 1974 and 1979, there was an average 40 percent increase in the number of referrals each year. If, as Kroth (1979) notes, there is no recidivism in 98 percent of all families reported for incest, regardless of the type of treatment they receive, providing a program that will attract families from their bonds of secrecy is beneficial in itself. The value of a program like the CSATP for encouraging the reporting of child sexual abuse was demonstrated by Barth and Schleske (1985), who compared the child sexual abuse reporting rates in California counties. Before comprehensive treatment programs were developed in some counties, there were no differences in reporting rates. Between 1972 and 1981, those counties that developed comprehensive treatment programs had significantly more referrals than did those without such a program. Thus it can be argued that programs like CSATP that encourage the reporting of incest by providing important and meaningful services to all family members help to reduce the number of incestuous families.

James and Nasjleti (1983) describe a treatment program that intersperses family sessions among the individual, group, and dyadic sessions throughout the course of treatment rather than having family sessions follow individual and dyadic therapy. Initial family sessions are carefully structured and controlled by the therapist. In contrast, the format of later sessions is more freely determined and is shaped more by the family's needs and style. It is interesting to note how the authors' writing style is analogous to their process of therapy. The description of the first family session takes five pages and includes specific guidelines and instructions—even specifying the phrases that a particular therapist should say to a particular family member at a particular point in the session. The last session is described in half a page, which basically tells clinicians to follow the lead of the family.

The first family session comes early in the therapy process, as soon as the victim feels "strong enough to confront the father" (p. 72). It is devoted to two tasks: having the family communicate openly and confronting the incest for the first time. A commitment to reunite the family is also made at this time if appropriate. The victim begins, with support from the clinicians if necessary, by describing her emotional reactions to the incest and her feelings about her father. The father is then asked to respond to the victim's statements. The mother and each sibling are then asked to respond to what the victim has said, to describe their understanding of the victim's experiences, and to express any ambivalent emotions about the victim, the perpetrator, and the incest. Needless to say, this is usually an emotionally laden session. Clinicians are cautioned not to try to reduce the intensity or pain of the emotions because it is important for them to be experienced fully by each family member.

The second session takes place two to four weeks later. This amount of time is long enough for each family member to process feelings in individual or group therapy yet short enough so that they do not forget the emotional experience of the first session. (Although not discussed by James and Nasjleti, the processing of the first session may be just as difficult and important for the siblings as for the victim and parents, and their inclusion in other forms of therapy may be essential if this course of therapy is to be pursued.) The second family session is devoted to defining the pattern of the abuse behavior. The father is asked to describe specifically when and under what circumstances the first act of abuse took place, such as where they were and who was or was not at home. The victim is then asked to describe actions that other family members could have taken to protect her from the abuse, such as taking her with them and not leaving her home alone with her father or installing a lock on her bedroom door. The victim is then asked to describe other abuse situations that occurred and ways that she could have been protected from them. Other family members are asked to recall times that they were aware that the abuse was occurring and whether it was ever discussed with the victim. At the end of the session, the clinicians review the molestation pattern of the family and the ways that the pattern could have been broken. Knowledge of this pattern will be important to help the family avoid similar situations when family visits by the perpetrator begin.

The third session takes place after the legal aspects of the case are settled; thus, it may not occur for several months after the abuse is reported. This session is devoted to the formulation by the family of a plan for the future. A list of both short- and long-term goals is developed, with each family member contributing.

Establishing a plan for visitation by the father is the task of the fourth session. Initially, the father will return home for three or four half-day visits. After the clinicians review the success of these visits, the father is allowed to have day-long visits. Later, he may be allowed to return home for weekend visits (without overnight stays), overnight visits, full weekend visits, and finally a trial family reunification. After three or four instances of each type of visit, the clinicians review the reactions of each family member, and if the visits have been successful, the next type of visitation is allowed. During the fourth session, definite plans for only the half-day visits are made, although tentative plans for other visits can be made as a way of encouraging the family. Key concerns are the feelings of the victim and defining a set of ground rules for the visits so that the victim feels safe. Participation by the family in this process, rather than determination of schedules and rules by the clinicians, allows the members to begin to take responsibility for the direction of the family.

The fifth session takes place after a number of successful visits by the father or if family members feel that the visits are unsatisfactory. The progress of the family is reviewed at this time. Families that are having difficult times or those in which a number of ground rules have been broken may require a number of meetings to work out the difficulties. The authors note that some testing of the ground rules will probably have occurred. The testing should be viewed as an important process; the victim can test her safety, and the perpetrator and other family members can test the clinicians' ability to react appropriately to their behavior. Clinicians must confront the rule breaker with the behavior and require that it stop, but the occasional breaking of rules should not be seen as a sign of treatment failure. Feelings that are behind the testing should be explored.

Once the visitation schedule has been completed, and when the family members and clinicians feel that it is appropriate, the family can be reunited. At this point, a new phase of the therapy begins, with the clinicians shifting to some extent away from concentrating on the sexual abuse and toward providing a general restructuring of the family.

The next set of sessions constitute the sixth step of treatment and focus on the family's adjustment after reunification. Both the strengths and limitations of the family are discussed, and an open communication system is nurtured. The structure and dynamics of the parents' families can be explored as a way of helping them to gain insight into their own behavior. Anxiety that the victim may have over the possibility of the recurrence of the abuse should be explored by having the victim and other family members each relate a situation in which they were concerned that the abuse might have happened again. This exploration should also help the family to identify the ways in which it has grown protective of the victim and other children. Throughout these sessions, strengthening of the parental bond and of the appropriate use of parental authority is fostered as a way of reestablishing a proper hierarchy within the family. In addition, the family may be afraid to touch, and helping them to develop ways of nonsexual, physical nurturing is an important process.

Termination should be a gradual process, as incestuous families are often sensitive to rejection and abandonment. In a final termination session the family reflects on its changes, celebrates, and looks forward to the future. In this session the clinicians stress that any member should feel free to request further intervention by contacting the clinicians and that recurrence of the abuse is not necessary before other sessions are requested.

Therapeutic Issues

Timing of Family Reunification. In some cases, a clinician may be asked to advise on whether the father or victim should be allowed to return home. This decision will be based on the subjective judgment of the clinician about the current state of the family and relations between individuals within the family. Such a decision may be quite difficult to make, and the clinician may feel pressure from the family, the perpetrator, and social service and child protective agencies to respond in certain ways.

If family therapy has begun before a request for reunification is made, the clinician may be able to base his or her judgment on the behaviors observed in therapy. In some cases, the goal of reunification can be used to encourage the family during difficult family therapy sessions, with those that successfully work through a number of issues being allowed to reunite (Anderson and Shafer, 1979). As described by James and Nasjleti (1983), family sessions can be used to plan for and evaluate the success of visits home by the missing family member, with the success of those visits being used as one indicator of the appropriateness of reunification.

O'Connell (1986) describes a gradual reunification process similar to that of James and Nasjleti (1983), along with specific rules for the perpetrator to follow during each stage. As part of this interesting and informative description, O'Connell makes one statement that we believe is controversial and deserves considerable attention: "If the offender is to have more than an occasional and brief interaction with other children [friends of his children], the parents of those children should be informed of his offense and the behavioral measures [rules] he is following to prevent reoffense" (p. 383). O'Connell provides no reason for this instruction, but apparently gives it because of concerns about the father's sexual orientation and the belief that other parents have the right to be aware of the possible threat to their children. Such an action may have several negative consequences, especially if there is little knowledge of the incest outside the family. Both the victim and family may become further isolated from their neighbors and friends because of their embarrassment or the friends' refusal to let their children play with the victim and siblings. The victim may also become the center of unwanted attention as she is asked repeatedly by other children to explain what happened. One also can imagine the additional burden on a mother who must visit several neighbors and explain the occurrence of the incest. We believe that clinicians must carefully consider these possible negative consequences before requiring a family to follow these procedures. It may be possible to implement rules for the perpetrator that protect other children and are similar to those that provide security for the victim, or to limit the amount of contact that the offender has with other children while he is home.

The amount of progress made toward the treatment goals may also be a critical factor to consider. Suitable progress indicates a movement toward healthy functioning for the family and also demonstrates the desire of family members to continue their growth. Thus, according to a number of treatment plans, a couple will need to become more able than they were before to work together as parents, to clearly define a hierarchy of authority in the family with both parents over the children, and to establish firm boundaries between the children and parents. As discussed in Chapter Ten, an increasing number of clinicians support the assessment of perpetrators' arousal patterns and advocate treatment to change the patterns of those for whom children are the primary source of arousal (although, as noted, this process has not gained general acceptance). Clinicians with this perspective often urge that the reunification of families with fathers whose primary arousal remains children be considered skeptically.

When the father has been removed from the home, the wishes of the victim and the mother may also play an important part in the decision to reunite. The clinician may want to be careful in this regard however. Recall that mothers often feel great financial pressure when the father is out of the home, and this pressure may force them to ask for reunification. As noted before, victims often feel pressured to retract an accusation of abuse so that the father can remain in the home, and they may feel similar pressure to allow the father to return. Consequently, although the wishes of the mother and victim should be considered, basing the decision to reunite mainly on the desires of the mother and victim may raise their level of stress.

The safety of the victim must also be considered. Herman (1983) writes that the child's safety is assured only when the mother feels strong enough to protect the victim and when the victim's relationship with the mother is such that she is willing to turn to her for protection. Thus, the self-esteem and self-confidence of the mother and the state of the mother/victim relationship may be important factors that need to be assessed carefully. Ryan (1986) also considers the mother's attitudinal and emotional state as central when considering reunification. The mother should have developed a lessened reliance on the father, so that the father cannot use such reliance to insist upon renewing sexual relations with his children. Ryan uses the paradoxical sign of the mother's growing doubt about taking the father back as an indication that reunification may be appropriate.

Clearly, the subjective decision about when to allow reunification may be a difficult one. In some cases, individual family members should be given a chance to discuss reunification away from other family members and the pressure that may be present when the entire family is together.

Close monitoring of a newly reunified family is usually desirable, and the possibility that reunification was attempted too soon should be entertained by the clinician as the family is observed. A thorny issue is the weight that should be given to the victim's comfort with the reunification when deciding whether it should continue. Basing a decision to remove the father after reunification primarily on the victim's discomfort may place the victim in an inappropriately powerful position in the family, which may make successful parenting impossible. The source of the victim's discomfort may provide clues to the actions that should be taken by the clinician. If discomfort is occurring because rules that were set for reunification are being broken—either literally or in spirit—then the discomfort may be given considerable weight and reseparation may be called for. If the discomfort is due to some vague concerns of the victim, work with the victim or the parents or both to reduce the discomfort may be appropriate.

Termination of Treatment. The termination of treatment has both therapeutic and legal ramifications. In many locales, the father can receive a reduced or suspended prison sentence if he or he and the family successfully complete treatment. Because of the idiosyncratic nature of each clinical case, however, it may be impossible to develop specific therapeutic criteria that the father can fulfill to satisfy his treatment requirement. Certainly, no specific criteria have been suggested in the literature. Thus, the father may find his ability to stay out of prison entirely dependent on the subjective views of a clinician. As a consequence, the legal requirement for treatment faced by one father may bear no resemblance to the legal requirement faced by another. This situation may be ethically questionable and may involve a mixing of roles that clinicians should avoid (Goldstein, Freud, Solnit, and Goldstein, 1986). Nevertheless, it is a vexing problem, and one for which no easy solution, or perhaps any solution, can be found.

Several factors may enter into the clinician's decision that termination is appropriate. Some of these will be the same as those considered by a clinician contemplating termination for any family, such as the clear delineation of parent and child subsystems and an appropriate pattern of communication between members. In addition, the extent to which the victim feels safe with the father may need to be considered. After formal termination, the clinician may suggest that the family consider continuing in self-help or support groups with which the members have become involved. Some clinicians may feel that requiring family members to continue in this way is appropriate. As James and Nasjleti (1983) note, letting the family know that they can turn to the clinicians for further help and that a major problem does not have to develop before they do so should be reassuring for the members. Ryan (1986) writes that preparatory discussions before termination are important and suggests that planning for termination with the family should begin six months prior to its projected occurrence.

On a pessimistic note, Herman (1983) states: "The father's internal controls should never be considered sufficient to ensure safety for the child; if the family decides to reunite, mother and daughter should be explicitly prepared for an attempt to resume the incestuous relationship. Some degree of outside supervision should probably be maintained as long as children remain in the home" (p. 90). Although some programs (such as that of Giarretto, 1981) appear to eliminate the recurrence of sexual abuse in families that complete treatment, not enough data on the overall success of treatment programs have been gathered to ensure that the warnings of Herman should not be heeded. However, the ramifications of permanent outside supervision on the functioning of the family have not been determined either. Certainly if the goal of treatment is an autonomous, well-functioning family, such supervision would suggest that such a goal had not been achieved and that it is not considered achievable.

CHAPTER THIRTEEN

Preventing
Child Sexual Abuse

Numerous programs to prevent child sexual abuse have been implemented in response to research indicating the prevalence of such abuse. Most programs have been designed for elementary school children, although a few have been designed for preschoolers or students in junior or senior high school. Plummer (1984b) suggests that nearly half a million children have been reached nationwide by preventive-education programs in schools alone. As the first programs did not appear until the late 1970s (Finkelhor, 1986), prevention programs are clearly among the fastest growing components of the movement to cope with child sexual abuse. Preventive interventions have much appeal because of their ability to reach large numbers of children in a relatively cost-efficient fashion and because of their potential for reducing the number of children affected by child sexual abuse.

The literature suggests that the programs have as goals both primary prevention (keeping the abuse from ever occurring) and secondary prevention (encouraging disclosure of past and ongoing sexual abuse so that children can receive early intervention and protection). In this chapter, we summarize several of those programs that have been evaluated and review research regarding their effectiveness. For every program that has included some sort of systematic evaluation, many have included none. Thus, whatever their shortcomings, those that have been evaluated are among the elite of prevention programs. We conclude with a discussion of several of the underlying assumptions that power these programs and that are frequently accepted as fact even though they are based mainly on clinical anecdote and "best guess."

Programs for School Children

Programs for children generally cover these topics: explaining what sexual abuse is; broadening awareness of who possible abusers are—not only strangers but also people the children know and like; teaching that children have the right to control the access of others to their bodies; describing a variety of "touches" that a child can experience—which are good, bad, confusing; stressing actions that children can take—for example, saying no to adults who want to touch them in a way that makes them feel uncomfortable, leaving or running away, resisting in some fashion; teaching that some secrets should not be kept; and stressing that the child should tell a trusted adult if touched in an inappropriate manner and should keep telling someone until something is done to protect the child (Conte, Rosen, and Saperstein, 1984; Finkelhor, 1986).

Finkelhor (1986) notes a general effort to skirt the emotionally charged topic of sexuality and sex education in sexual abuse prevention programs. Therefore, child sexual abuse prevention is usually approached from a protective, rather than a sexual, standpoint. The concepts of good and bad touching are often taught through discussions of bullies and people such as relatives who forcefully try to kiss a child. Intimate or long-term sexual abuse tends to be ignored as are specific discussions of molestation by parents. Also generally missing is the information that some "bad" touches can actually feel good. The presentations are entertaining, with occasional injections of humor. These tactics are used to keep the presentations from overly frightening the children or from including material that may be confusing. No investigations have studied the advantages and disadvantages of excluding any of this material or of presenting the programs in an entertaining fashion.

Excluding sexual material has some possible negative ramifications: Children may not learn the proper vocabulary and therefore may not tell anyone because they do not have the words; many children will realize that explicit sexual content is being avoided and thus receive the message that adults do not want to discuss intimate types of sexual activity in which the children may find themselves; and the covert message is that sex of any sort is negative (Finkelhor, 1986). Preventers are aware of these ramifications but claim that compromises must be made and that many schools might not adopt programs that are too closely linked with sex education.

In addition to program content, other factors play a major role in gaining community acceptance. Johnson (1987) suggests that the community-organization principles of innovation and partialization may be critical. Innovation refers to the idea of keeping a new program within the norms of a community and its elite, while partialization refers to presenting an innovative program on a partial basis—that is, a program that is given a trial will be better accepted by the community than a program presented without a trial. Two other factors are also important: citizen control and involvement. A program should have preliminary viewing by community leaders who can comment on its suitability. Training of teachers and parents and involving them as much as possible also contribute to the likelihood of acceptance. By following these guidelines, Johnson has been able to implement successfully a prevention program through the schools in several midwestern rural communities.

Prevention programs vary in a number of ways. Some involve only one presentation (Conte, Rosen, and Saperstein, 1984); one of the longest programs is a series of thirty-eight short sessions (Committee for Children, 1983). Shorter programs generally deal only with the topic of sexual abuse prevention, while longer programs (such as the Committee for Children, 1983) present a number of topics, the general theme of which is the child's right to be assertive with others in certain situations. Conte, Rosen, and Saperstein (1984) state that the length of the program depends on the number of concepts and skills to be covered and on the age of the children. They also suggest that programs aimed at primary prevention may need to be longer than those whose major goal is identification, because some abused children identify themselves after even brief prevention efforts (for example, several children in Seattle identified themselves after viewing a thirty-second public service announcement on television). Primary prevention skills and concepts are usually being taught in the abstract and are frequently difficult for the children to grasp because they have no concrete reference point.

Prevention programs come in many formats, including slide presentations, movies, plays, discussions, and role play, as well as various types of printed material, such as pamphlets or comic books, which may be distributed. Among the most widely used materials are a curriculum guide entitled *Preventing Sexual Abuse* (Plummer, 1984a); a guidance coloring book, *My Very Own Book About Me* (Stowell and Dietzel, 1982); the book *No More Secrets* (Adams and Fay, 1981), which provides practical information for parents and teachers; the special 1985 *Spiderman* comic book on the prevention of sexual abuse (National Committee for Prevention of Child Abuse, 1986); and the play *Bubbylonian Encounter* (Mackey, 1980), which has been presented to younger audiences with puppets and to older youth with actors. Type of format is usually determined by the resources and predilections of the group most involved in bringing the program to a community. Such groups are most often composed of community members who are part of a task force on sexual abuse or are organized by individuals such as the health coordinator of a school district. Most prevention educators (for example, Koblinsky and Behana, 1984) recommend high-interest, nonthreatening formats, such as plays, puppets, and stories, which are often the most expensive.

The presenters of the programs also vary. Some are individuals from groups specially formed for that purpose, such as members of a community task force on sex abuse, while others are teachers, police officers, mental health professionals, or community volunteers specially trained for the program (Conte, Rosen, and Saperstein, 1984). The reasons for using particular presenters include their familiarity with the children, expertise in the topic, and their standing as authority figures in the community who have the children's respect. Most programs take place through the schools and attempt to make use of teachers because of their ongoing contact with the children, their possible ability to deal with a sensitive topic in the best way for their class, and their role in identifying and supporting abused children. In addition, for those programs that provide follow-up discussions with the children in small groups, teachers are potentially ideal discussion leaders. Specially trained volunteers or police officers or employees of a particular group making a presentation have been used because it is assumed that their special training will enable them to impart the most accurate information in a pleasing or entertaining manner. Unfortunately, neither the type of format nor the identity of the presenter has been systematically investigated in order to judge the effectiveness of either. Evaluations are needed regarding these central components, including the differentiation of advantages and disadvantages according to the age of the children.

Programs for Parents and Other Adults

Finkelhor (1986) stresses the value of prevention programs aimed at parents and professionals involved with children. Programs for parents may help them to identify signs that their children are being abused and to react in a constructive manner if abuse is discovered. Moreover, if parents are the educators, children will probably receive repeated exposures to information from a trusted source. The importance of educating parents about sexual abuse was highlighted by Finkelhor's (1984) research finding that only 29 percent of his random sample of 521 parents of children aged six to fourteen had talked with them about sexual abuse. Moreover, only 53 percent of those parents who had talked about sexual abuse had mentioned that the abuser might be someone whom the child knew, and only 22 percent had indicated that a family member might be involved. In other words, only 6 percent of the total sample had ever suggested that a family member might be an abuser.

In spite of the possible advantages, relatively few efforts

have been made to involve parents. One reason may be that parents have a difficult time talking to their children about sexual topics of all sorts. In addition, Finkelhor's (1984) survey found that most parents tend to think of their own children as well supervised and able to avoid danger, and they do not want to frighten their children unnecessarily. Moreover, parents who are likely to attend such educational programs may be better informed and more likely to discuss these issues with their children than those who do not. For example, in the first evaluation of a parent workshop program, Porch and Petretic-Jackson (1986) found that among forty-four parents who completed questionnaires before and after the workshop significantly more parents discussed sexual abuse with their children, used increased specificity in their discussions, and provided more useful information than they had done before the workshop. These results were achieved even though 57 percent of these parents had discussed sexual abuse with their children before the workshop took place, a percentage double that found by Finkelhor (1984). This higher rate was probably caused by the fact that Finkelhor's sample was not selected in conjunction with a prevention program as was the Porch and Petretic-Jackson sample. Thus, although positive results were achieved with this sample, these individuals may have been much more motivated than an average group of parents. If these programs are to reach a broad cross section of parents, prevention educators may need to devise innovative means for delivering them, such as through places of employment or through community service clubs like Kiwanis and Rotary. Such innovations would also have the potential advantage of reaching males, the major perpetrators and the parents less likely to attend the usual evening sessions held in schools, churches, or other community centers. One immediate benefit may be to discourage men from becoming abusers if they believe that children are likely to tell someone of an approach (Finkelhor, 1986).

Prevention programs aimed at teachers, pediatricians, daycare workers, clergy, and the police can provide information that allows these professionals to detect sexual abuse in a child and to react in a constructive manner. Although such programs exist (Finkelhor, 1986), with the exception of Hazzard's (1984) evaluation of a six-hour training program for elementary school teachers, which covered all sorts of abuse prevention, and Swift's (1983) evaluation of an extensive sexual abuse prevention program for a variety of community professionals, there do not seem to have been any evaluations of prevention programs targeted specifically at these groups. Nevertheless, these two evaluations are encouraging. Hazzard found that trained teachers, compared with a control group of untrained teachers, increased significantly in knowledge about child abuse and were more likely to report talking with individual students to assess whether abuse was occurring and talking with colleagues about abuse situations. However, they were no more likely to report cases to protective services. In contrast, Swift found that reporting rates from seventy-one trained school counselors and nurses increased 500 percent, from ten cases during the twelve-month pretraining period to fifty cases during the twelve-month posttraining period. Hazzard and Angert (1986) suggest that Swift's dramatic results may be partially due to both the intensive training received and the community networking that was encouraged by training professionals in several agencies. An issue that was not addressed, however, was the percentage of unfounded reports in the totals. If there was not an increase in founded reports, was the increased reporting a benefit? Some would answer in the affirmative because such reporting may influence unconvicted abusers to cease and desist. Others (such as Goldstein, Freud, and Solnit, 1979) would argue that more harm than good can be done to the families of the children and alleged perpetrators and that family privacy rights may be abridged inappropriately.

Outcome Research on School-Based Programs

Several school-based prevention programs have evaluated the effectiveness with which the children learned the material presented. Conte, Rosen, Saperstein, and Shermack (1985) evaluated a program consisting of three one-hour presentations given by specially trained deputy sheriffs at a private daycare center in Cook County, Illinois. The participant group consisted of ten four- and five-year olds, and ten six- to ten-year-olds, with a similarly composed wait-list control group. One week before the presentation, each child was interviewed by one of four social work graduate students, three of whom were unaware of the child's group. Interviews were conducted again by the graduate students after the presentation. The authors do not say how much time elapsed between the end of the program and these interviews or whether the graduate students remained unaware of the children's grouping. The presentations by the sheriffs were tape recorded and compared with the model used in their training.

Following the program, children in the participating group had significantly increased their knowledge about the concepts and skills that the authors believed would help them avoid becoming victims of child sexual abuse. The older children made a larger gain than the younger children, as was the case in Saslawsky and Wurtele's (1986) evaluation of sixty-seven children from four elementary grades who viewed the Illusion Theater Company's film *Touch*. Conte and his colleagues note, however, that although the children's knowledge increased significantly, the average number of correct responses was only 50 percent for the participating group on the posttest (as opposed to 25 percent on the pretest). They suggest that further investigations into which concepts are not learned or which types of students are least likely to learn the concepts are still needed.

Analysis of the content of the presentations by the sheriffs indicated that assault by a stranger was stressed more than had been intended and that several presenters told "horror stories" to illustrate their points, although these were not included in the model. This information indicates the importance of good training and ongoing monitoring for the presenters if a goal is to ensure that the presenter's beliefs do not modify the presentation. In other words, any program should be monitored to ensure that it is being presented as described, a practice seldom adhered to in this or any other type of human services intervention (Reppucci, 1985; Sechrest, White, and Brown, 1979).

Plummer (1984b) evaluated a preventive program that consisted of three one-hour presentations to 112 fifth-grade students. Sixty-nine children completed pre- and posttests that dealt with the concepts of the program. Posttests were given immediately after the program and then at two- and eight-month follow-ups. More students gave correct answers to fourteen of the twenty-three questions on the posttest immediately following the program than on the pretest, and the answers to the other nine questions either approached significance or had been correct on the pretest. However, there was a significant lowering of knowledge on some items at the two- and eight-month follow-ups. Most of the concepts were still retained at the eight-month follow-up, but there were significantly fewer right answers to questions about breaking promises, whether molesters were often people whom the child knew, and who was to blame if the child was touched in a sexual way than on the previous posttest. Particularly disturbing is the fact that these three concepts are crucial. These findings, when combined with those of Ray (1984) that a booster training session significantly increased children's retention of prevention knowledge, clearly suggest that some sort of review work after the initial presentation increases retention and that prevention researchers should employ follow-up procedures to determine the durability of effects. They also suggest the possibility that programs not including review sessions may not permanently instill the most crucial elements of prevention programs.

Another study that indicated the importance of follow-up evaluation was conducted by Borkin and Frank (1986). These investigators evaluated the retention of basic information about what to do when somebody touches you in a "not okay" way. The eighty-three children (twenty-five three-year-olds, thirty four-year-olds, and twenty-eight five-year-olds) who responded had all seen an adaptation of the play *Bubbylonian Encounter* enacted by hand puppets of Ernie, a character from the popular "Sesame Street" television program, and Miss Piggy, one of the most popular Muppet characters, six weeks before. Answers scored as correct were "say no," "run away," or "tell someone" in response to the question "What should you do if someone tries to touch you in a way that doesn't feel good?" Only one (4 percent) three-year-old offered a correct answer, while thirteen (43 percent) of the four-year-olds and twelve (43 percent) of the five-year-olds did. Clearly more of the older children than the younger children retained some of the critical information taught by the play, but with all three of these young age groups, less than 50 percent of the children retained any of the information. These results again raise the issue of whether a one-time presentation is useful for teaching concepts to such young children even when it is done in an interesting way. Moreover, without a pretesting, there is no way to determine whether many of the four- and five-year-olds learned anything because some unknown percentage of the 43 percent who answered the question correctly probably would have answered it correctly without ever seeing the play.

Ray and Dietzel (1984) evaluated a sexual abuse prevention program in Spokane, Washington, that consisted of a slide presentation, a movie, and the distribution of a workbook that the students were encouraged to take home and discuss with their parents. The effectiveness of the program was evaluated using a twelve-item questionnaire covering the concepts taught to 191 third-grade participants from eight classes. Half the students had seen a follow-up film two weeks after the initial presentation that reinforced the concepts taught initially. Some of the students were pretested, some posttested immediately following the presentation, and all were posttested one month and six months after the presentation.

The authors found that, as a group, the students answered more questions correctly on the posttest immediately after the program than on the pretest. Students who saw the follow-up movie had significantly higher scores on the one-month and six-month posttesting, indicating, as did Plummer's (1984b) study, the importance of review sessions. There was no overall decrease in knowledge between the immediate posttest and the six-month posttest for any group, with the review group scoring slightly higher on the six-month follow-up than on the immediate follow-up. One problem in interpreting these results is presented by the questionnaire that was used. The average number correct on the pretesting was about nine out of the twelve questions, indicating that the students already knew many of the program's concepts before it took place. Consequently, the questionnaire had only a small amount of increased knowledge that it could measure. Similarly, with an average correct response of about 11.5 on the posttests, it is impossible to tell whether the small number of questions created a ceiling above which the amount of student's knowledge could not be measured. Thus, although the number of questions answered correctly on the posttest was statistically significantly more than on the pretest, it is unclear whether the small rise in absolute terms (about two and a half questions more on the posttest) indicates a meaningful rise in knowledge. However, the children may have learned more than was revealed by the limited-item questionnaire. Ceiling effects on knowledge questionnaires have been noted by several investigators (for instance, Conte, 1984b; Hazzard and Angert, 1986; Kleemeier and Webb, 1986).

In one of the few investigations to use a nontreatment control group, Wolfe, MacPherson, Blount, and Wolfe (1986) found that in comparison with this control group, fourth- and fifth-grade children who saw a single presentation of two five-minute skits and participated in a one-hour classroom discussion had more knowledge of the correct actions to take in an abusive situation. However, even though the differences were statistically significant on several questions, the number of children in the participating group answering each question correctly was never more than 10 percent higher than the number in the control group giving the correct answer. Thus, the results raise questions about costs and benefits. Does a less than 10 percent difference in the number of children correctly answering questions about what preventive action to take in a hypothetical abusive situation justify the expense, the time away from class, and any possible negative consequences of the presentations?

Saslawsky and Wurtele's (1986) evaluation of the film *Touch* also used a nontreatment control group and found significant differences favoring the participating group. Again, although significant statistically, the differences between the control and participating groups were less than two points on both a thirteen-point personal-safety questionnaire and a thirty-two-point scoring scale for four vignettes. Thus, the question of meaningful change and cost/benefit issues must be raised again. This study did find that the gains were maintained at a three-month follow-up assessment, and these investigators are the first to report the psychometric properties of their measuring instruments, a major methodological improvement.

Swan, Press, and Briggs (1985) evaluated the effectiveness of a thirty-minute presentation of the play *Bubbylonian Encounter* with a group of sixty-three second- through fifth-grade students in a private, urban, Catholic school. Forty-four children were shown five videotaped vignettes depicting inappropriate and appropriate touch (two examples of positive touching, one of negative touching, and two of sexual abuse) before and immediately after the play, while nineteen children participated in the posttest assessment only. All children were asked to identify the type of touch portrayed in each vignette. The children were correct a high percentage of the time on the pretest; 72 percent for vignettes showing nonsexual touching and 92 percent for those showing sexual abuse. According to the authors, these high scores made it impossible to find significant improvement from pre- to posttesting. However, on the posttest the children were able to answer significantly more often than on the pretest that sexual abuse can occur within one's family and that they should tell someone if they experience sexual abuse. With no long-term follow-up, there is no evidence for the durability of these relatively scant results.

The Swan, Press, and Briggs (1985) study appears to be one of only three that evaluated possible negative effects. When the children were asked about their reaction to the play, only 6 percent said that they did not like it. Because the school would not allow the researchers to question the parents of the children who had been evaluated, a separate sample of parents whose children had also seen the play were contacted by telephone within a week of the play's presentation and asked whether they noticed any adverse reactions to the play in the children, such as "loss of sleep or appetite, nightmares, or expression of fear," and whether their children had discussed the play with them at home. Only 7 percent of the children in this sample said that they did not like the play, and only 5 percent of the parents said that their children had shown adverse reactions; 42 percent of the children had discussed the play at home.

Kleemeier and Webb (1986) used a follow-up questionnaire with parents of elementary school children who had participated in a sexual abuse prevention program. Although the investigators summarized their results as showing "few negative reactions," the data suggest otherwise. More than one-third of the parents reported that their children showed anxiety and irritability, and 20 percent described negative behavioral responses, such as rudeness to strangers, disobedience, reluctance to being touched, and nightmares.

In the only other study that examined possible negative effects, Garbarino (1987) evaluated the impact of the special edition of the *Spiderman* comic book, which contains two stories dealing with sexual abuse. In one story, a girl runs away from home because she is being sexually abused by her father, and her mother refuses to believe her when she attempts to tell. The girl is eventually found by a group of children who have "super powers." These children encourage her to tell their parents, who do believe her and promise to assist her and her family in dealing with the incest. In the second story, Spiderman discovers a boy who is being sexually abused by his teenage female babysitter. Spiderman tells the boy the previously secret tale of his own experience of childhood sexual abuse by a young adult male who befriended him. With Spiderman's support, the boy tells his parents about the incident with the babysitter. (More than fifteen million copies of this comic have been distributed nationwide either as a comic book or as a comic strip in daily newspapers, making it one of the most widely distributed prevention materials yet produced.)

Garbarino used male and female undergraduate students to conduct interviews with a sample of thirty-six boys and thirty-seven girls in the second, fourth, and sixth grades who had read the comic after it was distributed to them in school. Even the second graders answered more than 80 percent of the questions dealing with sexual abuse correctly. As part of the interview, the children were asked whether the comic aroused worry or fear in them. Girls in the second and sixth grades reported feeling worried or scared more than their male counterparts (35 percent versus 17 percent in second grade and 30 percent versus 17 percent in sixth grade). Among fourth graders, 50 percent of both boys and girls reported these feelings. These feelings seemed to be based mainly on the children's realization that "it" might happen to them. At first glance this result may appear to be a negative side effect; certainly Garbarino appears to have interpreted it this way. However, it can also be interpreted as positive in that the comic book may have made a lasting impression on the children. As with fairy tales, the most enduring stories are frequently those that are somewhat disturbing to their young audience because they provide a warning about some harmful event that could happen.

Although not a sexual abuse prevention program per se, a program devised by Fryer, Kraizer, and Miyoshi (1987a, 1987b) is worth noting for its results and techniques. The program consisted of eight daily twenty-minute sessions to reduce children's susceptibility to stranger abduction. Children were taught four concrete rules to follow if approached by a stranger when they were not with a caretaking adult (the children were encouraged to interact with those they met when with a caretaking adult). These rules were: Stay an arm's length away, don't talk or answer questions, don't take anything, and don't go anywhere. Twenty-three kindergarten, first-, and second-grade students participated in the program initially and formed the experimental group, while twenty-one nonparticipating children from the same grades formed the control group and were given the program later. The day before and after the program, each child was sent on an errand by the teacher and met one of the researchers (a stranger) who asked the child to accompany him to his car to help him carry something into the school (the *in vivo* abduction situation). (The researchers went to extraordinary lengths before, during, and after the program to inform parents and to protect children from any anxiety associated with meeting the stranger.)

Pretest results showed that about half the children in each group agreed to accompany the stranger. Posttest results showed no change in the control group, but only 22 percent of the experimental group agreed to go. Six months later, experimental children who had failed the posttest (four children) and all the children in the control group participated in the training program. Children from all groups were then subjected to a new *in vivo* abduction situation. All the experimental children who had passed the original posttest, all the control children, and two of the four retrained experimental group children resisted the abduction situation. The authors conclude that the testing showed that the children had developed the ability to avoid stranger abduction of the type used.

We have reviewed this study in some detail because several components that led to the success of this program may be of importance in sexual abuse prevention programs. First, this program taught specific, concrete rules and steps to follow through the use of role-play techniques. These rules may be easier for young children to comprehend than the less concrete good touch/bad touch idea (with some bad touches feeling good). Also, the touch concept is often taught by means of puppet shows or other sorts of passive-learning techniques. Wurtele, Marrs, and Miller-Perrin (1987) provide evidence that this type of teaching does not work well with young children. Kindergarten children who were taught self-protective skills through modeling and active rehearsal learned these skills better than did a control group who passively watched an experimenter model the skills. Second, the pretesting and posttesting may have "set up" and then reinforced the skills taught by the program. The control students had been approached by a stranger two times before the program, and none of these students agreed to accompany the stranger after the program. Perhaps they were able to reflect on their own experience when taught the skills, and the repetition of the event increased the retention of the skills. Third, a few children were less able than the others to learn the skills; this finding highlights the need to assess which children may need additional instruction to make a prevention program meaningful to them. Lastly, the authors showed that it is possible to provide a meaningful *in vivo* test of the effectiveness of a program. The evaluation procedure and assuring that the children were not harmed by it took great care and considerable time, but the result was a demonstration of the value of the program.

Nevertheless, a word of caution is necessary about the use of *in vivo* studies to assess children's behavior in potentially dangerous situations, because such studies may have unintended negative consequences. For example, a design such as Fryer, Kraizer, and Miyoshi's (1987a, 1987b) might have resulted in desensitizing children to strangers or in arousing fears. Moreover, there is no guarantee that such skills as avoiding strangers in particular situations will generalize to other gambits that molesters might use, especially since there is evidence that perpetrators of sexual abuse commonly use sophisticated strategies of persuasion and social reinforcement (Wolf, Berliner, Conte, and Smith, 1987). As Melton (in press-c) points out, "The sorts of rules taught in the [Fryer, Kraizer, and Miyoshi] program provide little guidance to a child involved in a complex social interaction with a strange adult."

In summary, these evaluations as a whole provide some limited support for the efficacy of various sexual abuse prevention programs. The most common finding was a slight, yet often statistically significant, increase in knowledge about sexual abuse following exposure to a program. The fact learned the most was that family members or friends could engage in abusive activities; however, this was also the fact that was forgotten the most on the follow-up measures. The instruments used to measure change all seemed to have a ceiling effect in that most children answered a high percentage of the questions accurately even before they participated in the program. Thus, it may be that the children learned more than the tests measured (in which case improved assessment instruments are needed) or that children know more of the basic concepts than prevention educators think they do (in which case the need for the programs may be questioned).

In the few studies that examined differences between older and younger children, the younger children learned significantly less. These results raise questions as to whether the programs are useful for preschool children.

Booster or review sessions seemed to increase retention of

learning (as measured by three- to six-month follow-ups) for all but the youngest age groups. In fact, without such sessions, durability of learning seems so weak that it is questionable whether there is any value to prevention programs, particularly those involving only one presentation, even if there are immediate gains. The one exception to this general finding of lack of durability was the Fryer, Kraizer, and Miyoshi (1987a, 1987b) study, which used role-play techniques and *in vivo* abduction situations.

Most of the evaluations had basic design problems. For example, in only one study were the psychometric properties of the measuring instruments provided. Individual item analyses were often used without any concern for the relationship between items. Although a few studies did use nontreatment control groups, most did not; therefore, there is no way to ascertain whether the programs were responsible for any changes that might have occurred. Other flaws included small samples, interviewers not blind to the assignment of groups, and the lack of pretesting to establish a baseline of knowledge. Sophisticated research designs are necessary before we can make any claims regarding the overall positive impact of these interventions.

Finally, even though no investigator discussed the issue, the question of costs and benefits needs to be raised. Although these programs appear to have a great deal of face validity, the results are meager. Attention needs to be paid to different types of programs for different-aged children and to their impact in relation to their costs—both the financial costs and the possible negative consequences to the participants.

Untested Assumptions

As we have seen, initial research efforts seem to indicate that most prevention programs increase students' knowledge of the prevention concepts viewed as important by the programs' designers, at least to a limited degree. Unfortunately, we know little else, although the expanding number of studies holds promise for the future. Some evidence indicates that booster sessions are beneficial; investigations of other program variations have not been made, though. We do not have such basic information as whether the amount of knowledge gained by the students was affected by the length of the program or the identity of the presenter. The advantages and disadvantages of various formats (film, play, discussion, comic book) is not known, although there is some evidence that active participation in self-protective programs may be more effective than passive participation (Fryer, Kraizer, and Miyoshi, 1987a; Wurtele, Marrs, and Miller-Perrin, 1987). Valuable information might be gained by systematically varying these and other variables within a given program, or by using the same measures of effectiveness in several different programs. Also, developmental differences among children demand different instructional formats and different goals. Yet some programs used the same presentation for first and fifth graders as though there were no differences between the two groups of children.

Most preventive programs have a foundation in anecdotal clinical information (Conte, 1984b) and therefore are based on several untested assumptions (Reppucci, 1987). One of these assumptions is that we know what types of skills will lessen children's susceptibility to sexual abuse. However, as discussed in Chapter Three, research into the incidence of child sexual abuse clearly suggests that sexual abuse has many different forms. It is possible that skills useful for preventing one type of abuse are not useful in preventing a different type, or some skills may be useful for children of one age but not for children of another age. Clarity as to the specific skills and behaviors that prevention programs should teach is needed. This clarity should be achieved by assessing what happens in abusive situations. However, *in vivo* situations are difficult to construct because of various ethical problems, not the least of which is that subjecting children to sexual abuse situations is not acceptable.

Another assumption is that children will be able to translate the knowledge gained from prevention programs into effective action when needed. This assumption has also not been proven. In fact, Downer (1984) found that although 94 percent of the children in her evaluation study could define assertiveness after prevention training, only 47 percent could provide an example of an assertive response to an abusive situation. Most individuals, including adults, are aware of situations in which they acted quite differently from the way they knew they should act. Thus, even if Downer's children had been able to provide an effective response, there is no evidence that in a real abusive situation they would have responded appropriately. Prevention programs are powered by the ideas that increasing children's knowledge about abuse, providing them with action alternatives such as giving them permission to say no and get help, and bringing the dangers of abuse to their attention may be important in preventing sexual victimization, but there is insufficient evidence to demonstrate that these ideas prevent abuse.

A third assumption is that prevention programs have no negative effects or, at least, that the negative effects are insignificant when compared with the positive effects. We do not know whether programs about the incorrectness of some forms of touching will adversely affect the children in a number of ways; they may not, for example, be comfortable with nonsexual physical contact with their parents and other relatives or with exploratory sexual play with other children. Although Swan, Press, and Briggs (1985) did ask parents about negative consequences seen in their children, the behaviors that they asked the parents to recall seem to be ones that would indicate extreme and immediate negative effects. Garbarino (1987) also found that a sizable percentage of his sample did express worry and fear after reading the *Spiderman* comic book. In addition, anecdotal evidence suggests that at least some children have temporary negative reactions as a result of being exposed to a prevention program. For example, Conte (1984b) reports that after exposure some preschool children have been afraid to ride home from school with anyone but their parents. The following vignette also demonstrates this concern:

> A first-grade child generalized the message that she had the right to say no to all realms of behavior. For several weeks following the prevention program she frequently told her parents that she had the right to say no to any requests that she did not

like or that made her feel uncomfortable. The parents reported much anguish and frustration on their part about this behavior and about the fact that they had to punish her in order to convince her that she did not have the right to disobey them whenever she wanted to.

We also do not have any empirical or anecdotal evidence about long-term or subtle effects. Although it may be unlikely that most children are adversely affected in any way, these examples do suggest that the risk of negative consequences, such as increased fearfulness or disruption of children's understanding of their world, warrants their investigation (Melton, in press-c).

The crux of the matter is whether any of the programs have achieved either of their major goals—that is, primary or secondary prevention. No evidence, not even one published case example, indicates that primary prevention has ever been achieved. It is often assumed that these programs work because well-meaning professionals and parents believe that they do. For example, Swan, Press, and Briggs (1985) found that over 99 percent of a sample of 225 parents and professionals rated the play *Bubbylonian Encounter* as a helpful tool in teaching prevention concepts, but then these investigators inappropriately concluded on the basis of these endorsements that the play "can be effective in teaching children sexual abuse prevention concepts" (p. 404).

In comparison, there are some reported instances of successful secondary prevention—individual cases of ongoing or past abuse have been discovered as a result of the interventions.

At the conclusion of a standard interview evaluating a prevention program using the *Spiderman* comic on the prevention of sexual abuse, a fourth-grade boy said, "This is just what happened to me." And he proceeded to tell of being sexually molested by a teenage neighbor over a period of a year and a half starting when he was in the second grade. He was silent over that period to protect his mother from the harm the neighbor threatened to inflict upon her if he told. The boy concluded, "He said he would put soap suds in her eyes and put her in the washing machine and he has a black belt in karate and he said he would get her." Finally the boy was asked if having had the *Spiderman* comic at the time would have made a difference. "Yes," he replied, "I would have told my mom about it. I wouldn't have been so afraid. I would have known that it was right to tell" [Garbarino, 1987, p. 148].

Such cases are often cited as justifying preventive interventions; Garbarino did in this instance, even though he also found a significant percentage of the participating children reporting worry and fear as a result of the intervention. The judgment that must be made on some sort of ethical balancing scale is whether the uncovering of a small number of cases of abuse, such as this one, compensates for the seemingly minor negative consequences that have now been documented for up to 50 percent of participants (Garbarino, 1987). Is this a small price to pay in order to uncover and alleviate the possible severe abuse of a few, as documented by case examples? This is not an easy judgment. Recall the vignette we presented in Chapter One of the girl who after exposure to a prevention program mentioned to her teacher that her father had made sexual advances toward her several years previously; and the result was the near disintegration of her family. This example confronts us with the fact that in some instances even exposure of earlier sexual abuse may have negative consequences for the child and the family. Thus, the resolution of this dilemma is not as obvious as it may seem on first encounter.

Conclusion

Without definitive information about these untested assumptions and thorough evaluations of ongoing prevention programs, we cannot be sure that preventive programs are working, nor can we be sure that they are causing more good than harm.

This harm may come in two forms. As mentioned, the programs may adversely affect children's positive relationships with meaningful people in their lives or cause children undue worry or fear, at least in the short run. Also, these programs may increase the risk of sexual abuse for some children if we incorrectly assume that they are protected because of these programs and consequently become less vigilant than we now are about the problem (Wald and Cohen, 1986).

Extensive investigations of the full range of effects of these preventive programs must be undertaken in the future; we cannot continue to assume that they accomplish their goals. Since the safety of children is the goal of these programs, we need to know which ones work to teach which skills to which children. We have raised questions about the programs not to stop prevention efforts but to encourage those involved to begin to ascertain whether they are in fact helping children. Without these efforts we risk developing programs that make adults feel good but that do not protect children. Schools are under pressure continually to add to their curriculum or expand currently existing topics of instruction. Unless sexual abuse prevention programs can demonstrate their usefulness, they risk being replaced by other programs to solve other problems faced by school children.

Part *4*

LEGAL ISSUES

*T*he bond between the mental health and legal fields is becoming increasingly strong. Specifically, as discussed in Chapter Seven, clinicians have increased their involvement in the legal process through their assessments of the credibility of a child's accusation of sexual abuse. Some clinicians have also become involved as advocates of legal reform in order to lessen what they perceive to be the negative consequences of children's involvement in the prosecution of alleged abusers. In the next two chapters, we examine several issues pertaining to the trials of alleged perpetrators, first addressing the role of the child victim and clinician as witnesses, and then discussing the clinical and legal ramifications of courtroom procedural reforms that have been enacted in some states.

As in many legal controversies, balancing the rights of the defendant, the victim, and society is a difficult process in child sexual abuse cases. In 1984, the Minnesota Supreme Court stated, "We understand and recognize the State's concern about the sexual abuse of children. These cases are difficult to prosecute because of the age of the victims and the lack of eyewitnesses. Such crimes are indeed detestable and society demands prosecution of these abusers. However, a sexual abuse charge alone carries a large stigma on the accused and conviction provides a serious penalty. In interpreting our Rules of Evidence, we must not only be aware of the needs of society but also the defendant's right to a fair trial" (*State* v. *Meyers,* 1984, p. 97).

In order to appreciate the views of both victims and defendants, we would like to suggest that the reader think about the issues raised in these chapters from two perspectives. First, be the parent of a four-year-old girl who has been repeatedly sexually abused by a neighbor. Your daughter and you are both traumatized by the abuse, and you fear that her involvement with the legal system will have long-lasting negative consequences. You are distressed by what appears to be more legal concern for the abuser than for your daughter. Second, be a parent of a sixteen-year-old boy who has been babysitting for a neighbor's girl for three years. One evening he returns from babysitting and reports that he had a difficult time with the girl and had to send her to bed early. The next morning, two police officers come to arrest your son on a charge of child sexual abuse filed by the neighbors after their daughter reported that your son has been sexually abusing her for the past two years. You are convinced that the girl is lying because of having to go to bed early, yet the girl and her parents continue to maintain that she is telling the truth. You are distressed by new legal procedures that appear to deprive your son of some of his constitutional rights. Keeping these two perspectives in mind will help the reader understand the strong stands that are taken by both sides in the legal controversies now embroiling state legislatures and state and federal courts.

CHAPTER FOURTEEN

Children and Helping Professionals as Witnesses

S ince the 1970s, prosecutions of alleged perpetrators of child sexual abuse have significantly increased. This trend has meant both that a growing number of children must testify in court and that a growing number are denied the opportunity to testify because they are found to be incompetent. Clinicians' role in the courtroom has also expanded. In this chapter we outline the controversy that has surrounded the increased use of both children and clinicians as witnesses in child sexual abuse trials.

The Clinician as an Expert Witness

Clinicians are being called as expert witnesses in child sexual abuse trials either to tell the jury about sexual abuse in general or to comment on the probability that a particular child is telling the truth about an alleged abuse experience. Courts in different states have varied in their response to the clinician as an expert witness. In this section we review the reasons and requirements for having a clinician appear as an expert witness and discuss the various types of expert testimony that a clinician can give.

In order to be admitted as evidence in any type of case,

an expert's testimony must satisfy three requirements. These requirements are enforced because of the added weight that a jury may give to the testimony of an expert and the prejudicial effect that it might have on the outcome of the trial, which in our system is not to be decided by experts but by peers of the accused. Consequently, the trial judge must find that the value to the jury of the expert's testimony exceeds its possible prejudicial effect before it is admitted. The first requirement of expert testimony is that it be about an area that is not common knowledge. Clearly, if the testimony is common knowledge, its introduction into a trial will be of little additional value to the jury, which heightens the chance that it will be more prejudicial than probative. This requirement may be met by having a lawyer outline the expert's testimony to the judge and arguing which aspects of it are not common knowledge. The second requirement is that the expert have sufficient knowledge about the subject matter to be considered an expert. This requirement is usually satisfied by having experts describe the experiences that constitute the basis of their knowledge, such as number of years working in the field and articles or books published. The third requirement is that the opinion offered by the expert be based on information that is generally considered to be reliable in the scientific community in which it is used (Hensley, 1986). Through this requirement it is hoped that acceptable "fact," rather than an expert's idiosyncratic interpretations, will be introduced. As repeatedly seen in trials, however, a fact acceptable to one group of experts is often discounted by another, especially in many of the mental health professions, resulting in a debate among experts about the facts that the jury must resolve (Aber and Reppucci, 1987).

Expert testimony can take several forms in child sexual abuse cases: supplying general information about child sexual abuse, presenting statistical evidence, evaluating the competence or credibility of a child witness, and identifying a particular child as being a victim of sexual abuse. Opinions differ among commentators and courts on the appropriateness of these various types of testimony. With no federal court ruling on them, the admissibility of expert testimony has varied among the states.

Supplying General Information. In one form of testimony, the clinician may be asked to make general comments about the behaviors of many child sexual abuse victims. These comments are often intended to explain aspects of a victim's behavior that the defense has raised in order to diminish the efficacy of the claims of abuse by the victim. One frequent topic in this type of testimony is the delay that often occurs between the abuse and the child's report of the abuse (Roe, 1985). Defense lawyers may argue that any child who experiences abuse will report it immediately. Expert testimony that delayed reporting often happens in child sexual abuse cases has been accepted by courts as not being general knowledge and is viewed as valuable information for the jury members, who may assume that not reporting the abuse immediately indicates that the child is making up the story (*Smith* v. *Nevada*, 1984; *Washington* v. *Petrich*, 1984). Another topic is the reasons children reveal sexual abuse only in bits and pieces over time and the reasons for many children's retractions and reaffirmations of the abuse. Again, this information has been assumed to be out of the realm of general knowledge and important to help the jury understand the possible reasons for the actions of a victim (*California* v. *Roscoe*, 1985; *Oregon* v. *Middleton*, 1983).

This type of expert testimony has been more generally accepted than the other types outlined in this section. One reason is that it often occurs in response to the defense's attempts to discredit the child as a witness, and thus the defense brings the expert testimony on itself (McCord, 1986). Of greater importance is the fact that this type of testimony is not used to assert that the particular child witness is a victim but rather to assert that the child's behavior is not unlike that of other victims. This is a subtle yet crucial difference. With this type of expert testimony, the jury must rely on other facts in order to find that the child is a victim. If the expert were to assert that the child's behavior indicated that the child was a victim, then the expert could be seen as taking over the role of the jury by deciding that a crime took place. However, when the expert helps the jury understand the child's behaviors and the jury believes, from other facts, that the child is a victim, then the purview of the jury is maintained.

Presenting Statistical Evidence. Although clinicians have been asked to provide statistical information about child sexual abuse, such information has typically been disallowed by the courts, mainly because of a concern that the use of statistics may prejudice a jury against a defendant. Each defendant has a right to be tried as an individual, and placing a defendant within a group that has a high rate of a certain crime associates him or her with the crime merely because of group membership and thus unfairly increases the chance of conviction. For instance, information that a certain percentage of abuse is committed by fathers, as a way of indicating to a jury that a defendant father may have committed the abuse, would be considered prejudicial because it does not address whether that particular father molested that particular victim. "Our concern over this evidence is not with the adequacy of its foundation, but rather with its potentially exaggerated impact on the trier of fact. Testimony expressing opinions or conclusions in terms of statistical probabilities can make the uncertain seem all but proven, and suggest, by quantification, satisfaction of the requirement that guilt be established 'beyond a reasonable doubt' " (*State* v. *Carlson*, 1978, p. 197). In two cases in Washington, the state supreme court reversed convictions of child sexual abuse based on the prejudicial effect of a clinician's report of the frequency of sexual abuse perpetrated by someone known to the victim (Roe, 1985).

Another problem involves the inconsistency of research findings about perpetrators of child sexual abuse. Recall from Chapter Three that there are meaningful differences between the estimates from clinical and empirical studies about the identity of the perpetrator as well as differences in the results of different empirical studies. Although clinical reports often indicate that a father or father figure is the perpetrator in most cases, empirical studies generally find that the father is the perpetrator in less than 10 percent of the cases. In empirical studies of urban women, Russell (1984) found that only 11 percent had been abused by a stranger, while Wyatt (1985) found that 43 percent had been abused by a stranger. Thus, even if such statistical testimony were not found to be prejudicial, no consensus among researchers has been reached that would allow for accurate testimony.

Advising on the Competence or Credibility of a Child Witness. Another area of expert testimony involves clinicians' assessments of the competence or credibility of a child witness (the competence of a child witness is discussed later in this chapter). This area can be divided into two topics, expert testimony concerning the truthfulness of a child witness, and testimony concerning the general ability of children or the particular witness to supply meaningful and accurate testimony (McCord, 1986).

In a number of cases, experts have testified that a child told the truth during previous testimony. This testimony was accepted in one case as being nonprejudicial and out of the knowledge of the jury (*Hawaii* v. *Kim,* 1982). However, all other courts have ruled such testimony inadmissible (for instance, *New York* v. *Fogarty,* 1982; *Washington* v. *Fitzgerald,* 1985). Of primary concern is that such testimony improperly usurps the responsibility of the jury to determine the truthfulness of each witness. It has also been argued that experts have no easier time identifying when a person is lying than the general public, and thus they are not truly expert in this area (McCord, 1986).

A second type of testimony is expert opinions about the child witness's general ability to recognize and tell the truth. The crucial distinction of this type of testimony is that the child's previous testimony is not analyzed, and the jury must still decide, given the expert's testimony about the child's general ability, whether the child told the truth when testifying. Case law is more supportive of this type of expert testimony than of the previous type (see *Roberts* v. *Arizona,* 1983). Some authors have advocated an expanded role for clinicians in this regard (Haugaard, 1988; McCord, 1986). Melton (in press-b), however, disagrees, stating that even this type of testimony can be prejudicial and improperly impinges on the responsibility of the jury.

Identifying the Child as a Victim of Sexual Abuse. Perhaps the most controversial aspect of expert testimony in child sexual abuse cases is a clinician's opinion about whether a child has been sexually abused. This testimony can come in two forms: The clinician can comment on the credibility of previous testimony from the child or can state that the child exhibits behaviors indicating that he or she is a victim of sexual abuse. In a number of cases, courts have been asked to admit testimony that children's symptoms indicate that they exhibit a Child Sexual Abuse Accommodation Syndrome (a group of symptoms first discussed by Summit, 1983, and described in Chapter Four).

Some authors suggest that introduction of expert testimony on behaviors exhibited by the child is warranted (Hensley, 1986). They maintain that the Child Sexual Abuse Accommodation Syndrome has been generally accepted by those working in the field and thus has demonstrated reliability. Its need is defended because of the difficulty many children have giving convincing testimony in trials. A major concern about such admission is that the syndrome itself is flawed (see Chapter Four for details) and its acceptance into testimony is prejudicial to the defendant. In the trial of a stepfather, the supreme court of Hawaii allowed the testimony of a clinician regarding a thirteen-year-old victim who exhibited many of the signs of sexual abuse (*Hawaii* v. *Kim,* 1982). In a juvenile court dependency hearing, a California appellate court upheld the admissibility of expert testimony that a girl had been sexually abused (*In re Cheryl H.,* 1984). However, the following year, similar testimony was disallowed in a California criminal trial, with the differences between a dependency hearing and a trial (which might result in incarceration of the defendant) cited as the reason for the conflicting rulings (*People* v. *Roscoe,* 1985). Many legal scholars concerned with these issues expect that this sort of reasoning will preclude such evidence in the future.

Roe (1985) states that the admissibility of testimony from a clinician about whether a child has been sexually abused may be bad policy. One reason is that the determination of whether a crime has been committed is the responsibility of the jury. An expert testifying that the crime has occurred usurps that function. Melton (in press-a) is adamant about this point, arguing that because a jury is capable of determining whether a child has been sexually abused, this determination should not be relegated to an expert: "Such 'diagnoses' of sexual abuse are essentially legal conclusions based on common sense inferences. As a matter of law, they should not be admitted, and, as a matter of ethics, they should not be proffered, because they exceed experts' competence as mental health professionals." The rebuttal to this point is that the defense can also produce an expert witness to counterbalance the prosecution's expert (Hensley, 1986). Roe, however, is also concerned about this possibility. She notes that in any case where one side can produce a witness to say "black," the other can produce one to say "white." She writes that added stress can be placed on a child victim who is subjected to several batteries of tests by experts for the prosecution and the defense as they develop evidence for their arguments and that the testimony of several experts on each side will do nothing to clarify the question for the jury.

Although Roe believes that expert testimony concerning the general dynamics of abuse victims can provide a jury with valuable information, she suggests that because "interpreting human behavior is far more of an art than a science" (1985, p. 112), testimony by clinicians about whether a child has been sexually abused should not be admissible (see also Cohen, 1985). Her point seems to be well taken considering the problems associated with basing judgments on clinical samples (see Chapter Three), the wide range of symptoms that child sexual abuse victims exhibit (see Chapter Four), and the variety of symptoms and behaviors that clinicians have used to identify victims (see Chapters Six and Seven). We emphasize that the concept of the Child Sexual Abuse Accommodation Syndrome is flawed in that many of the symptoms could have numerous causes totally unrelated to being sexually abused, and the symptoms vary inconsistently depending on such factors as the age of the victim, whether the abuse was perpetrated by a family member, whether it was violent or nonviolent, and whether it lasted for a short or long time.

Competence of the Child Witness

In the 1970s and 1980s, the federal government and a number of state governments amended their rules of evidence regarding children's competence to testify in criminal proceedings. Basically these changes have reversed the presumption that young children, usually children under the age of ten, are incompetent to testify. In this situation, the legal definition of an incompetent witness is one who provides testimony so unreliable that the jury would be misled. It is important to distinguish between the competence and the credibility of a child witness. Competence pertains to the child's general capacity to observe, recollect, and communicate the truth. The judge has the responsibility to rule on competence and has broad powers to exclude any witness deemed incompetent. It is the responsibility of the jury to determine the credibility of the witnesses whom it hears. A number of factors other than the child's general capacity are important in determining credibility, including the witness's veracity or bias and any reasons the particular event in question might have reduced the witness's ability to observe and recollect accurately. In addition, the biases of jury members may affect their perception of a witness's credibility (as we will see in the last section of this chapter).

The impetus for these changes has come mainly from those concerned about the difficulties of successfully prosecuting adults accused of child sexual abuse. The child victim's testimony in sexual abuse trials is usually crucial because there is seldom any physical evidence or other witness, and the exclusion of some young child victims from testifying has irreparably harmed the prosecution of those accused of abusing them. Those favoring these changes regarding children's testimony have asserted that psychological evidence indicates few if any meaningful differences between children and adults in the capabilities needed to provide legally competent testimony, and that prosecutions of those accused of child sexual abuse would more often be successful if judicial screening of young witnesses ceased and each child victim was allowed to testify.

History and Process of Judicial Determination of Children's Competence

The traditional common law practice has been that children below a certain age, usually ten years, are presumed incompetent to testify. It was assumed that testimony given by young children would mislead the jury. In 1895, the Supreme Court ruled that young children could not be declared incompetent per se; rather, the admissibility of their testimony should be determined by the trial judge on a case-by-case basis through an examination of the child outside the presence of the jury. Competence was to depend on "the capacity and intelligence of the child, his appreciation of the difference between truth and falsehood, as well as his duty to tell the former" (*Wheeler* v. *United States*, 1895, p. 524). Until recently, in most states young children were presumed incompetent to testify, although this incompetence could be challenged by a party wishing to use a child as a witness. Under a challenge, competence was judicially determined using four general criteria: an understanding by the child of the difference between truth and falsity and an understanding of the responsibility to speak the truth on the witness stand; the capacity of the child at the time of the occurrence to perceive events accurately; the ability of the child to retain an independent recollection of the occurrence; and the capacity of the child to translate the recollection into words and be able to answer simple questions about it (Bulkley, 1982; Weithorn, 1984).

Judicial determination has not been unanimously accepted. Several legal commentators state that the jury, rather than the judge, should determine the competence of a witness (McCormick, 1972; Wigmore, [1940] 1976). "The major reason for disqualification of [children] to take the stand is the judge's distrust of a jury's ability to assay the words of a small child. . . . Conceding the jury's deficiencies, the remedy of excluding such a witness, who may be the only person available who knows the facts, seems inept and primitive. Though the tribunal is unskilled and the testimony difficult to weigh, it is better to let the evidence come in for what it is worth, with cautionary instructions" (McCormick, 1972, pp. 140–141).

Recently enacted rules of evidence governing children's competence have attempted to move away from judicial determination by changing the presumed incompetence of young children to a presumed competence. Federal Rule of Evidence 601 states that no one can be declared incompetent on the basis of age. This rule is often cited as a model law that eliminates the challenges to children's competence. However, it does require that each witness meet the four criteria mentioned in the previous paragraph. Thus, this new rule does not allow every child to testify, because each child must still meet the requirements of every other person who wishes to testify. As a result, even under the new rules many children must undergo a judicial determination of their competence before testifying (Melton, 1985). One advantage to the new rule is that the burden of proof now falls on a different party because the child must be found incompetent rather than competent (Mahady-Smith, 1985).

Before children can testify in court, they are often interviewed by the judge or attorneys or both in a so-called competence examination to predict the accuracy of their testimony. If the judge decides the child is incompetent as a witness, the child is not allowed to testify. Questions such as "Do you know the difference between the truth and a lie?" and "What would happen if you told a lie?" are often asked. In the one empirical study directly related to these questions, Goodman, Aman, and Hirschman (1987), as part of a larger study, asked several of these questions to determine whether they predicted the accuracy of the testimony of their sample of forty-eight three- to six-year-old children. The results indicated that they were poor predictors. Only two of a possible twenty-five correlations were significant. The authors conclude that these findings support the trend toward dropping the requirement of a competence examination because of the inability of the examination to detect children who cannot testify competently.

Are Children as Competent to Testify as Adults?

Laboratory Studies. A body of research indicates that under certain circumstances, children as young as six, and sometimes as young as three, have the capacities needed to provide legally competent testimony: They can distinguish between the truth and a lie, and they have the ability to perceive, remember, and recall events.

Evidence supporting several theories of moral development indicate that children are able to comprehend the difference between the truth and a lie and to understand the importance of telling the truth, although their reasons for doing so change as they mature (for instance, Colby, Kohlberg, Gibbs, and Leiberman, 1983). Some evidence suggests that age does not influence cheating on an academic test; and this may be an indicator for honesty in general (for a review, see Burton, 1976).

Children's performance on purposeful memory tasks shows that they make more errors of omission than adults and that, as they become older, the number of omissions decreases. Children as young as three have made no more errors of commission than adults, however. In sum, the amount that young children remember is less than adults, but the accuracy of their memory is often as high as that of adults (for reviews, see Goodman and Rosenberg, in press; Johnson and Foley, 1984; Melton, Bulkley, and Wulkan, 1985). Children's memories for tasks about which they are more familiar than adults are sometimes better than the adults' (Chi, 1978; Lindberg, 1980). During free recall, young children's memories are often disorganized, but the amount of their recall can be increased if the questioner provides a clear and logical structure for their memories (Emmerich and Ackerman, 1978; Kobasigawa, 1974).

Limitations of Laboratory Studies. Because this research has dealt with the capabilities of children and adults in the lab, it has examined them in situations that are far removed from those that a child would face when testifying in a sexual abuse trial. Consequently, the capabilities demonstrated by children in the laboratory may not represent those that they would have in a trial situation. The length of time between the event and the recall in these studies is less than the time in a trial situation. Also, there was no overt pressure on the child to answer in a certain way in the lab, but the sexually abused child may perceive pressure from a number of people, including parents and lawyers, to testify in a certain way. Child victims may also be coached about how to testify, are questioned repeatedly about the abuse, and may be badgered on the witness stand; none of this activity occurred in the studies. These situational factors may have considerable influence on the child's competence to testify, and little research has been done about their effects.

Because studies directly related to children's tendency to

tell the truth while witnesses have not been made, somewhat related studies, such as those on academic cheating, must be relied on to provide information in this area. Some other related work, however, raises concerns about young children's abilities to testify as witnesses. Empirical evidence based on both cognitive/developmental (Kohlberg, 1976) and social learning theories (Mischel and Mischel, 1976) indicates that young children's moral behavior is often influenced by what they believe the specific consequences of their acts will be. Children, therefore, may be inclined to lie if they believe that a significant adult wants them to, although this possibility has not been substantiated by research. Other studies have shown that honesty can be adversely affected by the presence of a parent (Burton, 1976). Also, young children's definitions of the truth may affect their testimony. If a young child believes that the truth is what a parent says happened, then the child could speak the "truth" on the witness stand yet not relate what actually happened. As yet, no studies have examined children's conceptions of the truth when parents are encouraging them to say something false, and information in this area is needed before generalizations about children's honesty as witnesses can be made.

The studies by Goodman and her colleagues are more relevant than many to this discussion because they examine children's memories of situations similar to those about which a child would testify. In the first study (Goodman and Reed, 1986), six- and twenty-two-year-old subjects showed a similar ability to answer objective questions about their interaction with an unfamiliar man four days earlier and to identify a photograph of the man. Three-year-olds, however, were significantly poorer at both these tasks. The second investigation (Goodman, Reed, and Hepps, 1985) studied the memories of three- to seven-year-olds about a frightening event (having blood drawn in a hospital) or a nonfrightening event (visiting the same hospital but only having a design rubbed on their arms). They found that although the groups were similar in amount of overall recall three days later, the frightened group recalled more central details about the activity, while those not frightened recalled more peripheral details. This study showed that the fear that some young children feel in an abuse situation may not affect their memory significantly. The lack of a group of similarly treated adults, however, does not allow for a comparison of children's and adults' memories in frightening situations.

In a third study (Goodman, Aman, and Hirschman, 1987), each of forty-eight three- to six-year-old children who were pre-scheduled for an inoculation either as part of normal medical care or as a requirement to attend public school was escorted into the inoculation room by a parent. When receiving the shot from the nurse, the children were usually restrained on their parent's lap or held down on a medical examination table. The event lasted about three to four minutes. Children were brought in for questioning after a three- to four-day or seven- to nine-day delay. They were asked to recall the event, answer objective and suggestive questions, and identify the nurse from a six-person photo lineup. The results indicated no significant age differences in the children's ability to recall the event, nor was there deterioration in recall over time. Moreover, the reports were quite accurate. Older children did, however, answer more objective questions correctly and were less likely to lose the ability to identify the culprit (nurse) over time. Thus, this study provides corroborating evidence that young children are quite able to recall a stressful event accurately after a short period of time.

Suggestibility. Of critical importance to young children's ability to maintain an independent memory of an event is their suggestibility. Do parents', lawyers', or therapists' questions that contain some information about an event affect children's memory of the event? Raising this issue does not imply that those questioning a child would purposefully try to manipulate the child into giving false testimony, although such manipulation has occurred. Suggesting incorrect information to a child may occur in a perfectly innocent way. For instance, a number of case reports give examples in which a young child's answer to a particular question was misinterpreted by an adult. If the adult questioner assimilates this false information into the story that is being constructed about the abuse and then repeats this "fact" over and over to the child while the rest of the story is being brought out, the misinterpretation may begin to be incorporated by the child as the truth.

Studies comparing children's and adults' suggestibility

have yielded conflicting results. Duncan, Whitney, and Kunen (1982) showed that first graders were less affected than third-grade, fifth-grade, or college students by both incorrect and correct information given during the course of a series of questions about story slides that they had just seen. This result implies that young children may be less suggestible than adults in some situations. Marin, Holmes, Guth, and Kovac (1978), however, found no significant differences in young children's and adults' abilities to resist a suggestive question about an incident they observed, both immediately and two weeks after the incident. On the opposite side, Cohen and Harnick (1980) found that nine-year-olds were more suggestible than twelve- or eighteen-year-olds when answering questions about a movie depicting a petty crime, both immediately and one week after seeing the movie. In the study by Goodman and Reed (1986) already mentioned, three- and six-year-olds were both more suggestible than adults when answering questions about an interaction they had had with an unfamiliar man, although the children were more suggestible mainly on questions concerning peripheral information. Consistent with this result was the Goodman, Aman, and Hirschman (1987) finding that older children in their inoculation study showed greater resistance to misleading information than did younger children, and that suggestibility was greater for characteristics of the room in which the event occurred than for the actions that took place or the physical characteristics of the culprit.

The inconsistency of the results of these studies is difficult to reconcile because they involved different situations and children of different ages. Consequently, no firm statements about young children's suggestibility can be made at this time. However, the studies by Goodman and her colleagues have one clear advantage: They examine children's testimony in situations that mimic victimization—the children are under stress, highly involved, and unaware that their memory is being tested.

One common limitation of all these studies is that the suggestions were not given by adults who were meaningful in the children's lives. A suggestion made by a parent or a therapist may be more influential than one made by an unknown experimenter, especially if it is repeated over time. Although some research has shown that adults are more suggestible when questioned by a person in authority than when questioned by a person who is not (for instance, Loftus, 1979), no reports of the ability of children to resist the suggestions of a significant adult have been made.

The information that will be the most difficult to obtain is on the effect multiple suggestions can have on a child over time. It would be unethical in a study to subject children to the type of subtle or overt pressure that some victims experience just to see how they react. Although some assumptions may be made based on other studies, this crucial aspect of children's ability to resist suggestion may have to go untested.

Summary. Although social scientists have provided some laboratory evidence suggesting that even children as young as three may be able to provide competent testimony about some situations, these studies were done in settings quite different from those of a trial. Consequently, we do not have sufficient evidence to justify conclusive statements about children's competence to testify or about the most effective way to present their testimony in court. Further research using relevant paradigms, such as the work of Goodman and her colleagues, would allow for the formation of policy more on evidence than on assumption.

How Do Adult Jurors Weigh Children's Testimony?

A commonsense assumption that is held by most professionals and laypeople is that an older child is a more credible witness than a younger one. This assumption has been confirmed by Goodman, Golding, and Haith (1984), who report that younger children are significantly less credible as eyewitnesses in a simulated vehicular homicide case than are adults. Goodman and others (1987) replicated this finding in three additional laboratory experiments in which the eyewitnesses were aged six, ten, and thirty. However, since the child was not the victim bringing the complaint in any of these studies, they differed considerably from a child sexual abuse case.

In a novel experiment, Levine and his graduate students (Duggan and others, in press) assessed the credibility of children of different ages as witnesses in a simulated sexual abuse trial. Videotapes of a child sexual abuse trial were developed in cooperation with lawyers familiar with sexual abuse cases. Child actresses aged five, nine, and thirteen years were employed to play the role of the victim. The same story line and allegations were used in each scenario: The child alleged that she had been touched illicitly while sitting on the lap of an adult male who was telling her a ghost story in the woods behind her home. In one set of tapes, there was no other witness corroborating the child's story; in a second set, there was corroboration in the form of testimony from a nine-year-old girl identified as a friend of the victim-witness; and in a third set, a woman identified as a neighbor of the victim-witness corroborated her story. The alleged perpetrator was identified in one version as the child's stepfather, in another as a neighbor. Thirty-six juries, each consisting of three female and three male jurors with a mean age of forty-two, selected from voter registration rolls, saw one of the eighteen child sexual abuse trial videotapes and then deliberated on the case for fifteen to forty-five minutes. Each deliberation was videotaped. Half of the juries filled out a questionnaire both before and after the deliberation, and the other half filled it out only after the deliberation. All jurors were paid for their participation.

Of the thirty-six juries, thirteen reached a unanimous verdict, twelve finding the defendant guilty and one finding the defendant not guilty. The nine-year-old was the most credible witness, while the thirteen-year-old was the least credible. Specifically, six of these guilty verdicts were reached in the case of the nine-year-old victim-witness, four in the case of the five-year-old, and two in the case of the thirteen-year-old. The one acquittal was rendered by the jury considering the uncorroborated testimony of the thirteen-year-old alleged victim about non-incestuous abuse. Eight of the guilty verdicts were given in cases where there was a child corroborator, one in a case with an adult corroborator, and two where there was no corroborator (in one of these latter two, the victim was five and in the other, nine). The relation of the alleged perpetrator to the victim was not a deciding factor.

This finding that the thirteen-year-old is the least believed witness contradicts findings (Goodman and others, 1987) that an older child witness is more credible than a younger witness. Although, because the law places sole responsibility on the adult for refraining from sex with a child, the issue of responsibility should not be a factor in a sexual abuse crime, Duggan and others (in press) suggest that jurors may hold a thirteen-year-old partially responsible for what occurred and that this judgment may affect their verdict. Thus, in sexual abuse cases, the credibility of victims may not increase as they approach their teens; indeed, it may decrease. Also, the fact that a child was a more credible corroborating witness than an adult again contradicts data that Goodman and others (1987) have reported. Finally, Duggan and others (1987) report obtaining results similar to their earlier findings, by asking persons comparable to their sample jurors to assess the credibility of child witnesses at different ages using a questionnaire format only. Clearly, the results of this study suggest that researchers must take into account the child's role as a plaintiff, and the nature of the offense involved, before suggesting that older child witnesses are given greater credibility. In summary, a witness's age is a significant factor that jurors weigh in considering testimony, but under specific circumstances—for example, with allegations of sexual abuse, younger children may be more credible witnesses than older ones. Further research is clearly necessary to confirm these surprising results.

CHAPTER FIFTEEN

Procedural Reforms in the Courtroom

*T*he view of many clinicians involved with child victims is
that the children are often further traumatized by their involvement in the prosecution of their abuser. In some instances,
parents have chosen not to report the sexual abuse of their child
because they believe that to do so would compound the overall
stress experienced by the child. As a result, many reports of
child sexual abuse are not made to the police, possibly allowing
the abuser to continue molesting other children. Even when a
report of child sexual abuse is made and the perpetrator is arrested, successful prosecution is difficult because the child, who
is frequently young and the only witness to the abuse, is often
unable to be a credible witness in the eyes of the jury (Bulkley,
1982, 1985b; Melton, 1981, 1985; *Harvard Law Review*, 1985;
Mitchell Law Review, 1985; Mahady-Smith, 1985). Consequently, the child may experience great stress in a trial that may be
unsuccessful in convicting a guilty perpetrator.

In response to these problems, considerable effort has
been focused on modifying trial procedures to make them less
stressful for the child than in the past. It should be noted, however, that few sexually abused children testify in open court
(Rogers, 1982), and, even for those children, participation in
the trial is a relatively minor part of their overall interaction

with the legal authorities (Melton, in press-a). Although changes have also been made in other aspects of the child's legal involvement (such as training investigators to be understanding of the victims), much attention has been paid to changes in trial procedures because they have the potential to change meaningfully the rights of defendants, not only in sexual abuse trials but perhaps also in other trials involving child victims. Goodman and Rosenberg (in press), for instance, question procedural changes in only child sexual abuse trials when other children, such as those who witness the killing of a parent, may be equally or more traumatized by the event and by having to testify about it.

Three changes in trial procedures have been enacted in some states to reduce the trauma to child witnesses and to increase the possibility of successful prosecution of offenders: a broadening of the types of out-of-court statements that can be admitted, increased use of videotaping of the child's testimony outside the court, and shielding the child from the defendant during the child's courtroom testimony. All three innovations involve restrictions on the rights afforded the accused in a criminal trial, particularly the Sixth Amendment right "to be confronted with the witnesses against him." This confrontation clause eliminates the dangers to the defendant of being convicted on the basis of hearsay evidence and, most importantly, provides the defendant with the opportunity for cross-examination. "Confrontation: (1) ensures that the witness will give his statements under oath—thus impressing him with the seriousness of the matter and guarding against the lie by the possibility of a penalty for perjury; (2) forces the witness to submit to cross-examination, the 'greatest legal engine ever invented for the discovery of truth'; (3) permits the jury that is to decide the defendant's fate to observe the demeanor of the witness in making his statement, thus aiding the jury in assessing his credibility" (*California* v. *Green,* 1970, p. 158).

Because these innovations often conflict with the defendant's right to confrontation, the courts and legislatures are faced with balancing the rights of the defendant against the rights of the victim and the community at large. Before discussing the arguments for and against each of these procedural reforms as well as the limited case law associated with each, it is worth noting that some techniques for demystifying the courtroom can be introduced without statutory reform. For example, the physical environment of the courtroom can be modified by such changes as providing a small chair for the child and having the judge sit on a level with the child or wear business clothes instead of a judicial robe (Whitcomb, 1985). As noted in Chapter Ten, careful preparation of the child before testifying by introducing the child to the judge, briefing the child on the roles of the people in the courtroom, taking the child on a tour of the courtroom, and allowing the child to sit in the witness chair and speak into the microphone can also reduce the potential for trauma.

Use of Out-of-Court Hearsay Statements

The innovation that has the most potential for being misused is the admissibility of hearsay statements because it raises major constitutional questions regarding defendants' rights. Hearsay is defined as "a statement, other than one made by the declarant while testifying at the trial or hearing, offered into evidence to prove the truth of the matter asserted" (Federal Rule of Evidence 801). To use an example relevant to child sexual abuse: A child tells her mother that a neighbor has been fondling her during the last few months. If the mother is allowed to testify during the neighbor's trial that the daughter told her of the abuse and the daughter does not testify, the neighbor has lost his ability to confront his accuser (the daughter) by cross-examining her about the accusation (the abuse). Cross-examining the mother would not suffice because the mother is merely relaying what her daughter said. The mother can be cross-examined only about the exchange between her and her daughter, not about any alleged sexual abuse that occurred between the neighbor and the daughter.

Strictly speaking, any use of hearsay would seem to be prohibited by the Sixth Amendment, which was drawn to ensure that a person could not be tried *ex parte* through affidavits and depositions (Mahady-Smith, 1985). The Supreme Court, however, has not viewed the prohibition of hearsay evidence as absolute: "General rules of law of this kind, however beneficial in their operation and valuable to the accused, must occasionally give way to considerations of public policy and the necessities of the case" (*Mattox* v. *United States,* 1895, pp. 242–243). Although there are well-established hearsay exceptions, such as dying declarations, "spontaneous utterances," and a "residual exception" (Clark-Weintraub, 1985), the Court has never espoused a definite theory balancing the confrontation clause with hearsay exceptions. Some guidelines have been given however. Following the precedent of *Mattox,* in *Ohio* v. *Roberts* (1980), the Court held that out-of-court statements do not deny the accused the right to confrontation if two requirements are met: the witness is unavailable (which shows the necessity of the admission of the out-of-court statement) and the statement has "sufficient indicia of reliability" (*Mitchell Law Review,* 1985, p. 812); therefore, each request for an exception must be determined individually by the trial judge taking into account these two requirements.

Unavailability. For hearsay to be considered, the child must be found "unavailable" by the trial judge. Children can be found unavailable for several reasons. If they are found to be incompetent to testify, then they are unavailable. If they are competent to testify, other criteria may make them unavailable: "Unavailability as a witness includes situations in which the declarant . . . (1) is exempted by ruling of the court on the ground of privilege from testifying; . . . or (2) persists in refusing to testify concerning the subject matter of his statement despite an order of the court to do so; or (3) testifies to a lack of memory of the subject matter of his statement; or (4) is unable to be present or to testify at the hearing because of death or then existing physical or mental illness or infirmity; or (5) is absent from the hearing and the proponent of his statement has been unable to procure his attendance . . . by process or other reasonable means" (Federal Rule of Evidence 804).

Most often, a child is found unavailable because he or she (a) is too young to testify (and thus is incompetent), (b) was mentally infirm at the time (such as being very emotionally upset), or (c) would be meaningfully emotionally harmed as a result of having to testify. A child who "freezes" on the stand, either during examination by the prosecution or during cross-examination by the defense, can also be found unavailable.

Indicia of Reliability. If the child is found to be unavailable, the statement that was made by the child must have indicia of reliability. Because the child will not be cross-examined about the statements in court, there must be a clear indication that they are reliable before being admitted as hearsay. In *Dutton* v. *Evans* (1970), the Supreme Court enunciated four criteria for the assessment of the reliability of out-of-court statements made by witnesses, although subsequent lower court rulings have held that not all must be met for reliability to be declared (Bulkley, 1985c). The four criteria are: The statement contains no express assertion of facts previous to the incident described; cross-examination would not indicate that the witness had a lack of knowledge of the incident; there is only a remote possibility that the witness's recollection is faulty; and the statement is such that there is no reason to suppose that the witness purposely misrepresented the defendant's involvement. No further rulings by the Court have more clearly defined these criteria, and it is up to the individual trial judge to interpret the criteria for each individual case.

The Washington supreme court (*State* v. *Ryan,* 1984) found that statements made by a person declared to be incompetent are inherently unreliable. Thus, if a child is found to be unavailable on the basis of incompetence to testify, then another witness may not be substituted for the incompetent child because the hearsay is inherently unreliable. Although no exception was spelled out in the decision, it would seem logical that an excited utterance (see the next section for a definition), which does not depend on memory, could still be supplied by another witness who heard it, even if the child was found to be incompetent to testify.

Current Hearsay Exceptions. Through the years, the courts have developed several hearsay exceptions, in which hearsay evidence, given the unavailability of the witness, can be admitted. Typical situations in which hearsay evidence may be desired in a sexual abuse trial include those where the child has told a parent, doctor, therapist, or other person about the sexual abuse. The prosecution may wish to call the other person either to support a child's testimony or to testify in place of the child. If the child also testifies, there is little trouble with the hearsay evidence presented by the other person because the person giving the hearsay can be cross-examined about hearing it and the child can be cross-examined about the abuse. However, when the child cannot testify, the admissibility of the hearsay is questionable, especially if the account was elicited through questioning and was not spontaneously made by the child. The hearsay exemptions that generally occur in child sexual abuse trials are those involving "excited utterances" or *res gestae* and statements made to a physician during the diagnosis and treatment for an injury. A "residual" exemption also exists that allows for other hearsay evidence if it can be shown to be reliable.

Black's Law Dictionary (1979) defines an excited utterance as a "spontaneous declaration made by a person immediately after an event and before the mind has an opportunity to conjure a falsehood" (p. 1173); in other words, it should be an emotional reaction to an event. Most hearsay in child sexual abuse trials has been admitted under this exemption. A typical example is that of a child who runs home to tell her mother that a neighbor has just molested her. In order to ascertain the spontaneity of the utterance, the court must consider the length of time between the situation and the child's statement about it. In *United States* v. *Nick* (1979), for instance, a three-year-old boy's statements to his mother about a sexual assault he had experienced an hour or two before were deemed admissible (as given by the mother) because the child was found to be too young to testify. Similarly, in *United States* v. *Iron Shell* (1980) a nine-year-old girl's statements to her mother about abuse she had experienced an hour before were considered excited utterances and admitted into testimony. In some states such as Virginia, statements made by the victim several hours after the abuse can be admitted as excited utterances only in rape cases (*Leybourne* v. *Commonwealth of Virginia*, 1981).

Statements made to a physician in the course of a physi-

cal examination for an injury are admissible to the extent that
the information gathered by the doctor was needed for the
proper diagnosis and treatment of the injury (Bulkley, 1985c).
In *U.S.* v. *Iron Shell* (1980), the court held that statements
made to a child's physician when she was being examined two
days after her attempted rape for injuries sustained during the
experience were admissible under this traditional exemption to
the hearsay rule.

*Statutes Creating Special Hearsay Exemptions in Child
Sexual Abuse Cases.* Seven states have enacted special hearsay
statutes for child sexual abuse trials since 1982 (Bulkley, 1985b)
to increase the number of admissible hearsay statements. The
language of the Washington statute served as a model for the
laws of several other states:

> A statement made by a child when under the age
> of ten describing any act of sexual contact per-
> formed with or on the child by another, not other-
> wise admissible by statute or court rule, is admissi-
> ble in evidence in criminal proceedings . . . if:
>   (1) the court finds, in a hearing conducted
> outside the presence of the jury that the time, con-
> tent, and circumstances of the statement provide
> sufficient indicia of reliability; and
>   (2) the child either:
>   (a) testifies at the proceedings; or
>   (b) is unavailable as a witness, provided that,
> when the child is unavailable as a witness, such
> statement may be admitted only if there is corrob-
> orative evidence of the act [Graham, 1985, p. 164].

The adoption of a statute in this form serves several purposes. It facilitates the prosecution of sex offenses against children because courts are no longer required to stretch the requirements of the excited-utterance exemption. Also, it gives
clear judicial guidelines for the admission of hearsay evidence,
resulting in increased certainty as to which types of out-of-court
statements will be admissible. It helps to avoid the wrongful

conviction of alleged perpetrators by requiring either direct testimony by the child or other corroborative testimony; the statement of one adult who was not witness to the abuse cannot be
used alone to convict the defendant. Finally, it discourages constitutional challenges to the statute by closely following the
guidelines enunciated by the Supreme Court (*Harvard Law Review*, 1985; *Mitchell Law Review*, 1985). The Washington statute has been held constitutional by the Washington supreme
court but has not been reviewed by a federal court (*Harvard
Law Review*, 1985).

Use of Videotaped Testimony

The use of videotaped testimony is quite different from
the use, during a trial, of videotapes of children's earlier interactions with a clinician, which were described in Chapter Seven.
Whereas taped interactions with a clinician may be introduced
in a few instances, they are not designed to take the place of the
testimony of the child, and the child often must testify in court
for the tapes to be admitted. In this section, we discuss the use
of videotaped testimony taken outside the courtroom that is designed to take the place of the testimony of the child in open
court.

Statutes allowing for the videotaping of a child's testimony are based on the assumption that the act of testifying in a
strange situation in front of a large number of strangers is, in itself, traumatic for the child and consequently reduces the value
of the child's testimony (Bulkley, 1982, 1985b; *Harvard Law
Review*, 1985; *Mitchell Law Review*, 1985). As a typical example, the New Mexico statute, enacted in 1978, reads: "In any
prosecution for criminal sexual penetration or criminal sexual
contact of a minor, upon motion of the district attorney and
after notice to the opposing counsel, the district court may, for
a good cause shown, order the taking of a videotaped deposition
of any alleged victim under the age of sixteen years. The videotaped deposition shall be taken before the judge in chambers in
the presence of the district attorney, the defendant, and his attorneys. Examination and cross-examination of the alleged vic-

tim shall proceed . . . in the same manner as permitted at trial.
. . . Any videotaped deposition taken under the provision of this
act . . . shall be viewed and heard at the trial and entered into
the record in lieu of the direct testimony of the alleged victim"
(*Harvard Law Review,* 1985, p. 814). The intent of the statute
is to keep the essential aspects of the trial situation (presence of
the judge, defendant, and lawyers, and the ability of the defendant to cross-examine the child) while eliminating the public
aspect of the trial, which occurs if the child must testify in an
open court.

Videotaped testimony is technically hearsay testimony
because it is made outside the presence of the jury (Federal
Rule of Evidence 801). However, although it is a substitution
for open-court testimony, cross-examination of the child is still
possible, which strikingly differentiates it from other forms of
hearsay testimony. States vary in their requirements for admissible videotaped testimony. For instance, the Texas, Kentucky,
and Arizona statutes do not allow the defendant face-to-face
confrontation with the child during the videotaping, although
the defendant can hear the testimony from an adjacent room
and the defendant's attorney is present with the child. These
statutes also prohibit the calling of the child as a witness during
the trial once a videotape is made (Clark-Weintraub, 1985). Several states require that the trial judge make a ruling that the
child is unavailable to testify before allowing the videotaping of
the child's testimony. At least eight states do not require the
finding of unavailability and provide that the child's testimony
should be taped at the request of the child or the prosecuting
attorney.

Although the various statutes providing for the videotaping of children's testimony have not been challenged in the federal courts, several have been challenged in state courts. In *State
v. Melendez* (1982), an Arizona appellate court upheld the use
of a videotaped deposition of a seven-year-old girl. The court
noted that the child had expressed fear about testifying and
that a clinical psychologist had testified that the child would
likely become uncommunicative if testifying in open court. The
court then stated that because the defendant and his counsel

were present during the deposition and cross-examined the witness, the defendant's rights of confrontation were upheld (*Harvard Law Review*, 1985). Similarly, in *Commonwealth* v. *Stasko* (1977), a Pennsylvania court approved the constitutionality of videotaped testimony, noting that the three purposes of confrontation—administration of the oath, cross-examination, and observation of demeanor—were all served (*Mitchell Law Review*, 1985).

Armstrong (1976) argues that the use of videotaped testimony severely infringes on defendants' rights and on the ability of jury members to gather all the information needed to reach the best decision. He notes that the camera becomes the jurors' eyes during the videotaping, selecting and commenting on what the members are allowed to see. He cites television production experts who maintained that "composition, camera angle, light direction, colour renderings will all affect the viewer's impressions and attitudes to what he sees in the picture" (p. 575). He states that videotape is unable to transmit, in the detail needed, all the nuances of the testimony and the witness's demeanor during it. Although an argument can be made that the quality of videotaping has improved dramatically since 1976, Armstrong also argues that the videotaping statutes do not mandate the quality of the videotape, and thus high quality, even if possible, is not guaranteed. Many legal scholars consider videotaping much less of a threat to a defendant's rights than the hearsay exemption. The major threat of videotaping is that in states that do not require the defendant's presence during the child's testimony, the jury may draw inappropriate inferences about the defendant's guilt, because of the harm that it appears the court is suggesting will be caused by the child's seeing the defendant.

Some commentators suggest that components of some state statutes may make them unconstitutional (Clark-Weintraub, 1985; *Harvard Law Review*, 1985). The provisions for removing the defendant from the room in which the videotaping takes place and allowing videotaping without a previous finding of witness unavailability are the ones most often cited as possibly unconstitutional. The general view among legal commentators, however, is that the statutes that require unavailability and videotaping in the presence of the defendant will probably be found constitutional.

Although videotaping has been highly praised by its proponents, Whitcomb (1985) points out that it is seldom used in states where it is authorized. She suggests that many prosecutors consider the environment at a deposition before the trial to be more traumatic than in a courtroom for several reasons: Depositions often take place in small rooms, which bring the child and the defendant into closer physical proximity than in the courtroom; the judge may not be present to monitor the behavior of the defendant or his counsel; and victim advocates may not be permitted to attend. In addition, if a court finding of emotional trauma or unavailability is a prerequisite to a videotaping testimony, the child may have to undergo a battery of psychiatric or medical tests or both by examiners for the state and the defense. Thus, some prosecutors believe that a child who can successfully endure the investigation process leading up to the deposition or preliminary hearing can succeed at trial as well.

Shielding the Child Witness from the Defendant

Several states have enacted statutes allowing the defendant to be screened from the child witness during the child's testimony. Some of the statutes require that the defendant be able to see the witness (such as through a one-way mirror), while others merely mandate that the defendant be able to hear the witness. In other states, the child can testify via closed-circuit television, allowing the judge, jury, and defendant to see the child, while the child is unable to see into the courtroom (Bulkley, 1985c; *Harvard Law Review*, 1985). As an example, the Texas statute reads:

> The court may on the motion of the attorney of any party order that the testimony of the child be taken in a room other than the courtroom and be televised by closed circuit equipment in the courtroom to be viewed by the court and the finder of

fact in the proceeding. Only the attorney for the defendant and for the state, persons necessary to operate the equipment, and any person whose presence would contribute to the welfare and well-being of the child may be present in the room with the child during his testimony. Only the attorneys may question the child. The persons operating the equipment shall be confined to an adjacent room or behind a screen or mirror that permits them to see and hear the child during his testimony but does not permit the child to see or hear them. The court shall permit the defendant to observe and hear the testimony of the child in person but shall ensure that the child cannot hear or see the defendant [Graham, 1985, p. 190].

At issue with this procedural change is whether the defendant has a right to face-to-face confrontation with a witness. Although the Supreme Court has never declared that face-to-face confrontation is required at all stages of a court proceeding, it has stated that such confrontation is preferable at trial (Clark-Weintraub, 1985). In *Mattox* v. *United States* (1895) the Court stated that one advantage of confronting a witness was that of "compelling him to stand face-to-face with the jury in order that they may look at him and judge by his demeanor upon the stand and the manner in which he gives his testimony whether he is worthy of belief" (pp. 242–243). On appeal of a robbery trial four years later, the Court stated, "A fact which can be primarily established only by witnesses cannot be proved against an accused . . . except by witnesses who confront him at the trial, upon whom he can look while being tried" (*Kirby* v. *United States,* 1899, p. 54). As noted, recent rules have held that although face-to-face confrontation may be preferable, it is not essential to the confrontation clause. In a trial not related to child sexual abuse, the Court held that "an adequate opportunity for cross-examination may satisfy the confrontation clause even in the absence of physical confrontation" (*Douglas* v. *Alabama,* 1965, p. 418).

Although the constitutionality of the lack of face-to-face confrontation in child sexual abuse cases has not been reviewed in federal court, the issue has been raised in several state courts, with differing results. In 1981, the Iowa supreme court allowed the screening of a defendant from a child witness during open-court testimony. The court rejected a confrontation clause argument, arguing that the defendant's attorney was able to cross-examine the child and that the jury could observe the demeanor of the child (Bulkley, 1985c). However, in the same year, the California supreme court reversed the conviction of a man for sexual abuse on the grounds that during the trial he was seated so that he could hear but not see the child witness and thus was not afforded his right of confrontation (*Herbert* v. *Superior Court*, 1981). In order to protect the defendant's right to confront an accuser, California law now requires that in instances where the child testifies from another room via closed-circuit television, the defendant's face must appear on a television monitor in the room where the child is located.

Some legal commentators have argued for the use of modern techniques such as closed-circuit television on the grounds that they meet all the requirements set forth by previous Supreme Court decisions regarding confrontation; they merely do so in a way inconceivable when the requirement of confrontation was first enunciated. Mahady-Smith (1985) argues that the goal of the confrontation clause, ensuring the reliability of the witness's testimony, may be lessened by insisting on face-to-face confrontation. She reasons that in many cases the intimidating force of the defendant in the courtroom may make the child's testimony less reliable than it would otherwise be. She notes that the Supreme Court has never held that the right to confront is equal to the right to intimidate a witness and argues that the defendant should not be allowed to intimidate the child witness through confrontation.

Armstrong's (1976) concerns, noted previously, about the effect that the camera may have on the child's videotaped testimony also apply in this area. In addition, concerns expressed in *Hochieser* v. *Superior Court* (1984) are relevant: "Also it is quite conceivable that the credibility of a witness whose testimony is presented via closed-circuit television may be enhanced by the phenomenon called status-conferral; it is recognized that the media bestows prestige and enhances the authority of an individual by legitimizing his status. . . . Such considerations are of particular importance when, as here, the demeanor and credibility of the witness are crucial to the state's case" (p. 286).

Perhaps the key argument against shielding the defendant from the victim, through the use of either closed-circuit television or a physical barrier between them during the child's testimony, is the extent to which the procedure itself suggests to the jury that the defendant is guilty (Graham, 1985). The necessity of shielding a child from the defendant because of the trauma that is caused by the child's seeing the defendant can easily be interpreted by the members of the jury as indicating that the child has good reason to be afraid of the defendant, and hence that the defendant must be guilty. Even if the jury is warned against the development of such an attitude by the court, it may develop and improperly bias the jury against the defendant, who must be presumed innocent until proven guilty.

Conclusions

Notably missing from our discussion of procedural reforms was empirical evidence, psychological or legal, to buttress the positions taken by the reform advocates or opponents. Although the legislative and judicial branches of the government have never been known for their extensive use of empirical data, the lack of such data in these situations is problematic at the least. Melton (1981, 1985) argues that the abridging of defendants' rights that takes place with each of the reforms is serious and should be undertaken only because of pressing need. No available empirical evidence indicates the percentage of children traumatized by testifying, which children are at the greatest risk for trauma, the types of sexual abuse experiences that cause the most trauma to a child testifying about them, or the value of these new procedures for reducing this trauma.

Research projects could be undertaken to answer some of

the questions raised about the effects of the new procedures. For instance, concern has been registered about the effect of testimony via closed-circuit television or videotape. In an experimental situation, it would be possible to present a child's testimony live to one group of adults (representing a jury) and at the same time videotape it to show to another group of adults. Differences in the adults' reactions to the testimony, if any, would provide preliminary information about the effects of videotaped testimony. In a similar type of situation, the reactions to testimony given by a child who is shielded from a "defendant" could be compared with the reactions to the same testimony given while the child is able to see the "defendant." Although such research would be difficult to carry out, it would provide an objective evaluation of these new procedures.

Some of the new procedures seem to have the potential to infringe significantly on a defendant's rights, while others simply make a surface change. For instance, inclusion of hearsay evidence may have a large impact on a defendant's rights because basically no confrontation of the defendant's accuser is possible. Also, shielding the defendant from the witness may meaningfully prejudice a jury because it clearly suggests that the child is afraid of the defendant. However, allowing videotaped testimony of the child, made in the presence of the judge, the defendant, and both counsels, may not have much impact if it is viewed as necessary because of the problems that the child has being in the courtroom (as opposed to being near the defendant). There is often a tendency to assume that a defendant is guilty simply because enough evidence has been accumulated to allow for a trial, despite the fact that we all know that presumption of innocence is one of the cornerstones of our judicial system. Such a tendency may be even stronger when the crime is one of child sexual abuse. This tendency must be guarded against, however, when making policy because changes made in one trial or for one type of crime can often have major ripple effects throughout our legal system.

CHAPTER SIXTEEN

Conclusion: Toward Further Research and Intervention Strategies

*I*n Chapter One, we noted that child sexual abuse has only recently been accorded widespread attention in both the professional and lay communities. We have also discussed throughout this book the extent to which the variety of abuse experiences and the idiosyncratic nature of the victim and perpetrator increase the complexity of the field. Because of the recency of attention and the complexity of the subject, we still have much to learn. Such a situation is a boon for those who are actively looking for answers to many of the questions that remain, because there is still so much of interest to be investigated. Simultaneously, it is a problem for those who need the answers in order to provide meaningful interventions or make sensible policy, because they must use incomplete and scattered information. We believe that the current level of knowledge about child sexual abuse requires certain attitudes and behaviors from those involved in both research and intervention, and we conclude this book by discussing these requirements briefly.

Definitional Issues

One of the advantages of labels or categories, especially in a clinical sense, is that they provide a common meaning for a certain phenomenon. This common meaning can facilitate commu-

nication among those interested in that phenomenon by providing a common language for all to use. For instance, when two
psychologists discuss a client with agoraphobia they generally
know that, although agoraphobics have some unique qualities
and there may be differences in the ways in which the agoraphobia is manifested in different individuals' lives, there is a
certain core group of behaviors and experiences that agoraphobics have in common that set them apart from those without
agoraphobia. As discussed in Chapter Two, such a common
meaning for child sexual abuse has not been developed. The
term has been applied to children who have been approached
unsuccessfully about a sexual encounter, to those required to
watch a pornographic film, to those seeing an exhibitionist one
time, to young children engaging in mutually consenting sexual
encounters with older children, and to children repeatedly
forced to have intercourse with adults over a period of years. It
is difficult to see meaningful commonalities of experience
uniquely present within this diverse group. Referring to child
sexual abuse victims is analogous to referring to phobics: Although it gives some rudimentary information about the experience of the individual, the types of experience can be so disparate that little useful information is imparted. We argued in
Chapter Two that more circumscribed definitions are required
and that *child sexual abuse* should be used only in the most general sense.

Carefully defining what we want to study, treat, or prevent is essential before we can adequately perform these functions. Although it may be hard for a researcher to gather nar-
rowly defined groups of victims for study, the results of a more
easily constructed investigation with a heterogeneous group
may be relatively meaningless. Effective prevention programs,
especially those of short duration, must target specific types of
abuse to be prevented because a general presentation may not
stop any type of abuse. A specific intervention program may be
effective with a certain type of victim and ineffective with another, and this relative effectiveness can be determined only by
judging the effectiveness of specifically defined strategies used
with specific types of victims.

The victims of child sexual abuse form a heterogeneous group. Rather than deciding on a specific definition of child sexual abuse as a way of handling this heterogeneity, we need to develop and use regularly a hierarchy of definitions and labels that becomes increasingly specific. Use of such a hierarchy will allow professionals and laypersons concerned about this issue to increase their ability to communicate with each other because they will know specifically what is being described. We need to define clearly which child sexual abuse victims are the targets of research and intervention so that we can begin to understand the meaning of the phenomenon for the many types of individuals who form this diverse group. Definitional clarity is a requirement for meaningful future work.

Theoretical Issues

We have reviewed the variety of theories that have been put forward to explain the mechanisms that cause the negative consequences seen in many abuse victims and to explain the process by which some families become incestuous. Some of these theories are derived from different views of a particular phenomenon. Several authors have begun to compare the usefulness of these theories. Some are relatively narrow and thus can be used to understand only certain types of sexually abused children. Perhaps in response, other theories are broad and attempt to encompass most or all situations and victims. The limitation of the broad theories is that because they try to explain the entire phenomenon, they must be so encompassing that they risk becoming meaningless as explanations of a particular victim.

When reviewing the various and sometimes competing theories, we have argued that there is evidence supporting each theoretical position and that each theory may be useful in explaining some aspect of sexual abuse experiences. We believe that theories that appear to be competing are only doing so if the assumption is that one theory should emerge to explain all of child sexual abuse. We prefer to view many of the theories as explaining well the experiences of some and explaining poorly the experiences of others. We see no problem with acknowledging the usefulness of several theories to explain this diverse area of inquiry, and we believe that circumscribed theories will be useful guides for the treatment of those victims whom the theory adequately describes. Conceivably a theory that adequately explains the consequences to a four-year-old boy abused by his mother will not be useful in explaining the consequences to a sixteen-year-old girl abused by her father. The individual developmental differences of the child and the perpetrator, and the family developmental differences in cases of incest, may make different theories not only useful but necessary.

Rather than continuing the search for the one best theory or working to demonstrate the superiority of one theory over another, the most promising path appears to be accepting the fact that the diversity of those involved in child sexual abuse can best be understood through a diversity of theoretical approaches. Delineating which theories appear to best explain the consequences found in a certain group of victims will provide specific directions for research and intervention with those victims. Such delineation will occur when theorists present their theories along with hypotheses about the types of victims to which the theories are the most and least applicable. We would argue that for an author to acknowledge that a theory is not applicable to certain victims is not a sign of weakness but a sign of strength and reasonable thinking.

Research Issues

Before introducing empirical or clinical evidence in the preceding chapters, we had to discuss the limits of both types of evidence. Unfortunately, this discussion often took several pages because of the many gaps in our knowledge. All social science research has multiple limitations; one cannot study as complex a topic as human interaction in an absolutely controlled manner. The limitations in the area of child sexual abuse often appear even more numerous than in many others, not because of the inability of the researchers but because of the sensitive nature of the topic and the consequent inability of researchers, for moral and ethical reasons, to use the methods that have been shown to have the highest validity and reliability in other areas of social science inquiry.

Much relatively valid data about child sexual abuse could be obtained from interviewing large groups of children (such as was done with adults in the large-scale studies described in Chapter Three) and then following these groups over time. For instance, research into the consequences of child sexual abuse would be most valid if a large sample of children could be given a battery of psychological measures and could have their environmental circumstances recorded annually, with the changes in those who experience abuse during the course of the study being noted. Of course, such research is unlikely because of the difficulty of obtaining parental permission for the children's participation and ethical concerns about repeatedly testing and asking children about being abused. Consequently, we must fall back on less reliable retrospective reports of how a child was before or after an abuse experience, or we must try to compare abused children with nonabused children who may vary on many factors besides the abuse.

As noted in Chapter Three, only a minority of sexually abused children come to the eventual attention of researchers, and these children do not appear to be representative of sexual abuse victims in general. There are also questions about the representativeness of adults who volunteer for child sexual abuse research and about the representativeness of some large-scale studies, particularly those involving college students. The danger comes as investigators use findings from these limited and unrepresentative samples to describe the entire group of child sexual abuse victims and to develop public policy recommendations. Even defining the phenomenon specifically will be of little help in this regard, as it is likely that, for instance, identified eight-year-old female victims of incestuous intercourse are not representative of all such victims. It is important for investigators to both recognize the limitations of their research and relate this information in their reports so that the consumers of the research are not misled.

The difficulty of doing research in this area may lessen somewhat as investigators develop increasingly elaborate or sensitive research plans, but the major limitations to research will remain. As a result, data on the variety of aspects of child sexual abuse that warrant study will probably improve in quality but remain flawed. We hope to continue to learn as time goes on but recognize that important gaps in our knowledge will continue to exist. The consequence is that we must always incorporate research findings with a knowledge of their limitations. Researchers who claim that they have discovered the answers to the questions about child sexual abuse will in all likelihood be overstating their case. Consumers of this research should be aware that investigators will not be able to give them unimpeachable facts. This is not to say that additional research is not necessary or that current research should be ignored. Some of the information that has and will be provided is meaningful and should be understood; it is just not accurate enough to reveal *the* truth.

Rather than suggest specific research topics, we would like to comment on the importance of the use of clear definitions and the value of the use of specific theories in guiding research programs. Researchers can add important information to the field by testing theory. Theory should be used to direct research, with the research results being used to modify theory. Much current research appears devoid of theory and thus may not be making as meaningful a contribution as possible. For instance, research into the consequences of the legal process on child victims can be guided by clinical, cognitive, and developmental theory hypothesizing about why a particular aspect of the legal process results in a particular consequence for certain children and perhaps in different consequences for other children, with the results of the research used to refine the theory.

Intervention Issues

One of the most striking aspects of the information presented in Part Three is the extent to which the intervention strategies of various clinicians differed and the strategies reported all appeared to be successful. One conclusion is that there is not one best way of intervening with victims and their families. This conclusion is not surprising, because there appear to be many ways of successfully intervening with a variety of therapy clients.

Undoubtedly, part of the reason for the success of many types of interventions is that they match the styles, beliefs, and theoretical positions of the clinicians who employ them. It may be that the clinician's warm and caring attitude toward the client and the clinician's belief that a particular treatment will be of benefit to the client are essential ingredients in the treatment program and that their presence greatly increases the chance that many types of interventions will be successful. We suspect that another factor in the success of many treatments is that each of them may work more or less effectively with different clients because of the clients' abuse experiences, personalities, and dispositional characteristics. If this is the case, an elaboration of the characteristics of clients with whom a particular intervention has been successful and unsuccessful would be an important and needed addition to the treatment literature.

In the introduction to Part Three we discussed ethical reasons cited by some authors to explain the lack of outcome research in child sexual abuse cases. Although we raised some questions about these ethical reasons, we realize that most clinicians are uncomfortable with the experimental manipulations that often accompany outcome research. We would like to suggest that one way of providing valuable outcome data without using an experimental paradigm would be for clinicians to report their cases in the literature, specifically detailing the methods that they employed and their successes and failures. As we argued in a preceding section, acknowledging failures is not a sign of weakness but a recognition that no approach works for all clients. Ryan (1986) has written "Problems, Errors, and Opportunities in the Treatment of Father-Daughter Incest," outlining therapeutic attempts that were later found to be mistakes —a wonderful article for helping other clinicians avoid making the same errors. We would encourage clinicians who write about the subject in the future to be even more specific and outline procedures that have been found valuable for some clients but not for others. This information would provide some guidance to other clinicians in their efforts to diversify their treatment strategies to match the diversity of their clients.

A Cautious and Positive Conclusion

This chapter may be viewed by some as a rather negative way to end a book like this. We have stated that (a) we have much to learn in order to understand this vague phenomenon labeled child sexual abuse, (b) our knowledge will always be flawed, and (c) consequently, it is important to recognize that few statements should ever be accepted as representing a truth about this field. Unfortunately, the current literature is rife with authors' assumptions that are presented as truth or permanent knowledge, and we believe that this tendency is dangerous. Even basic assumptions—such as, any sexual encounter with an adult is harmful to a child, or therapy is beneficial to all victims of child sexual abuse—should not be accepted as fact. Although statements made in the literature may sometimes or often or nearly always be true, there is no reason not to think that in some important cases they will be false. Those working in this field must therefore approach each case with as open a mind as possible and consciously assemble information about each case in a manner that keeps personal biases acquired from previous cases from coloring their thinking about a new case. Creative integration of existing theory and knowledge and personal experience should be the goal.

This is clearly not a field of endeavor for the faint-hearted. It is also not a field for those who need to understand a phenomenon fully before dealing with it or who require specific directions that they can use to deal with any type of situation. It is, however, a field where much needs to be learned and done. Those who are willing to forge ahead despite the roadblocks to success will find their contributions useful and helpful to many.

REFERENCES

Abel, G. G., Becker, J. V., and Cunningham-Rather, J. "Complications, Consent, and Cognitions in Sex Between Children and Adults." *International Journal of Law and Psychiatry,* 1984, *7,* 89–103.

Abel, G. G., Becker, J. V., and Skinner, L. J. "Behavioral Approaches to Treatment of the Violent Sex Offender." In L. H. Roth (ed.), *Clinical Treatment of the Violent Person.* New York: Guilford, 1987.

Abel, G. G., Becker, J. V., Murphy, W. D., and Flanagan, B. "Identifying Dangerous Child Molesters." In R. B. Stuart (ed.), *Violent Behavior: Social Learning Approaches to Prediction, Management, and Treatment.* New York: Brunner/ Mazel, 1981.

Aber, J. L. "The Socio-Emotional Development of Maltreated Children." Unpublished doctoral dissertation, Department of Psychology, Yale University, 1982.

Aber, M. S., and Reppucci, N. D. "The Limits of Mental Health Expertise in Juvenile and Family Law." *International Journal of Law and Psychiatry,* 1987, *10,* 167–184.

Adams, C., and Fay, J. *No More Secrets: Protecting Your Children from Sexual Assault.* San Luis Obispo, Calif.: Impact, 1981.

Adams, M. S., and Neel, J. V. "Children of Incest." *Pediatrics,* 1967, *40,* 55–62.

Adams-Tucker, C. "Proximate Effects of Sexual Abuse in Child-hood: A Report on Twenty-Eight Children." *American Journal of Psychiatry,* 1982, *139,* 1252–1256.

Adams-Tucker, C. "Early Treatment of Child Incest Victims." *American Journal of Psychotherapy,* 1984, *38,* 505–515.

Aguilera, D. C., and Messick, J. M. *Crisis Intervention: Theory and Methodology.* St. Louis, Mo.: Mosby, 1982.

Alexander, P. C., and Lupfer, S. L. "Family Characteristics and Long-Term Consequences Associated with Sexual Abuse." *Archives of Sexual Behavior,* 1987, *16,* 235–245.

Alfaro, J. "Impediments to Mandated Reporting of Suspected Child Abuse and Neglect in New York City." Paper presented at the Seventh National Conference on Child Abuse and Neglect, Chicago, 1985.

Altias, R., and Goodwin, J. "Knowledge and Management Strategies in Incest Cases: A Survey of Physicians, Psychologists, and Family Counselors." *Child Abuse and Neglect,* 1985, *9,* 527–533.

American Psychiatric Association. *Diagnostic and Statistical Manual of Mental Disorders (DSM III).* Washington, D.C.: American Psychiatric Association, 1980.

Anderson, L. M., and Shafer, G. "The Character Disordered Family: A Community Treatment Model for Family Sexual Abuse." *American Journal of Orthopsychiatry,* 1979, *49,* 436–445.

Anderson, L. S. "Notes on the Linkage Between the Sexually Abused Child and the Suicidal Adolescent." *Journal of Adolescence,* 1981, *4,* 157–162.

Araji, S., and Finkelhor, D. "Explanations of Pedophilia: Review of Empirical Research." *Bulletin of the American Academy of Psychiatry and the Law,* 1985, *13,* 17–37.

Aries, P. *Centuries of Childhood: A Social History of Family Life.* New York: Vintage Books, 1962.

Arkin, A. M. "A Hypothesis Concerning the Incest Taboo." *Psychoanalytic Review,* 1984, *71,* 375–381.

Armstrong, J. J. "Constitutionality of Videotaping of Testimony in Criminal Trials." *Oregon Law Review,* 1976, *55,* 555–583.

Asch, S. E. "Opinions and Social Pressure." In E. Aronson (ed.), *The Social Animal.* San Francisco: W. H. Freeman, 1972.

Atteberry-Bennett, J. "Child Sexual Abuse: Definitions and Interventions of Parents and Professionals." Unpublished doctoral dissertation, Institute of Clinical Psychology, University of Virginia, Charlottesville, 1987.

Atteberry-Bennett, J., and Reppucci, N. D. "What Does Child Sexual Abuse Mean?" Paper presented at the 94th annual meeting of the American Psychological Association, Washington, D.C., Aug. 1986.

Avery, B. E., and Sand, M. J. "The Rights of Children in Custody Proceedings in Modern American Family Law." Paper presented at the Law and Psychology Seminar, University of Louisville, 1975.

Avery-Clark, C. A., and Lewis, D. R. "Differential Erection Response Patterns of Sexual Child Abusers to Stimuli Describing Activities with Children." *Behavior Therapy*, 1984, *15*, 71–83.

Bagley, C. "Incest Behavior and Incest Taboo." *Social Problems*, 1969, *16*, 505–519.

Bales, J. "Brief Stresses Competence of Minors." *APA Monitor*, Apr. 1987, p. 35.

Bander, K., Fein, E., and Bishop, G. "Child Sex Abuse Treatment: Some Barriers to Program Operation." *Child Abuse and Neglect*, 1982, *6*, 185–191.

Barry, M. J., and Johnson, A. M. "The Incest Barrier." *Psychoanalytic Quarterly*, 1958, *27*, 485–500.

Barth, R. P., and Schleske, D. "Comprehensive Sexual Abuse Treatment Programs and Reports of Sexual Abuse." *Child Abuse and Neglect*, 1985, *7*, 285–298.

Bauer, H. "Preparation of the Sexually Abused Child for Court Testimony." *Bulletin of the American Academy of Psychiatry and the Law*, 1983, *11*, 287–289.

Bazelon, D. "Veils, Values, and Social Responsibility." *American Psychologist*, 1982, *37*, 115–121.

Bender, L., and Blau, A. "The Reaction of Children to Sexual Relations with Adults." *American Journal of Orthopsychiatry*, 1937, *7*, 500–518.

Bender, L., and Grugett, A. E. "A Follow-Up Report on Children Who Had Atypical Sexual Experiences." *American Journal of Orthopsychiatry*, 1952, *22*, 825–837.

Benedek, E. P. "The Role of the Child Psychiatrist in Court Cases Involving Child Victims of Sexual Assault." *Journal of the American Academy of Child Psychiatry*, 1982, *21*, 519–520.

Benedek, E. P., and Schetky, D. H. "Allegations of Sexual Abuse in Child Custody and Visitation Disputes." In D. H. Schetky and E. P. Benedek (eds.), *Emerging Issues in Child Psychiatry and the Law.* New York: Brunner/Mazel, 1985.

Benedek, E. P., and Schetky, D. H. "Problems in Validating Accusations of Child Sexual Abuse." Unpublished manuscript, Center for Forensic Psychiatry, Ann Arbor, Mich., 1986.

Berlin, F. S., and Meinecke, C. F. "Treatment of Sex Offenders with Antiandrogenic Medications: Conceptualization, Review of Treatment Modalities, and Preliminary Findings." *American Journal of Psychiatry*, 1981, *138*, 601–607.

Berliner, L., and Ernst, E. "Group Work with Preadolescent Sexual Assault Victims." In I. R. Stuart and J. G. Greer (eds.), *Victims of Sexual Aggression: Treatment of Children, Women, and Men.* New York: Van Nostrand Reinhold, 1984.

Bernard, F. "A Study of Pedophiliac Relationships." In L. M. Constantine and F. Martinson (eds.), *Children and Sex: New Findings, New Perspectives.* Boston: Little, Brown, 1981.

Bess, B. E., and Janssen, Y. "Incest: A Pilot Study." *Hillside Journal of Clinical Psychiatry*, 1982, *4*, 39–52.

Black's Law Dictionary. 5th ed. New York: Western, 1979.

Blick, L. C., and Porter, F. S. "Group Treatment with Female Adolescent Incest Victims." In S. M. Sgroi (ed.), *Handbook of Clinical Intervention in Child Sexual Abuse.* Lexington, Mass.: Lexington Books, 1982.

Block, D. A., Silbert, E., and Perry, S. E. "Some Factors in the Emotional Reaction of Children to Disaster." *American Journal of Psychiatry*, 1956, *113*, 416–422.

Boat, B. "Correspondence Between Doll Users and Behaviors of Nonabused and Sexually Abused Children with Anatomical Dolls." Paper presented to the Society for Research in Child Development, Baltimore, Apr. 1987.

Boekelheide, P. D. "Sexual Adjustment in College Women Who Experience Incestuous Relationships." *Journal of the American College Health Association*, 1978, *26*, 327–330.

Borgman, R. "Problems of Sexually Abused Girls and Their Treatment." *Social Casework,* 1984, *65,* 182–186.

Borkin, J., and Frank, L. "Sexual Abuse Prevention for Preschoolers: A Pilot Program." *Child Welfare,* 1986, *6,* 75–83.

Bourne, R., and Newberger, E. H. "Family Autonomy or Coercive Intervention? Ambiguity and Conflict in the Proposed Standards for Child Abuse and Neglect." *Boston University Law Review,* 1977, *57,* 670–706.

Brassard, M. R., Tyler, A. H., and Kehle, T. J. "School Programs to Prevent Intrafamilial Child Sexual Abuse." *Child Abuse and Neglect,* 1983, *7,* 241–245.

Bresee, P. B., Stearns, G. B., Bess, B. H., and Packer, L. S. "Allegations of Child Sexual Abuse in Child Custody Disputes: A Therapeutic Assessment Model." *American Journal of Orthopsychiatry,* 1986, *56,* 560–569.

Browne, A., and Finkelhor, D. "The Impact of Child Sexual Abuse: A Review of the Research." *Psychological Bulletin,* 1986, *99,* 66–77.

Browning, D. H., and Boatman, B. "Incest: Children at Risk." *American Journal of Psychiatry,* 1977, *134,* 69–72.

Bruckner, D. F., and Johnson, P. E. "Treatment for Adult Male Victims of Childhood Sexual Abuse." *Social Casework,* 1987, *68,* 81–87.

Bulkley, J. *Recommendations for Improving Legal Interventions in Intrafamilial Child Sexual Abuse Cases.* Washington, D.C.: National Legal Resource Center for Child Advocacy and Protection, 1982.

Bulkley, J. "Analysis of Civil Child Protection Statutes Dealing with Sexual Abuse." In J. Bulkley (ed.), *Child Sexual Abuse and the Law.* (5th ed.) Washington, D.C.: American Bar Association, 1985a.

Bulkley, J. (ed.). *Child Sexual Abuse and the Law.* 5th ed. Washington, D.C.: American Bar Association, 1985b.

Bulkley, J. "Evidentiary and Procedural Trends in State Legislation and Other Emerging Legal Issues in Child Sexual Abuse Cases." *Dickinson Law Review,* 1985c, *89,* 721–749.

Burgdorf, K. *Results of the National Incidence Study.* Washington, D.C.: National Center on Child Abuse and Neglect, 1981.

Burgess, A. W. (ed.). *Child Pornography and Sex Rings.* Lexington, Mass.: Lexington Books, 1984.

Burgess, A. W., Groth, A. N., Holstrom, L. L., and Sgroi, S. M. (eds.). *Sexual Assault of Children and Adolescents.* Lexington, Mass.: Lexington Books, 1978.

Burgess, A. W., Groth, A. N., and McCausland, M. P. "Child Sex Initiation Rings." *American Journal of Orthopsychiatry,* 1981, *51,* 110–119.

Burgess, A. W., Hartman, C. R., McCausland, M. P., and Powers, P. "Impact of Child Pornography and Sex Rings on Child Victims and Their Families." In A. W. Burgess (ed.), *Child Pornography and Sex Rings.* Lexington, Mass.: Lexington Books, 1984a.

Burgess, A. W., Hartman, C. R., McCausland, M. P., and Powers, P. "Response Patterns in Children and Adolescents Exploited Through Sex Rings and Pornography." *American Journal of Psychiatry,* 1984b, *141,* 656–662.

Burgess, A. W., and Holstrom, L. L. "Interviewing Young Victims." In A. W. Burgess, A. N. Groth, L. L. Holstrom, and S. M. Sgroi (eds.), *Sexual Assault of Children and Adolescents.* Lexington, Mass.: Lexington Books, 1978.

Burgess, A. W., Holstrom, L. L., and McCausland, M. P. "Child Sexual Assault by a Family Member: Decisions Following Disclosure." *Victimology,* 1977, *11,* 236–250.

Burgess, A. W., Holstrom, L. L., and McCausland, M. P. "Counseling Young Victims and Their Families." In A. W. Burgess, A. N. Groth, L. L. Holstrom, and S. M. Sgroi (eds.), *Sexual Assault of Children and Adolescents.* Lexington, Mass.: Lexington Books, 1978.

Burke, J. D., and others. "Changes in Children's Behavior After a Natural Disaster." *American Journal of Psychiatry,* 1982, *139,* 1010–1014.

Burton, R. V. "Honesty and Dishonesty." In T. Lickona (ed.), *Moral Development and Behavior: Theory, Research, and Social Issues.* New York: Holt, Rinehart and Winston, 1976.

Buskirk, S., and Cole, C. F. "Characteristics of Eight Women Seeking Therapy for the Effects of Incest." *Psychology in the Schools,* 1983, *12,* 145–153.

Byrne, J. P., and Valdiserri, E. V. "Victims of Childhood Sexual

Abuse: A Follow-Up Study of a Non-Compliant Population." *Hospital and Community Psychiatry,* 1982, *33,* 938–940.

California v. *Green,* 399 U.S. 149 (1970).

California v. *Roscoe,* 215 Cal. Rptr. 45 (1985).

Canepa, G., and Bandini, T. "Incest and Family Dynamics: A Clinical Study." *International Journal of Law and Psychiatry,* 1980, *3,* 453–460.

Caplan, N., and Nelson, S. "On Being Useful: The Nature and Consequences of Psychological Research on Social Problems." *American Psychologist,* 1973, *28,* 199–211.

Cavallin, H. "Incestuous Fathers: A Clinical Report." *American Journal of Psychiatry,* 1966, *122,* 1132–1138.

Chandler, S. M. "Knowns and Unknowns in Sexual Abuse of Children." *Journal of Social Work and Human Sexuality,* 1982, *1,* 51–68.

Chasnoff, I. J., and others. "Maternal-Neonatal Incest." *American Journal of Orthopsychiatry,* 1986, *56,* 577–580.

Chi, M.T.H. "Knowledge Structures and Memory Development." In R. S. Siegler (ed.), *Children's Thinking: What Develops?* Hillsdale, N.J.: Erlbaum, 1978.

Christopherson, R. J. "Public Perception of Child Abuse and the Need for Intervention: Are Professionals Seen as Abusers?" *Child Abuse and Neglect,* 1983, *7,* 435–442.

Clark-Weintraub, D. "The Use of Videotaped Testimony of Victims in Cases Involving Child Sexual Abuse: A Constitutional Dilemma." *Hofstra Law Review,* 1985, *14,* 261–296.

Cohen, A. "The Unreliability of Expert Testimony on the Typical Characteristics of Sexual Abuse Victims." *Georgetown Law Journal,* 1985, *74,* 429–456.

Cohen, R. L., and Harnick, M. A. "The Susceptibility of Child Witnesses to Suggestion." *Law and Human Behavior,* 1980, *4,* 201–210.

Colby, A., Kohlberg, L., Gibbs, J., and Leiberman, M. "A Longitudinal Study of Moral Judgment." *Monographs of the Society for Research in Child Development,* 1983, *48,* 1–124.

Committee for Children. *Talking About Touching: A Personal Safety Curriculum,* 1983. Available from the Committee for Children, P.O. Box 15190, Seattle, Wash. 98115.

Committee on Sexual Offenses Against Children and Youth.

Sexual Offenses Against Children. Ottawa: Canadian Government Publishing Centre, 1984.

Commonwealth v. *Stasko,* 370 A.2d 350 (1977).

Conerly, S. "Assessment of Suspected Child Sexual Abuse." In K. MacFarlane and others (eds.), *Sexual Abuse of Young Children.* New York: Guilford, 1986.

Constantine, L. M. "The Effects of Early Sexual Experiences: A Review and Synthesis of Research." In L. M. Constantine and F. Martinson (eds.), *Children and Sex: New Findings, New Perspectives.* Boston: Little, Brown, 1981.

Conte, J. R. "Progress in Treating the Sexual Abuse of Children." *Social Work,* 1984a, *84,* 258–263.

Conte, J. R. "Research on the Prevention of Sexual Abuse of Children." Paper presented at the Second National Family Violence Research Conference Researchers, Durham, N.H., Aug. 1984b.

Conte, J. R., Rosen, C., and Saperstein, L. "An Analysis of Programs to Prevent the Sexual Victimization of Children." Paper presented at the Fifth International Congress on Child Abuse and Neglect, Montreal, Sept. 1984.

Conte, J. R., Rosen, C., Saperstein, L., and Shermack, R. "An Evaluation of a Program to Prevent the Sexual Victimization of Young Children." *Child Abuse and Neglect,* 1985, *9,* 319–328.

Conte, J. R., and Schuerman, J. R. "Factors Associated with an Increased Impact of Child Sexual Abuse." *Child Abuse and Neglect,* 1987, *11,* 201–211.

Cook, M., and Howells, K. (eds.). *Adult Sexual Interest in Children.* London: Academic Press, 1981.

Cormier, B. M., Kennedy, M., and Sangowicz, J. "Psychodynamics of Father-Daughter Incest." *Canadian Psychiatric Association Journal,* 1962, 7, 203–217.

Corsini-Munt, L. "Sexual Abuse of Children and Adolescents." In *Childhood and Sexuality: Proceedings of the International Symposium.* Montreal: Editions Etudes Vivantes, 1980.

Coulter, M. L., Runyan, D. K., Everson, M. D., and Edelsohn, G. A. "Conflicting Needs and Interests of Researchers and Service Providers in Child Sexual Abuse Cases." *Child Abuse and Neglect,* 1985, *9,* 535–542.

Courtois, C. A. "The Incest Experience and Its Aftermath." *Victimology*, 1979, *4*, 337–347.

Day, D. "Termination of Parental Rights Statutes and Void for Vagueness Doctrine: A Successful Attack on the *Parens Patriae* Rationale." *Journal of Family Law*, 1977–1978, *16*, 213–219.

DeJong, A. R. "The Medical Evaluation of Sexual Abuse in Children." *Hospital and Community Psychiatry*, 1985, *36*, 509–512.

DeJong, A. R., Emmett, G. A., and Hervado, A. R. "Sexual Abuse of Children." *American Journal of Diseases of Children*, 1982, *136*, 129–134.

Delson, N., and Clark, M. "Group Therapy with Sexually Molested Children." *Child Welfare*, 1981, *60*, 175–182.

deMause, L. *The History of Childhood.* New York: Psychohistory Press, 1974.

DeVoss, J. A., and Newlon, B. J. "Support Groups for Parents of Sexually Abused Children." *The School Counselor*, 1986, *34*, 51–56.

DeYoung, M. *Sexual Victimization of Children.* Jefferson, N.C.: McFarland, 1982.

DeYoung, M. "Counterphobic Behaviors in Multiply Molested Children." *Child Welfare*, 1984, *68*, 333–339.

DeYoung, M. "A Conceptual Model for Judging the Truthfulness of a Young Child's Allegation of Sexual Abuse." *American Journal of Psychiatry*, 1986, *56*, 550–559.

Dietz, C. A., and Craft, J. L. "Family Dynamics of Incest: A New Perspective." *Social Casework*, 1980, *61*, 602–609.

Dietz, S. R., and Sissman, P. L. "Investigating Jury Bias in a Child Molestation Case." *Behavioral Sciences and the Law*, 1984, *2*, 423–434.

Dixon, K. N., Arnold, E. L., and Calestro, K. "Father-Son Incest: Underreported Psychiatric Problem?" *American Journal of Psychiatry*, 1978, *135*, 835–838.

Douglas v. *Alabama*, 380 U.S. 415 (1965).

Downer, A. "Development and Testing of an Evaluation Instrument for Assessing the Effectiveness of a Child Sexual Abuse Prevention Curriculum." Unpublished master's thesis, Department of Psychology, University of Washington, Seattle, 1984.

Duggan, L. M., III, and others. "The Credibility of Children as Witnesses in a Simulated Child Sex Abuse Trial." In S. J. Ceci, D. F. Ross, and M. P. Toglia (eds.), *Perspective on the Child/Witness.* New York: Springer-Verlag, in press.

Duncan, E. M., Whitney, P., and Kunen, S. "Integration of Visual and Verbal Information in Children's Memories." *Child Development,* 1982, *53,* 1215–1223.

Dutton v. *Evans,* 400 U.S. 74 (1970).

Earls, C. M., and Marshall, W. L. "The Current State of Technology in the Laboratory Assessment of Sexual Arousal Patterns." In J. G. Greer and I. R. Stuart (eds.), *Sexual Aggression: Current Perspectives on Treatment.* New York: Van Nostrand Reinhold, 1982.

Eberle, P., and Eberle, S. *The Politics of Child Abuse.* Secaucus, N.J.: Stuart, 1986.

Ellerstein, N. S., and Canavan, J. W. "Sexual Abuse of Boys." *American Journal of Diseases of Children,* 1980, *134,* 255–257.

Elwell, M. E., and Ephros, P. H. "Initial Reactions of Sexually Abused Children." *Social Casework,* 1987, *68,* 109–116.

Emans, S. J., Woods, E. R., Flagg, N. T., and Freeman, A. "Genital Findings in Sexually Abused, Symptomatic and Asymptomatic Girls." *Pediatrics,* 1987, *79,* 778–785.

Emery, R. E. "Interparental Conflict and the Children of Discord and Divorce." *Psychological Bulletin,* 1982, *92,* 310–330.

Emmerich, H. J., and Ackerman, B. P. "Developmental Differences in Recall: Encoding or Retrieval?" *Journal of Experimental Child Psychology,* 1978, *25,* 514–525.

Enos, W. F., Conrath, T. B., and Byer, J. C. "Forensic Evaluation of the Sexually Abused Child." *Pediatrics,* 1986, *78,* 385–398.

Erikson, E. H. *Identity, Youth and Crisis.* New York: Norton, 1967.

Farber, E. D., and others. "The Sexual Abuse of Children: A Comparison of Male and Female Victims." *Journal of Clinical Child Psychology,* 1984, *13,* 294–297.

Feldman-Summers, S., Gordon, P. E., and Meagler, J. R. "The

Impact of Rape on Sexual Satisfaction." *Journal of Abnormal Psychology,* 1979, *88,* 101–105.

Ferenczi, S. "Confusion of Tongues Between the Adult and the Child." *International Journal of Psychoanalysis,* 1949, *30,* 225–231.

Feshbach, N. D., and Feshbach, S. "Toward an Historical, Social, and Developmental Perspective on Children's Rights." *Journal of Social Issues,* 1978, *34,* 1–7.

Festinger, L. "Cognitive Dissonance." In E. Aronson (ed.), *The Social Animal.* San Francisco: W. H. Freeman, 1972.

Finch, S. M. "Sexual Abuse by Mothers." *Medical Aspects of Human Sexuality,* 1973, *7,* 191–197.

Finkelhor, D. *Sexually Victimized Children.* New York: Free Press, 1979.

Finkelhor, D. "Risk Factors in the Sexual Victimization of Children." *Child Abuse and Neglect,* 1980a, *4,* 265–273.

Finkelhor, D. "Sex Among Siblings: A Survey on Prevalence, Variety, and Effects." *Archives of Sexual Behavior,* 1980b, *9,* 171–194.

Finkelhor, D. (ed.). *Child Sexual Abuse: New Theory and Research.* New York: Free Press, 1984.

Finkelhor, D. "Prevention: A Review of Programs and Research." In D. Finkelhor and others (eds.), *A Sourcebook on Child Sexual Abuse.* Beverly Hills, Calif.: Sage, 1986.

Finkelhor, D. "The Trauma of Child Sexual Abuse: Two Models." *Journal of Social Issues,* in press.

Finkelhor, D., and Araji, S. "The Prevention of Child Sexual Abuse: A Review of Current Approaches." Unpublished manuscript, Family Research Laboratory, Horton Social Science Center, University of New Hampshire, Durham, 1983.

Finkelhor, D., and Browne, A. "The Traumatic Impact of Child Sexual Abuse." *American Journal of Orthopsychiatry,* 1985, *55,* 530–541.

Finkelhor, D., Gomes-Schwartz, B., and Horowitz, J. "Professionals' Responses." In D. Finkelhor (ed.), *Child Sexual Abuse: New Theory and Research.* New York: Free Press, 1984.

Finkelhor, D., and Redfield, D. "How the Public Defines Sexual

Abuse." In D. Finkelhor (ed.), *Child Sexual Abuse: New Theory and Research.* New York: Free Press, 1984.

Finkelhor, D., and Associates. *A Sourcebook on Child Sexual Abuse.* Beverly Hills, Calif.: Sage, 1986.

Fischer, M. "Adolescent Adjustment After Incest." *School Psychology International,* 1983, *4,* 217–222.

Forseth, L. B., and Brown, A. "A Survey of Intrafamilial Sexual Abuse Treatment Centers: Implications for Intervention." *Child Abuse and Neglect,* 1981, *5,* 177–186.

Fowler, C., Burns, S. R., and Roehl, J. E. "The Role of Group Therapy in Incest Counseling." *International Journal of Family Therapy,* 1983, *5,* 127–135.

Fox, J. R. "Sibling Incest." *British Journal of Sociology,* 1962, *13,* 128–150.

Freud, A. "A Psychoanalyst's View of Sexual Abuse by Parents." In P. B. Mrazek and C. H. Kempe (eds.), *Sexually Abused Children and Their Families.* Elmsford, N.Y.: Pergamon Press, 1981.

Freud, S. *The Complete Introductory Lectures on Psychoanalysis.* (J. Strachey, ed. and trans.) New York: Norton, 1965. (Originally published 1933.)

Freund, K., McNight, C. K., Langevin, R., and Cibiri, S. "The Female Child as a Surrogate Object." *Archives of Sexual Behavior,* 1972, *2,* 119–133.

Friedrich, W. N., Beilke, R. L., and Urquiza, A. J. "Behavior Problems in Young Sexually Abused Boys: A Comparison Study." *Journal of Interpersonal Violence,* in press.

Friedrich, W. N., and Reams, R. A. "Course of Psychological Symptoms in Sexually Abused Young Children." *Psychotherapy,* in press.

Friedrich, W. N., Urquiza, A. J., and Beilke, R. L. "Behavior Problems in Sexually Abused Young Children." *Journal of Pediatric Psychiatry,* 1986, *2,* 47–57.

Fritz, G. S., Stoll, K., and Wagner, N. N. "A Comparison of Males and Females Who Were Sexually Molested as Children." *Journal of Sex and Marital Therapy,* 1981, *7,* 54–59.

Fromuth, M. E. "The Relationship of Childhood Sexual Abuse with Later Psychological and Sexual Adjustment in a Sample of College Women." *Child Abuse and Neglect,* 1986, *10,* 5–15.

Fryer, G. E., Kraizer, S. K., and Miyoshi, T. "Measuring Actual Reduction of Risk to Child Abuse: A New Approach." *Child Abuse and Neglect,* 1987a, *11,* 173–179.

Fryer, G. E., Kraizer, S. K., and Miyoshi, T. "Measuring Children's Retention of Skills to Resist Stranger Abduction: Use of the Simulation Technique." *Child Abuse and Neglect,* 1987b, *11,* 181–185.

Furniss, T. "Family Process in the Treatment of Intrafamilial Child Sexual Abuse." *Journal of Family Therapy,* 1983a, *5,* 263–278.

Furniss, T. "Mutual Influence and Interlocking Professional-Family Process in the Treatment of Child Sexual Abuse and Neglect." *Child Abuse and Neglect,* 1983b, *7,* 207–223.

Furniss, T. "Organizing a Therapeutic Approach to Intrafamilial Child Sexual Abuse." *Journal of Adolescence,* 1984, *7,* 309–317.

Furniss, T., Bingley-Miller, L., and van Elburg, A. "Goal-Oriented Group Treatment for Sexually Abused Adolescent Girls." *British Journal of Psychiatry,* in press.

Gagnon, J. "Female Child Victims of Sex Offenses." *Social Problems,* 1965, *13,* 176–192.

Ganzarian, R., and Buchele, B. "Countertransference When Incest Is the Problem." *International Journal of Group Psychotherapy,* 1986, *36,* 549–566.

Garbarino, J. "Children's Response to a Sexual Abuse Prevention Program: A Study of the *Spiderman* Comic." *Child Abuse and Neglect,* 1987, *11,* 143–148.

Garbarino, J., and Gilliam, G. *Understanding Abusive Families.* Lexington, Mass.: Lexington Books, 1980.

Garbarino, J., Guttman, E., and Seeley, J. W. *The Psychologically Battered Child: Strategies for Identification, Assessment, and Intervention.* San Francisco: Jossey-Bass, 1986.

Garrett, T. B., and Wright, R. "Wives of Rapists and Incest Offenders." *Journal of Sex Research,* 1975, *11,* 149–157.

Gelinas, D. J. "The Persisting Negative Effects of Incest." *Psychiatry,* 1983, *46,* 312–332.

Gelles, R. J. "Violence in the Family: A Review of Research in the Seventies." *Journal of Marriage and the Family,* 1980, *42,* 873–885.

Giarretto, H. A. "Humanistic Treatment of Father-Daughter Incest." *Journal of Humanistic Psychology,* 1978, *18,* 59–76.

Giarretto, H. A. "A Comprehensive Child Sexual Abuse Treatment Program." In P. B. Mrazek and C. H. Kempe (eds.), *Sexually Abused Children and Their Families.* Elmsford, N.Y.: Pergamon Press, 1981.

Giarretto, H. A. *Integrated Treatment of Child Sexual Abuse.* Palo Alto, Calif.: Science and Behavior Books, 1982.

Giovannoni, J. M., and Becerra, R. M. *Defining Child Abuse.* New York: Free Press, 1979.

Giovannoni, J., Conklin, J., and Iiyama, P. *Child Abuse and Neglect: An Examination from the Perspective of Child Development Knowledge.* Palo Alto, Calif.: R and E Research Associates, 1978.

Gold, E. R. "Long-Term Effects of Sexual Victimization in Childhood: An Attributional Approach." *Journal of Consulting and Clinical Psychology,* 1986, *54,* 471–475.

Goldstein, J., Freud, A., and Solnit, A. *Before the Best Interests of the Child.* New York: Free Press, 1979.

Goldstein, J., Freud, A., Solnit, A. J., and Goldstein, S. *In the Best Interests of the Child.* New York: Free Press, 1986.

Gomes-Schwartz, B., Horowitz, J. M., and Sauzier, M. "Severity of Emotional Distress Among Sexually Abused Preschool, School-Age, and Adolescent Children." *Hospital and Community Psychiatry,* 1985, *36,* 503–508.

Goodman, B., and Nowak-Scibelli, D. "Group Treatment for Women Incestuously Abused as Children." *International Journal of Psychotherapy,* 1985, *35,* 531–544.

Goodman, G. S. "The Child Witness: Conclusions and Future Directions for Research and Legal Practice." *Journal of Social Issues,* 1984, *40,* 157–175.

Goodman, G. S., Aman, C., and Hirschman, J. "Child Sexual and Physical Abuse: Children's Testimony." In S. J. Ceci, M. P. Toglia, and D. F. Ross (eds.), *Children's Eyewitness Memory.* New York: Springer-Verlag, 1987.

Goodman, G. S., Golding, J. M., and Haith, M. M. "Jurors' Reactions to Child Witnesses." *Journal of Social Issues,* 1984, *40,* 139–156.

Goodman, G. S., and Reed, R. S. "Age Differences in Eyewitness Testimony." *Law and Human Behavior,* 1986, *10,* 317–322.

Goodman, G. S., Reed, R. S., and Hepps, D. "The Child Victim's Testimony." In R. Toglia (chair), *Current Trends in Children's Eyewitness Testimony Research.* Symposium presented at the 93rd annual meeting of the American Psychological Association, Los Angeles, Aug. 1985.

Goodman, G. S., and Rosenberg, M. S. "The Child Witness to Family Violence." In D. J. Sonkin (ed.), *Domestic Violence on Trial: The Legal and Psychological Dimensions of Family Violence.* New York: Springer-Verlag, in press.

Goodman, G. S., and others. "When a Child Takes the Stand: Jurors' Perceptions of Children's Eyewitness Testimony." *Law and Human Behavior,* 1987, *11,* 27–40.

Goodwin, J. (ed.). *Sexual Abuse: Incest Victims and Their Families.* Boston: John Wright, 1982a.

Goodwin, J. "The Use of Drawings in Incest Cases." In J. Goodwin (ed.), *Sexual Abuse: Incest Victims and Their Families.* Boston: John Wright, 1982b.

Goodwin, J. "Post-Traumatic Symptoms in Incest Victims." In S. Eth and R. S. Pynoos (eds.), *Post-Traumatic Stress Disorder in Children.* Los Angeles: American Psychiatric Association, 1985.

Goodwin, J., McCarthy, T., and DiVasto, P. "Prior Incest in Mothers of Abused Children." *Child Abuse and Neglect,* 1981, *5,* 87–96.

Goodwin, J., and Owen, J. "Group Treatment Approaches." In J. Goodwin (ed.), *Sexual Abuse: Incest Victims and Their Families.* Boston: John Wright, 1982.

Goodwin, J., Sahd, D., and Rada, R. T. "Incest Hoax: False Accusations, False Denials." *Bulletin of the American Academy of Psychiatry and the Law,* 1978, *5,* 269–276.

Gottlieb, B., and Dean, J. "The Co-Therapy Relationship in Group Treatment of Sexually Mistreated Adolescent Girls." In P. B. Mrazek and C. H. Kempe (eds.), *Sexually Abused*

Children and Their Families. Elmsford, N.Y.: Pergamon Press, 1981.

Graham, M. H. "Child Sex Abuse Prosecutions: Hearsay and Confrontation Clause Issues." In J. Bulkley (ed.), *Papers from a National Conference on Legal Reforms in Child Sexual Abuse Cases.* Washington, D.C.: American Bar Association, 1985.

Green, A. H. "True and False Allegations of Sexual Abuse in Child Custody Disputes." *Journal of the American Academy of Child Psychiatry,* 1986, *25,* 449–456.

Greene, N. B. "A View of Family Pathology Involving Child Molest—From a Juvenile Probation Perspective." *Juvenile Justice,* 1977, *13,* 29–34.

Greenleaf, B. K. *Children Through the Ages: A History of Childhood.* New York: McGraw-Hill, 1978.

Groff, M. G., and Hubble, L. M. "A Comparison of Father-Daughter and Stepfather-Stepdaughter Incest." *Criminal Justice and Behavior,* 1984, *11,* 461–475.

Gross, M. "Incestuous Rape: A Cause for Hysterical Seizures in Four Adolescents." *American Journal of Orthopsychiatry,* 1979, *49,* 704–708.

Groth, A. N. "The Adolescent Sexual Offender and His Prey." *International Journal of Offender Therapy and Comparative Criminology,* 1977, *21,* 249–254.

Groth, A. N. "Patterns of Sexual Assault Against Children and Adolescents." In A. W. Burgess and others (eds.), *Sexual Assault of Children and Adolescents.* Lexington, Mass.: Lexington Books, 1978.

Groth, A. N. *Men Who Rape.* New York: Plenum, 1979.

Groth, A. N. "Treatment of the Sexual Offender in a Correctional Institution." In J. G. Greer and I. R. Stuart (eds.), *The Sexual Aggressor, Current Perspective on Treatment.* New York: Van Nostrand Reinhold, 1983.

Gruber, K. J., Jones, R. J., and Freeman, M. H. "Youth Reactions to Sexual Assault." *Adolescence,* 1982, *67,* 541–551.

Gumaer, J. *Counseling and Therapy for Children.* New York: Free Press, 1984.

Gundlach, R. H. "Sexual Molestation and Rape Reported by

Heterosexual and Homosexual Women." *Journal of Homosexuality,* 1977, *2,* 367–384.

Harvard Law Review. "The Testimony of Child Victims in Sex Abuse Prosecutions: Two Legislative Proposals." *Harvard Law Review,* 1985, *98,* 806–836.

Haugaard, J. J. "The Consequences of Child Sexual Abuse: A College Survey." Unpublished manuscript, Department of Psychology, University of Virginia, Charlottesville, 1987.

Haugaard, J. J. "Judicial Determination of Children's Competency to Testify. Should It Be Abandoned?" *Professional Psychology: Research and Practice,* 1988, *19* (1).

Haugaard, J. J., and Reppucci, N. D. *Child Sexual Abuse: A Review of the Research for the Clinician,* 1986. Available from the Virginia Treatment Center for Children, Box 1-L, Richmond, Va. 23201.

Hawaii v. *Kim,* 645 P.2d 1330 (1982).

Hazzard, A. "Training Teachers to Identify and Intervene with Abused Children." *Journal of Clinical Child Psychology,* 1984, *13,* 288–293.

Hazzard, A., and Angert, L. "Child Sexual Abuse Prevention: Previous Research and Future Directions." Paper presented at the 94th annual meeting of the American Psychological Association, Washington, D.C., Aug. 1986.

Hazzard, A., King, E. H., and Webb, C. "Group Therapy with Sexually Abused Adolescent Girls." *American Journal of Psychotherapy,* 1986, *40,* 213–223.

Hensley, K. L. "The Admissibility of 'Child Sexual Abuse Accommodation Syndrome' in California Criminal Courts." *Pacific Law Journal,* 1986, *17,* 1361–1392.

Herbert v. *Superior Court,* 117 Cal. App. 3d 661 (1981).

Herman, J. *Father-Daughter Incest.* Cambridge: Harvard University Press, 1981.

Herman, J. "Recognition and Treatment in Incestuous Families." *International Journal of Family Therapy,* 1983, *5,* 81–91.

Herman, J., Russell, D.E.H., and Trocki, K. "Long Term Effects of Incestuous Abuse in Childhood." *American Journal of Psychiatry,* 1986, *143,* 1293–1296.

Herman, J., and Schatzow, E. "Time Limited Group Therapy for Women with a History of Incest." *International Journal of Group Psychotherapy*, 1984, *34*, 605–616.

Herold, E. S., Mantle, D., and Zemitis, O. "A Study of Sexual Offenses Against Females." *Adolescence*, 1979, *14*, 65–72.

Hochieser v. *Superior Court*, 208 Cal. Rptr. 273 (1984).

Hoorwitz, A. N. "Guidelines for Treating Father-Daughter Incest." *Social Casework*, 1983, *64*, 515–524.

Horowitz, M. J. *Stress Response Syndromes.* New York: Aronson, 1976.

In re Cheryl H., 200 Cal. Rptr. 789 (1984).

Ingram, M. "Participating Victims: A Study of Sexual Offenses with Boys." In L. M. Constantine and F. Martinson (eds.), *Children and Sex: New Findings, New Perspectives.* Boston: Little, Brown, 1981.

Jaffee, A. C., Dynnesson, R. N., and ten Bensel, R. W. "Sexual Abuse of Children." *American Journal of Diseases of Children*, 1975, *129*, 689–692.

James, B., and Nasjleti, M. *Treating Sexually Abused Children and Their Families.* Palo Alto, Calif.: Consulting Psychologists Press, 1983.

James, J., and Meyerding, J. "Early Sexual Experience as a Factor in Prostitution." *Archives of Sexual Behavior*, 1977, *7*, 31–42.

James, K. L. "Incest: The Teenagers' Perspective." *Psychotherapy: Theory, Research, and Practice*, 1977, *14*, 146–155.

Janoff-Bulman, R. "The Aftermath of Victimization: Rebuilding Shattered Assumptions." In C. R. Figley (ed.), *Trauma and Its Wake: The Study and Treatment of Post-Traumatic Stress Disorder.* New York: Brunner/Mazel, 1985.

Jason, J., Williams, S. L., Burton, A., and Rochat, B. "Epidemiologic Differences Between Sexual and Physical Child Abuse." *Journal of the American Medical Association*, 1982, *247*, 3344–3348.

Jehu, D., and Gazan, M. "Psychosocial Adjustment of Women Who Were Sexually Victimized in Childhood or Adolescence." *Canadian Journal of Community Mental Health*, 1983, *2*, 71–81.

Johnson, B. B. "Sexual Abuse Prevention: A Rural Interdisciplinary Effort." *Child Welfare*, 1987, *66*, 165–173.

Johnson, M. K., and Foley, M. A. "Differentiating Fact from Fantasy: The Reliability of Children's Memory." *Journal of Social Issues*, 1984, *40*, 33–50.

Jones, B. M., Jenstron, L. L., and McFarlane, K. *Sexual Abuse of Children: Selected Readings.* Washington, D.C.: U.S. Department of Health and Human Services, 1980.

Jones, D. P. "Individual Psychotherapy for the Sexually Abused Child." *Child Abuse and Neglect*, 1986, *10*, 377–385.

Jones, D. P., and McQuiston, M. *Interviewing the Sexually Abused Child*, 1985. Available from the Kempe Foundation, 1205 Oneida St., Denver, Colo. 80220.

Jones, R. J., Gruber, K. J., and Timbers, G. D. "Incidence and Situational Factors Surrounding Sexual Assault Against Delinquent Youth." *Child Abuse and Neglect*, 1981, *5*, 431–440.

Julian, V., and Mohr, C. "Father-Daughter Incest: Profile of the Offender." *Victimology*, 1979, *4*, 348–360.

Justice, B., and Justice, R. *The Broken Taboo.* New York: Human Science Press, 1979.

Kalichman, S. C., and Craig, M. E. "Mental Health Professionals' Attitudes and Tendency to Report." Paper presented at the Second World Congress for Victimology, Orlando, Fla., 1987.

Kalichman, S. C., Craig, M. E., and Follingstad, D. R. "Mental Health Professions' Treatment of Child Abuse: Why Professionals May Not Report." Paper presented at the Third World Congress for Victimology, San Francisco, 1987.

Katan, A. "Children Who Were Raped." *Psychoanalytic Study of the Child*, 1973, *28*, 208–224.

Kaufman, I., Peck, A. L., and Tagiuri, C. K. "The Family Constellation and Overt Incestuous Relations Between Father and Daughter." *American Journal of Orthopsychiatry*, 1954, *24*, 266–279.

Kelleum v. State, 396 A.2d 166 (1986).

Kelley, S. J. "Drawings: Critical Communications for Sexually Abused Children." *Pediatric Nursing*, 1985, *11*, 421–426.

Kelly, R. J. "Behavioral Reorientation of Pedophiles: Can It Be Done?" *Clinical Psychology Review*, 1982, *2*, 387–408.

Kempe, C. H., and others. "The Battered-Child Syndrome." *Journal of the American Medical Association,* 1962, *181,* 17–24.

Kendall-Tackett, K. A., and Simon, A. F. "Perpetrators and Their Acts: Data from 365 Adults Molested as Children." *Child Abuse and Neglect,* 1987, *11,* 237–245.

Kercher, G. A., and McShane, M. "The Prevalence of Child Sexual Abuse Victimization in an Adult Sample of Texas Residents." *Child Abuse and Neglect,* 1984, *8,* 495–501.

Kilpatrick, D. G., and Best, C. L. "Some Cautionary Remarks on Treating Sexual Assault Victims with Implosion." *Behavior Therapy,* 1984, *15,* 421–423.

Kinsey, A. C., Pomeroy, W. B., Martin, C. E., and Gebhard, P. H. *Sexual Behavior in the Human Female.* Philadelphia: Saunders, 1953.

Kirby v. *United States,* 174 U.S. 47 (1899).

Kirkwood, L. J., and Mihaila, M. E. "Incest and the Legal System: Inadequacies and Alternatives." *University of California, Davis, Law Review,* 1979, *12,* 673–699.

Kleemeier, C., and Webb, C. "Evaluation of a School-Based Prevention Program." Paper presented at the 94th annual meeting of the American Psychological Association, Washington, D.C., Aug. 1986.

Klein, M. W. "Deinstitutionalization and Diversion of Juvenile Offenders: A Litany of Impediments." In N. Morris and M. Tonry (eds.), *Crime and Justice: An Annual Review of Research.* Vol. 1. Chicago: University of Chicago Press, 1979.

Knittle, B. J., and Tuana, S. J. "Group Therapy as a Primary Treatment for Adolescent Victims of Intrafamilial Sexual Abuse." *Clinical Social Work Journal,* 1980, *8,* 236–242.

Kobasigawa, A. "Utilization of Retrieval Cues by Children in Recall." *Child Development,* 1974, *45,* 127–134.

Koblinsky, S., and Behana, N. "Child Sexual Abuse: The Educator's Role in Prevention, Detection, and Intervention." *Young Children,* 1984, *39,* 3–15.

Kocen, L., and Bulkley, J. "Analysis of Criminal Child Sex Abuse Statutes." In J. Bulkley (ed.), *Child Sexual Abuse and the Law.* (5th ed.) Washington, D.C.: American Bar Association, 1985.

Kohan, M. J., Pothier, P., and Norbeck, J. S. "Hospitalized Children with a History of Sexual Abuse: Incidence and Care Issues." *American Journal of Orthopsychiatry,* 1987, *57,* 258–264.

Kohlberg, L. "Moral Stages and Moralization: The Cognitive-Developmental Approach." In T. Lickona (ed.), *Moral Development and Behavior: Theory, Research, and Social Issues.* New York: Holt, Rinehart and Winston, 1976.

Krafft-Ebing, R. *Psychopathia Sexualis: A Medico Forensic Study.* New York: Putnam, 1965. (Originally published 1886.)

Krener, P. "After Incest: Secondary Prevention." *Journal of the American Academy of Child Psychiatry,* 1985, *24,* 231–234.

Krieger, M. J., and Robbinis, J. "The Adolescent Incest Victim and the Judicial System." *American Journal of Orthopsychiatry,* 1985, *55,* 419–425.

Krieger, M. J., Rosenfeld, A. A., Gordon, A., and Bennett, M. "Problems in the Psychotherapy of Children with Histories of Incest." *American Journal of Psychotherapy,* 1980, *34,* 81–88.

Kroth, J. A. *Child Sexual Abuse: Analysis of a Family Therapy Approach.* Springfield, Ill.: Thomas, 1979.

LaBarbera, J. D. "Seductive Father-Daughter Relationships and Sex Roles in Women." *Sex Roles,* 1984, *11,* 941–951.

Lacayo, R. "Sexual Abuse or Abuse of Justice?" *Time,* May 11, 1987, p. 49.

Lamb, S. "Treating Sexually Abused Children: Issues of Blame and Responsibility." *American Journal of Orthopsychiatry,* 1986, *56,* 303–307.

Landis, J. "Experiences of 500 Children with Adult Sexual Deviants." *Psychiatric Quarterly Supplement,* 1956, *30,* 91–109.

Langevin, R. *Sexual Strands.* Hillsdale, N.J.: Erlbaum, 1983.

Langsley, D. G., Schwartz, M. N., and Fairbairn, R. H. "Father-Son Incest." *Comprehensive Psychiatry,* 1968, *9,* 218–226.

Lanyon, R. I. "Theory and Treatment in Child Molestation." *Journal of Consulting and Clinical Psychology,* 1986, *54,* 176–182.

Larson, N. R., and Maddock, J. W. "Structural and Functional

Variables in Incest Family Systems: Implications for Assessment and Treatment." In T. S. Trepper and M. J. Barrett (eds.), *The Assessment and Treatment of Intrafamilial Sexual Abuse.* New York: Haworth Press, 1985.

Lewis, M., and Sarrel, P. M. "Some Psychological Aspects of Seduction, Incest, and Rape in Childhood." *Journal of the American Academy of Child Psychiatry*, 1969, *8*, 606–619.

Leybourne v. *Commonwealth of Virginia*, 282 S.E.2d 12 (1981).

Libai, D. "The Protection of the Child Victim of a Sexual Offense in the Criminal Justice System." *Wayne Law Review*, 1969, *15*, 977–986.

Lincoln, S. G., Teilmann, K., Klein, M., and Labin, S. "Recidivism Rates of Diverted Juvenile Offenders." Paper presented at the National Conference on Criminal Justice Evaluation, Washington, D.C., 1977.

Lindberg, F. H., and Distad, L. J. "Post Traumatic Stress Disorders in Women Who Experienced Childhood Incest." *Child Abuse and Neglect*, 1985a, *9*, 329–334.

Lindberg, F. H., and Distad, L. J. "Survival Responses to Incest: Adolescents in Crisis." *Child Abuse and Neglect*, 1985b, *9*, 521–526.

Lindberg, M. A. "Is Knowledge Base Development a Necessary and Sufficient Condition for Memory Development?" *Journal of Experimental Child Psychology*, 1980, *30*, 401–410.

Lindzey, G. "Some Remarks Concerning Incest, the Incest Taboo, and Psychoanalytic Theory." *American Psychologist*, 1967, *22*, 1051–1059.

Litin, E. M., Giffin, M. E., and Johnson, A. M. "Parental Influences in Unusual Sexual Behavior in Children." *Psychoanalytic Quarterly*, 1956, *25*, 37–55.

Loftus, E. F. *Eyewitness Testimony.* Cambridge, Mass.: Harvard University Press, 1979.

Long, K. A. "Cultural Considerations in the Assessment and Treatment of Intrafamilial Abuse." *American Journal of Orthopsychiatry*, 1986, *56*, 131–136.

Lubell, D., and Soong, S. "Group Therapy with Sexually Abused Adolescents." *Canadian Journal of Psychiatry*, 1982, *27*, 311–315.

Lukianowicz, N. "Incest I: Paternal Incest." *American Journal of Psychiatry*, 1972, *120*, 301–313.

Lustig, N., Dresser, J. W., Spellman, S. W., and Murray, T. B. "Incest: A Family Group Survival Pattern." *Archives of General Psychology*, 1966, *14*, 31–40.

Lyon, E., and Cassady, L. "Speaking of Sex: Child Abuse Treatment and Team Development." Paper presented at the 94th annual meeting of the American Psychological Association, Washington, D.C., Aug. 1986.

McCarthy, L. M. "Mother-Child Incest: Characteristics of the Offender." *Child Welfare*, 1986, *65*, 447–458.

McCauley, J., Gorman, R. L., and Guzinski, G. "Toluidine Blue in the Detection of Perineal Lacerations in Pediatric and Adolescent Sexual Abuse Victims." *Pediatrics*, 1986, *78*, 1039–1043.

McCord, D. "Expert Psychological Testimony About Child Complainants in Sexual Abuse Prosecutions: A Foray into the Admissibility of Novel Psychological Evidence." *The Journal of Criminal Law and Criminology*, 1986, *77*, 1–68.

McCord, J. "A Thirty-Year Follow-Up of Treatment Effects." *American Psychologist*, 1978, *33*, 284–289.

McCormack, A., Janus, M. D., and Burgess, A. W. "Runaway Youths and Sexual Victimization: Gender Differences in an Adolescent Runaway Population." *Child Abuse and Neglect*, 1986, *10*, 387–395.

McCormick, C. E. *McCormick's Handbook of the Law of Evidence.* (2nd ed.) St. Paul, Minn.: West, 1972.

McDonald, R. P. *Factor Analysis and Related Methods.* Hillsdale, N.J.: Erlbaum, 1985.

MacFarlane, K. "Program Considerations in the Treatment of Incest Offenders." In J. G. Greer and I. R. Stuart (eds.), *The Sexual Aggressor: Current Perspectives on Treatment.* New York: Van Nostrand Reinhold, 1983.

MacFarlane, K. "Diagnostic Evaluations and the Use of Videotapes in Child Sexual Abuse Cases." *University of Miami Law Review*, 1985, *40*, 136–165.

MacFarlane, K., and Krebs, S. "Techniques for Interviewing and Evidence Gathering." In K. MacFarlane and others (eds.), *Sexual Abuse of Young Children.* New York: Guilford, 1986a.

MacFarlane, K., and Krebs, S. "Videotaping of Interviews and Court Testimony." In K. MacFarlane and others (eds.), *Sexual Abuse of Young Children.* New York: Guilford, 1986b.

MacFarlane, K., and others (eds.). *Sexual Abuse of Young Children.* New York: Guilford, 1986.

McGuire, L. S., and Wagner, N. N. "Sexual Dysfunction in Women Who Were Molested as Children: One Response Pattern and Suggestions for Treatment." *Journal of Sex and Marital Therapy,* 1978, *4,* 11-15.

Machotka, P., Pittman, F. S., and Flomenhaft, K. "Incest as a Family Affair." *Family Process,* 1967, *6,* 98-116.

McIntyre, K. "Role of Mothers in Father-Daughter Incest: A Feminist Analysis." *Social Work,* 1981, *81,* 462-466.

Mackey, G. *Bubbylonian Encounter,* 1980. Available from Theater for Young America, 7204 W. 80th St., Overland Park, Kan. 66204.

MacVicar, K. "Psychotherapeutic Issues in the Treatment of Sexually Abused Girls." *Journal of the American Academy of Child Psychiatry,* 1979, *18,* 342-353.

Mahady-Smith, C. M. "The Young Victims as Witness for the Prosecution: Another Form of Abuse?" *Whittier Law Review,* 1985, *7,* 639-661.

Malinowski, J. *Sex and Repression in Savage Society.* London: Routledge & Kegan Paul, 1927.

Mann, E. M. "The Assessment of Credibility of Sexually Abused Children in Criminal Court Cases." *American Journal of Forensic Psychiatry,* 1985, *6,* 9-15.

Margolis, M. "A Case of Mother-Adolescent Son Incest: A Follow-Up Study." *Psychoanalytic Quarterly,* 1984, *53,* 355-385.

Marin, B. V., Holmes, D. L., Guth, M., and Kovac, P. "The Potential of Children as Eyewitnesses: A Comparison of Children and Adults on Eyewitness Tasks." *Law and Human Behavior,* 1978, *3,* 295-306.

Marshall, W. L., Earls, C. M., Segal, Z., and Darke, J. "A Behavioral Program for the Assessment and Treatment of Sexual Aggressors." In K. D. Craig and R. J. McMahon (eds.), *Advances in Clinical Behavior Therapy.* New York: Brunner/Mazel, 1983.

Mattox v. *United States,* 156 U.S. 237 (1895).

Mayhall, D. D., and Norgard, K. E. *Child Abuse and Neglect: Sharing Responsibility.* New York: Wiley, 1983.

Meiselman, K. C. *Incest: A Psychological Study of Causes and Effects with Treatment Recommendations.* San Francisco: Jossey-Bass, 1978.

Melton, G. B. "Psycholegal Issues in Child Victims' Interaction with the Legal System." *Victimology,* 1981, *5,* 274–284.

Melton, G. B. "Sexually Abused Children and the Legal System: Some Policy Recommendations." *American Journal of Family Therapy,* 1985, *13,* 61–67.

Melton, G. B. "Children's Testimony in Cases of Alleged Sexual Abuse." In M. Wolraich and D. K. Routh (eds.), *Advances in Developmental and Behavioral Pediatrics.* Greenwich, Conn.: JAI Press, in press-a.

Melton, G. B. "Children, Ecology, and Legal Contexts: A Reply to Haugaard." *Professional Psychology: Research and Practice,* in press-b, *19* (1).

Melton, G. B. "The Improbability of Prevention of Sexual Abuse." in D. J. Willis, E. W. Holden, and M. S. Rosenberg (eds.), *Child Abuse Prevention.* New York: Wiley, in press-c.

Melton, G. B., Bulkley, J. A., and Wulkan, D. "Competency of Children as Witnesses." In J. A. Bulkley (ed.), *Child Sexual Abuse and the Law.* (5th ed.) Washington, D.C.: American Bar Association, 1985.

Melton, G. B., and Limber, S. "Psychologists' Involvement in Cases of Child Maltreatment: Limits of Role and Expertise." Unpublished manuscript, Department of Psychology, University of Nebraska, Lincoln, 1987.

Mian, M., and others. "Review of 125 Children, Six Years of Age and Under, Who Were Sexually Abused." *Child Abuse and Neglect,* 1986, *10,* 223–229.

Miller, G. R. "The Effects of Videotaped Trial Materials on Juror Responses." In C. Berman, C. Neimeth, and N. Widmar (eds.), *Psychology and the Law.* Lexington, Mass.: Lexington Books, 1976.

Mischel, W., and Mischel, H. N. "A Cognitive Social-Learning Approach to Morality and Self-Regulation." In T. Lickona (ed.), *Moral Development and Behavior: Theory, Research, and Social Issues.* New York: Holt, Rinehart and Winston, 1976.

Mitchell Law Review. "Minnesota's Hearsay Exception for Child Victims of Sexual Abuse." *William Mitchell Law Review,* 1985, *11,* 799–823.

Monahan, J. (ed.). *Who Is the Client?* Washington, D.C.: American Psychological Association, 1980.

Morey, R. W. "The Competency Requirement for the Child Victim of Sexual Abuse: Must We Abandon It?" *University of Miami Law Review,* 1985, *40,* 245–284.

Mrazek, D. A. "The Child Psychiatric Examination of the Sexually Abused Child." *Child Abuse and Neglect,* 1980, *4,* 275–284.

Mrazek, P. B. "Special Problems in the Treatment of Child Sexual Abuse." In P. B. Mrazek and C. H. Kempe (eds.), *Sexually Abused Children and Their Families.* Elmsford, N.Y.: Pergamon Press, 1981.

Mrazek, P. B., and Kempe, C. H. (eds.). *Sexually Abused Children and Their Families.* Elmsford, N.Y.: Pergamon Press, 1981.

Muldoon, L. *Incest: Confronting the Silent Crime.* Minneapolis: Minnesota Program for Victims of Sexual Assault, 1981.

Mulvey, E. P., and Haugaard, J. J. *Report of the Surgeon General's Workshop on Pornography and Public Health.* Washington, D.C.: U.S. Public Health Service, 1986.

Murdock, C. *Social Structure.* New York: Macmillan, 1949.

Nasjleti, M. "Suffering in Silence: The Male Incest Victim." *Child Welfare,* 1980, *59,* 269–275.

National Committee for Prevention of Child Abuse. *NCPCA Summary Report: Spiderman and Power Pack Comic on the Prevention of Sexual Abuse.* Chicago: National Committee for Prevention of Child Abuse, 1986.

National Legal Resource Center for Child Advocacy and Protection. *Child Sexual Exploitation: Background and Legal Analysis.* Washington, D.C.: Young Lawyers Division, American Bar Association, 1984.

Nelson, J. "The Impact of Incest: Factors in Self-Evaluation." In L. Constantine (ed.), *Children and Sex.* Boston: Little, Brown, 1981.

New York v. *Fogarty,* 86 A.2d 617 (1982).

Nichols, M. P. *Family Therapy: Concepts and Methods.* New York: Gardner, 1984.

Nielson, T. "Sexual Abuse of Boys: Current Perspectives." *The Personnel and Guidance Journal,* 1983, *62,* 139–142.

O'Carroll, T. *Paedophelia: The Radical Case.* London: Owen, 1982.

O'Connell, M. A. "Reuniting Incest Offenders with Their Families." *Journal of Interpersonal Violence,* 1986, *1,* 374–386.

Ohio v. *Roberts,* 448 U.S. 56 (1980).

Oregon v. *Middleton,* 657 P.2d 1215 (1983).

Orlando, J. A., and Koss, M. P. "The Effects of Sexual Victimization on Sexual Satisfaction: A Study of the Negative Associative Hypothesis." *Journal of Abnormal Psychology,* 1983, *92,* 104–106.

Orr, D. P., and Downes, M. C. "Self-Concept of Adolescent Sexual Abuse Victims." *Journal of Youth and Adolescence,* 1985, *14,* 401–409.

Owens, T. H. "Personality Traits of Female Psychotherapy Patients with a History of Incest: A Research Note." *Journal of Personality Assessment,* 1984, *48,* 606–608.

Parker, H., and Parker, S. "Father-Daughter Sexual Abuse: An Emerging Perspective." *American Journal of Orthopsychiatry,* 1986, *56,* 531–549.

Parsons, T. "The Incest Taboo in Relation to Social Structure and the Socialization of the Child." *British Journal of Sociology,* 1954, *5,* 101–117.

Pelletier, G., and Handy, L. C. "Family Dysfunction and the Psychological Impact of Child Sexual Abuse." *Canadian Journal of Psychiatry,* 1986, *31,* 407–412.

People v. *Roscoe,* 215 Cal. Rptr. 45 (1985).

Peters, J. J. "Children Who Are Victims of Sexual Assault and the Psychology of Offenders." *American Journal of Psychotherapy,* 1976, *30,* 398–421.

Peters, S. D., Wyatt, G. E., and Finkelhor, D. "Prevalence." In D. Finkelhor and others (eds.), *A Sourcebook on Child Sexual Abuse.* Beverly Hills, Calif.: Sage, 1986.

Pierce, L. H. "Father-Son Incest: Using the Literature to Guide Practice." *Social Casework,* 1987, *68,* 67–74.

Pierce, L. H., and Pierce, R. L. "Race as a Factor in the Sexual Abuse of Children." *Social Work Research and Abstracts,* 1984, *19,* 9–14.

Pierce, R. L. "Child Pornography: A Hidden Dimension of Child Abuse." *Child Abuse and Neglect,* 1984, *8,* 483–493.

Pierce, R. L., and Pierce, L. H. "The Sexually Abused Child: A Comparison of Male and Female Victims." *Child Abuse and Neglect,* 1985, *9,* 191–199.

Plummer, C. *Preventing Sexual Abuse: Activities and Strategies for Working with Children and Adolescents.* Holmes Beach, Fla.: Learning Publications, 1984a.

Plummer, C. "Preventing Sexual Abuse: What In-School Programs Teach Children." Unpublished manuscript, 1984b.

Poche, C., Brouwer, R., and Swearington, M. "Teaching Self-Protection to Children." *Journal of Applied Behavioral Analysis,* 1981, *14,* 169–176.

Porch, T. L., and Petretic-Jackson, P. A. "Child Sexual Assault Prevention: Evaluation of Parent Education Workshops." Paper presented at the 94th annual meeting of the American Psychological Association, Washington, D.C., Aug. 1986.

Porter, F. S., Blick, L. C., and Sgroi, S. M. "Treatment of the Sexually Abused Child." In S. M. Sgroi (ed.), *Handbook of Clinical Intervention in Child Sexual Abuse.* Lexington, Mass.: Lexington Books, 1982.

Pynoss, R. S., and Eth, S. "Developmental Perspective on Psychic Trauma in Childhood." In C. R. Figley (ed.), *Trauma and Its Wake: The Study and Treatment of Post-Traumatic Stress Disorder.* New York: Brunner/Mazel, 1985.

Quinsey, V. L., Chaplin, T. C., and Carrigan, W. F. "Sexual Preferences Among Incestuous and Nonincestuous Child Molesters." *Behavior Therapy,* 1979, *10,* 562–565.

Quinsey, V. L., Chaplin, T. C., and Carrigan, W. F. "Biofeedback and Signalled Punishment in the Modification of Sexual Age Preferences." *Behavior Therapy,* 1980, *11,* 567–576.

Quinsey, V. L., and Marshall, W. L. "Procedures for Reducing Inappropriate Sexual Arousal: An Evaluative Review." In J. G. Greer and I. R. Stuart (eds.), *The Sexual Aggressor: Current Perspectives on Treatment.* New York: Van Nostrand Reinhold, 1983.

Racusin, R. J., and Felsman, J. K. "Reporting Child Abuse: The Ethical Obligation to Inform Parents." *Journal of the American Academy of Child Psychiatry,* 1986, *25,* 485-489.

Ray, J. *Evaluation of the Child Sexual Abuse Prevention Program,* 1984. Available from the Rape Crisis Network, N1226 Howard, Spokane, Wash. 99201.

Ray, J., and Dietzel, M. "Teaching Child Sexual Abuse Prevention." Unpublished manuscript, 1984.

Reich, J. W., and Gutieries, S. E. "Escape/Aggression Incidence in Sexually Abused Juvenile Delinquents." *Criminal Justice and Behavior,* 1979, *6,* 239-243.

Reinhart, M. A. "Sexually Abused Boys." *Child Abuse and Neglect,* 1987, *11,* 229-235.

Renshaw, D. C. "Evaluating Suspected Cases of Child Sexual Abuse." *Psychiatric Annals,* 1987, *17,* 262-270.

Reposa, R. E., and Zuelzer, M. B. "Family Therapy with Incest." *International Journal of Family Therapy,* 1983, *5,* 111-126.

Reppucci, N. D. "Psychology in the Public Interest." In A. M. Rogers and C. J. Scheier (eds.), *The G. Stanley Hall Lecture Series.* Vol. 5. Washington, D.C.: American Psychological Association, 1985.

Reppucci, N. D. "Prevention and Ecology: Teen-Age Pregnancy, Child Sexual Abuse, and Organized Youth Sports." *American Journal of Community Psychology,* 1987, *15,* 1-22.

Riemer, S. "A Research Note on Incest." *American Journal of Sociology,* 1940, *45,* 566-575.

Rimsza, M. E., and Niggemann, E. H. "Medical Evaluation of Sexually Abused Children: A Review of 311 Cases." *Pediatrics,* 1982, *69,* 8-14.

Roberts v. *Arizona,* 677 P.2d 280 (1983).

Roe, R. J. "Expert Testimony in Child Sexual Abuse Cases." *University of Miami Law Review,* 1985, *40,* 97-113.

Rogers, C. "Child Sexual Abuse and the Courts: Preliminary Findings." *Journal of Social Work and Human Sexuality,* 1982, *1,* 145-153.

Rogers, C., and Terry, T. "Clinical Intervention with Boy Victims of Sexual Abuse." In I. R. Stuart and J. G. Greer (eds.),

Victims of Sexual Aggression: Treatment of Children, Women, and Men. New York: Van Nostrand Reinhold, 1984.

Roland, B. C., Zelhart, P. F., and Cochran, S. W. "MMPI Correlates of Clinical Women Who Report Early Sexual Abuse." *Journal of Clinical Psychology,* 1985, *41,* 763–766.

Rosen, H. "How Workers Use Cues to Determine Child Abuse." *Social Work Research and Abstracts,* 1981, *16,* 27–33.

Rosenberg, M., and Hunt, R. D. "Child Maltreatment: Legal and Mental Health Issues." In N. D. Reppucci and others (eds.), *Children, Mental Health, and the Law.* Beverly Hills, Calif.: Sage, 1984.

Rosenberg, M. S., and Reppucci, N. D. "Abusive Mothers: Perceptions of Their Own and Their Children's Behavior." *Journal of Consulting and Clinical Psychology,* 1983, *51,* 674–682.

Rosenfeld, A. A. "Sexual Misuse and the Family." *Victimology,* 1977, *2,* 226–235.

Rosenfeld, A. A. "Clinical Management of Incest and Sexual Abuse of Children." *Journal of the American Medical Association,* 1978, *242,* 1761–1764.

Rosenfeld, A. A., Nadelson, C. C., and Krieger, M. "Fantasy and Reality in Patients' Reports of Incest." *Journal of Clinical Psychiatry,* 1979, *46,* 159–164.

Ruch, L. O., and Chandler, S. M. "The Crisis Impact of Sexual Assault on Three Victim Groups: Adult Rape Victims, Child Rape Victims, and Incest Victims." *Journal of Social Service Research,* 1982, *5,* 83–100.

Runyan, D. K., and others. "Impact of Legal Intervention on Sexually Abused Children." Paper presented at the Third National Family Violence Research Conference, Durham, N.H., July 1987.

Russell, D.E.H. "The Incidence and Prevalence of Intrafamilial and Extrafamilial Sexual Abuse of Female Children." *Child Abuse and Neglect,* 1983, *7,* 133–146.

Russell, D.E.H. *Sexual Exploitation, Rape, Child Sexual Abuse, and Work Place Harassment.* Beverly Hills, Calif.: Sage, 1984.

Ryan, T. S. "Problems, Errors, and Opportunities in the Treatment of Father-Daughter Incest." *Journal of Interpersonal Violence,* 1986, *1,* 113–124.

Rychtarik, R. G., Silverman, W. K., Landingham, W. P., and Prue, D. M. "Further Considerations in Treating Sexual Assault Victims with Implosion." *Behavior Therapy,* 1984a, *15,* 423–426.

Rychtarik, R. G., Silverman, W. K., Landingham, W. P., and Prue, D. M. "Treatment of an Incest Victim with Implosive Therapy: A Case Study." *Behavior Therapy,* 1984b, *15,* 410–420.

Sandfort, T. G. "Sex in Pedophiliac Relationships: An Empirical Investigation Among a Nonrepresentative Group of Boys." *Journal of Sex Research,* 1984, *20,* 123–142.

Sanfilippo, J. S., and Schikler, K. N. "Identifying the Sexually Molested Preadolescent Girl." *Pediatric Annals,* 1986, *15,* 621–624.

Saslawsky, D. A., and Wurtele, S. K. "Educating Children About Sexual Abuse: Implications for Pediatric Intervention and Possible Prevention." *Journal of Pediatric Psychology,* 1986, *11,* 235–245.

Saulsbury, F., and Campbell, R. "Evaluation of Child Abuse Reporting by Physicians." *American Journal of Diseases of Children,* 1985, *139,* 393–395.

Scherzer, L. N., and Lala, P. "Sexual Offenses Committed Against Children." *Clinical Pediatrics,* 1980, *19,* 679–685.

Schlesinger, B. "Sexual Abuse of Children: Knowns and Unknowns." *Conciliation Courts Review,* 1983, *21,* 71–80.

Schroeder, T. "Incest in Mormonism." *The American Journal of Urology and Sexology,* 1915, *11,* 409–416.

Schultz, L. G. "The Child Sex Victim: Social, Psychological and Legal Perspectives." *Child Welfare,* 1973, *52,* 147–157.

Schuman, D. C. "False Accusations of Physical and Sexual Abuse." *Bulletin of the American Academy of Psychiatry and the Law,* 1986, *14,* 5–21.

Schwartzman, J. "The Individual, Incest, and Exogamy." *Psychiatry,* 1974, *37,* 171–179.

Scott, R. L., and Stone, D. A. "MMPI Measures of Psychological Disturbance in Adolescent and Adult Victims of Father-Daughter Incest." *Journal of Clinical Psychology,* 1986a, *42,* 251–259.

Scott, R. L., and Stone, D. A. "MMPI Profile Constellations in

Incest Families." *Journal of Consulting and Clinical Psychology*, 1986b, *54*, 6–14.

Sebold, J. "Indicators of Child Sexual Abuse in Males." *Social Casework*, 1987, *68*, 75–80.

Sechrest, L., White, S. O., and Brown, E. (eds.). *The Rehabilitation of Criminal Offenders: Problems and Prospects.* Washington, D.C.: National Academy of Sciences, 1979.

Sedney, M. A., and Brooks, B. "Factors Associated with a History of Childhood Sexual Experience in a Non-Clinical Female Population." *Journal of the American Academy of Child Psychiatry*, 1984, *23*, 215–218.

Seemanova, E. "A Study of Children of Incestuous Matings." *Human Heredity*, 1971, *21*, 108–128.

Selby, J. W., and others. "Family of Incest: A Collation of Clinical Impressions." *International Journal of Social Psychiatry*, 1980, *26*, 7–16.

Serrano, A. C., Zuelzer, M. B., Howe, D. D., and Reposa, R. E. "Ecology of Abusive and Nonabusive Families." *Journal of Child Psychiatry*, 1979, *75*, 175–179.

Sesan, R., Freeark, K., and Murphy, S. "The Support Network: Crisis Intervention for Extrafamilial Child Sexual Abuse." *Professional Psychology: Research and Practice*, 1986, *17*, 138–146.

Sgroi, S. M. "Comprehensive Examination for Child Sexual Assault." In A. W. Burgess and others (eds.), *Sexual Assault of Children and Adolescents.* Lexington, Mass.: Lexington Books, 1978.

Sgroi, S. M. "Family Treatment of Child Sexual Abuse." *Journal of Social Work and Human Sexuality*, 1982a, *1*, 109–128.

Sgroi, S. M. (ed.). *Handbook of Clinical Intervention in Child Sexual Abuse.* Lexington, Mass.: Lexington Books, 1982b.

Sgroi, S. M., and Dana, N. T. "Individual and Group Treatment of Mothers of Incest Victims." In S. M. Sgroi (ed.), *Handbook of Clinical Intervention in Child Sexual Abuse.* Lexington, Mass.: Lexington Books, 1982.

Sgroi, S. M., Porter, F. S., and Blick, L. C. "Validation of Child Sexual Abuse." In S. M. Sgroi (ed.), *Handbook of Clinical Intervention in Child Sexual Abuse.* Lexington, Mass.: Lexington Books, 1982.

Shamroy, J. A. "Interviewing the Sexually Abused Child with Anatomically Correct Dolls." *Social Work*, 1987, *32*, 165-166.

Shapiro, S. "Self-Mutilation and Self-Blame in Incest Victims." *American Journal of Psychotherapy*, 1987, *41*, 46-54.

Sheldon, J., and Hill, J. P. "Effects on Cheating of Achievement Anxiety and Knowledge of Peer Performance." *Developmental Psychology*, 1969, *1*, 449-455.

Showers, J., and others. "The Sexual Victimization of Boys: A Three Year Survey." *Health Values*, 1983, *7*, 15-18.

Shultz, L. G. "The Child Sex Victim: Social, Psychological, and Legal Perspectives." *Child Welfare*, 1973, *52*, 147-157.

Silbert, M. H., and Pines, A. M. "Sexual Abuse as an Antecedent to Prostitution." *Child Abuse and Neglect*, 1981, *5*, 407-411.

Silbert, M. H., and Pines, A. M. "Pornography and Sexual Abuse of Women." *Sex Roles*, 1984, *10*, 857-868.

Simrel, K., Berg, R., and Thomas, J. "Crisis Management of Sexually Abused Children." *Pediatric Annals*, 1979, *8*, 59-72.

Sivan, A. B. "Interactions of Nonabused Children with Anatomically Correct Dolls." Paper presented to the Society for Research in Child Development, Baltimore, Apr. 1987.

Smith v. *Nevada*, 688 P.2d 326 (1984).

Solin, C. A. "Displacement of Affect in Families Following Incest Disclosure." *American Journal of Orthopsychiatry*, 1986, *56*, 570-576.

Spencer, W. J., and Dunklee, P. "Sexual Abuse of Boys." *Pediatrics*, 1986, *78*, 133-138.

Spiegel, L. *A Question of Innocence.* Los Angeles: Unicorn, 1987.

State v. *Carlson*, 267 N.W.2d 170 (1978).

State v. *Melendez*, 661 P.2d 654 (1982).

State v. *Meyers*, 359 N.W.2d 60 (1984).

State v. *Ryan*, 691 P.2d 197 (1984).

Steward, M. S., and others. "Group Therapy: A Treatment of Choice for Young Victims of Child Abuse." *International Journal of Group Psychotherapy*, 1986, *36*, 261-277.

Stowell, J., and Dietzel, M. *My Very Own Book About Me.* Spokane, Wash.: Lutheran Social Services, 1982.

Sturkie, K. "Structured Group Treatment for Sexually Abused Children." *Health and Social Work*, 1983, *4*, 299-309.

Sugar, M. "Sexual Abuse of Children and Adolescents." *Adolescent Psychiatry,* 1983, *11,* 199–211.

Summit, R. C. "The Child Sexual Abuse Accommodation Syndrome." *Child Abuse and Neglect,* 1983, 7, 177–193.

Sutherland, E. H. "The Diffusion of Sexual Psychopath Laws." *American Journal of Sociology,* 1950, *56,* 142–146.

Sutton v. Commonwealth of Virginia, 324 S.E.2d 665 (1985).

Swan, H. L., Press, A. N., and Briggs, S. L. "Child Sexual Abuse Prevention: Does It Work?" *Child Welfare,* 1985, *64,* 395–405.

Swanson, L., and Biuggio, M. K. "Therapeutic Perspectives on Father-Daughter Incest." *American Journal of Psychiatry,* 1985, *142,* 667–674.

Swift, C. *Consultation in the Area of Child Sexual Abuse.* NIMH Report 83-213. Washington, D.C.: National Institute of Mental Health, 1983.

Symonds, C. L., Mendoza, M. J., and Harrell, W. C. "Forbidden Sex Among Kin." In L. L. Constantine and F. M. Martinson (eds.), *Children and Sex: New Findings, New Perspectives.* Boston: Little, Brown, 1981.

Taubman, S. "Incest in Context." *Social Work,* 1984, *29,* 35–40.

Taylor, J. W. "Social Casework and the Multimodal Treatment of Incest." *Social Casework,* 1986, *66,* 451–459.

Taylor, R. "Marital Therapy in the Treatment of Incest." *Social Casework,* 1984, *65,* 195–202.

Tedesco, J. F., and Schnell, S. V. "Children's Reactions to Sex Abuse Investigation and Litigation." *Child Abuse and Neglect,* 1987, *11,* 267–272.

Terr, L. C. "The Child Psychiatrist and the Child Witness: Travelling Companions by Necessity, If Not by Design." *Journal of the American Academy of Child Psychiatry,* 1986, *25,* 462–472.

Tester, M. A. "The Scott County Sexual Abuse Cases: A Closer Look at What Went Wrong." Unpublished manuscript, Department of Psychology, University of Virginia, 1986.

Tilelli, J. A., Turek, D., and Jaffee, A. C. "Sexual Abuse of Children: Clinical Findings and Implications for Management." *New England Journal of Medicine,* 1980, *302,* 319–323.

Topper, A. B., and Aldridge, D. J. "Incest: Intake and Investigation." In P. B. Mrazek and C. H. Kempe (eds.), *Sexually Abused Children and Their Families.* Elmsford, N.Y.: Pergamon Press, 1981.

Trepper, T. S., and Barrett, M. J. "Vulnerability to Incest: A Framework for Assessment." *Journal of Psychotherapy and the Family,* 1986, *2,* 13–26.

Truesdell, D. L., McNeil, J. S., and Deschner, J. P. "Incidence of Wife Abuse in Incestuous Families." *Social Work,* 1986, *86,* 138–140.

Tsai, M., Feldman-Summers, S., and Edgar, M. "Childhood Molestation: Variables Related to Differential Impacts on Psychosexual Functioning in Adult Women." *Journal of Abnormal Psychology,* 1979, *88,* 407–417.

Tsai, M., and Wagner, N. N. "Therapy Groups for Women Sexually Molested as Children." *Archives of Sexual Behavior,* 1978, *7,* 417–427.

Tufts' New England Medical Center, Division of Child Psychiatry. *Sexually Exploited Children: Service and Research Project.* Washington, D.C.: U.S. Department of Justice, 1984.

United States v. *Iron Shell,* 633 F.2d 77 (1980).

United States v. *Nick,* 604 F.2d 1199 (1979).

VandenBos, G. R. *American Psychologist,* 1986, *41* (2) (entire issue).

Wald, M. S. "State Intervention on Behalf of 'Neglected' Children: A Search for Realistic Standards." *Stanford Law Review,* 1975, *27,* 985–1040.

Wald, M. S., and Cohen, S. "Preventing Child Abuse: What Will It Take?" *Family Law Quarterly,* 1986, *20,* 281–302.

Walh, C. W. "The Psychodynamics of Consummated Maternal Incest." *Archives of General Psychiatry,* 1960, *3,* 96–101.

Wallerstein, J., and Kelly, J. *Surviving the Breakup: How Children and Parents Cope with Divorce.* New York: Basic Books, 1980.

Washington v. *Fitzgerald,* 694 P.2d 1117 (1985).

Washington v. *Petrich,* 683 P.2d 173 (1984).

Wattenberg, E. "In a Different Light: A Feminist Perspective on the Role of Mothers in Father-Daughter Incest." *Child Welfare,* 1985, *64,* 203–211.

Wayne, J., and Weeks, K. K. "Groupwork with Abused Adolescent Girls: A Special Challenge." *Social Work with Groups,* 1984, *7,* 83–104.

Webb-Woodard, L., and Woodard, B. "Incest: Treatment in the Larger System." *Journal of Strategic and Systematic Therapies,* 1982, *2,* 28–37.

Weisberg, D. K. "The 'Discovery' of Sexual Abuse: Experts' Role in Legal Policy Formation." *University of California, Davis, Law Review,* 1984, *18,* 1–57.

Weiss, E. H. "Incest Accusation: Assessing Credibility." *The Journal of Psychiatry and the Law,* 1983, 305–317.

Weithorn, L. A. "Children's Capacities in Legal Contexts." In N. D. Reppucci and others (eds.), *Children, Mental Health, and the Law.* Beverly Hills, Calif.: Sage, 1984.

Westermarck, E. *A Short History of Marriage.* London: Macmillan, 1926.

Wheeler v. *United States,* 159 U.S. 523 (1895).

Whitcomb, D. "Prosecution of Child Sexual Abuse: Innovations in Practice." In *Research in Brief.* Washington, D.C.: National Institute of Justice, 1985.

White, L. A. "A Definition and Prohibition of Incest." *American Anthropology,* 1948, *15,* 416–435.

White, S., Santilli, G., and Quinn, K. "Child Evaluator's Roles in Child Sexual Abuse Assessments." Paper presented to the Society for Research in Child Development, Baltimore, Apr. 1987.

Wigmore, J. H. *Evidence in Trials at Common Law.* (Revised by J. Chadborn.) Vol. 6. Boston: Little, Brown, 1976. (Originally published 1940.)

Wilcox, B. "Remarks." Paper presented at the symposium "Evaluation of Suspected Child Abuse," Society for Research in Child Development, Baltimore, Apr. 1987.

Will, D. "Approaching the Incestuous and Sexually Abusive Family." *Journal of Adolescence,* 1983, *6,* 229–246.

Wolf, S. C., Berliner, L. C., Conte, J., and Smith, T. "The Victimization Process in Child Sexual Abuse." Paper presented at the Third National Family Violence Research Conference, Durham, N.H., 1987.

Wolfe, D. A., Aragona, J., Kaufman, K., and Sandler, J. "The Importance of Adjudication in the Treatment of Child

Abusers: Some Preliminary Findings." *Child Abuse and Neglect*, 1980, *4*, 127-133.

Wolfe, D. A., MacPherson, T., Blount, R., and Wolfe, U. V. "Evaluation of a Brief Intervention for Educating School Children in Awareness of Physical and Sexual Abuse." *Child Abuse and Neglect*, 1986, *10*, 85-92.

Wood, S. P., and Rhodes, C. "Sexual Abuse Prevention for Children: A Critical Overview." Paper presented at the 94th annual meeting of the American Psychological Association, Washington, D.C., Aug. 1986.

Wulkan, D., and Bulkley, J. "Analysis of Incest Statutes." In J. Bulkley (ed.), *Child Sexual Abuse and the Law.* (5th ed.) Washington, D.C.: American Bar Association, 1985.

Wurtele, S. K., Marrs, S. R., and Miller-Perrin, C. L. "Practice Makes Perfect? The Role of Participant Modeling in Sexual Abuse Prevention Programs." *Journal of Consulting and Clinical Psychology*, 1987, *55*, 599-602.

Wyatt, G. E. "The Sexual Abuse of Afro-American and White-American Women in Childhood." *Child Abuse and Neglect*, 1985, *9*, 507-519.

Wyatt, G. E. "The Relationship Between the Cumulative Impact of a Range of Child Sexual Abuse Experiences and Women's Psychological Well-Being." *Victimology*, in press.

Wyatt, G. E., and Peters, S. D. "Issues in the Definition of Child Sexual Abuse Research." *Child Abuse and Neglect*, 1986, *10*, 231-240.

Yates, A. Y. "Children Eroticized by Incest." *American Journal of Psychiatry*, 1982, *139*, 482-485.

Yates, A. Y. "Should Young Children Testify in Cases of Sexual Abuse?" *American Journal of Psychiatry*, 1987, *144*, 476-479.

Yates, A. Y., Beutler, L. E., and Crago, M. "Drawings by Child Victims of Incest." *Child Abuse and Neglect*, 1985, *9*, 183-189.

Yorukoglu, A., and Kemph, J. P. "Children Not Severely Damaged by Incest with a Parent." *Journal of the American Academy of Child Psychiatry*, 1966, *5*, 111-124.

Zefran, J., and others. "Management and Treatment of Child Sexual Abuse Cases in a Juvenile Court Setting." *Journal of Social Work and Human Sexuality*, 1982, *1*, 155-170.

NAME INDEX

SUBJECT INDEX

A

Accusations of abuse: analysis of evaluating, 148-180; assessment issues for, 165-179; background on, 148-151; and emotional and behavioral indicators, 156-179; indicators of truth or falsehood of, 174-177; and interview process, 157-165; and objective and projective tests, 171-174; and physical indicators, 151-158; retraction of, 178-179, 224-225; summary on, 179-180; and syndrome use, 177-178

Adults: abused as children, group therapy for, 286-292; prevention programs for, 317-319; responsibility of, 192-196, 240

Alabama, witness shielded from defendant in, 365

American Psychiatric Association, 94, 128

American Psychological Association, 16, 75

Anatomically correct dolls: in individual treatment, 245-246; in interviews, 159-160, 164; and language, 169

Anger: as consequence for victim, 65; displaced, 192; in group therapy, 266, 268, 273; in individual treatment, 239, 243, 257; in women abused as children, 257

Anxiety, as consequence for victim, 65, 93

Appalachia, incidence research in, 53

Arizona: competence of witness in, 341; incidence research in, 55; videotaped testimony in, 362-363

Attorney General's Commission on Pornography, 80

B

Baltimore, incidence research in, 55

Battered child syndrome, attention to, 3

Beck Depression Inventory, 70

Behavior: checklist of, 172; as indication of abuse, 137-139, 156-179; and individual treatment, 242; sexualized, reactions to, 189-190; syndrome of emotions and, 177-178; victimized, reactions to, 190-191